WOMEN WHO RULED THE WORLD

WOMEN WHO RULED THE WORLD

5000 YEARS OF FEMALE MONARCHY

ELIZABETH NORTON

FOOTNOTE

First published in 2025 by Footnote Press

Footnote Press
An imprint of Bonnier Books UK
5th Floor, HYLO, 103–105 Bunhill Row, London, EC1Y 8LZ

Owned by Bonnier Books
Sveavägen 56, Stockholm, Sweden

First printing
1 3 5 7 9 10 8 6 4 2

Copyright © 2025 Elizabeth Norton

The right of Elizabeth Norton to be identified as the author of this work has been asserted in accordance with the Copyright, Designs and Patents Act 1998.

All rights reserved. No part of this publication may be reproduced, stored in a retrieval system, or transmitted in any form or by any means without the written permission of the publisher, nor be otherwise circulated in any form of binding or cover other than that in which it is published and without a similar condition being imposed on the subsequent purchaser.

A CIP catalogue record for this book is available from the British Library.

ISBN (hardback): 9781804441138
ISBN (ebook): 9781804441145

Design and Typeset by Envy Design Ltd
Printed and bound in Great Britain by Clays Ltd, Elcograf S.p.A.

The authorised representative in the EEA is
Bonnier Books UK (Ireland) Limited.
Registered office address: Floor 3, Block 3, Miesian Plaza,
Dublin 2, D02 Y754, Ireland
compliance@bonnierbooks.ie
www.bonnierbooks.co.uk

For all the women who have dared to rule.
And for those that will come after.

'Ladies from the past, the present, and the future:
you may all live here.'
—Christine de Pizan

CONTENTS

Author's Note   xi
Preface: The Women Who Ruled the World   1

CHAPTER 1: MIGHTY LADIES AND RIGHTEOUS (FEMALE) HUSBANDS   17
Merneith of Egypt, Matilda of England, Margrete I of Denmark, Norway and Sweden, and Tecuichpotzin (Isabel Moctezuma) of the Mexica

CHAPTER 2: THE MALE RELATIVE PROBLEM   37
Cleopatra VII of Egypt, Charlotte of Cyprus, and Blanca II and Leonor of Navarre

CHAPTER 3: SNATCHING THE THRONE   57
Hatshepsut of Egypt, Irene of Byzantium, and Elizaveta and Catherine II of Russia

CHAPTER 4: CHILD QUEENS   83
Maria and Isabella II of Jerusalem, Mary Queen of Scots, Teri'imaevarua II of Bora Bora and Wilhemina of the Netherlands

CHAPTER 5: A LION'S CUBS ARE LIONS ALL   107
Tamar of Georgia, Jeanne of France (alias Juana II of Navarre) and Maria Theresia of Austria-Hungary

CHAPTER 6: THE PHOENIX'S CHOICE   133
Wu Zetian of China and Elizabeth I of England and Ireland

CHAPTER 7: MONSTROUS REGIMENTS   157
Athaliah of Judah, Arsinoë IV of Egypt and Mary Queen of Scots

CHAPTER 8: WARRIOR QUEENS   181
The Kandakes of Kush, Zenobia of Palmyra, Isabel I of Castile and Juana la Beltraneja

CHAPTER 9: QUEEN HIMIKO'S MIRRORS   201
The Eight Reigning Empresses of Japan

CHAPTER 10: QUEENSHIP AND COLONISATION   223
Victoria of the United Kingdom, Lili'uokalani of Hawaii and the Rain Queens of the Balobedu

CHAPTER 11: AGE OF EMPRESSES   247
The Nawab Begums of Bhopal, Victoria of India, Cora Gooseberry (Caroo) of Sydney, Ranavalona I of Madagascar

CHAPTER 12: QUEENS OF THE TWENTIETH CENTURY   275
Wilhelmina of the Netherlands, Sālote Tupou III of Tonga, Elizabeth II of the United Kingdom and Margarethe II of Denmark

Afterword: The Women Who Will Rule the World   297
Bibliography   309
Endnotes   339
Acknowledgements   389
Index   391

AUTHOR'S NOTE

You may find some of the names used here for the reigning queens and other people in their lives are unfamiliar. Given the global span of the book, I have tried in the main to use the names by which individuals called themselves. So, we have Maria Theresia of Austria rather than Maria Theresa, Isabel I of Castile rather than the Anglicised Isabella (although, strictly speaking, an Anglicisation would be Elizabeth), Margrete I of Denmark, Norway and Sweden rather than Margaret or Margarethe and Elizaveta of Russia rather than Elizabeth.

There are a few exceptions to this. Catherine II of Russia, famously Catherine the Great, is pronounced Ekaterina in Russian. When using the Latin alphabet, however, the German-born empress used the spelling 'Catherine', so I have used that here. Since she is so well known as Catherine, this seemed sensible while also serving to differentiate her from her husband's grandmother, Ekaterina (Catherine) I. Charlotte of Cyprus, too, used the French Charlotte herself due to her ancestry, even though many of her subjects would have called her 'Carlotta'. I have therefore continued to use that form of her name.

WOMEN WHO RULED THE WORLD

On occasion, I have had to take a decision on which form of someone's name to use. Francois Etienne of Lorraine, Holy Roman Emperor and husband of Maria Theresia, could just as well be rendered as Franz Stefan, but the French form of his name seemed correct given his French origins. Place names are rendered in their English versions for ease of reference.

Japan's reigning emperors and empresses are accorded posthumous names, which replace the use of the names used during their lifetimes. As a result, their contemporary names tend not to be widely known. I have therefore used the posthumous names here for Japan's reigning empresses and male members of that royal family, in accordance with longstanding Japanese tradition. They are not, however, names that they would have recognised for themselves.

I have chosen to call Cora Gooseberry by this name rather than her birthname of Caroo. This is because, as will become apparent, her queenship was largely a construct of the British settlers to the new colony of New South Wales. The identity, 'Cora Gooseberry', was simiarly constructed by the British settlers in an attempt to interact with the Aboriginal Australian population of the area. It was a name imposed upon Caroo, but it remains the name by which she is best known today.

Mary Queen of Scots was Mary I of Scotland (with her reign followed by Mary II, who also ruled in England and Ireland, between 1689 and 1694). She is frequently confused with her contemporary queen and cousin, Mary I of England (reigned 1553–1558). For this reason, I have continued to refer to her as Mary Queen of Scots.

Finally, some individuals are so well known that it seems problematic not to use the names by which they are remembered. Mark Antony – in reality Marcus Antonius – is a case in point.

PREFACE

THE WOMEN WHO RULED THE WORLD

It was a dull September day in 2022 when I noticed a missed call on my phone from the United Arab Emirates. Then, it rang again. This time the number came from the United States. The next, London, then Australia, and later Qatar. Was I available – right now – for a telephone interview or a discussion over Zoom? Could I get to Buckingham Palace, where the world's major news organisations were already assembling in portacabins arranged in an arc around zealously tended flowerbeds from Canada Gate to the Mall? It was 8 September 2022, and Buckingham Palace had informed the world that the health of Elizabeth II, who had so recently celebrated her Platinum Jubilee, was failing. The Queen, who was the world's longest-reigning living sovereign and, as far as records allow, the longest-ruling woman in history, died at Balmoral in Scotland later that afternoon with her family around her.

In London, it rained heavily all through the night, but crowds were already gathering at the gilded gates of Buckingham Palace the next morning. Leaving my post in the press area, I walked over, past the great memorial to another queen, Victoria, who sits sculpted and blank-faced, looking away from the seat of the British monarchy. There were flowers and messages, as well as people – shell-shocked, grieving or simply curious. As the days drew on, the crowds became immense, while people queued for long hours to pay their respect to the monarch in ancient, solid Westminster Hall. The most famous human being on the planet had been a woman. She was also a reigning queen. Indeed, her fame and visibility, augmented by her longevity and the fact that the world's monarchies are diminishing, was *because* she was a reigning queen. In 1952, when Elizabeth, *The* Queen, took up her throne, she became the member of a select club of powerful women. When we look at photographs of the Queen with world leaders from throughout her seventy-year reign, she is almost always the only woman in the room.

When Elizabeth II came to the throne in 1952, a woman had never been elected as a head of state or as a head of government anywhere in the world.* When Margrethe II of Denmark, who attended Elizabeth II's funeral in Westminster Abbey, became queen in 1972, there had still never been a female elected head of state. Vigdís Finnbogadóttir, who trailblazed her way to Iceland's presidency in 1980, holding office for sixteen years (still a record for a female elected head of state), was the first woman to be directly elected to a presidency. She is now in her mid-nineties. The first male elected head of state died centuries before the birth of Christ. Non-royal female power is recent, and it is fragile. For almost all of recorded history, female monarchs were the only women to head states and nations. We must look to these royal women to tell us about female power.

*

---

* Prime ministers are heads of government and serve under a head of state, who is either a monarch or a president. Although in this book I will note the power and importance of elected heads of government, the role of head of state is of more symbolic importance since they are at the very top of the nation.

THE WOMEN WHO RULED THE WORLD

Fables tell us of the Amazons, who inhabited a world of women and made brave warriors quake.[1] They were led by their great queen, Hippolyte, daughter of the war god Ares, while her mother, Otrera, was the Amazons' founding ruler. Hippolyte was mighty, fearsome and wise but, crucially, ultimately vanquished by the 'heroes' – first Heracles and then Theseus – who sought her out. The point of these women was to make the men they encountered look mighty, with their taming essential to the proper order, as the mythmakers understood it. A warrior race so fierce that they removed their right breasts to allow them to better draw a bow were worthy adversaries indeed. The Amazons exist in the realms of myth and legend, amongst Trojan horses and three-headed hellhounds, but it is notable that in the brave Hippolyte, Otrera and their successors, the people of Ancient Greece were able to conceive of a world ruled by women.

For a long time, Europeans thought that California was an island, presided over by a bloodthirsty queen to rival anything of the Amazonian imagination.[2] This Queen Calafia ruled her island with an iron grip, barring men from inhabiting her lands, while she and the other 'black women' lived an Amazonian lifestyle with their 'energetic bodies and courageous, ardent hearts', according to an early sixteenth-century Spanish account, *The Labors of the Very Brave Knight Esplandián*.[3] It was in this work that the name 'California', coined from the mythical queen, was first used and is a rare departure from the safety of a saint's name in Spanish geographic nomenclature. The women there had tamed griffins, which they used as guard dogs to defend against men daring to land on their island. The 'pagan' Calafia, 'who was bigger and more beautiful than the other women on the island', voyaged across the ocean to aid the Muslim besiegers of Constantinople, with the queen appearing before the city walls clad in golden armour and accompanied by her attack-griffins.[4] That Constantinople had, in fact, fallen long before Spain's realisation that the Americas even existed should have been enough to raise suspicions about Calafia's historicity, but it made a good story. People have always been drawn to fables of female power, as they are to the rare beasts in a zoo. Why else would the story of Hippolyte, or Dido, the mythical foundress of Carthage, still resonate if they were not exotic and *other*.

As with the Amazons, Calafia was eventually domesticated, converting to Christianity and settling down to wedded bliss with a male co-ruler. This taming of Calafia is echoed by the housebreaking of Hippolyte, who appears as a genteel and cultured queen excited about her upcoming wedding as a character in Shakespeare's *A Midsummer Night's Dream*, which was first performed in 1595/6.

We can romanticise about Amazons, living in their female-run Utopia, but no such place has ever existed. *Homo sapiens* is a sexually dimorphic and highly patriarchal species, something that is reinforced in the Abrahamic faiths that dominate much of the world. Even so-called matrilineal societies tend to mask this fundamental truth at their core. The Trobriand people of Papua New Guinea, who were the darlings of countless anthropology departments in the twentieth century and a staple of the first year of my degree in archaeology and anthropology at Cambridge University, are a case in point. A chief would be succeeded by his sister's son, and so on through his female lineage, but it was still the male members of the clan who held the authority. A reigning woman is therefore a departure from the norm: a 'monstrous regiment' according to the sixteenth-century misogynist John Knox. He exaggerated. Female rulers have hardly overrun the planet.

There is something supremely unusual, and special, about a woman who overthrew the established order and dared to rule alone. The queens in this book, for the most part, had no man to hide behind. When they acted, they acted for themselves and in their own interests, something that flew, and still flies, in the face of the patriarchy that framed their lives. They may not all have built their own Xanadus, with paradise's stately pleasure domes and incense-bearing trees of Samuel Taylor Coleridge's dreamy imaginings, but the attempts were potent in themselves.

The rarity of ruling queens likely accounts for their visibility. They stand out from the crowd. Visit London's Kensington Palace today and you can view a painting by David Wilkie depicting the first council meeting held by Queen Victoria on the day that she succeeded to the throne.[5] In his depiction, the teenaged queen sits at the head of a table, surrounded by middle-aged men in dark morning suits. To further emphasise the eighteen-year-old queen, Wilkie changed the colour of her black dress to vivid white. He hardly needed to bother. Eyes would always be drawn to the only female in the room. It has been the same throughout time. Cleopatra VII of Egypt inevitably drew the attention of chroniclers away from her brother and co-ruler, the equally wily Ptolemy XIII. Caratacus, the chief of the Catuvellauni who led a first-century CE revolt against the Roman administration in Britain can never hope to outshine Boudicca, Queen of the Iceni, who surged out of East Anglia to burn London, St Albans and Colchester. It is his capture, at the hands of Cartimandua, reigning Queen of the Brigantes, for which he is best known.

This very much continues. Shortly after giving a talk on the reign of Elizabeth I in front of a group of interested tourists, I joined them for dinner, sitting at one of those big round tables you find in hotels. Over the course of the meal, someone asked me what I was currently working on. I told them I was writing a book on reigning queens, looking at the ways in which they established themselves (or didn't) and whether we could see similarities and differences across time and across the world. My neighbour nodded sagely. 'You are going to include the Queen of Tonga, aren't you? She was marvellous at the coronation.' This wasn't the first time this reigning queen, who entered legend by riding proudly through the rain of Elizabeth II's coronation in 1953 in an open carriage, had been mentioned to me by those old enough to remember. There were two stars of that day: Elizabeth II in her robes of state and the headachingly heavy Imperial State Crown, but also Sālote Tupou III of Tonga (whom we will meet in Chapter 12). Reigning queens have always been notable and remarkable. A man shared the Tongan queen's carriage that day, getting equally drenched, but all eyes were on her.

The English language does not have a specific word to describe Hippolyte's role in her Amazonian queendom, nor Elizabeth II's in her twenty-first-century state. They are queen regnants, but this term is not without its complications – it is a description rather than a form of address. 'Queen', which comes from Old English, was initially applied only to the wives of male rulers. In France, *'reine'* is used for king's wives, as is the German *'königin'*. These king's wives are consorts rather than reigning monarchs, but they are not distinguished from reigning queens by the way that they are addressed. Queen Victoria and her daughter-in-law, Queen Alexandra, had wildly different statuses, but this is concealed by the common title applied to them.

This is not to say that queen consorts could not be powerful and political figures. Many of the women described in this book began their careers as consorts, such as Matilda of England, Hatshepsut of Egypt, Irene of Byzantium and Catherine the Great, while the wives of male rulers could still wield immense power. Matilda of Boulogne, the wife of England's King Stephen who snatched the crown away from Matilda of England in 1135, is a good example. Stephen could not have secured victory over his rival nor regained his freedom without his wife's high political acumen and powerful contacts. She was a strong woman standing in the shadow of a weak man. And yet a consort was very different to a reigning queen. It is also notable that a king outranks a queen, even if he is the husband of a reigning queen. There are many examples of king consorts stepping over their wives in terms of precedence and prestige, as Mary Queen of Scots would find after her marriage to the lower born Henry, Lord Darnley.

'Female king' is probably a better term than queen regnant, although it qualifies a role which is usually absolute: no one refers to a male king. Tamar of Georgia called herself a king and was identified as such. She was far from the only woman to be acknowledged in this way: Maria was crowned as King of Hungary in 1382 and her sister, Jadwiga, was enthroned as King of Poland in 1384. Margrete I of Denmark, Norway and Sweden was called 'husband' of her kingdoms, a name that undoubtedly conferred authority but fell short of identifying her as a ruler. As we shall see, it is all too common to deny women the title of monarch, regardless of the role that they play. The diversity of terms used is itself interesting, indicating an understanding that these women had to be called something, even if a full acknowledgement of their status was not felt appropriate by the men that traditionally wrote the history books. Reigning queen, the term that will primarily be used here, is clunky and imprecise, but it is the best that English can do.

So, what is a reigning queen? Why are Hippolyte and Elizabeth II included in this book but Eleanor of Aquitaine, the Queen of France and then England and ruler in her own right of approximately one-third of modern France, excluded? The simple fact is that, while there have always been powerful women, it is rarer for such women to act in their own name. Eleanor, although she inherited and ruled Aquitaine, had husbands and sons who claimed her duchy as their own even during her lifetime, masking her own very considerable autonomy. At the same time, Aquitaine, although wealthy and sizeable, was under the aegis of the King of France, who was its overlord, a position that was made inherently more complex when he also became her ex-husband. Eleanor was a ruling duchess rather than a reigning monarch, a queen consort rather than a reigning queen.

WOMEN WHO RULED THE WORLD

Throughout the book, I have attempted to include only those women who appear to me to be heads of state, a role which is defined in the *Oxford English Dictionary* as 'the chief public representative of a country (sometimes also the head of the government), such as a president or a monarch)'. This need not be an entirely independent state, although some form of monarchy must be recognised at a subnational level (effectively a state within a state), something which became increasingly an issue when the Imperial powers of the nineteenth and early twentieth centuries took out their rulers to draw straight line national borders on maps of Africa and other parts of the world. The Rain Queens of the Balobedu, in South Africa, exist within a larger nation, with their queenship and the Balobedu's independent existence (within the framework of the larger state) recognised by the South African government. Cora Gooseberry of Sydney, whom we will meet in Chapter 11, was an unwilling resident of Britain's newly established New South Wales colony, but she was recognised as a community leader and as a queen by those same Europeans who sailed into Sydney Harbour in 1787. She did not exactly have a state, but the role that was thrust upon her was considered to be a key one in community relations by the leaders of the British colony, which overlaid her traditional authority.

There is an element of the colonising Europeans attempting to fit their own understanding of monarchy and status to the people they encountered at the edges of the (to them) known world. Like Cora Gooseberry, a number of Native American chiefs were female and recognised by the title of queen by the Europeans who encountered them. These included Queen Aliquippa, ruler of the Seneca tribe, who reigned 'with great authority', according to one German-born settler who met her in 1748.[6] As an important ally of the British in the first half of the eighteenth century, Aliquippa was feted, with the Colonial Authorities receiving an official report of her death in December

1754 ('Aliquippa the old queen, is dead'). She also received a visit from George Washington in December 1753, graciously accepting a matchcoat and a bottle of rum from the future president (with the second gift, according to Washington's own account, 'thought much the best Present of the two').[7] Yet, while Aliquippa may not have been called a queen by her own people, she was undoubtedly a powerful and independent ruler and recognised as such by both the Seneca and the Europeans that she encountered.

What about female rulers such as Shah Jahan Begum of Bhopal who reigned under a colonial power – in this case, the Indian Empire of Victoria, Queen of the United Kingdom? Given Bhopal's continuing high level of independence, I think she should be included, particularly since Bhopal, a semi-independent princely state, had begun its unprecedented century of female rule long before Victoria claimed an Indian imperial crown to add to a British queenly diadem. Shah Jahan remained the ultimate authority in Bhopal, albeit under British supervision. I include, too, and with enthusiasm, women whose queenship was denied during their lifetimes, such as Margrete I of Denmark, Norway and Sweden, or who were disavowed later, such as Japan's eight ruling empresses who are usually referred to as regents today (and, thus, ruling on behalf of another – often – male relative), although they reigned during their lifetimes and were acknowledged as empresses.

A queen can be recognised as a head of state without being afforded power. Some queens, like Juana 'La Loca', the unfortunate daughter of Isabel I of Castile (whose sad story of captivity and disenfranchisement we will encounter in Chapter 8) had limited agency, but she was the acknowledged queen of the constituent kingdoms of Spain and treated, officially at least, as such. The conquistador Hernan Cortes wrote dutifully to Queen Juana back home, even if he likely did not expect her to read his letters or respond. For form's sake, she had to be informed. The poor woman spent the first half of the sixteenth century 'reigning' over all the kingdoms of a newly united Spain, but had so little autonomy that her son, the Holy Roman Emperor Charles V, on occasion plundered her possessions. She was, as we will see, far from the only reigning queen to be disenfranchised by a close male relative.

The mere fact of being head of state is not, in itself, enough for inclusion here. Otherwise, Mary Robinson of the Republic of Ireland or Droupadi Murmu of India, amongst other female presidents, should be covered. As such, the second element of my definition must be that the women, these heads of state, also rule or reign, within the confines of a monarchy. What do I mean by this? Wu Zetian of China and Ekaterina I of Russia, for example, were certainly not born royal, but they acquired royalty. In their cases, through concubinage and, later, marriage. It is hard, in fact, to think of a lower born reigning queen than Ekaterina, an illiterate Lithuanian peasant woman. Wu, too, was an astoundingly unlikely Empress of China, having been born the daughter of a lumber merchant in an insignificant province. Yet, just by saying their marriage vows they acquired a royal status that set them apart from their peers.**

You may not agree with my inclusions in every case, but I hope this two-part definition will at least provide a somewhat coherent picture of such a fascinating group.

I do not include regents, queen mothers or powerful consorts. This was always the acceptable face of female power, with women dutifully taking on political responsibilities in the names of husbands, brothers, sons and nephews. These cases are interesting. The most notable, perhaps, being the Empress Dowager Cixi, who was China's *de facto* head of state during the last years of the nineteenth century and the early years of the twentieth. She was a highly politically astute woman, and her story is unprecedented, but she always ruled through an emperor.

** This is the major twist in Disney's *The Princess and the Frog*, but I won't spoil the ending.

THE WOMEN WHO RULED THE WORLD

Wu Zetian, China's only reigning empress, was able to dispense with such an appendage. She ruled alone. There is a story to be told about regents and other powerful royal women, such as Isabella of France, who deposed and murdered her husband, the fourteenth-century English king, Edward II, but this is not the place. In the 1980s, Queen Ntfombi ruled capably as regent of Eswatini (formerly Swaziland), appearing as one of the four *Reigning Queens* of Andy Warhol's series of paintings completed in 1985 (the others being Beatrix of the Netherlands, Margrethe II of Denmark and Elizabeth II of the United Kingdom). She ruled on behalf of her young son, who appointed her to the official role of Queen Mother when he reached adulthood in 1986. She has always held great power, but not on her own behalf.

To be born female was, at least until the late twentieth century, a major disadvantage for anyone born into a reigning family. The disaster of bearing a mere girl cost Anne Boleyn, the mother of Elizabeth I, her head. This was an extreme reaction, but countless royal women have been displaced by baby brothers or other male relatives. Ang Mei, who reigned as Queen of Cambodia in the first half of the nineteenth century, was perceived by many as a puppet of the occupying Vietnamese, her reign used to facilitate 'the identification of female political power with national humiliation'.[8]

Women have served as reigning queens around the world and across time, save South America, which never really seems to have embraced reigning queenship.[***] And you will, I think, forgive me that I have not found a queen amongst the penguins and icebergs of Antarctica. Though a royal female ruler could usually expect to face considerable opposition. Rameses II of Egypt, known as Rameses the

---
[***] Maria I of Portugal served as Brazil's only reigning queen from 16 December 1815 until her death on 20 March 1816. She was resident in Brazil during her brief reign, but she had long been considered mentally incapacitated.

Great, who plainly disapproved of female rule, went so far as to remove his kingdom's reigning queens from the official records. He must have turned in his grave when his granddaughter Tausret took the throne in 1191 BCE.

As far as records allow, reigning queenship began in the desert sand of Egypt approximately 5000 years ago, although earlier queens, predating the development of writing, are highly likely. There are countless examples of African reigning queens before we can name a single European example.**** While Amanirenas, who ruled from Meroë, the capital city of the ancient kingdom of Kush (what is mostly now modern-day Sudan) is not a household name, she probably should be. The nineteenth-century Ranavalona I of Madagascar undoubtedly deserves to be better known, with the ferocity of her reputation a decisive factor in her country's continuing independence in the face of European colonisation. Cleopatra VII is, of course, an African queen who needs no introduction, but Hatshepsut who reigned in Egypt more than 1000 years earlier can also speak to us about the role of queen.

Other parts of the world also had rich traditions of reigning queenship, with 277 female rulers identified by the historian Stefan Amirell in the islands of the Indian Ocean and along its coastline from the fourteenth to the nineteenth centuries.[9] Just what made these island nations so willing to accept female rule is not entirely clear. At least two women reigned as *sheha*, or headwoman, on Tumbatu Island in the Zanzibar Archipelago in the nineteenth century, though Mwana wa Mwana, who ruled there in the early 1800s was 'pressured' into a political marriage with the ruler of a neighbouring island to provide her island with a male monarch, suggesting that female rule was not necessarily desired.[10]

**** In medieval Europe, the first truly acknowledged reigning queen is Urraca, Queen of Leon and Castile and self-styled Empress of All Galicia. For more on this truly fascinating figure, see Bernard F. Reilly, *The Kingdom of León-Castilla under Queen Urraca, 1109-1126* (Princeton: Princeton University Press, 1982).

Although 277 female rulers sounds like a lot, given the vastness of the territory covered by this Indian Ocean World, there were still many more male rulers in the period than female.

Most cultures have had a strong disinclination to female rule, with the matrons of Classical Rome kept firmly (at least in theory) away from power, as were the women of the imperial harem in China, although this proved no bar to Wu Zetian's rise to empress in the seventh century CE. It is rare to find a reigning queen in the Islamic world, with the Abrahamic faiths usually staunch in their antipathy towards female dominance. There were some Islamic queens, however. We will meet the nawab begums of Bhopal in Chapter 11, while the thirteenth-century Radiyya, Sultana of Delhi, is another example. Her near contemporary Shajar al-Durr also enjoyed a remarkable career, encompassing a childhood in slavery before rising to become Sultana of Egypt in 1250. While women do feature in the Qur'an, the only woman mentioned by name is Maryam (Mary), the mother of Jesus, who became the central figure in medieval (and later) Christianity.[11]

Royal women did, however, tend to be amongst the best travelled of anyone in the medieval period and earlier, thanks to their commodification in the international marriage market. Princesses, such as Matilda of England, Margrete I of Denmark, Norway and Sweden and Isabella II of Jerusalem, were traded in wedlock, often in the expectation that they would never return home or see their families again. Cleopatra VII, Arsinoë IV, Zenobia and Matilda of England all visited Rome, which was considered the centre of the world from the Christian and the Classical perspective. They went for different reasons, but in all cases the travel would have seemed remarkable to their contemporaries. Royal women were mobile and urbane in so many cases. Elizabeth II famously received news of her accession to the British throne in 1952 while sleeping in a treehouse in Kenya. Her seventy-year reign would see her crisscross the globe. On many occasions she walked (often unwittingly) in the footsteps of the queenly sisters who had gone before her.

The cult of the Virgin Mary arguably went some way to improving women's status in medieval Europe, with the coronation of the Virgin as Queen of Heaven a very common motif.[12] While unscriptural, by the eighth century it largely appears to have been established in the Western church that Mary would reign alongside Christ in Heaven for eternity, giving the sense that she was herself a reigning queen rather than a consort. It was first depicted (as far as we can tell) in the tenth-century *Benedictional of St Aethelwold* in an attempt to glorify and promote Aelfthryth, a particularly powerful English queen consort, with the association between the Virgin and queenship longstanding.[13] Mary I of England and Ireland, who was crowned in 1553 – the first time an Englishwoman secured a coronation in her own right – shared her name with the Virgin, making it natural for her contemporaries to draw comparisons. The resemblance was explicitly made clear in literature, with the earthly queen benefitting from the association with her heavenly counterpart, who was considered the most ideal of women.[14] Her half-sister, Elizabeth I, too, despite her Protestant rejection of Marianism as unscriptural, made the association to bolster her own prestige on occasion.[15] This could be a double-edged sword, with Christ's mother creating a model of feminine perfection that it was impossible for anyone to live up to. In Chapter 7, as we will see, Mary I and the other British reigning queens from the period were more likely to be designated as Jezebels or Athaliahs than Virgin Marys. Mary I endures her own notoriety as Bloody Mary, a reputation that is not entirely just (and one that is less likely to be applied to a man – we don't speak of 'Bloody Henry VIII').

Attempts to identify parallels between royal women and religious figures are not particularly surprising, given the relative scarcity of women in public life with whom they could otherwise be compared.

THE WOMEN WHO RULED THE WORLD

While this book focusses on the queens as political figures, it should also be noted that many had (or have) a spiritual role. The Rain Queens of the Balobedu are as much deities or spiritual beings as rulers, while English, and later British, female monarchs from 1559 onwards have been the Supreme Governor of the Church of England. Japan's reigning empresses were semi-divine, as the descendants of the all-powerful sun goddess so central to Shintoism. A small sense of divine appointment or divinity itself arguably does not hamper a woman attempting to establish herself on a throne in a man's world.

Shakespeare's Hippolyte, as she appears in *A Midsummer Night's Dream*, is a strangely domesticated character, looking forward to her forthcoming wedding to the 'hero' Theseus, who had earlier vanquished her and her queenship. He had, he said, wooed her 'with my sword' and 'won thy love doing thee injuries'.[16] In a play that tips the world topsy-turvy, the portrayal of this once Amazonian queen is strangely conventional. Written in the realm of Elizabeth I, the play seeks explicitly to turn Hippolyte from ruler to consort, just as Elizabeth, too, had faced pressure to marry and furnish her kingdom with a king. Yet, the role of reigning queen itself must always hide an unconventionality just beneath the surface: such women were, by their very nature, unnatural. It is, however, a measure of how much times have changed that at her last formal engagement, two days before her death, Elizabeth II posed for smiling photographs with her fifteenth British prime minister – a woman. Reigning queens from the distant past to the twenty-first century have faced a unique set of pressures as people – both men and women – have struggled to make sense of a role so inherently alien. Across the globe and across time, I invite you to explore the lives of some of the women who reigned in an attempt to understand just what the role entailed and what its relevance is today. In their very existence, these queens are truly remarkable. They are the women who ruled the world.

CHAPTER 1:

MIGHTY LADIES AND RIGHTEOUS (FEMALE) HUSBANDS

Merneith of Egypt, Matilda of England, Margrete I of Denmark, Norway and Sweden, and Tecuichpotzin (Isabel Moctezuma) of the Mexica

Saqqara in Egypt is a city of the dead, which lies mostly buried, with the collapsed and crumbled mounds of small pyramids dotting the surface and doorways opening into desert rocks. The great Step Pyramid dominates the landscape, but Saqqara was already ancient when the pyramid builders came here. Three hundred years before the blocks were laid in Egypt's first pyramid, a woman walked these sands, selecting a suitable location for her own monument. To reach out to her, the first known reigning queen at the dawn of recorded history, we have to turn the clock of history back nearly 5000 years. The concept of a reigning queen is almost as old as the written word itself.

The great Flinders Petrie, who was the nineteenth century's foremost archaeologist, immeasurably expanded our knowledge of Egyptian history, overseeing his excavations in a Victorian formalwear that would not have been out of place in an English country house. He spent the 1900 season at Abydos, scraping back the layers of history with his trowel. He was excavating the tomb of a pharaoh, 'Meri-

Neith', in the royal burial ground outside the city's ruins. The burial chamber he discovered was positively opulent, even amongst the usual Ancient Egyptian concern for the comfort of the dead. There was a wooden ceiling, a rare luxury in a land where timber was scarce, and two stelae proudly bearing the name of its important occupant, as well as the bodies of forty-one servants, laid out neatly. This was, Flinders Petrie declared, the fifth king of Egypt's impossibly distant first dynasty.[1] Soon afterwards, it was discovered that 'Meri-Neith' was, in fact, the female 'Merit-Neith', or Merneith, and claims of her kingship were quietly allowed to drop. Her sex, as far as Flinders Petrie and his largely male contemporaries in the archaeology departments of their day were concerned, was an absolute bar to kingship. Indeed, the idea was preposterous. Excavations continued, but no attempt was made to interpret Merneith as anything more than a consort or queen mother. Flinders Petrie, whose own afterlife has been eventful with his mummified head now gathering dust on a shelf in the Royal College of Surgeons in London, took control of the narrative concerning this long-dead queen and fitted it to the Victorian and Edwardian sensibilities in which he was imbedded.

Was Merneith a powerful ruler in her own right? She undoubtedly took power in Egypt on the death of her (probable) husband, King Djet. But was she merely the queen regent, ruling on behalf of her young son, Den? This has, throughout history, often been the more acceptable face of female rule. The first woman in world history whose name we know, Neithhotep, ruled as regent for her son in Egypt right at the start of the First Dynasty, and it is entirely possible to interpret Merneith as a dutiful regent – many have done and still do.[2]

Those responsible for burying Merneith's son thought that she had reigned. An early king list, found in the impression of a cylinder seal (used to seal jar lids) in King Den's tomb includes Merneith.[3] The Palermo Stone, a Fifth Dynasty list of Egypt's past monarchs, also

MIGHTY LADIES AND RIGHTEOUS (FEMALE) HUSBANDS

names her as one of the First Dynasty's rulers. But in later eras, she seems to disappear from the record. The Abydos King List, compiled 1400 years after the end of the First Dynasty for Rameses II of Egypt, included the male First Dynasty rulers but omitted Merneith, along with any woman who could be said to have ruled Egypt. The high priest Manetho, Egypt's earliest historian, who wrote 2500 years later, made no mention of Merneith either. It seems that to Flinders Petrie, Rameses (with a synchronicity of thought that belies the differences of their eras and experience) and others, it was inconceivable that a woman could stand amongst the line of mace-wielding warrior kings at the dawn of recorded history.

Merneith is far from the only female monarch to be denied the title of king either during their lifetime or afterwards. We cannot always trust the ways in which women are interpreted and described by those that have written history, with the (usually) male writers of their times and later assessing them with their own biases and opinions. It is remarkable how frequently women acting as monarchs have been – and continue to be – dismissed as mere regents, princesses or placeholders. The title of monarch is denied them solely on the grounds of their sex, something which we must strive to look beyond if we wish to get a clearer picture of the history of female power. The queens in this chapter undoubtedly should 'count', regardless of how they have been historically presented. We can see this in Margrete I, 'husband' of her kingdoms in medieval Scandinavia, and with Merneith of Egypt, the male pharaoh who became a female regent when her sex was revealed to later observers. We can see it, too, in the Northern European kingdom of England.

Matilda was the only legitimate daughter of England's Henry I, the son of the famous William the Conqueror. She was married off in childhood to the Holy Roman Emperor Heinrich V, learning her trade as a ruler in forested Germany and mountainous Italy, assisting her husband in the governance of his widespread domains until his early death in 1125. By then, her own prospects had dramatically changed.

In the early twelfth century, England had no fixed system for the inheritance of the crown. William the Conqueror passed the throne to his second son, William 'Rufus', in 1087, who was then succeeded (in preference to his elder brother) by his younger brother, Henry I.* Henry's only legitimate son drowned in the notorious wreck of the *White Ship* in November 1120 (caused, one contemporary claimed, by the prince's excessive generosity in supplying the crew with wine). When a second marriage to a girl as young as his daughter failed to supply him with a new heir, Henry named Matilda as his successor and demanded his barons swear oaths in her support. Father and daughter had a tumultuous relationship, but both were committed to her accession. Matilda's cousin Stephen of Blois, however, who had been prominent amongst the oath-takers, was not.

When Henry I died suddenly on 1 December 1135, Stephen, who had fortuitously disembarked from the raucous *White Ship* before it sailed, after apparently suffering from a case of violent diarrhoea, slipped over the English Channel and had himself crowned as king. Matilda, who was in Normandy at the time and hampered by a recent pregnancy and her growing estrangement from her second husband, Geoffrey, Count of Anjou, was not prepared to let the matter drop.

There was no certainty that Matilda was even heir to the crown, with the Anglo-Saxon rulers, who had come before, considering only the sons of kings to be throne worthy. The world in which Matilda inhabited gave women power only grudgingly. Nonetheless, there were men prepared to admit that her claim, based on hereditary right, oaths sworn and the authority of the Church, was a powerful one,

---

* This succession was probably not Rufus's choice. He died after being shot in a hunting 'accident' in 1100, when his younger brother conveniently happened to be in the vicinity, allowing him to claim the royal treasury and the crown.

MIGHTY LADIES AND RIGHTEOUS (FEMALE) HUSBANDS

and offer their support. One thing that is both remarkable and clear is that Matilda meant to claim England for herself. Her ambition and determination resonate through the centuries, as do those of other women across the globe who attempted to fill a man's office. Although her circumvention of the gendered norms of the day did not extend as far as taking up arms herself, she was undoubtedly a war leader and active in promoting her claim. This was essential. To rule in twelfth-century Europe was to take on the trappings of male culture: women and monarchy were seen as a dichotomy.

Matilda's army captured her cousin and rival in 1141. With Stephen chained in her dungeon, Matilda secured recognition by the leading figures of the kingdom, including Stephen's brother, the Bishop of Winchester, as 'Lady of England'. This title did not quite admit her queenship, although at her proclamation in the marketplace at Winchester, the people saluted her 'as their lady and their queen'.[**4] While Matilda preferred the superior title of Empress, which had been bestowed on her during her first marriage, two charters suggest that she may have used the title Queen of England during this period. In any event, the name that she called herself or was called is immaterial. She was, as Charles Been notes in his gendered study of Matilda's rule, 'recognised as the sole source of royal authority for several months in the year 1141'.

To the male merchants of the hard-nosed Hanseatic League, a trading network that controlled much of the wealth of Europe, Margrete I of Denmark, Norway and Sweden was the 'Lady King', but this acceptance of her power had been grudging and sceptical.[5] During her lifetime, few

---

[**] Catherine Hanley, *Matilda: Empress Queen Warrior* (New Haven: Yale, 2019), p151 makes the pertinent point that Matilda herself might have rejected the title of queen since she risked using the same title as Stephen's wife, Matilda of Boulogne, and framing herself merely as a wife rather than as an independent monarch.

were prepared to admit that the first great independent female power in Western Europe was also a reigning monarch. Denmark, Europe's most continuously ancient monarchy, has witnessed almost sixty monarchs, but only two of them have been female and the queenship of the first, Margrete I, remains questioned.

One of the most significant figures in Scandinavian history, Margrete was born in 1353 in the wake of the Black Death, a bubonic plague that swept Europe, devastating the population, including that of her father's small, but populous, kingdom of Denmark. As her parents' youngest child, the idea of her ever taking power was improbable, and Margrete was betrothed aged only six to the teenaged heir to neighbouring Sweden and Norway. ('A game with dolls', considered the astute future saint Birgitta of Vadstena, who lamented that the children's marriage would bring bad luck to her homeland of Sweden.)[6] Princesses of Margrete's era expected to make an arranged marriage into an alien royal family, but even by the standards of the day, her betrothal, marked by warfare and the kidnapping of an alternative bride, was turbulent.[7] The couple finally wed in 1363 when Margrete was nine or ten.[8]

The child queen was taken to Norway, where she was raised by St Birgitta's daughter, a woman well prepared to whip Margrete to ensure her obedience.[9] With the death of her elder brother in 1363 and her husband's expulsion from Sweden the following year, Margrete's life was upturned again, with her father settling the succession on her deceased sister's son, Albrecht of Mecklenburg in 1371. This proof that a woman could at least transmit a claim to the Danish throne likely interested Margrete who, by this time, had given birth to her only child – a son, Oluf. A surviving letter that Margrete wrote to her husband around the time of the birth displays her dominant character, with the queen complaining of a lack of food and funds, as well as carefully going through the business she had conducted.[10] This is the first time that we can hear her voice, and it is a commanding one. When 'a mismanaged attack of gout' carried her father off in 1375, Margrete took decisive action, approaching the great Hanseatic League to secure a peace treaty between herself as a potential ruler and these central-and-northern-European merchants who controlled all trade in the region and could crush a ruler with sanctions and tariffs.[11] This took the merchants by surprise, since, as they admitted in correspondence, 'it seemed to them they were very important matters to entrust to the Lady', but money talked louder than any scruples they might have had about doing business with a woman.[12]

With his mother working tirelessly for his election, it was only a matter of time before little Oluf was declared King of Denmark. He also became King of Norway following his father's death in 1380. His mother, who had already shown 'exceptional political skill', as her recent biographer, Vivian Etting, notes, ruled on his behalf as regent.[13] Oluf died suddenly in 1387, just before reaching adulthood, something that unsurprisingly (but likely unfairly) raised suspicions over his mother's ambitions. With no king in Denmark or Norway Margrete became, to all intents and purposes, queen of both realms. There was no other ruler in her kingdoms but her.

Still, though, there was a contemporary reluctance to admit her reign.[14] For some years after Oluf's death, the kingdoms officially had no monarch, with Margrete styled as 'Almighty lady and husband and guardian for the whole kingdom of Denmark' and 'Mighty lady and righteous husband of Norway', both appointments – expressed as though she were the male head of a household – explicitly made for the term of her life.[15] While these suggest an interregnum rather than a reigning queen, Margrete's reign is clear.

There is much about the organisation of Egyptian society, as well as that of medieval Denmark or England, that the Mexica people of the Basin of Mexico would have recognised and understood. Better (but incorrectly) known as the Aztecs, their capital of Tenochtitlan, which lies beneath modern Mexico City, was one of the largest cities on earth before the Spanish Conquest in 1521, with a population of approximately 150,000 living on an island around two miles square in the centre of a great lake.[16] They had arrived from the north two centuries before, establishing an empire that would eventually see 25 million people under their sway.[17] This was driven, at least in part, by the desire to ensure a ready supply of captives for the shape-shifting god Huitzilopochtli. Feeding this deity with the blood of these prisoners kept the sun rising each morning, with the Mexica rulers expected to play an active role in a slaughter that could involve extracting the unfortunate victims' still-beating hearts.[18] To rule as Tlatoani of Tenochtitlan (a title which translates to 'king of the whole world') was to take on a masculine office in which the holder was expected to be an energetic and successful warrior, as well as to participate in the bloody religious ceremonies.

At first glance, there was no room for women in the politics of the Mexica Empire, with newborn girls presented with a spindle, whorl, broom and a small basket of cotton, while a brother would receive a buckler and arrows. Even empresses and princesses span cotton and embroidered, and spirited girls who would not sit quietly at their work risked having their feet tied together to prevent them from moving.[19] It was what was expected by the gods, while boys were cautioned to stay well away from the kitchen fire – the female domain – lest setting a foot down on the sooty hearth emasculated them.[20] The differences between the sexes are writ large in the archaeological record, where female skeletons often have deformed feet, suggesting a lifetime of kneeling with their body weight pushed back onto their toes. Even the goddesses of the Mexica were secondary, vastly outnumbered by their male counterparts.

It is therefore surprising that Acamapichtli, the first Tlatoani of Tenochtitlan appears to have ruled through his wife, Ilancueitl (whose name means, unromantically, 'old woman skirt'), in the late fourteenth century, with her royal birth giving legitimacy to his upstart claims.[21] Three generations later, the Mexica Princess Atotoztli almost certainly reigned as Tlatoani, even though – as a woman – she was considered unable to wield the wooden, obsidian edged clubs of her male counterparts, which could remove a horse's head with a single blow. The Mexica did not have a full writing system, with all sources for Atotoztli's reign postdating the Spanish conquest, but the evidence that she succeeded her father, Motecuhzoma I, in 1468 or 1469 is clear.[22] She stands out in the pictorial genealogies of the Mexica's rulers, with her white *cueitl* (calf-length skirt), *huipilli* (a loose-fitting blouse) and the braided hairstyle of a married woman, that was pinned to the top of the head to resemble two small horns, making her immediately distinctive amongst the images of men.[23] In one, she appears as a monarch with a turquoise diadem hovering above her head, in other sources her father was 'succeeded by a legitimate daughter' or that 'his daughter inherited the kingdom', while – explicitly – her son 'was king after his mother'.[24] All compelling evidence of the monarchy of a woman whom we know almost nothing about.

Atotoztli's great-granddaughter thought she reigned, with a sixteenth-century source with strong connections to her claiming that 'because she is a woman they do not put her in the annals but her son'.[25] This is the crux of the issue faced by so many women rulers. If a woman cannot be king (or pharaoh, or emperor or tlatoani) then they cannot be recognised as monarch when they do dare to take up the reins of power.

This great-granddaughter was Tecuichpotzin, who is arguably the last of the Mexica's rulers, born in the years before the Spanish Conquest of 1519 sent the world as she knew it crashing down around her head. As the only surviving child of the immensely famous Emperor

Motecuhzoma II by his premier wife Teotlalco, Tecuichpotzin, who is now better known by her baptismal name of Isabel Moctezuma, was a figure of huge interest to both her own compatriots and to the Spaniards who sailed into the Bay of Mexico on 'towers or small mountains floating on the waves of the sea'.[26] She witnessed firsthand the 'terror' of her father, who sent rich gifts and hospitality to the unwelcome visitors, something that was interpreted as worship by the Spaniards (although whether the Mexica truly believed that Hernan Cortes, the leader of the Spanish conquistadors, was the returning serpent-god Quetzalcoatl is highly disputed by scholars).[27] A demonstration by Cortes of the explosive power of his cannons ensured that he was invited to attend Motecuhzoma in the great city of Tenochtitlan.[28]

The Spanish crossing of the three causeways into Tenochtitlan (so large that men could ride eight abreast with ease) would change Tecuichpotzin's life, with her father going in person to meet them, a canopy carried over his head and mantles spread before him to prevent him touching the ground with his sandalled feet.[29] The Spanish were impressed, with one – writing forty years later that everything 'is so strongly imprinted in my memory, that it appears to me as if it had happened only yesterday'.[30] Motecuhzoma took his visitors sightseeing (including offering Hernan Cortes a complement of priests to carry him up the 114 steps to the top of the main, pyramid-shaped temple – a courtesy the conquistador, on looking at the queasily steep staircase, declined).***[31] From the top the Spanish were alarmed to see clear evidence of human sacrifice, but also gasped at the bird's-eye view of the city below, with its houses linked by wooden bridges and streets that were made up of canals down which canoeists paddled. The marketplace, with which goods from all over the Valley of Mexico were

---

*** Having climbed a Mexican pyramid (albeit a Mayan one – Ek Balam), I can testify to the terror they engender. The steps are alarmingly steep.

MIGHTY LADIES AND RIGHTEOUS (FEMALE) HUSBANDS

traded, particularly drew comment, with the Spaniards staring down awe-struck. Even those who had been to Rome or Constantinople exclaimed 'that for convenience, regularity, and population, they had never seen the like'. Cortes himself believed that 60,000 people came daily to buy and sell there, while he marvelled at 'shops like apothecaries, where they sell ready-made medicines as well as liquid ointments and plasters'.[32] The forests outside the city were rich with game, while the food was good and the houses neat and tidy. The Spanish were, in fact, particularly struck by the Mexica's cleanliness, noting with evident incredulity that Motecuhzoma II bathed daily and rested his clothes for at least four days before wearing them again.[33] Only a few years later, a Spanish ambassador would blame Elizabeth I of England's near fatal bout of smallpox on an uncharacteristic desire to take a bath. It is, of course, a virus and one that would be carried to Mexico by the Spaniards to appallingly devastating effect. Within two years of the Spaniards' arrival, glorious Tenochtitlan was in ruins and the fastidious Motecuhzoma was dead.

Tecuichpotzin was the symbol of the destruction wrought by Spain, as gold and treasures began to flow from the New World to the Old. On her father's death, she should have inherited his throne, but her sex made her a pawn.[34] There would later be claims that her horoscope had been cast at her birth with her father surprised to be told that his daughter would marry many husbands, but so it was to prove as Tecuichpotzin sought to navigate (or was navigated through) a world that was impossibly altered. First, she was married to two male relatives in turn who each claimed the throne, before being baptised as 'Isabel' (a name almost certainly chosen in honour of Spain's famous Queen Isabel I of Castile). She was twice widowed by the age of nineteen – her first husband, an uncle, died of smallpox after only sixty days of marriage, while her second, a cousin, was tortured and then hanged by the conquistadors. She bore Hernan Cortes a daughter in a relationship that may have been coercive before being married to a further three Spaniards in turn. The lack of agency is startling: Doña Isabel Moctezuma, as she became known, was one of, perhaps, 150 children born to her father, but crucially she was his only surviving legitimate heir.[35] As one Mexica poet writing after the conquest lamented, 'But who is that at the side of the Captain-General? Ah, it is Dona Isabel, my little niece! Ah, it is true; the kings are prisoners now.'[36] The Mexica viewed the new Doña Isabel as their rightful heir, even if her claims were pressed, or ignored, by the men in her life.

Tecuichpotzin/Doña Isabel's life was defined by the almostness of her monarchy. Her fifth and final husband, the Spaniard Juan Cano de Saavedra, promoted her 'rank and her legitimacy' through royal genealogies that were produced in her lifetime, with the stress laid on the fact that Mexica inheritance could pass through the female line.[37] Though she settled into life as a Spanish noblewoman, she and her husband continued to press her inheritance rights.[38] Forty years after her death, in 1590, Tecuichpotzin's heirs gained recognition of these claims, with Felipe II of Spain reaching a settlement with them in return for the renunciation of their rights as the heirs of Emperor Motecuhzoma II. This, at least, as one of Tecuichpotzin's biographers, Donald Chipman, has noted, 'vindicated Dona Isabel's decision, made more than half a century before, to link her destiny with that of the Spanish conquerors who had destroyed her nation and to contribute to the establishment of a new society on Mexican soil'.[39] It was more than this, too, with the payment, which came too late for Tecuichpotzin, a tacit acknowledgment that she, like her father and ancestors, had reigned – or at least that she should have done.

Tecuichpotzin, who was arguably the last ruler of the Mexica, lost her throne and her identity. She is now, largely, not even recognised as a queen.

MIGHTY LADIES AND RIGHTEOUS (FEMALE) HUSBANDS

While our knowledge of Tecuichpotzin is limited mostly due to the lack of a formal system of writing in Mexica culture, as well as their people's almost total erasure at the hands of Europeans, the details of Merneith's life are obscured by her position right at the beginning of written history. What we do know is scant and mediated through what has been dug out of the sand. Like Tenochtitlan, a city that expanded onto land reclaimed from a lake, the place that Merneith knew was well organised on a hitherto unheard-of scale. Egypt's annual Nile floods created a lush and verdant corridor of green, dissecting the red sands of Egypt's Western and Eastern deserts. Regular deposits of fertile river silt caused crops to flourish in the burning heat of the sun and grain stores, large enough to store a year's worth of wheat and barley, were dug into the ground and plastered with mud, before being lined with rush baskets.[40] It was these crop surpluses that allowed the building of a state.

Merneith is believed to be the daughter of King Djer and the great-granddaughter of King Narmer (also known as Menes), the latter famously uniting the two kingdoms of Upper and Lower Egypt. Wearing both crowns at once in his depiction on the famous Narmer Palette, he also holds his mace ready to strike down a kneeling captive – the king was frequently portrayed in such an aggressive stance. Fewer than ten women ruled alone in Egypt's 3000 years of pharaonic history (a paltry rate of around one every three centuries). And yet Merneith may even have been raised to reign: in the monument dedicated to her at Saqqara, thirteen impressions of a seal were found that displayed father's and daughter's names side by side and enclosed by serekhs – a symbol, shaped like a palace, which delineated the majesty of the pharaohs. Though she was likely not initially expected to rule alone, serving as wife and consort to King Djet, whose father is also thought to have been King Djer. Sibling marriages were common amongst the pharaohs, so it's entirely feasible that he was Merneith's brother, but it's also possible he attained his throne through her royal lineage. His was, in any event, a brief and unmemorable reign, by all accounts.[41] After his death, Merneith got down to the hum-drum business of ruling, employing her own inspector of canals, whose role involved managing irrigation work, designed to improve the agricultural capabilities of an already richly endowed land.[42]

Merneith, along with most First Dynasty pharaohs whose reigns followed the unification of the country, was provided with two funerary complexes, in Abydos and Saqqara, ceremonially located in Upper and Lower Egypt.[43] At Saqqara, her sacrificed servants were helpfully provided with grave goods to assist them in their everlasting labour, including paints for her artist, model boats for her shipmaster and pots for her potter. Merneith even had a nearly 60-foot-long boat to carry her spirit to the sun god Ra: she clearly intended to travel in style.

It would have been possible to learn more about Merneith had both her tombs not been all but destroyed by fire shortly after her death, with the conflagration at Saqqara so intense that the stone burst. There is evidence that it was deliberately started, suggesting that someone did not want this monarch to enjoy a peaceful afterlife with the gods or for her memory to echo down the millennia of eternity. Almost immediately after her death, Merneith's kingship was in question. This has continued to this day.[44] She was silenced and disenfranchised by deliberate destruction of her legacy and memory as surely as Tecuichpotzin was. So, too, was Empress Matilda of England.

The Bayeux Tapestry, that remarkable memorial of Matilda's grandfather's surprising conquest of England in 1066, is evidence of a society that similarly sharply differentiated between the sexes. This vibrant pictorial record – which is so long it has to snake round a corner in the purpose-built hall it is displayed in while visitors listen to an unpauseable audio guide to keep them moving – was worked by the

MIGHTY LADIES AND RIGHTEOUS (FEMALE) HUSBANDS

expert hands of Kentish embroideresses. However, just three women appear amongst the multitude of characters portrayed and these are (respectively) weeping, denigrated and victimised. Only one of these female figures was granted a name – Aelfgyva. She appears above an image of a naked man masturbating and pointing to her suggestively, which has almost unanimously been taken to suggest a scandalous reputation for this otherwise unknown woman. (Prudishly, the usually faithful full-scale Victorian copy now held in Reading Museum gave this small figure a pair of stripey shorts to cover his modesty.)[****] The Bayeux Tapestry was once commonly held to have been the work of Matilda's namesake grandmother and it remains known in France as 'La tapisserie de la reine Mathilde'.

Culturally, Anglo-Norman women did not ride into battle and received no martial training; royal women of the period were much more likely to work with a needle than a sword.[45] For the (male) chroniclers of the day, a female ruler was unacceptable, but so were any perceived masculine traits in a woman. One recalled Matilda 'with a grim look, her forehead wrinkled into a frown, every trace of a woman's gentleness removed from her face, blazed into unbearable fury'.[46] What was seen as strong rulership in a man was not necessarily viewed positively in a woman.

Matilda was forced by circumstances to free her cousin Stephen in late 1141, but she continued to press her rights for some years, before returning to Normandy and passing on her claim to her eldest son – who would eventually become King Henry II of England after Stephen's death. Matilda's arrival in England triggered a decade and a half of civil war. Victorians called this period the Anarchy and, while not contemporary, it is a somewhat apt term.

[****] This censorship was done on the photographs of the original tapestry which were supplied to the embroideresses by the V&A Museum in London rather than by the embroideresses themselves. They copied the images supplied.

WOMEN WHO RULED THE WORLD

Matilda's queenship has been obscured and hidden, with the sources on her life brief and often contradictory and always presented through a male lens. She looks like a monarch, acted like a monarch and the record shows she was recognised as such by some of her leading contemporaries. Yet, even now, Matilda's queenship remains frequently denied.[47] She rarely appears on king lists or sticker sets of monarchs sold in gift shops; even the *Horrible Histories* monarchs' song skips speedily from Stephen to Henry II.

That this position began to change in the latter years of the twentieth century and, certainly, in academic circles in the early years of the twenty-first, can probably be linked to the growth of the feminist movement. As early as 1851, one academic, publishing a study of Matilda's coinage considered her omission to be 'ungallant', while Catherine Hanley subtitled her 2019 biography of Matilda *Empress, Queen, Warrior*.[48] Yet, the work of Marjorie Chibnall, who devoted her career to Matilda and recognised her significant political role, is subtitled merely *Queen Consort, Queen Mother and Lady of the English*.[49] Even her epitaph, paid for her by her son, Henry II, references the men in her life: 'Great by birth, greater by marriage, greatest in her offspring: here lies Matilda, the daughter, wife and mother of Henry.' It hardly does her justice. Matilda's sex made her queenship disputed and possible to ignore. It was the same when Flinders Petrie accepted 'Meri-Neith' and relegated Merneith or when Tecuichpotzin morphed into Doña Isabel.

Denmark's 'Lady King' certainly wielded power on her own behalf, regardless of claims of her regency. Margrete I was an ambitious and expansionist ruler, not content simply with her two kingdoms of Denmark and Norway, but also determined to reacquire Sweden, which had been lost by her husband not long after their marriage – she never abandoned her title (by marriage) of Queen of Sweden, while she allowed her son to call himself 'lawful successor to the

MIGHTY LADIES AND RIGHTEOUS (FEMALE) HUSBANDS

kingdom of Sweden' in the 1380s. She intervened surreptitiously in the kingdom's affairs, including facilitating the appointment of her friend, Peder Jensen Lodehat, as Bishop of Växjö in 1382, by racing the chapter's messengers to the Pope when they attempted to elect their own candidate.[50]

Following her son's death, Denmark and Norway's 'righteous husband' continued in her attempts to retake Sweden, encouraging rebellion in the kingdom and courting its powerful nobility. In March 1388, a delegation from Sweden's royal council arrived in Denmark to formally elect Margrete as 'the almighty lady and true husband of Sweden'. The decisive battle came on 24 February 1389 when Margrete's forces defeated those of King Albrecht of Sweden, the man who had deposed her husband.[51] For Margrete, it was her greatest triumph, although she was still defined by some chroniclers in relation to the men in her life; she was, said one, 'the daughter of a wolf', referring to her father's notable cunning.[52] Even those who praised Margrete expressed their surprise in the outcome due to her sex, with one declaring, 'Praise be to God forever and ever, who gave the defeated an unexpected punishment in the hand of a woman, that is, kings in fetters and their nobles in iron cuffs.'[53] She would revere St Matthias, on whose feast day the battle had been fought, for the rest of her life.

For all her might, Margrete faced considerable pressure to provide a male ruler, eventually permitting her great-nephew, the somewhat hopeless Erik of Pomerania, to be declared King of Denmark, Norway and Sweden in 1396. However, while she lived, he served as merely a puppet. It was Margrete who created the Kalmar Union of the Scandinavian kingdoms in 1397, which would endure for more than a century after her death and placed the countries under one joint crown (with the component parts to 'remain in concordance and love').[54] It was an ambitious project and is a testament to Margrete's supreme power – effectively, she formed the first European Union. Tellingly, although young Erik was crowned as king of the union on 17 June in Kalmar, the treaty itself was published on 20 June: the feast day of St Margaret of Antioch.[55] The glory belonged to Margrete.

Denmark in the late fourteenth century was far from a cultural backwater, building alliances through marriage and trade across much of Western Europe, with a population of approximately one million citizens. The kingdom's herring, which passed through Danish waters in their millions every autumn, was the envy of Europe, with 40,000 boats setting out to catch, salt and sell them each year to feed the Christian world during Lent.[56] These lucrative herring markets were a bustling space tightly regulated by Margrete who decreed that anyone caught using 'false measures' would be executed, while she also confirmed in ordinances the amount of wine that should be poured into thirsty shopper's glasses.[57]

Margrete was a shrewd ruler. And yet, in this highly stratified society in which there was a strict delineation of the roles of the sexes, despite her undeniable power and authority, she eschewed the title of queen; even in her herring market ordinances, referring to herself as merely 'King Valdemar's daughter'. Despite her achievements, Margrete of Denmark was also excluded from the king lists for Denmark, with her quarter century rule glossed over as a regency or interregnum. Did this exclusion matter to her? Probably not, but it may have rankled to see her hapless great-nephew Erik feted solely on account of his sex.

So perhaps the last word of this chapter should be with Queen Margrethe II of Denmark who was, at the time of her abdication in January 2024, the world's only undisputed reigning queen. When she took the throne in 1972, a feat that was accomplished only when the law was changed to allow female succession, the queen chose her regnal number 'II', immediately promoting Margrete the 'regent' to Queen Margrete I.[58] At the stroke of a pen (or, in this case, the announcement of an accession from the balcony of the Christiansborg

MIGHTY LADIES AND RIGHTEOUS (FEMALE) HUSBANDS

Palace), Margrete joined, or rejoined, the long line of Danish monarchs, something that was denied this 'Lady King' during her lifetime.

Merneith, Matilda, Margrete and Tecuichpotzin have long seen their queenships disputed and denied, with the definition of monarch closed to them due to their sex. This reluctance to call a queen a queen is an almost universal theme. Would we say that any of these women did not rule (or at least attempt to do so) if they were men? It speaks of the disinclination of polities the world over to accept a female ruler, particularly if there was a male alternative, as the next chapter will show all too clearly.

CHAPTER 2:
THE MALE RELATIVE PROBLEM

Cleopatra VII of Egypt, Charlotte of Cyprus, and Blanca II and Leonor of Navarre

Charlotte of Cyprus had already endured years of troubles when, in late 1461, she boarded a ship to Rome to appeal directly to the Pope himself for assistance in her dispute with her half-brother over her island throne. This was a drastic decision, with many, including her parents-in-law, furious at her presumption in lobbying on her own behalf. ('How is it decent for a young woman to leave her husband and sail from the east to the west? To ask hospitality from so many strangers?' they railed.)[1] She was still only seventeen years old but had been widowed and wed again and crowned as a queen. She was hanging on to her throne by her fingertips. The stakes were high for her as she threw herself to the ground weeping and kissing the pontiff's feet. 'Her conversation,' he noted, 'came pouring out like a torrent.' She had the manner of a queen, considered Pope Pius II, who was himself a querulous and self-righteous figure. However, while he sympathised with her concerns, there was the small matter of the 'slights' done to him by her father-in-law and husband on previous occasions. 'A throne is an unstable thing,' summed up the Pope sagely, and 'in our opinion you are paying the penalty for the sins of your father-in-law and your husband'. What, exactly, these 'sins' done to the Pope by her male in-laws had to do with Charlotte and her reign in Cyprus is difficult to comprehend, but the Pope clearly thought it relevant that her reign should rise or fall on the behaviour of the men in her life. Male relatives were invariably a problem for reigning queens.

With few exceptions before the modern era, women reigned only when there were no viable male candidates. This is the reason queens were often the full stop at the end of a dynasty or emerged during times of dynastic turmoil – a reigning queen was the product, not the cause, of such a maelstrom. In inheritance systems favouring male primogeniture, this was even more certain, with the princesses of medieval Europe aware that they ranked below their male siblings (and, frequently, uncles or their own sons) in the succession. As we saw in the previous chapter, those women who did succeed in taking, or attempting to take, a throne were often overlooked or disparaged, with queens such as Matilda of England criticised for her lack of femininity when carrying out what was viewed as a male role. This is still the case today, with strong women often being described using terms such as 'shrill', a trait almost never ascribed to men, and undoubtedly designed (sometimes unconsciously) to silence them.[2] This is ancient. Even Hera, Queen of the Gods, was ordered by her brother-husband, Zeus, not to question his doings, according to Homer, the mysterious composer of *The Iliad*.[3] Such criticism extended well beyond the actual accession of these women, with Charlotte's 'torrent' of speech to the Pope a more archaic form of the claim that women talk too much. In reality, they speak up far too little.

Even those women who succeeded in claiming a throne needed to be cautious, since the men in their lives would frequently seek to attack, control or silence them: their thrones were very often seen as fair game. A half-sibling with no obvious claim to the throne, an uncle,

THE MALE RELATIVE PROBLEM

a father, a cousin: all were potentially dangerous to reigning queens who could rarely rely on the disinterested support of their male family members. A crown was too enticing a prize. That this was a fact for female kings across the world and across the eras is all too apparent. The world's most famous reigning queen, Cleopatra VII of Egypt (whose recognisability stands in stark contrast to her ancient predecessor, Merneith), is viewed today as a powerful woman who manipulated the men in her life with her sexuality as a means of furthering her wishes and ambitions. And yet, surprisingly, she too had to negotiate the 'male relative problem' and never actually ruled alone. There was a general presumption in Ptolemaic Egypt that there should be a king and a queen, even if one dominated the other. Cleopatra's 'manipulation' was often simply a tactic of ensuring her own survival in one of the most fiercely ambitious dynasties of all time.

Incest was an accepted practice in Egypt's pharaonic dynasties, allowing a close male relative to rule with the support of a similarly royal female. The Ptolemies, Egypt's final dynasty, adopted this practice as a means of ensuring that their royal blood was not diluted. This dynasty, of which Cleopatra VII was a part, worked hard to ensure the legitimacy of what had, initially, been a shaky claim to the throne. They arrived in Egypt in the wake of Alexander III of Macedon, the ancient world's all-famous conquering hero known as Alexander the Great. Alexander's general (and self-proclaimed half-brother) Ptolemy I snatched up Egypt after the former's death in 323 BCE, declaring himself pharaoh and basing himself in the new city of Alexandria. The Ptolemies, who were Greek by descent and culture, looked out from their capital at the Mediterranean Sea. That city today is a faded power, where monuments to the distant, Ptolemaic past stand amongst modern tower blocks in need of more than a lick of paint. Yet, walk around the monuments still dotted around, or go deep into the subterranean world of the Catacombs of Kom el Shoqafa, where families would bring picnics to share with the dead, and it all looks unmistakeably, self-consciously Ancient Egyptian. The new arrivals enthusiastically bought into the model of pharaonic rulership, though Cleopatra VII was closer in time to iPhones and aeroplanes than she was to the building of the Great Pyramid of Giza.

When Ptolemy II married his sister, one poet accused him of 'shoving your prick into an unholy hole', an outspoken statement, which led to the speaker being sealed into a lead jar and dropped into the sea.[4] While it was clearly a touchy subject, incest did increase the status of royal women, although it was still assumed that a man would succeed in preference to any sisters. Ptolemaic Egypt saw an ostensibly high number of queens, though few were truly rulers, while those that did reign rarely did so alone. There are exceptions to this: for example, Berenice III began her career as a co-ruler to her father, Ptolemy IX, but was able to retain the throne after his death in 81 BCE, most probably thanks to her wild popularity in Alexandria.[5] Her people still struggled to conceive of a female king with no male consort and she was pushed into marrying a cousin, who promptly murdered her before being torn apart by a furious mob. A generation or so later, supporters of Berenice IV ousted her father, Ptolemy XII, in 58 BCE, with the queen then reigning jointly with either her mother (Cleopatra V) or sister (Cleopatra VI), though which it was remains unclear.*[6] With her co-ruler's death, Berenice was required to marry a boorish cousin, before having him strangled during their honeymoon.[7] She held the throne alone until her father returned with an army in 55 BCE, ordering her immediate execution and handing the succession to his favourite daughter – Cleopatra VII.

Cleopatra was a complex figure.[8] She remains renowned as a famous beauty, temptress and seductress, although her surviving contemporary

---

* The identity of Berenice IV's co-ruler is not entirely certain. Most scholars believe Cleopatra VI did not exist.

THE MALE RELATIVE PROBLEM

portraiture gives few hints of this (we do not entirely know what she looked like. She seems to have had a prominent nose and may have been a redhead based on the limited portrait evidence which tends to depict her as a typical Roman matron). She was highly intelligent and very possibly the only member of the Ptolemaic dynasty to speak Egyptian fluently.

Cleopatra faced similar obstacles to her immediate female predecessors in asserting her rule. On her father's death four years after his return to Alexandria, she took the throne jointly with her brother, Ptolemy XIII. (They were also probably married, as was customary, but no evidence has been found to confirm this.)[9] At eighteen years old, she had the advantage of seniority over her eleven-year-old brother, although it was expected that the king would eventually become the dominant ruler.[10] The early years of their joint reign were troubled with food shortages, while the queen was increasingly seen as a Roman puppet, particularly when, in 49 BCE, she agreed to supply the Roman general and statesman, Pompey, who was the great rival of Gaius Julius Caesar (better known as simply Julius Caesar), with military aid. Seizing this chance, young Ptolemy expelled Cleopatra from Alexandria and removed her from the throne. That he had the power to do this highlights clearly Cleopatra's need to vie for power with a close male relative. Hers might be one of the most recognisable names in history, but she still forced to struggle to assert herself against the men in her life.

For her part, Charlotte of Cyprus was a self-possessed woman with manners 'such as became a lady of royal station'.[11] Her assertiveness in travelling to Rome to apply for the pontiff's support for her rule was perhaps partly down to her claim that 'as the only daughter of their marriage my parents brought me up in the expectation of ruling', though this placed her in an anomalous position: her sun-parched island kingdom actively discouraged female succession.[12] There had never been a female heiress to Cyprus before and it was not a prospect that the estimated 120,000 citizens of the island relished.[13] While she seems to have had some hope of actually ruling rather than serving as a mere figurehead, the focus in Cyprus was very much on the question of her marriage and the king that this would provide.

Cyprus may have been lacking in reigning queens, but – like Egypt – it had always known powerful women. Not least, Charlotte's mother, the Byzantine princess, Helena Palaiologina. She dominated her husband, Charlotte's father, Jean II of Cyprus, and was renowned as 'a virago'.[14] Helena, who 'acted more as king than queen' (according to her contemporary, Pope Pius II), was a force to be reckoned with. One, most likely apocryphal, story has her biting off the nose of her husband's mistress, Marietta of Patras.[15]

The kings of Cyprus had traditionally looked towards Western Europe for their brides, but Helena was entirely Greek in both culture and sympathies. She shocked the Pope by strenuously attempting to promote the Greek church. The Lusignan dynasty who ruled Cyprus had traditionally patronised only Roman Catholicism, although the Greek Orthodox Church was dominant amongst the populace. The two Christian faiths largely ran alongside each other successfully. Indeed, a German friar breaking his journey to the Holy Land in Cyprus in 1483 stopped to rest in a Greek Orthodox Church and was horrified to discover that his host – a monk – 'was curate of both churches, the Greek and the Latin, and performed indifferently the offices of either rite'. On Sundays 'he first said Mass in the Latin church, and consecrated the Host, as do the Westerns in unleavened bread. This done, he went over to the Greek church and consecrated as do the Easterns, in leavened bread.'[16] This was par for the course in the cultural mix of Cyprus, even if Helena Palaiologina did attempt to tip the balance towards the Greek faith. She was, according to one contemporary, 'a terrible Greek', suggesting that much of the criticism

THE MALE RELATIVE PROBLEM

was due to xenophobia.[17] There was, undoubtedly, a considerable element of misogyny too.

Helena was a colossus in the politics of 1440s and 1450s Cyprus, but she was no reigning queen. She also would have been seen to have failed as a queen consort in the most fundamental way, bearing no sons. Instead, it was the apparently nose-less Marietta of Patras, her husband's mistress, who succeeded, producing a son – Jacques – who was an acknowledged member of the dynasty, even if he was not earmarked as the heir to the kingdom.

In the late medieval period, Cyprus's ruling Lusignan dynasty was a relatively stable one. While at least one Cypriot king had succeeded through a female line, there was a clear preference for male succession, even when a woman had – ostensibly – a better claim. In light of this, Charlotte's mother looked warily at Jacques, a handsome and charismatic boy a year or two older than Charlotte – and her most obvious rival.

The appointment of this boy as Archbishop of Nicosia when he was barely a teenager may have been a deliberate solution to the problem of the existence of Jacques the Bastard, since holy orders would bar him from the throne. If so, it was an ill-calculated one. In April 1457, only a year after taking up his position, he murdered the royal chamberlain, Iacopo Urri, forcing him to abandon his see and flee to Rhodes.[18] He was soon pardoned and permitted to return home. It was plain to see that Jean II adored his illegitimate son. Most crucially of all: he acknowledged him. While Jean II had committed himself to his daughter's succession, a male relative – even an illegitimate one – always held the potential to be a significant challenge to Charlotte's future reign.

With an older brother, Carlos, the future Blanca II of Navarre was, unlike her Cypriot counterpart, not born to reign in the nearly forgotten tiny mountainous kingdom, which sat high in the Pyrenees in what is now north-eastern Spain, amidst such other vanished polities as Castile, Aragon, Granada and Leon. Instead, both Blanca and her younger sister, Leonor, were intended for diplomatic marriages, the usual lot of a medieval European princess.

Through mischance and bad luck, the kingdom had proved early that female succession was acceptable. Premature deaths and accidents happened so frequently in the Navarrese royal family (including a baby prince being dropped from a window) that, by the fifteenth century, it was almost a queendom. Blanca's mother, Blanca I, was married to the future Juan II of Aragon, an ambitious spider-like prince determined not to give up one inch of any land that passed into his grasping fingers. The kingdom, centred on picturesque, pretty Pamplona, which is now most famous for its running of the bulls (and subsequent gorings), might have accepted female monarchs, but few of them can be said to have ruled entirely independently, with Juan ruling alongside his wife. Following the deaths of her mother and brother, Blanca II, the couple's eldest daughter, was to find that her greatest rival was to be her own father, who was determined to ensure that Navarre's ancient throne remained firmly in his grip.

But first came Blanca's marriage. The family hedged their bets, choosing a wealthy French nobleman for Leonor and a Spaniard for Blanca. Accordingly, in the early autumn of 1440, the sixteen-year-old Blanca set out for Valladolid in Castile, accompanied by her mother and brother at the head of a great number of Navarrese lords. There, they were given 'a very great welcome', with hunting, feasting and tournaments lavishly arranged.[19] It was, on the face of it, a sparkling match for a princess from a tiny Pyrenean kingdom, but the bridegroom shocked everyone by furiously refusing to attend the wedding banquet. Matters did not improve. The morning after the wedding, it was widely reported that the future Enrique IV of Castile, who is remembered by the nickname 'el Impotente', had left his bride 'as she was born'.[20] This, one contemporary chronicler reported, made everyone 'very angry', but there was nothing to be done except wait and see whether the marriage could ever succeed.[21] It soon became apparent that it could not.

As a monarch, Enrique IV's reputation was smeared by propaganda, as we will see in Chapter 8. However, there is little doubt that he was unable to fully validate his marriage to Blanca through sexual intercourse. A twentieth-century biographer of Blanca's father, Juan II, considered that it was Enrique's suspicion of his father-in-law's ambitions that led to his failure to sleep with his wife, while Elena Woodacre in her masterful study of the reigning queens of Navarre has concluded the same.[22]

Blanca's mother died not long after the wedding, in 1441. This only served to further consolidate the power of Blanca's father, Navarre's king consort. Blanca I had recognised first her son, Carlos, and then her two daughters as her heirs. However, she surprisingly requested in her will, which she had signed over two years before, that 'although the said prince, our very dear and very beloved son, may, after our death, by reason of inheritance and recognised right, be titled and name yourself King of Navarre and Duke of Nemours, however to maintain the honour due to the king your father, we beg you, with the greatest tenderness we can, not to wish to take these titles without the consent and blessing of the said lord your father'.[23] Given Juan's great ambition (he had actually abandoned a betrothal with Blanca I's younger sister when the heiress to Navarre unexpectedly came on the marriage market), this attempt to delay Carlos's accession was a recipe for disaster.[24] Maybe, as Juan's leading biographer Jaume Vicens Vives has suggested, she did it either due 'to her exquisite devotion or to an inextinguishable love for the person of her husband', but it was contrary to the laws of Navarre and, indeed, to what most contemporaries would consider natural justice.[25] Carlos's fury was compounded when his father unexpectedly succeeded to the throne of Aragon in 1458, but still would not pass Navarre over to him. Juan took a Castilian noblewoman as his second wife, producing a second family, including a son, Fernando, which raised suspicions even more in his first wife's kingdom that he meant to absorb Navarre into Aragon and pass it to his new heirs after his death.

For the younger Blanca, all of this must have been troubling – her family back in Navarre were at loggerheads over the succession and her own position in Castile was highly precarious. There were whispers (heartily endorsed by Enrique, who was anxious to avoid claims of his impotency) that her marriage was hexed or cursed, or that her husband had been bewitched, causing his lack of performance.[26] By the early 1450s, he was actively seeking a new marriage.[27] The case was heard by the Bishop of Segovia on 11 May 1453, with the royal couple sending separate lawyers to plead their cases. Enrique had, his attorney assured the bishop, attempted 'with all love and faithful will ... carnal copulation with the said lady Princess', but the years spent on these endeavours had been wasted.[28] It was not, the lawyer hastened to add, a problem with the prince. He was unable to consummate his relationship with Blanca but 'not with others'. However, since he wished to be a father, something had to be done.

Blanca's thoughts on all this are unknown, although she was compliant with the inquiry, admitting through her lawyer that she was 'an incorrupt virgin and as she had been born'. Both were prepared to swear oaths to this effect, but this was not enough for the thorough bishop. To prove the case, Blanca was required to undergo an intimate physical examination. For Enrique, it was more simple. His agents merely went to one of Segovia's brothels, recruiting a group of prostitutes who were prepared to attest to his 'firm, virile cock'.[29] With that, the marriage was pronounced dissolved and the couple free to marry other people. Enrique 'el Impotente' would later come to regret his willingness to admit to an inability to perform in the marriage bed. For Blanca, however, as was usually the case for women, it was much worse. She was returned to Navarre and, once again, found herself under the authority of her covetous father.

Royal marriages were almost always politically motivated in medieval Europe, with success invariably random. Charlotte of Cyprus, who began her own marital career only a few years after Blanca's ended, would find that she was no happier in matrimony than her Navarrese counterpart. In the mid-1450s, her father, Jean II, opened negotiations for her to wed Joao of Coimbra, a grandson of King Joao I of Portugal, who was then in his mid-twenties, a somewhat mysterious selection, given his lack of connection to Cyprus or any neighbouring realms. Nonetheless, the couple married in 1456, when Charlotte was twelve years old, with her new husband's position as *de facto* heir to the throne reinforced when he was created Prince of Antioch (a defunct Crusader state claimed by the Cypriot royal family) and Regent of Cyprus.[30]

Charlotte's new husband was soon at odds with her mother over his favouritism of the Latin Church over the Greek. As relations deteriorated, Joao fell sick, dying on 11 September 1457 in Nicosia after a year of marriage. Unsurprisingly, given their tense relationship, Queen Helena was widely believed to have poisoned her son-in-law. Charlotte would later describe the marriage as 'unfortunate', saying only that 'the husband I took from Portugal I lost by a sudden and untimely death'.[31] She made no further recorded comment about the stranger with whom she had once been expected to share her throne and her bed. Soon, negotiations opened for a marriage to her first cousin, Louis of Savoy, a match that would be equally unsatisfactory. Before anything could be agreed, Queen Helena died on 11 April 1458. 'Scarcely caring any more for sovereignty', the ineffectual Jean II followed her to the grave three months later.[32]

In less than a year, the just turned fourteen-year-old Charlotte had been both widowed and orphaned. Alone and unprotected, she immediately took steps to take control of Cyprus's fertile, rugged 3500 square miles, its economy dominated by its lucrative saltpans, the trade in luxury fabrics and – when the almost Biblical plagues of locusts allowed – the expansive wheatfields. Ostensibly a calm, sleepy place (although visitors habitually complained about the 'foul and almost pestiferous air'), Cyprus's size and location meant that it had long been viewed as prey by the various powers of the area. Prehistoric hunter-gatherers, Phoenicians, Pharaonic Egyptians, Persians, Greeks, Ptolemies, Romans, Byzantines: the list of the island's masters was a rollcall of the leading powers in that part of the world for millennia. Richard the Lionheart came, saw and conquered Cyprus during one frenetic month in 1191, but then he always lived his life at a frantic pace. He only spent six months in his other island kingdom, England, during a decade-long reign. Crusading was an expensive business and Richard paid his bills with the sale of Cyprus: first to the Templars, who were driven out by hostile islanders, and then to Guy de Lusignan, widower of Queen Sybilla of Jerusalem, whom we will meet in Chapter 4. The Lusignans added a frisson of Frankishness to an island that was already home to Greeks, Italians, Syrians, Armenians and exiles from the Latin kingdoms of the Holy Land.[33] It was a natural stopping point, too, for pilgrims on their way to Jerusalem. Saint's relics and holy sites drew tourists, just as the island's castles and other historic sites do for visitors today.

Initially, the Lusignans had paid homage to the Holy Roman Emperor, but in 1373 they were conquered by the Genoese. Just over fifty years later they were conquered again, this time by Egypt. Cyprus's King Janus, Charlotte's grandfather, who had been born in captivity in Genoa, found himself chained and paraded through the streets of Cairo.[34] The price of his freedom was 200,000 ducats and a substantial annual tribute to Egypt, making Cyprus a vassal of the Mamluk sultan. This would have profound implications for Charlotte.

Charlotte's coronation took place on 15 October 1458, although there were whispered murmurings when, as she left the ceremony on horseback, her horse reared and the crown fell from her head, which seemed to some like an inauspicious start. Charlotte was in no hurry to wed again, though she finally bowed to pressure and married Louis of Savoy on 7 October 1459, having ruled alone for a little over a year. It was politic to stand behind a male co-ruler, even one as cold, aloof and dislikeable as Louis of Savoy. Charlotte was clearly unenthusiastic about her charmless cousin, with the two vying for dominance by issuing their own coins as monarch that made no reference to the other.[35] It was a battle that Charlotte was never likely to win: the authority of a king, even a king by marriage, was invariably greater than that of a mere queen. Charlotte would later recall that, 'I succeeded my father and having been proclaimed queen ascended the throne together with my husband,' omitting to mention her year of ruling alone.[36]

Perhaps Charlotte felt extra pressure to rule alongside a king because of the challenge to her reign from her half-brother, Jacques, a considerably more charismatic figure than her husband, Louis. After attempting to assassinate Charlotte, Jacques fled the island. He sailed to Egypt along with his supporters, including William Goneme, a highly resourceful Augustinian friar, to lobby in person amongst Cyprus's Mamluk overlords.[37] He secured the friendship of Sultan Inal's son, as well as many of the more powerful emirs who surrounded the Mamluk sultan. Jacques' endeavours quickly bore fruit, with the sultan gifting fine robes of honour to Jacques and the Machiavellian Goneme. In the sultan's eyes, Jacques was King of Cyprus.

Thanks to the annulment of her marriage, Blanca II of Navarre did not have the somewhat dubious luxury of a man to potentially shore up her power. Back home in Navarre in 1453, she united herself with her brother, the ostensible Carlos IV of Navarre, in his struggle with their father.[38] In this she found herself opposed to her younger sister, Leonor, Countess of Foix, who along with her husband stood steadfastly with their remaining parent. Her loyalty was rewarded when, in Barcelona on 3 December 1455 Juan signed a document disinheriting Carlos and Blanca and leaving the throne of Navarre (after his death) to Leonor.[39] This was both illegal and at odds with the prevailing rights as Juan's contemporaries would have viewed it, but it had the desired effect of dividing the siblings even further, with Leonor and her husband, Gaston, Count of Foix, taking on the governance of the kingdom in her father's absence.

Amidst ongoing civil strife, Carlos died suddenly on 23 September 1461. It is hard not to suspect murder: his contemporaries certainly thought so. José Moret, in his *Anales del Reino de Navarra,* considered the prince's stepmother (who was anxious that her own young son should succeed to Aragon) was the poisoner, but others credited the deed to Leonor.[40] Carlos's restless ghost, which was seen (according to more than one source) walking the streets of Barcelona, cried out for revenge, but he was not to receive it. With his death, the focus of everyone opposed to Juan II turned towards Carlos's eldest sister who became, at least in the eyes of many, Queen Blanca II of Navarre. It was not to be a long reign.

Cleopatra's reacquisition of power in Alexandria stems from a substantial misstep on the part of her brother. When the Roman general Pompey, who Cleopatra had been supplying with miliary aid, unexpectedly arrived in Alexandria the following year, Ptolemy had him murdered. Julius Caesar, who himself arrived in Egypt's capital city shortly afterwards, was outraged to be presented with his rival's (and one time son-in-law's) head and ordered his troops to seize the

THE MALE RELATIVE PROBLEM

royal palace. The Roman statesman then ordered that both Ptolemy and Cleopatra appear before him so that he could decide the merits of their respective claims himself. Determined to plead her case to Caesar privately, Cleopatra famously had herself smuggled into the palace in a bundle of linen sheets (although it is unlikely that she was unrolled quite as dramatically as Elizabeth Taylor was in the 1963 epic *Cleopatra*). According to Plutarch, Caesar was 'captivated' at the first sight of Cleopatra, finding her 'a bold coquette'.[41] She was soon his mistress, with the Roman ordering Ptolemy to take Cleopatra back as his co-ruler. When Ptolemy heard of Cleopatra's success, he publicly tore off his crown, inciting the people of Alexandria to storm the palace, with the city tense and on edge.

Undoubtedly, Cleopatra was a skilled politician – as she needed to be, coming to power as she did at a time when Rome was eyeing her kingdom acquisitively. She won the support of Julius Caesar against her siblings, remaining as his mistress and claiming him as the father of her eldest child – an assertion that the Roman consul did not deny. Even then, having rid herself of Ptolemy XIII, she was required to rule alongside another little brother, Ptolemy XIV, whom she also probably married. He was likely murdered by his Cleopatra in 44 BCE, allowing her to proclaim her young son, Ptolemy XV 'Caesarion', as her co-ruler, who reigned alongside her for the rest of her life.

Following Julius Caesar's assassination in 44 BCE, Cleopatra allied herself with Caesar's close supporter the Roman general Marcus Antonius (better known today as Mark Antony), who took control of the eastern portion of the Roman Empire, while Caesar's nephew and heir, Octavian, the soon-to-become-Emperor Augustus, took the west. This proved to be a fatal miscalculation, since Mark Antony, who became Cleopatra's consort and fathered her youngest three children, was married to Octavian's sister. Although undoubtedly a powerful queen, she was never entirely able to assert her independence from the men in her life, with Cleopatra ultimately brought low by the ambitions of Mark Antony when Egypt was drawn into his dispute with Octavian. When Antony was defeated in the Battle of Actium in 32 BCE, their cause must have seemed hopeless. Both committed suicide in 30 BCE, with William Shakespeare romanticising the rather unlikely claim that Cleopatra died by inducing an asp to bite her. His Cleopatra – a complex portrayal of a highly sexualised and independent queen – underplays the Egyptian queen's political acumen and cunning while it overstates the independence of a woman who, to rule, always had to have a male figure at her side. She most likely died by drinking poison.

While Charlotte of Cyprus would take it upon herself to make the trip to Rome to try to secure the support of another foreign powerful man, Pope Pius II, her ability to make alliances and so shore up her control over her kingdom was severely limited by her sex. A problem that her brother did not, of course, have to surmount.

Charlotte was prepared to do battle for the crucial approval of her Mamluk overlord in Egypt but there was no way she could go there herself. Her hands were also tied by the fact that her husband, Louis, had singularly failed to take the initiative. She finally sent an embassy to Cairo in her husband's name in late 1459. Her envoys arrived in a city that was one of the largest in the world, teeming with life.[42] It was a city of markets, public baths and grand mosques, with their minarets rising high above the streets below. There were great riches but also poverty, with crowds of the poor – armed only with sieves – sifting the sand outside the sultan's palace, searching for a dropped trinket or, perhaps, even a fortune-making lost diamond. Charlotte's emissaries went straight to the sultan with their gifts and tribute before, in an enormous setback to their queen, promptly dying of plague. Undaunted, Charlotte immediately sent Peter Podocataro, who had previously represented her father with the sultan. He arrived for an audience at the same time

THE MALE RELATIVE PROBLEM

as Jacques' emissaries, with both groups kissing the ground before the Mamluk ruler, as required of non-Muslims at his court.[43]

Podocataro had rich gifts, of course, both for the sultan and for the most influential royal emirs. He promised, on Charlotte's behalf, that she would increase Cyprus's annual tribute in exchange for Egyptian recognition of her queenship, while John Dolfin, who had come as the emissary of the Knight's Hospitallers, relayed his Grand Master's orders that he should 'urge the sultan to reach an agreement with 'the king of Cyprus', by whom he meant Louis of Savoy. After some thought, the sultan declared in favour of Charlotte, ordering that robes be prepared to be sent to the queen as Egypt's vassal, as well as presents and letters confirming her accession. Jacques, who was present, burst into tears.

In many ways it was surprising that the sultan was prepared to decide in Charlotte's favour, since the Mamluk Sultanate had no concept of illegitimacy: in Egypt, the contest was simply viewed as one between the son and daughter of the former king, something which was hardly a contest at all.[44]

However, when Charlotte's emissaries arrived the next morning to collect the queen's robe everything had changed – they had been outbid. A natural inclination on the part of the sultan to favour the male candidate was helped in no small part by the fact that Jacques, spurred on by the urging of William Goneme, spent the whole of that night bribing the most influential emirs around the sultan. The 'newly bought' Mamluks, as one contemporary source calls them, tore the robes from Charlotte's ambassadors' hands and placed them on Jacques, declaring 'what, deprive the male, and give the lordship to the female?'. Faced with this pressure, the sultan capitulated. Amidst cries of 'long live King Jacques', the sultan promised to support Charlotte's half-brother, sending him back to Cyprus with a Mamluk fleet. Scandalously, he also invited Jacques, an 'infidel', to attend the festivities to mark the birthday of the Prophet Muhammed.[45] Jacques' ability to present in person and charm the sultan and his court – something which Charlotte, as a woman – could not do, won the day.

Jacques had secured the recognition of Egypt, as well as military support, but Charlotte was not beaten. Civil war erupted in Cyprus in September 1460 when Jacques arrived with his Egyptian fleet, immediately making conquests. Jacques' strategy had been to present himself in Cyprus as the Greek candidate for the throne, using the Frankishness of the Lusignan dynasty against his sister. Charlotte, on the other hand, depicted the conflict in religious terms, as demonstrated in the way she declared to the pontiff that she and her husband were 'waging war with the enemies of the Cross of Christ'. Religion was always seen as the proper sphere for female activities, but in Charlotte's case she failed to inspire a Crusade against her 'Pseudo-Christian' brother (as she called him). Even her parents-in-law, whom she visited in Savoy to request aid, rebuffed her, remonstrating with her for her presumption in soliciting aid herself since 'it was more fitting for a husband to seek to do that'.[46] Charlotte, as all reigning queens have found, was held to higher standards of behaviour than a male ruler. Ashamed by this hostility, she abandoned plans to travel on to France. Soon afterwards, her kingdom was finally lost. Jacques was crowned as King of Cyprus in 1464 after Charlotte and Louis fled. She would never again enjoy more than the pretence of royal power.

Blanca II faced a similar barrier to claiming her power. With her 'accession', the ire of her father, sister and brother-in-law immediately turned directly towards her. Her very presence in Navarre was a threat to the pretensions of all three. In early 1462, the decision was taken to move Blanca out of Navarre and into France, presumably to ensure that she could no longer press her claims. On being told that she was to wed the Duke of Berry, brother of Louis XI of France, she angrily refused. They took her anyway and it is on 23 April 1462, when she arrived under guard at the monastery of Roncesvalles, that we get a glimpse of

THE MALE RELATIVE PROBLEM

just how impressive a monarch Blanca could have been. Bravely, for she was essentially a prisoner, she sat down to write a lengthy document, protesting at her treatment, which she clearly intended as a statement of her plight to the world.

She was, she said, the granddaughter and heir of Carlos III 'of laudable memory', whose kingdom had been damaged by Juan II, who had also harmed her brother, Carlos IV, showing 'great hatred against him and his people'. Since Carlos was now dead, after long periods of imprisonment, she asserted her rights: 'I am the owner and Lady and heir of the said kingdom.'[47]

It was a brave assertion of her rights as a reigning queen, but it did little to protect her from attack from her father, her sister and her brother-in-law. Blanca herself noted the impossibility of her position. In her protest, she was forced to turn to the one man who likely despised her father nearly as much as she did: her former husband, who had become Enrique IV of Castile. She would, she said, make him her heir, asking him to enter Navarre and recover her kingdom for her, since only war could 'obtain the freedom of my person and recover the blessed kingdom of Navarre entirely'. It was a last desperate throw of the dice.

As she was moved further away from Pamplona, her position appeared even more hopeless. On 30 April, she attempted to abdicate in favour of Enrique IV, apparently hoping at least to keep Navarre out of the hands of her father and sister. It was not to be. Amidst civil war, Castilian invasion and diplomatic manoeuvring, Blanca quietly died on 2 December 1464. Unsurprisingly, Leonor was the main suspect in this 'pitiful death'.[48]

Yet, Leonor would never succeed in emerging from beneath her father's domineering shadow and benefitted very little from her loyalty to him. When Juan II died on 20 January 1479, at the advanced age of eighty, she finally succeeded to her mother's throne. Leonor was crowned in Pamplona eight days later but died on 12 February after a reign of only three weeks.[49] It is hard to disagree with the statement of one chronicler that, 'She was not very happy during her reign. Because among all the kings and queens of Navarre she was the one who reigned the least, being perhaps the one who wanted it the most.'[50] Her reputation remains 'unsavoury': she was effectively the public face of her father's regime.

Although she held authority for longer than her fifteenth-century European counterparts, Cleopatra's reign was ultimately a failure. The last and most famous of Egypt's female kings never reigned alone, ruling alongside two brothers and then her son.[51] Though never technically a sole monarch, she was the dominant party, relying initially on her friendship with Rome to build her independent position. She would almost certainly have had more success if she had been able to remain single.

Charlotte of Cyprus and Blanca II of Navarre are also (and more emphatically so) examples of failed queen regnants. Neither managed to retain either their thrones or their independence, in the face of fierce opposition from the men in their lives. They simply could not live up to the ideals of kingship in a way that their male relatives could: social pressure, but also real political power worked against women in their period and in other centuries. To be recognised as the heir to a throne was one thing: to take possession was often quite another, as Cleopatra, Charlotte, Blanca and Leonor were to find. It is therefore surprising that, in the face of all the pressures against female rule, some women were able to snatch their thrones from out of the hands of male rivals.

CHAPTER 3:

SNATCHING THE THRONE

Hatshepsut of Egypt, Irene of Byzantium, and Elizaveta and Catherine II of Russia

Today, the vast yellow-white stone temple complex is usually busy with tourists braving the steep steps in burning heat as they climb into a building constructed into the side of a giant cliff. Early photographs attest that this structure was once considerably more ruinous, but, like a great many other archaeological sites around the world, it has been rebuilt and restored. When it was first constructed, well over 3000 years ago, it shone in the beating sunlight of the city of Thebes, now Luxor in the centre of Egypt. Inside, painted scenes on plaster walls take you into the bedchamber of a pharaoh's wife, candidly witnessing her seduction by the great god Amun. On beholding a child born nine months after this liaison, the god declared, 'Thou art the king who takes possession of the diadem on the Throne of Horus of the Living, eternally.'[1] This prophesied monarch was Hatshepsut, Egypt's most successful female king.

Hatshepsut began her political career as a consort, but she neglected to stress her connection to her brother-husband, Thutmose II, who is remembered primarily for suffering from a disfiguring skin disease (he may also be the stubborn Biblical king described in Exodus). Hatshepsut's great mortuary temple, which is all pillars, stairs and open spaces, has little wall space, making this message of celestial endorsement all the more significant; it is what she wanted to tell the world.

What she did not want to relate, however, were the circumstances of her promotion from queen consort to king when she was already in her mid-thirties. While she lived, these were as shrouded as her scratched-out face on the monuments of her reign, an act most likely carried out by the man who was her predecessor, co-ruler and successor. Since across the world it was usually difficult for a woman to inherit a throne, it is perhaps not surprising that many came to power in circumstances that were less than neat and tidy. A relatively high number of queens effectively snatched their thrones.

Hatshepsut, as a royal princess, was at least born with a potential claim to the throne, with her sex the major obstacle. Three thousand years later, Catherine II of Russia, who remains wildly famous as Catherine the Great, faced barriers that were greater still: she was barely royal, not Russian and had no claim at all to the Russian crown – and she was a woman. When Sophia Augusta Frederica of Anhalt-Zerbst was born into provincial German obscurity in 1729, not one single person could have predicted that, by the age of thirty-three, she would be rechristened into the Orthodox Church as Catherine to rule over a realm of icons, ice and serfs. She would hold the greatest territorial empire that the world had hitherto seen. And yet, perhaps with the exception of the sixteenth-century Ivan the Terrible, she remains Russia's most well-known and memorable ruler – an Enlightened Despot, who corresponded with Voltaire and the other leading philosophers of the day. Even Catherine, whose own near-obsessive autobiographical writings worked and reworked her story as the years went by, seemed not entirely at ease with the twists and turns of her eventful path to the throne.[2]

Probably unwittingly, Catherine would follow in the footsteps of Irene, who ruled another Orthodox empire nearly 1000 years earlier. Irene, who was raised in Athens, would rule over the Byzantine Empire from within the walls of the mighty city of Constantinople. She is surprisingly relatively obscure today given the circumstances of her rise to power when she was already approaching her fifties. Yet, she proved to be a highly forceful figure, very much underestimated in the male-dominated court in which she found herself. She thrived in the whispers of conspiracies that floated through windows and were voiced in dark corridors.

Irene, Hatshepsut and Catherine were all mature women when they began their assent to power, having served long apprenticeships at their respective courts. Although more than 2000 years separated Hatshepsut from Irene and another 1000 years separated Irene from Catherine, there are parallels in the ways in which they grasped for their thrones. They must have been ambitious. Clearly, all three had the intensity of purpose and character needed to take the leap from consort or regent into a man's world of rule, but they also used the advantage afforded by the weakness of the men in their lives. Catherine could never have removed her husband's grandfather, Peter the Great from the throne, but weak Peter III was another matter. The women discussed in this chapter spotted an opportunity and they seized it.

Constantinople must have astounded the teenaged Irene as she viewed it from her ship in 769 CE, with the metropolis sitting on a triangular peninsula on the borders of Europe and Asia. No city in all the world was mightier. The harbour was guarded by a great iron chain that could be suspended across the waters in time of attack. Triple walls, too, ringed the city on land, making it almost impregnable. Every luxury that could be traded and bought was crowded into its fragrant marketplaces, with spices, fabrics and furs squeezed onto stalls filled with exotica. It was a place where the wealthy showed pride in their position through great public buildings and monuments, with triumphal arches proclaiming the city's power. Irene could have glimpsed in the forum the mighty statue of Constantine the Great, the city's namesake and unifier of the Roman Empire, depicted with a crown radiating out like the rays of the sun. Although monuments to the old gods remained in places, Constantinople had been founded as a Christian city, with its domed churches and steeples rising up in praise of Christ, who had reputedly won over the first Christian Roman emperor with a miracle. Of course, no church was greater than Hagia Sophia, which was already more than 200 years old and by far and away the largest church in the world. Now Istanbul's Grand Mosque, its dome still dominates the city today.

The Western Roman Empire had long since fallen by the time of Irene's birth in the 750s, having been replaced with a hotchpotch of warring duchies, petty princedoms and ambitious kingdoms, as well as walled city states and prosperous port cities. The eastern part, however, on whose edges she was born, continued to thrive. The people of the empire's capital, Constantinople (modern-day Istanbul), thought of themselves as Romans, called themselves Romans and were, indeed, essentially Roman, albeit with the Greek style that had always characterised the empire's eastern provinces.[3] The sixth-century Emperor Justinian I had reformed both the church and the state while his consort, the lowborn former 'actress' (which may be shorthand for prostitute), Theodora, set the scene for powerful empress consorts.[4] These imperial wives were sometimes able to establish themselves as regents, issuing their own decrees and minting their own coins, which had, unusually for the time, female faces glaring out at their owners.[5] Irene, who may have been selected in a 'bride show', which was a beauty contest for eligible girls, was likely aware of her famous predecessors and could have had legitimate expectations of power, albeit through her husband and male children. She was plucked from obscurity in 769 to wed the future Emperor Leo IV, travelling by sea from the provinces to a city that was then the centre of the world.[6]

Fifteen-year-old Catherine II arrived in Russia with her mother after a snowy journey overland in 1745, wrapped in furs and enveloped in an imperial sleigh. The immense landscape through which she travelled was vastly different from the miniature cities and tidy countryside that she had known in Germany, while the people who came out of their houses to watch her pass and their customs were alien to her. To her mother, the unfamiliarity was alarming, but to Catherine it was an opportunity to be embraced. Russia suited her – it fascinated her. The same could not be said for her fiancé, sixteen-year-old Grand Duke Peter who was heir to Russia's imperial throne and whom she met for the first time soon after her arrival. He was, like Catherine, German by birth, with no memory of his Russian mother, Anna Petrovna, daughter of Peter the Great, who had died when he was tiny. With a claim to the Swedish as well as the Russian throne, he was extraordinarily well connected. Yet, according to his future wife, he was locked in a state of 'perpetual childishness', playing make-believe games until well into his late teens.[7] He was an unhappy, orphaned boy, who had been removed from everything that he had known in childhood when he was summoned to Russia, becoming 'irredeemably Prussian' and emphasising his Germanness to compensate.[8]

Unlike Peter, Catherine, who was similarly cast adrift, thrived. She learned Russian, a language in which he was never fluent, and immersed herself in her studies of the Orthodox Church. ('I find,' she wrote reassuringly but inaccurately to her anxious father who had remained at home in Stettin, 'almost no difference between the Greek and Lutheran faiths.')[9] Years later, she would recall in her memoirs that she saw at once that Peter 'did not care much for the nation that he was destined to rule, that he clung to Lutheranism, did not like his entourage, and was very childish'.[10] There may well be a strong element of retrospective justification in this pen-portrait, with one biographer considering that too much reliance is placed on her words, through which she 'concealed her competition for power by demeaning an able opponent'.[11] But even his indulgent aunt, the Empress Elizaveta, who had adored her sister and wanted to love her son, had private doubts about his suitability to reign. It is hard not to conclude that Peter was but a poor shadow of his enlightened Russian grandfather.

Catherine's primary purpose was, of course, to supply an heir for the Romanov dynasty, which had held Russia's throne since 1613. This looked, initially, highly unlikely. A disfiguring bout of smallpox suffered by Peter shortly before the wedding probably did not help the marriage's chances. Catherine, however, won the initial favour of Elizaveta. When Catherine, too, fell ill before the wedding, her mother caused consternation by calling for a Lutheran preacher to attend her. Catherine, who was prepossessed even when struck down with pneumonia, cried out for her Orthodox teacher, writing later, 'This act gained me great favour in the opinion of the Empress and of the entire court.'[12]

Catherine's primary relationship in Russia proved not to be with her ineffectual husband but with his larger-than-life aunt, who dominated her court and country with the force of her personality. The women's relationship was one of extremes, with the Empress sometimes solicitous but at other times as sharp as the icicles that hung from the window ledges and balconies of the new Winter Palace in St Petersburg. She had nursed Catherine through her bout of pneumonia herself, holding a vigil at her bedside and stroking her hair, while she was also generous with gifts and money. Yet, as Catherine related in one of her memoirs, she once sat shivering in 'a damp cold in the church such as I have never felt in my life'. On seeing her shiver, Elizaveta called for her sable stoles and immediately put one around her own neck. Catherine recalled,

'I saw another one in the box; I thought that she was going to send it to me to put on, but I was mistaken. She sent it back; it seemed to me that this was a rather marked sign of ill will.'[13] On another occasion, Elizaveta sent Catherine as a gift an inferior pair of earrings, two rings and a necklace ('that I would have been ashamed to give to my ladies-in-waiting'), before pointedly asking how she liked them.[14] Even more cruelly, Catherine was forbidden to publicly mourn her father, who died in 1747, since he was 'not a king'.[15]

This capriciousness and the failure of her marriage sent Catherine into a melancholy, which she sought to overcome with reading, devouring the works of Voltaire, Montesquieu and other leading philosophers of the day, who, as she noted, 'produced a revolution in my thinking'.[16] Living under the shadow of the Empress Elizaveta for eighteen years provided Catherine with an apprenticeship in how to reign, with adversity driving her ambition forward. Elizaveta's gilded court, filled with glittering jewels, masked balls and the lengthy church services of which she was fond was a hotbed of intrigue, with the two women at its centre, locked in a near-silent battle of wills. The relationship is striking since it involved two of the most powerful women the world would ever see, with one at the pinnacle of her power and the other a student in sovereignty. As an absolute ruler, the empress could largely do as she pleased. Once, on objecting to the hairstyles of some of her maids she attacked the offending locks with scissors so violently that she cut into the women's skin. No one could ever be sure what temper they would find her in. Elizaveta was a figure both feared and loved in her country, with much of this due to the circumstances with which she had taken the throne.

Hatshepsut's life was initially a conventional one. She was born in around 1507 BCE, as the only child of Pharaoh Thutmose I by his Great Royal Wife (official queen consort), making her undoubtedly royal.

While still young, she was married to her half-brother, Thutmose II, with the marriage likely intended to bolster the new pharaoh's prestige as the son of an anonymous harem woman. As Great Royal Wife like her mother before her, Hatshepsut played a ceremonial role in governance and was a visible figure at court, but she, too, produced only a surviving daughter. As a result, when Pharaoh Thutmose II died, he was succeeded by a son born within his harem. Since this woman was not of suitable rank to rule Egypt on young Thutmose III's behalf, his aunt-stepmother, Queen Hatshepsut, stepped into the breach. As one contemporary source puts it, Thutmose III 'ruled on the throne of he who had begotten him. His sister, the God's Wife Hatshepsut, governed the land and the Two Lands were advised by her. Work was done for her and Egypt bowed its head.'[17] She gained a taste for reigning, and without warning (as far as we know from the limited historical records) took the throne for herself seven years into little Thutmose's reign, with the queen regent suddenly appearing in public as pharaoh in her own right. We can only speculate as to her motives. Perhaps she was concerned about losing power as the boy grew or considered her royal blood superior to that of the son and grandson of harem queens. She may simply have wanted the crown for herself.

Hatshepsut clearly did not view Thutmose III as a threat, allowing him to remain in place as her junior co-ruler, but she is always depicted first. So unorthodox was the situation that when both were shown on monuments (with Hatshepsut always the larger figure and Thutmose the smaller), the carvers sometimes mixed up their pronouns: they were so used to the king – a man – appearing before the queen – a woman – that subconsciously they ascribed those respective genders to the dominant queen and subservient king.

In many respects, this confusion was understandable since female monarchy was far from the norm in Egypt's millennia of pharaonic rule (although the office is truly ancient, we have, of course, already met Merneith). The pharaoh was believed to be the living embodiment of the god Horus, as well as the son of the sun god Re. He was a religious figure, essential to the maintenance of Maat, which was the equilibrium of the state, leading to prosperity and happiness.[18] The pharaoh was, therefore, conceived of as a male figure, semi-divine and distinct from those around him, including his Great Royal Wife and the lesser wives of his harem. As a result, it seemed only natural to the Egyptians that Thutmose III should succeed his father, even if his mother and paternal grandmother had been lowborn women. In taking the throne herself, Hatshepsut burst through the glass ceiling of tradition: she stepped over a male claimant to take her seat on the throne. Although Hatshepsut never ruled alone, all authority was vested in her.[19] She even appointed her daughter, Neferure, as her Great Royal Wife, ensuring that the important consort's role was performed following her elevation to the kingship. Thutmose probably resented his demotion, but he was not strong enough to challenge it. He would later be accused of attempting to obliterate her memory by scratching Hatshepsut's name from her monuments.

In the opulent palaces of imperial Russia, Catherine continued to learn how to rule from a master. Empress Elizaveta was known to have trouble sleeping, and as one contemporary put it, 'She durst not lie down to sleep till day-light appeared, because it was a nocturnal conspiracy which placed herself upon the throne.'[20] In daylight she was imperious, but the darkness brought only nightmares, with Elizaveta haunted by the continuing existence of an infant cousin, the former Ivan VI, who lived, effectively, as Russia's own version of the man in the iron mask.

Elizaveta was never entirely sure of her position on the Russian throne, looking for a conspiracy around every corner. Her father had been the formidable Peter the Great, who was famous both for bringing Western culture to his remote court and for his wild and ungovernable temper.[21] Only his second wife, the Livonia peasant-mistress turned bride, Marta Skavronska, could calm him, sometimes sitting with him for hours while he stroked her head in his lap.[22] He called her 'mother' or 'old girl' in his letters, while she referred to him as 'Mr Colonel', demonstrating a relationship that was clearly a love match and one of easy familiarity.[23] Illiterate and alcoholic, Marta, who took the Orthodox baptismal name of Ekaterina, was honoured by her husband with the first coronation of a Russian empress, which Peter based on Byzantine precedents. It was the fact of this crowning that was enough for Ekaterina to be declared Empress on Peter's death in 1725, when it emerged that the Tsar had not named a successor.[24]

Elizaveta was, thus, the daughter of two reigning monarchs, but her status was shaky since she had been born long before her parents' marriage. Her mother, whose own reign was short and ineffectual, set a precedent for female rule, with effusive praise for Ekaterina at her husband's funeral as 'our most gracious and autocratic sovereign, great heroine and monarch, mother of all Russians', overcompensating for the obvious inadequacies in Russia's first reigning empress.[25] She was, the mourners were assured, an 'identically minded ruler' to the dead Peter, suggesting almost a form of posthumous co-rule or a postscript to what had been both an exhilarating and exhausting reign. Elizaveta would later stress her own similarities to her gigantic father, but the Russians turned first to her young nephew, Peter II, on Ekaterina's death in 1727 and then her cousin, Anna Ivanova, in 1730 when they found themselves without an obvious successor once more.

Neither Ekaterina nor Anna had faced an adult male claimant, something which eased their path to the throne, although a baby tsar – Ivan VI – was selected on Anna's death in 1740, with his mother, Anna Leopoldovna, who was Empress Anna's niece ruling as his regent. In Russia, the emperor, or tsar (derived from Caesar) was always conceived of as male, something which encouraged 'ritualised cross-dressing' and some level of gender fluidity in the ways that the empresses presented themselves to their subjects.[26] Elizaveta took this on board when she donned a metal breastplate and simply walked into the palace one night in 1741, having won the allegiance of the palace guards and declared herself empress, gently waking the regent Anna Leopoldovna in her bed to inform her that she and her family were now state prisoners.[27] Although Anna died only five years into her strict imprisonment, her children would also suffer greatly, moving from fortress to fortress for the next forty years in an attempt to ensure that they were never in a position to claim Russia's crown.

Elizaveta was an intelligent and highly educated empress determined to retain her throne at all costs.[28] As an absolute monarch, reigning over one-sixth of the Earth's surface, she was a capricious character: a mass of contradictions. Famously, Elizaveta executed no one during her twenty-year reign, a remarkable feat for an eighteenth-century ruler, but she could be capable of cutting cruelty as Catherine found.[29] Deeply pious, she would walk for miles on pilgrimages while her court travelled beside her in coaches or sleighs, but she was also vain and high-handed. A literal giant in both height and (increasingly) girth, she was also a behemoth amongst the personalities of her court. With no child of her own, she brought her nephew to Russia and arranged his marriage. There was surprisingly little contemporary comment in Russia about the accession of another woman, something that was likely due to Elizaveta's popularity and her similarity in character and appearance to her revered father.[30] Nonetheless, a contemporary peasant toast declaring, 'Long live her most gracious empress, even though she is a woman!' suggests a certain degree of ambivalence.[31]

The eighteenth century was almost entirely a time of queens in Russia, but this does not mean that they were accepted as the norm. As late as the 1970s, a biographer of Empresses Ekaterina I, Anna and Elizaveta summed them up as 'a sot', 'a sadist' and 'a nymphomaniac'.[32]

This misogynist appraisal says more about the author than it does about his subjects.

Irene, who was still a teenager when she arrived in Constantinople, initially played second-fiddle to the men in her life, with her position uncertain until she gave birth to her only child, the future Constantine VI in 771.[33] As first daughter-in-law of the forceful Emperor Constantine V and then the wife of his successor, Leo IV, Irene entered a court that was (unsurprisingly) 'Byzantine' in its complexity. She learned the politics of the court from her eunuch servants, who existed as, essentially, an additional gender, with many castrated as children at their family's behests as a means of entrée into the royal court and as the first step to what could be a glittering political career.[34] They were granted privileged access to the women of the court due to their perceived reliability, having no (it was assumed) sexual desires, nor wives, nor children to distract them from their administrative roles at court. During her husband's brief reign, Irene built contacts, watched and learned. We know little of her time as consort although, as the mother of the emperor's heir, she was able to place herself in the perfect position to secure the regency on Leo IV's death in 780, ruling – ostensibly – with her young son.

This was the acceptable face of female power in Byzantium, with a child ruler's mother believed to be the person most likely to put his interests first.[35] There were many occasions where such a regency proved to work in Byzantium, with Irene's own decade as the power behind her son's throne notably productive. She was powerful enough that, in 787, she was able to call a church council to the city of Nicaea with the aim of putting to an end the greatest religious controversy of her era: the veneration of icons. Such religious matters can look petty to twenty-first-century eyes, but there were many in the Byzantine Empire who were prepared to die for their right to pray before vividly coloured images of Christ, the Virgin Mary and other saints, something which had been banned as idolatrous under the rule of Irene's father-in-law and husband.[36]

Irene used her regency in support of iconophilia, which may have been a genuinely held belief or one born out of the realisation that she needed to heal the rift in the church, while she was also aware that the public's desire to venerate icons was deeply held.[37] She helped shape the policy and the debate of her council, presiding in person over the final session, which was attended by 365 bishops and 132 monks, before it was agreed that the icons could be displayed and venerated once more.[38] As the only woman present and a highly visible one, Irene's participation drew open praise, comparing her to St Helena, the mother of Constantine the Great.[39] The well-connected historian Theophanes the Confessor, who wrote his chronicle during Irene's lifetime, lavished praise on 'the most pious Irene', while extolling a God who 'could work a miracle through a widow-woman and an orphan child'.[40] As Charlotte of Cyprus would find, the church was seen as the proper sphere for royal women, with some – notably Theodora, the powerful sixth-century wife of Emperor Justinian I – involving themselves in religious controversy.[41] We would remember a very different Irene had her career ended on the high of Nicaea. But she was unable to bring herself to relinquish power when her son reached manhood.

Catherine II's retrospective memoirs give the sense of her as a consummate actor, plotting a path to the throne, but the reality was likely much more organic. She was ambitious and eager to experience a bigger life than she could have in provincial Stettin where she was born, but she was also a natural politician. She even finally succeeded in producing an heir to Russia after nine years of marriage, though whether he was in fact Peter III's child is questionable. Elizaveta, whose throne the baby was expected to inherit, did not care. She removed the child at the moment of his birth so that she could raise him herself, a move that both satisfied a maternal need and ensured that she kept a potential heir under her close control. It would be almost a week before Catherine saw her son again, and then only as a visitor. A few years later, she gave birth to a daughter, Anna, who was almost certainly not her husband's, something which he himself perceived, saying out loud one day, 'God knows where my wife gets her pregnancies. I really do not know if this child is mine and if I ought to recognise it.'[42] The empress, however, was unconcerned, taking Anna into her custody at birth, just as she had done with Anna's elder brother.[*] Russia needed heirs and Catherine, as the wife of the Grand Duke, was expected to provide them in any way possible.

Empress Elizaveta railed against the loss of her once remarkable beauty, dying her blond hair black and rouging her face. Despite her efforts to remain looking young, she could not stop time, dying on 25 December 1761.[43] Peter III, now the tsar, had never been popular in his adopted homeland, but his overt Prussian sympathies became notably toxic in his new position. Almost immediately he ended Russia's years-long war with Prussia, agreeing to unfavourable terms. He also routinely dressed in Prussian military uniform.

More worrying for Catherine, he took to openly stating that he intended to discard her and marry his mistress, Elizaveta Vorontsova. Catherine's position was further hampered by the fact that, at the time of the empress's death, she was five months pregnant by the courtier, Grigory Orlov. Aware that Peter would use this as a pretext for divorce, Catherine employed ever more elaborate subterfuges to ensure that her condition went unnoticed. When she went into labour on 11 April 1762, her valet set fire to his own house on the opposite side of St Petersburg, aware that it would draw the pyromaniac

---

[*] M. de Rulhiere, *A History or Anecdotes*, pp11–12, a contemporary work which Catherine sought to suppress strongly hints that her eldest son, Pavel, was illegitimate.

emperor to spectate. The child, Alexis Grigorevich, was later privately acknowledged by his mother, but for the moment was hurried from the palace by her valet's wife, who took him out of the city. Catherine was able to resume official duties almost immediately. By the end of the month, even the veneer of civility had slipped between the imperial couple when Peter, who seated Catherine far from him in a state banquet, stood and called out that she was a 'fool'. Catherine understood that the end of her marriage – one way or another – was only a matter of time.

Irene of Byzantium's own son, Constantine VI, undoubtedly resented the continuing influence of his mother as he grew to manhood. He was a strong-willed but somewhat ineffectual monarch. It was Irene who broke off his engagement to Rotrud, daughter of Charlemagne, the powerful King of the Franks, while she also intervened in the subsequent bride show, making a choice that left the young bridegroom 'quite distressed'.[44] He would later show his displeasure by forcing his wife to become a nun so that he could wed his mistress. By the start of 790, the twenty-year-old Constantine had come to see 'that he had no power'.[45] Even Irene's contemporary Theophanes, who considered her to be a pious and godly woman, summed her up as 'power-hungry'.

With both parties locked uncomfortably in this joint rule, Irene was clearly working against her son.[46] As Theophanes records, she took the opportunity of the birth of Constantine's first son in late 796 to make her move. Rushing back to Constantinople to meet the child and, probably, proclaim him his co-emperor, Constantine made the fatal error of leaving his army with Irene, with his mother taking 'this opportunity to talk with the guards' officers; she piled up gifts and promises so she could oust her son and rule alone herself'.[47] Assembling the imperial guard, Irene informed her 'friends', whom she had secreted in her son's household to pounce, writing to them that, 'If you do not devise some way to betray him, I promise I will reveal to him your discussions with me.' Recognising the danger they were in, Irene's 'friends' seized Constantine, apparently while he was praying, and locked him in the chamber in which he had been born. On his mother's orders, he was blinded in 797, and, as Theophanes notes with more than a hint of judgment, 'in this way his mother Irene took power'.

In Byzantium, the mutilation of a political opponent was a means of disqualifying them from the throne. (Although not an entirely certain one – Justinian II had reigned from 705 in spite of having his nose cut off, while failed attempts were made to crown a blinded prince in 812.)[48] Previously, Irene had shown mercy to her husband's five half-brothers when they had challenged her regency in 780, ordering them to be ordained as priests and forcing them to administer communion before the court on Christmas Day, something which should have debarred them from the throne.[49] Yet, such leniency could be risky – as Irene was all too aware; Nikephoros, the eldest of these half-brothers, made a bid for the throne in 792 causing an order (given by Irene's son) that he also be blinded. Theophanes characterised Irene's decision as one of God's judgment on her son, noting of the blinding of Nikephoros that 'not for long did God's avenging justice permit this unjust act. For, five years later, Constantine was blinded by his own mother on a Saturday of the same month.'[50] Whether Irene can really be said to have been the agent of God's vengeance or not (and most undoubtedly thought not), the act damned her reputation in her lifetime and continues to do so today. Other Byzantine royals could be ruthless, but Irene stands alone as an unnatural and unwomanly figure by the standards of her time and later. To both contemporary and modern observers, it was one thing to blind a brother or an uncle, but quite another for a mother to damn her son's life to darkness.

Hatshepsut, too, has commonly been portrayed as an 'unnatural' figure following her decision to take the throne all those generations before Irene. Staring down at visitors today from her stunning temple in

Luxor, the city built on the ruins of ancient Thebes, are several colossal statues of the pharaoh wearing the red and white combined crown of Upper and Lower Egypt, bearded and arms crossed over her iron-flat chest. Such representations of Hatshepsut, as a male ruler, initially caused confusion amongst scholars who viewed her as a woman uncertain of her own gender or attempting to fool her subjects. One academic paper from the 1950s goes so far as to refer to her 'deviant personality and behaviour', characterising Hatshepsut as a cross-dresser with a 'forceful personality', obsessed with her 'masquerade change of sex'.[51] This rather misses the point and there is no evidence to suggest that Hatshepsut viewed herself as transgender. When shown as a male, she was not asserting maleness, instead she was depicting herself as a pharaoh. Hatshepsut took on elements of male kingship while remaining open about her sex in the names and inscriptions that adorned her temple walls.

There were good reasons for presenting herself as a man since Hatshepsut, like Irene, took a throne that was already occupied by a king.[52] Hatshepsut lived in a world divided on the grounds of sex, with men and women expected to perform different roles. They were even depicted differently, with men usually shown with red skin and women yellow.[53] The man was the head of the household, with society drawn on patriarchal lines as it would have been in countless civilisations across the globe (and, indeed, often still is). Yet, within this context, Egyptian women enjoyed a rare level of freedom that would have shocked their sisters in Classical Greece or Ancient Rome, or even, tens of centuries later, Tsarist Russia. Indeed, when the scholar Amelia Blandford Edwards embarked on a public lecture tour of the United States in 1889–90, she used the opportunity to speak on the remarkable freedoms of Ancient Egypt's women, in contrast to the constraints then still in place on the lives of women in Queen Victoria's Britain, the United States and other parts of the Western world.[54] While her claim regarding Egyptian women that 'we find her always free, respected, and in the full exercise of personal rights and as widely recognised as the personal rights of man' were perhaps a little too rosy, records survive of female businesswomen and traders, as well as a handful of female scribes – all occupations more traditionally associated with men. Women were treated equally by the law, while they could also inherit property. This was linked to the prominence of Egypt's goddesses, such as the important solar goddess Hathor, with whom queens were particularly associated. Of course, the most prominent of all was Isis, the sister-wife of Osiris and mother of Horus. As the Egyptian historian Manetho wrote towards the end of the pharaonic period, the Egyptians lived in a land of the gods, with their pharaohs their direct descendants.[55] The vast majority of Egypt's women are invisible in the archaeological or historical record, with even queens struggling to assert their place in the dynasty. In the case of Hatshepsut, one of the highest born of any Egyptian monarch, an infant boy, born to a woman of inferior social status, was still initially preferred to her on Egypt's throne, demonstrating the limits of acceptance of female power.

Much later, queens in Europe and other parts of the world, almost certainly quite independently, would similarly take on the trappings of male kingship to emphasise their role as a reigning queen, such as Elizabeth I of England who, in the sixteenth century CE, had 'the heart and stomach of a king' and 'the body but of a weak and feeble woman'.[56] Hatshepsut might be depicted with a male body or with the false beard of the pharaohs, but her subjects knew her sex, even if early Egyptologists were initially confused by her. Contemporary graffiti, found in a tomb close to Hatshepsut's temple crudely depicts a female pharaoh being penetrated from behind by a standing man. The workers on Hatshepsut's temple, at least, knew that she was female, with her depicted 'lover' perhaps being Senenmut, a lowborn man who rose in Hatshepsut's service to become tutor to her daughter and an important official. There were rumours about the relationship between the two.

Irene was certainly not confused about her gender, although she did occasionally use the title of Basileus (Emperor) rather than her preferred title of Basilissa (Empress).[57] In this, she was assisted by the fact that succession to the Byzantine throne was based on possession rather than hereditary right (something that positively encouraged emperors to name their sons as co-emperors in their cradles). Emperors were considered to hold their thrones due to God's favour, with Irene herself said to have acknowledged that she owed her position 'to God, through Whom Emperors reign and dynasts rule the world'.[58] As Judith Herrup has noted in her insightful study of female power in the Byzantine Empire, this concept, which can essentially be characterised as the divine right of kings, was potentially highly liberal in its application, with citizens accepting such disenfranchised individuals as common soldiers, peasants and even women as their ruler since 'once established, they were all considered to have been chosen by God to provide a short period of leadership, after which another would be chosen'.[59]

Although a woman, Irene was accepted in Byzantium, but this was not the case in the wider world, with Pope Leo III crowning the Frankish Charlemagne as Roman Emperor on Christmas Day in 800, arguing that the office – occupied only by a woman – was technically vacant. Irene made laws as emperor, including one banning third marriages, which was almost certainly aimed at the still troublesome (if now priestly) offspring of her much-married father-in-law. She would later have her husband's remaining half-brothers blinded in 799. She made official appointments too, particularly with regard to her eunuch servants, many of whom had worked for her for years. She was philanthropic, exempting orphanages, hostels, churches and other charitable institutions from the state's hearth taxes, while she also exempted military widows from, effectively, having to buy out their deceased husbands' remaining terms of service.[60]

Sources are somewhat limited for Irene's reign, making a detailed assessment difficult, but it is clear that the five years of her individual rule were a troubled period. In 802, her finance minister, Nikephoros, rose up against her, with an imprisoned Irene railing against a man who had been but 'yesterday an oathbreaking slave'.[61] On being told that Nikephoros had been crowned as emperor in her place, she yielded, telling him, 'I give back what was once mine. Now I give you reverence as Emperor, as you are pious and have been chosen by Him.'[62] It was likely only her sex, which was still a very considerable bar to the throne, which stopped Irene from suffering the mutilation that she had meted out on her own son and predecessor. Instead, she was placed under house arrest on Lesbos, where she died on 9 August 803.

Hatshepsut's reign, which had begun under similar circumstances to Irene's, was rather more successful. During her twenty years as the senior of the co-ruling pharaohs, she presided over a golden age of monument building, leaving behind not just her own vast temple but also countless elements of the great temple at Karnak, much of which stands today. It was Hatshepsut who commissioned and raised two gigantic obelisks that still stand as the most awesome monuments in a complex that is breathtaking in its size and scale. Hatshepsut ruled over a prosperous period in Egyptian history. Undertaking a few military expeditions, which was expected of Egypt's king, she presented a new face of kingship, launching a successful trading voyage to the mysterious land of Punt, which lay to the south of Egypt along the Red Sea.[63] Hatshepsut did not entirely sideline her stepson, with his title of king strictly noted in inscriptions of the pair together, but she built herself a splendid tomb, choosing to spend eternity in the Valley of the Kings rather than the nearby Valley of the Queens.[64] Hatshepsut – a usurping queen – proved to be one of Egypt's most successful rulers, in spite of the fact that her name was once largely lost to history due to the efforts of her male successors.

Peter III's reign would prove to be only a brief interlude in what was to be three-quarters of a century of female rule in Russia. Following her very public estrangement from her husband in April 1762, Catherine II continued to rally her supporters, building her own powerbase in the imperial court in opposition to a husband who had, she later claimed, 'lost what little intelligence he had'.[65] At five o'clock in the morning of 28 June 1762, Catherine was woken by Alexis Orlov, the influential soldier and brother of her lover, Grigory, who informed her that, 'It is time for you to get up; everything is ready for your proclamation.' Boarding a hired carriage with only her maid, her valet and Orlov, they set out for St Petersburg in a hurry, having first bribed a peasant to sell them his horses. On arriving at the barracks of the Izmailovsky Guards, Catherine was greeted by the guardsmen with whom she was popular, with the empress making a speech declaring that she acted only for the good of Russia, the Orthodox faith and for her young son, Pavel (better known in Western Europe as Paul). Those assembled swore an oath to her as Catherine II, but it was not as spontaneous an acclamation as might have appeared. As Catherine admitted in a letter to a former lover, 'The Guards had been mentally prepared. By the end, thirty to forty officers were privy to the secret, as were nearly 10,000 ordinary soldiers.'[66] Entering the Winter Palace, Catherine stood on the balcony with her son and was acknowledged by the crowds below as their sovereign. It was a strange kind of revolution, with one onlooker noting their surprise that, 'A whole city had changed its Sovereign, an army had revolted, yet without the least disorder.'[67]

She had been proclaimed in the capital in a burst of spontaneous affection, but Peter was still at large. Catherine, who had herself proclaimed as the colonel of the Preobrazhensky Guards, resolved to lead the forces sent to apprehend him, riding at their head in her green military uniform and on a white stallion. It must have been an incongruous sight, with the popular empress leading 14,000 troops. Peter, who was initially unaware of what had happened, vowed to defend himself on hearing the news, but the Holstein soldiers that he placed on the road to St Petersburg carried only wooden parade ground rifles, unaware that this was anything other than a drill. On attempting to reach the Kronstadt Fortress, which stood mighty on an island close to St Petersburg and had been built by his namesake grandfather, Peter was rebuffed at the walls. On identifying himself as the emperor, he was informed that 'we no longer have an emperor' before an officer called out, 'Long live the Empress Catherine II.' Terrified, Peter returned to his residence at Oranienbaum, where he wrote a letter to Catherine, surrendering to her and offering to share the throne. Soon he had abandoned even hopes of that, merely writing from captivity to request that Catherine permit him to depart for Germany with his mistress and his beloved violin. He died (improbably) of haemorrhoids on 6 July 1762, but everyone, of course, held Catherine responsible, with gossip spreading across the courts of Europe.** It hardly mattered. Popular, intelligent and a politician of considerable note, Catherine the Great – formerly the humble Sophia of Anhalt-Zerbst – was in full control of the largest empire that the world had hitherto seen.

Catherine the Great was judged by the harsh eyes of her contemporaries and later generations as unnatural, with her femininity difficult for many to reconcile with her undoubted ambition. Her contemporaries were eager to portray her in masculine terms, perhaps as a means of rationalising the incongruity of a woman who was also

---

** Catherine herself blamed haemorrhoids (see Catherine the Great, *Selected Letters*, p20); Simon Dixon, *Catherine the Great* (London: Routledge, 2001) p34 notes the lengths to which Catherine went to disassociate herself from Peter's death. She was unsuccessful. Horace Walpole, called her 'Catherine Slay-Czar'.

an unquestionably powerful ruler.[68] She had, noted the English Earl of Malmesbury, who was an ambassador to her court, a 'masculine force of mind', although in this he considered she was let down by possessing 'in a high degree the weaknesses vulgarly attributed to her sex – love of flattery, and its inseparable companion, vanity; an inattention to unpleasant but salutary advice; and a propensity to voluptuousness which leads to excesses that would debase a female character in any sphere of life'.[69] Others contrasted her unfavourably with her contemporary Maria Theresia of Austria-Hungary, whose rule was predicated by the fiction that she was only a co-ruler to either her husband or son.[70] Catherine certainly felt no compunction to keep either her husband nominally at her side or to prematurely promote her son, with whom she enjoyed a troubled relationship. She also deftly swerved early suggestions that she should further legitimise her reign by marrying the hapless lifelong prisoner, Ivan VI, who had been deposed by Empress Elizaveta and would finally be murdered in 1764 when an attempt was made to free him.

She did, however, carefully cultivate her image, allowing herself to be painted in male military attire, as in the stunningly effective painting by Vigilius Eriksen, which depicted her riding her favourite horse, Brillante, while dressed in the uniform of the Preobrazhensky Life Guards and which is now on display in Copenhagen. In this she was 'Amazon-like' and, it has been suggested, 'an immutable political emblem in eighteenth-century Russia'.[71] Catherine may well have learned these lessons from Elizaveta, who had symbolically donned a breastplate during the nighttime coup that had placed her on Russia's throne, while she also positively revelled in trampling over the strict gender roles of the day by hosting balls in which the men appeared dressed as women and the women as men. This served to reinforce the idea of the empress as more than a mere woman, something that was arguably necessary in a world that held women, particularly widows or spinsters as Catherine and Elizaveta were, in contempt. Catherine remains a colossus amongst the rulers of the eighteenth century, but she did not necessarily convince her contemporaries of the advantages of female rule. She was Russia's final reigning empress.

Irene's reign was highly unusual in Byzantine history, despite the elevated status and independence of the empire's women.[72] Was she a saint or a sinner? No one quite knows what to do with her. The fact of her deposition from the throne is not, in itself, a reason to denigrate her rule. Few Byzantine sovereigns of the period died of natural causes and while still reigning. Irene should rightly be viewed as the model for female power, with the sisters Zoe and Theodora Porphyrogenita, daughters of Constantine VIII, making their own bids for the throne in the eleventh century. Zoe, whose love life made for a complicated series of emperors-by-marriage, at one stage shared her throne directly with her sister; Byzantium was, for six weeks in 1042, ruled by two empresses. Theodora, who unlike the much-married Zoe remained single, took the throne alone at the advanced age of seventy-five in January 1055, reigning until her death the following year. Irene was no proto-feminist intent on an early bid for women's power, but she did base her authority on a long tradition of highly political Byzantine empress consorts.

Catherine the Great's memoirs, which she wrote and rewrote throughout her life, end jarringly midway through a private, 'long promised' interview with the Empress Elizaveta in 1759, three years before the *coup d'etat* that would place her on Russia's imperial throne. After promising to tell the elder empress – her political mentor and frequent tormentor – 'the most exact truth from my mouth', Elizaveta 'asked me for details about the Grand Duke's life', with Catherine's reminiscences stopping there abruptly.[73] Why should Catherine, an inveterate autobiographer, break off in a seemingly unimportant moment in an apparently unexceptional interview? Should Catherine's desire to justify and self-analyse be viewed in the context of the Enlightenment, the intellectual movement that changed the world and meant so much to her? Certainly, Monika Greenleaf, in her work on Catherine's corpus of writings considers that, 'Autobiography was perhaps the crowning genre in the Enlightenment system of genres, a strictly verbal proof of the power of individual reasoning to overcome external obstacles, examine its own consciousness, and submit a unified vision of life to the reason of the public.'[74] There was also likely a sense of Catherine wanting to tell her own story, one that she knew was controversial, before the world told it for her. If that is the case, however, why did she, time and again, stop short of the circumstances of her accession? It is a question that can never be fully answered and perhaps she did not know herself.

Catherine's life, just as the lives of Irene and Hatshepsut centuries before her, was defined by the circumstances in which she took the throne. Reigning as Russia's favourite enlightened despot for over thirty years, she cannot have looked back at the events that brought her to the throne with regret, but they certainly sharply delineated the life that she led before and the one that came after. Hatshepsut was subjected to a form of *damnatio memoriae*, while Irene was silenced and deposed. Mighty Catherine the Great was posthumously muted too when, in 1797, her son and successor, Pavel, banned subsequent women from the throne. Russia never saw the like of Catherine the Great again.

CHAPTER 4:
CHILD QUEENS

Maria and Isabella II of Jerusalem, Mary Queen of Scots, Teri'imaevarua II of Bora Bora and Wilhemina of the Netherlands

Lying in his bed at Falkland Palace, a fine Renaissance-style residence built as a monument to his impeccable taste, King James V of Scotland was dying. His decline came in the wake of a crushing military defeat at Solway Moss only shortly before, when many of his men, bogged down in marshland, had drowned in the rout. James, whose father had died in battle when he was himself an infant, was still only thirty and had known his fair share of tragedy. In December 1542, the last person in the direct line of Scotland's unlucky Stewart dynasty simply began to waste away. The cause has never truly been ascertained, though he was clearly depressed, perhaps never entirely having recovered from the loss of his two little sons on consecutive days in April 1541. The news on 8 December 1542 that he was once again a father failed to rouse him. On hearing the tidings that his wife had borne a third child, the king reputedly commented, 'Adieu, fare well, it came with a lass, it will pass with a lass,' predicting that the Stewart dynasty, which had acquired the throne through Margery, daughter of Robert the Bruce, would end with his newborn daughter.[1] Six days later, he was dead. The baby, Mary, still less than a week old, had become Queen of Scots.

No kingdom wanted a child monarch, of either sex, with the ancient Northern European kingdom of Scotland understanding that better than most at the time of little Mary's accession. The ruling Stewarts, who had come to power in 1371, had witnessed one child sovereign after another in the seventeen decades that it had been in power. From James I, who became king aged twelve in 1406, until James V, who succeeded to the throne aged seventeen months in 1513, no monarch had become king as an adult.* Long minorities were a recipe for political instability, just as (the contemporary wisdom held) were women's reigns. In both cases, the actual monarch was not expected to wield power themselves, with a governor or regent (usually a male relative, although sometimes their mother) appointed for a child ruler and a husband taking control for a woman. There was commonly disagreement over just who should rule on behalf of the monarch, either relating to the choice of governor or the choice of marriage partner. A child queen, who incorporated both these major disadvantages, was potentially disastrous.[2] So in many respects, Mary's very existence was a substantial problem for the Scots. If she had never been born, they would at least have had the option of selecting an adult male from amongst her distantly related kin, while controversy over who she would wed (and, who would therefore become the next King of Scots) began before she was even weaned.

A baby even younger than Mary became Queen of the Crusader kingdom of Jerusalem, 330 years before Mary's birth. Isabella II (who is sometimes called Yolanda in surviving sources) was hours or, at most, a few days old, when her mother, Maria, the kingdom's reigning queen died following complications in childbirth. Scotland had only

---

* James IV, the eldest at his accession, had been fifteen. He alone did not require a regent.

once contemplated a female monarch before – a little Norwegian princess, Margaret, in 1286 only for her to die of seasickness (or, more likely, food poisoning) in the Orkneys in 1290 on her way to claim her maternal grandfather's throne. Female succession was, however, an all too common by-product of the instability of the Latin kingdom of Jerusalem, which was surrounded on all sides by hostile neighbours. Maria, who had probably not yet turned twenty when she died, had herself been a child queen, inheriting the throne aged twelve on the death of her mother, Isabella I, in 1205.

At the time of Queen Maria's death, Jerusalem was the leading Christian state in the Holy Land, carved out in the religious zeal (and, undoubtedly, land lust) of the First Crusade of the late eleventh century.[3] It was a cosmopolitan place once the initial carnage of the First Crusade had subsided, with mosques and synagogues appearing in the same streetscapes, while Orthodox Christians socialised with the Frankish Catholics (from whom the monarchs were drawn) who owned more than 90 per cent of the land but made up only a tiny fraction of the population.[4] These Frankish masters, who could pride themselves in the knowledge that they had 'liberated' the geographic backdrop to Christ's life from its Muslim occupants, were constantly on their guard and always wary. It was a dangerous place to carve out a life, with the major cities walled and villagers living under the constant shadow of raids from their Islamic neighbours, which would see them scurrying for the stone towers that dotted their settlements.[5] Kings' reigns were all too frequently nasty, brutal and short.

As a military society, in which kings were expected to lead their subjects into battle, there was room for female political agency. The kingdom's first resident queen consort, Morphia, took decisive action in 1124 to secure the release of her husband, Baldwin II, after he was captured in war, although his freedom came at immense personal cost with their youngest daughter sent to replace him as hostage.[6]

With knights liable to serve their king for up to a year if necessary, women were often left behind in the cities or fields of the kingdom to attend to daily matters and, all too commonly, grieve for the deaths of husbands, brothers and sons. They were given freedoms out of necessity rather than any desire to subvert the accepted patriarchy of their world: women could wield power and agency only on behalf of men.

Baldwin II successfully named his eldest daughter, Melisende, as his heir, but only after the much older Fulk, Count of Anjou, had been dispatched from France to marry her.

This ill-assorted couple, who were jointly crowned in 1131, spent the next five years vying for power before establishing an uneasy co-rule.[7] In widowhood, Melisende was required to share her throne with her young son, who later forced her into retirement. She was the most powerful woman the kingdom of Jerusalem ever witnessed, but her authority was always qualified and subject to the men in her life. Early deaths and misfortunes would see Melisende eventually followed by a further four female monarchs. As Sarah Lambert has noted in her study of Jerusalem's reigning queens, 'The problem of female succession was to recur with almost monotonous regularity in the dynasty which ruled the kingdom of Jerusalem from 1099 until 1228.'[8] Even adult reigning queens struggled to assert any independence in a kingdom created and maintained on knightly exploits. As a largely military society, it was considered essential that the kingdom have a man at the helm to defend it, but these were in short supply in the royal dynasty in the late twelfth century. The crown's independence would reach its nadir in the reigns of the child queens Maria and Isabella II.

Wilhelmina, growing up as a happy only child beloved by her parents, never actually met the older half-brother whose death changed her life. Her father, the sixty-one-year-old King Wilhelm III of the Netherlands had scandalised his family and court when, in 1879 he married twenty-year-old Emma of Waldeck-Pyrmont, a minor princess from a tiny German duchy.[9] Against the odds, it was a happy union, with the intellectual Emma working a great improvement on the rather morose monarch.

The relatively recent kingdom of the Netherlands, whose rulers had gained their crown at the end of the Napoleonic Wars in 1815, employed a semi-salic system of inheritance which prioritised all males in the royal dynasty over females.**[10] However, by the time Wilhemina was three, her father had lost two sons, two brothers and an uncle.[11] Then, on Saturday 21 June 1884, the Prince of Orange – who was 'sickly, eccentric & plain' according to the private jottings of his acquaintance Queen Victoria – died of typhus. He was the last male heir to the House of Orange-Nassau and so his death rendered the royal house extinct in the male line, save for the king himself. Wilhelmina was now suddenly promoted in his place; her accession, which was likely to happen sooner rather than later, considering her father's age, was almost a certainty.

Wilhemina would later write of the cherished hour of each day when she was taken to spend time with the king: 'I was taken to my father's study by way of the main staircase and the big drawing-room; and then the fun started!'[12] She reminisced about a happy family unit, about pony-carriage rides and flower picking, but it was increasingly overshadowed by her father's infirm health. 'During these last few years,' she recalled, 'Father hardly ever left the house. I remember his last walk, when he was so weak that he could go no further than one of the copper beeches on the way to the chalet.'[13]

She surely must have had an inkling of what was coming, but Queen Emma did her best to shield her, with Wilhemina writing, 'The last night she did not come to bed at all – I had been sleeping in

---

** Wilhemina was third in line to the throne at birth, after her surviving half-brother and her father's brother.

her room for some time – and that night I felt that something terrible was happening upstairs in Father's room. People tried to hide it from me, but yet I knew what that terrible thing was.'[14] On 23 November 1890, Wilhelmina, who was only ten years old, became Queen of the Netherlands. She was the first Dutch reigning queen, something that, at the time of her birth, would have seemed almost impossible to countenance. She was also the kingdom's only child monarch. Even at the end of the nineteenth century, when princesses were no longer forcibly married off and knights had ceased to ride into battle, this was a problem. The Dutch constitution required an active and involved monarch. There were strong doubts that a woman could fulfil this role, let alone a ten-year-old girl.

Maria of Jerusalem would have seemed a similarly unlikely future reigning queen at her birth in 1192. Her mother, Isabella I, had inherited a depleted kingdom two years before thanks to the conquests of the mighty Salah-al-Din, Sultan of Egypt and Syria, who had conquered the City of Jerusalem and pushed the Crusaders back to a narrow strip of coastline around 20 miles wide.[15] All possible male heirs were dead, including the kingdom's famous 'Leper King', Baldwin IV, who had been crowned in 1174 aged thirteen in spite of his already alarming symptoms. Blind and debilitated, he would later have himself carried into battle in a litter.*** Unable to father children of his own, he was succeeded by a child nephew and then his sister, Sybilla, whose husband, Guy de Lusignan, ruled on her behalf. 'The wife of King Guy' (as one contemporary puts it) was succeeded by her half-sister, Isabella.[16]

Isabella I was informed at her accession that 'she could not be lady

---

*** Baldwin's condition was suspected when his tutor, the Chronicler William of Tyre, noticed that he felt no pain in his right arm when pinched. He was not, however, formally diagnosed until after his accession, likely due to the common (but not universal) stigma attached to leprosy in the medieval period; For a contemporary usage of the nickname 'the Leper King', see 'The Old French Continuation of William of Tyre, 1184–97' in *The Conquest of Jerusalem and the Third Crusade: Sources in Translation*, ed. Peter W. Edbury (Aldershot: Routledge, 1998), p27.

of the kingdom' if she did not leave her husband, who was deemed unsuitable to be Jerusalem's king.[17] The queen was forced into an annulment, with a contemporary writer commenting that 'God knows if this sentence [of annulment] was in accord with the law, for the lady was not in the power of her husband but was in the power and control of the marquis [Conrad de Montferrat, Queen Maria's father] who married her as soon as sentence had been given.'[18] Even as an adult, Isabella I was a cipher to power, with Jerusalem's barons becoming increasingly used to the idea of selecting their own king, who would seal their choice by marrying the queen.

Maria was a posthumous child, with her father's murder in the weeks before her birth forcing her mother to remarry again on the orders of her barons. Her stepfather was far from gallant. On hearing that his bride was pregnant he complained that, if she bore a son and heir, 'I shall be stuck with the woman' and without the kingdom.'[****] He was only appeased by the assurance that Conrad's child would be stepped over in favour of the sons that Isabella would bear him.[19] Since Isabella bore no surviving son in any of her four marriages, Maria succeeded her aged twelve on 5 April 1205. She was immediately placed under the control and regency of her uncle, Jean of Ibelin, who became king in all but name.[20] She was never expected to reign alone. Queens had become the means by which a suitable male could be 'co-opted into the dynasty'.[21] This position was far from unique to medieval Jerusalem.

By the mid-nineteenth century, the Tahitian islands had fallen under the influence of France which claimed them as a protectorate in 1843, forcing Queen Pomare IV of Tahiti, who had herself come to the throne

---

[****] Natasha R. Hodgson, *Women, Crusading and the Holy Land in Historical Narrative* (Woodbridge: Boydell, 2007), p82 notes that 'when Henry of Champagne [Maria's stepfather] went to assert his authority over the cities and castles now under his dominion, he took Isabella with him' as he needed her 'physical presence' to take control of the kingdom.

as a fourteen-year-old, to sign away her rights to the kingdom.*****[22] She reacted with understandable fury and 'hoisted her flag' in opposition, writing at once to Queen Victoria to request aid, with the British monarch agreeing privately in her journal with regard to the French actions that, 'We cannot acquiesce in this act, the Queen [Pomare] having strong claims upon us.'[23] Pomare was disappointed therefore to receive only a carriage and a set of drawing-room furniture, which, as the son of her British advisor would later recall, the French governor was quick to confiscate on driving the queen from her palace, since he 'was not too fastidious to use them'.[24]

Pomare, who was soundly patronised and belittled by both her French enemies and her British allies (almost certainly on account of her sex), was a shrewd politician and quickly came to the conclusion that she could not rely on any foreign support.[25] Appearing as a 'South Sea Victoria', she promoted the comparisons between her and her fellow monarch, with images produced of the queen in full skirts and a bonnet looking suspiciously like her British counterpart, while it has also been suggested that she deliberately 'whitened' herself as a political strategy to garner sympathy and, crucially, support.[26] Eventually coming to terms with the French, she was able to negotiate to receive the vast sum of around 37,000 Francs per year and to remain, effectively, as absolute monarch of her islands.[27]

Restored to her throne in 1847, she had already turned her attention to the dominance of the surrounding polities. Thanks to Pomare IV's politicking, she was able to manoeuvre her one-year-old granddaughter, Teri'imaevarua II, onto the throne of Bora Bora in February 1873, a tiny island kingdom of only 12 square miles and dominated by orange groves, coconut trees and banana plants, as well as the highly prized pigs, which slept in their owner's huts each night

---

***** Pomare was more of a title and was used by male and female rulers. Pomare IV was the first reigning queen of the islands.

for protection.[28] The infant queen's sole purpose was to perpetuate the Pomare dynasty in the region: the fact that she was a child and, thus, could not rule alone, undoubtedly helped her grandmother to continue to dominate Tahiti's political life.

Teri'imaevarua was born into a highly stratified society, whose traditional life had been disrupted by the arrival of Europeans: first the Dutch, then the British, the French and the Spanish in the 1760s and 1770s. These successive waves of fluttering white sails would change everything for the islands, lying as a 'constellation of marine peaks and atolls scattered over a million square miles of Pacific ocean'.[29] Initial contact between Tahitians and their European visitors had been hostile, although trade was established by the 1770s when ornate red feathers, mostly taken from parakeets, were being used as currency.[30] Later, of course, the islanders, aware 'that all that glitters is not gold', demanded French silver coins and silks in their trading.[31] Soon, they were receiving regular visits from Europe and the wider world and, while this was often on the Europeans' terms, a strong leader such as Pomare could ensure some measure of continuing autonomy and the perpetuation of traditional life. As part of this, it suited Pomare to ensure that Bora Bora, which was an independent state but part of the wider Tahitian diaspora, should be under her control.

Her little granddaughter's kingdom, which should more correctly be called Porapora in the local language, had a proud and ancient history, having first been settled by at least 300 BCE by people migrating across the Pacific. The islanders there had a reputation for hostility amongst their neighbours, with the first European explorers to Tahiti informed of regular waterborne attacks (every month or six weeks) with paddles deliberately muffled to add to the element of surprise.[32] There were naval battles, too, with the great war canoes of Bora Bora engaging with their neighbours in bloody conquests; not for nothing were the islands known as 'Porapora the destroyer of Fleets'.[33] Pomare had enough trouble with French pressure and British indifference: ensuring a compliant client-monarch in Bora Bora looked, to her, like a sensible decision and, after all, who could be more compliant and less likely to cause trouble than an infant? The circumstances of Teri'imaevarua's queenship should undoubtedly be viewed in this context.

Centuries separated them, but Mary Queen of Scots was as entirely oblivious of her accession as her Bora Boran counterpart would be. There never seems to have been any question of simply stepping over her in the succession, with her hereditary right acknowledged, if not entirely welcomed. In this, she was probably fortunate in the Stewart dynasty's lack of fecundity. Her father had no surviving full siblings, while neither did her grandfather. To find the next heir to the throne it was necessary to go all the way back to the descendants of James II, who had died in 1460. As such, it was really Mary or no-one as far as the Stewart dynasty was concerned, with her guardianship the central question. Whoever controlled the little queen would control the nation, with the success – or failure – of Mary's reign resting on the abilities of this central figure. There was, unsurprisingly a contest, with her mother, Marie of Guise, and her Scottish relatives fighting over the governorship of the young queen.

By January 1543, hereditary claim rather than ability had won out, with the baby queen's distant relative James Hamilton, Earl of Arran, confirmed as governor, someone who was disparagingly described as 'but a simple man' by one contemporary, while there were also strong questions over his legitimacy.[34] For good reason, Mary's mother opposed this appointment, commenting in March 1543 to the English ambassador Ralph Sadler that, 'It hath been seldom seen, that the heir of a realm should be in the custody of him that claimeth the succession of the same, as the governor is now established by parliament the second person of this realm, and if her daughter fail, looketh to be king of the same.'³⁵ Infant heirs were undoubtedly vulnerable. It had been reported soon after Mary's birth that she was 'a very weak child and not like to live', while it has also been suggested that she was somewhat premature.³⁶ Marie very pointedly ordered her daughter to be stripped naked so that Sadler could confirm her health to his master, King Henry VIII of England. Sadler, who had begun his career as the protegee of the Machiavellian first minister, Thomas Cromwell, thought she was 'as goodly a child as I have seen of her age, and as like to live, with the grace of God'.

Wilhelmina of the Netherlands was highly fortunate that, unlike Mary Queen of Scots, she was entrusted to her mother's regency. This had not been a foregone conclusion, with members of the government pushing for a male regent to be appointed, doubting the capacity of a woman to reign, even on behalf of her own child. Nonetheless, in spite of opposition, the all-male assembly of the States General, which met on 8 December 1890, recognised Emma as queen regent, allowing her to take control of her daughter's government during her childhood and, crucially, also retaining custody of the child-queen's person. She was a woman determined that her daughter, against the odds, should succeed, ensuring that Wilhelmina made regular public appearances and that she toured both her kingdom and abroad extensively. As one commentator has noted, Emma's role was a difficult one. It was her belief 'that a strict adherence to protocol would keep courtiers and politicians who might be inclined to take a woman on the throne less seriously, in their place'.³⁷

Emma sailed her ship of regency safely through choppy waters and undoubtedly acted with her daughter's best interests at heart. As Wilhelmina herself would later recall, 'Soon after Father's death she took me into her confidence and sometimes discussed the worries and problems of her Regency with me.'³⁸ Watching her daughter be inaugurated at the Nieuwe Kerk in Amsterdam, not far from the palace in the city, on 6 September 1898, Emma could pride herself on a job well done.[39] There was, by the time of Wilhelmina's eighteenth birthday, no question of naming a different ruler, with the young queen swearing her oath to uphold the Dutch Constitution before making a speech in which she promised 'to devote all my strength to the wellbeing and growth of the Fatherland so precious to me'. Since her accession, Wilhelmina had been trained in her future role as monarch, carrying out her first official engagement on 29 May 1891 when the ten-year-old queen laid the foundation stone for a new hospital, to be named in her honour, in Amsterdam, while soon afterwards she hosted a visit by the German kaiser, Wilhelm II.[40] It was, however, a lonely life, as Wilhelmina would later candidly admit in her autobiography. While her mother attempted to arrange for other children to visit the palace to play with the young queen, Wilhelmina later regretted that, 'I was far from accommodating, and in fact I disliked these visits heartily.' She lamented that 'normal companionship with children was unthinkable in the cage'.[41] All of the child queens discussed here, from diverse places and far-removed times, existed similarly in captivity. A crown could add bejewelled lustre, but it also drew covetous attentions and was fraught with danger. To be a queen while still a child never provided either stability or the hope of power. It simply created distance and uncertainty.

Maria of Jerusalem, who succeeded to her throne at the age of twelve, had no input into her marriage – the central question of her life – with her barons' choice settling on the relatively undistinguished French nobleman, Jean of Brienne, who was almost twenty years her senior and far below her in rank.[42] Crucially, however, as a landless younger son, he was willing to settle in Jerusalem and to take on the role of warrior king, although he is a classic example of a man promoted above his abilities. (In a meteoric but perplexing career, he would later be appointed to Latin Emperor of Constantinople – a role that, as in

Jerusalem, he did not excel in.) Crowned jointly on 3 October 1210, Maria seems to have consented to almost every one of Jean's policies and she is almost entirely absent from the records of their joint reign.[43] She never really had a chance, dying in childbirth in late 1212 at the age of only twenty.[44] Maria's was a brief and indistinct life and she never managed to assert independent authority.

The same can certainly be said for her newborn daughter, Isabella II, on whose behalf Jean simply continued to rule, calling himself King of Jerusalem.[45] This was not necessarily a good thing for the beleaguered kingdom, with Jean's leadership of the Fifth Crusade, which began in the autumn of 1217, proving to be a long-running disaster. Poor harvests meant that the Jerusalemites, marooned on their narrow strip of coastline, struggled even to feed themselves, let alone the influx of zealous and heavily armed Crusaders. Jean had also married again, to Stephanie, the heiress to the Armenian kingdom of Cilicia, and he found his attention divided as he vied with his second wife's younger half-sister, who had been named heir on their father's deathbed, for the crown. There may have been domestic strife, too, with one chronicler claiming that Stephanie had tried to poison Isabella, perhaps to clear the way for her own son's accession to Jerusalem, something over which he would have no hereditary right as the son of a mere king consort. According to this source, when Jean discovered her actions, he beat his wife to death.[46] While this story is likely apocryphal, Isabella's childhood was dangerous and unstable, with her father sailing for the West to rally support in 1222 when she was approaching her tenth birthday. He also went to find 'a powerful man for his daughter'.[47]

From her own experience, Pomare IV would have known that during her childhood Teri'imaevarua, inserted into the politics of tiny Bora Bora in the face of growing French colonialism, would be powerless, leaving a vacuum that she herself intended to fill. As a child queen herself, Pomare had been married to Tapoa the eldest son of the reigning King of Bora Bora, who was around six or seven years older than her. In class-conscious Tahiti and its neighbouring islands, where chiefly status set apart the elite from the kingdoms' 30–40,000 other inhabitants, it was an obvious match, but personally an unhappy one.[48] It had only been in 1831 when she reached her twenties that Pomare was independent enough to annul the marriage – on the grounds of Tapoa's fertility, with the queen then taking a second husband from amongst Tahiti's chiefly class and producing nine children in quick succession.[49] Pomare had made the jump from child cipher to adult ruler, with her magnetism still holding the discarded Tapoa, who had succeeded as King Tapoa II of Bora Bora shortly after their divorce, firmly within her orbit. He joined with her to dine on board the HMS *Grampus* with Captain Henry Byam Martin of the British Royal Navy in October 1846, for example, struggling with the weather because 'it seemed as if the flood gates of heaven were once more opened'.[50] The Captain warmed to his 'jolly' Bora Boran guest, calling him 'my fat friend Tapoa' in his journal and advising him to treat separately with the French since he feared that Pomare was attempting 'to get him into the same scrape as herself'.[51]

There was doubtless more to Tapoa's decision to ally with Pomare against the French than Captain Martin surmised, with even the naval officer referring to the Bora Boran king as a cunning 'old fox'.[52] It suited him to adopt her only surviving daughter, Teri'imaevarua I, and tie his micro-kingdom to the queen's broader dynastic scheme. As well as arranging the adoption, Pomare made her son, Tamatoa, king of the neighbouring island of Raiatea in 1857, while her eldest son was intended to eventually succeed her in Tahiti itself.[53] Teri'imaevarua I succeeded to Bora Bora on her adoptive father's death in 1860, having been married aged thirteen to a member of a high-ranking chiefly family on Bora Bora in order to smooth her path to the throne. It proved to be childless, with Teri'imaevarua I adopting her namesake niece, the daughter of her brother Tamatoa, who was born in 1871. There is a clear pattern – stemming from Pomare herself – of tying Bora Bora to her dynasty. With a minor queen on the throne – first, her own daughter and then her granddaughter – it would be impossible for the Bora Borans to ally with the French in opposition to her, as Captain Martin had foreseen.

Teri'imaevarua II's new home was a turquoise sea paradise 'overgrown with trees, and with coco palms fringing the beaches', while the women dressed with banana leaf wreaths, strewn with flowers (ensuring that, as one visitor in 1846 noted, 'a gathering of women is always sweet smelling').[54] Music and dance was important to the islands' culture, with drumming continuing day and night during the crisis of the French take-over of the islands.[55] She succeeded her aunt before she had reached the age of two, ensuring a long minority under the regency of her aunt's widowed husband.[56] Her obituary would later claim that 'although a child, she reigned as absolute monarch', but there is little evidence of Teri'imaevarua II ever establishing herself as the true authority on the island.[57] Her youth made her a figurehead only, albeit an important one: for the estimated 600 inhabitants of her pint-sized kingdom, she was a symbol of their continuing independence and traditional rule, though it was mediated through the Pomare dynasty of neighbouring Tahiti.[58]

Following his second marriage in 1876, her uncle-regent stepped down from his position, with the kingdom ruled on Teri'imaevarua's behalf until, aged twelve, she was married to another Bora Boran chief. Their divorce only three years later may have been an attempt by the young queen to assert her adult authority, but, in reality, she had little time left to reign. Her grandmother, Pomare IV had died in September 1877, while her father, 'a gigantic brawler in moments of wrath, and on evenings of feasting a famous carouser', lost the island kingdom of Raiatea into which he had been inserted in 1871.[59] As one commentator has noted, 'Pomare IV's dynastic ambitions crumbled, and at the end of her life she witnessed the dissolution of the chiefly power she had fought for her entire life.'[60] Her son and successor, Pomare V, an alcoholic and ineffectual ruler, would hand Tahiti over to the French government in 1881. Teri'imaevarua, amongst Pomare IV's descendants, actually held out the longest, but she could not stand against the tide, with her youth and inexperience likely to have led to her first being overlooked by the French colonising powers. On 17 April 1888, the sixteen-year-old queen witnessed the formal annexation of her kingdom by France, ending its independence forever.[61]

Teri'imaevarua II remained in French-owned Bora Bora, still nominally queen until 1895 when her 'reign' formally came to an end, and she was forced to leave the only home she had ever really known. Taking ship to Tahiti, a place that she cannot have remembered, she settled in a small bungalow, close to the capital, Papeete, set within a picturesque grove of coconut palms, which had been 'part of the ancestral domain of the Pomare family long before Cook dropped anchor in Matavai Bay' and set in motion the destruction of the world that she and her family knew.[62] As one of the obituaries in the local paper after her death in 1933 noted, she had lived 'a virtual exile from Borabora, with only her memories and a few retainers to remind her of a past greatness'.[63] Her story, that of a 'fallen princess', was not so different from those of the child queens who had gone before her.[64] Had she ruled for longer, perhaps she could have proved a second Pomare IV, morphing from hapless child queen to powerful political juggernaut. But Teri'imaevarua never had the chance to rule as an adult, with her reign brought prematurely to a close by decisions taken by others. She never had the chance to reign at all.

Such had always been the lot of child queens, with no guarantee that they would successfully transition into adult independence. In fact, most child queens were Teri'imaevaruas rather than Pomares. No one truly expected little Mary Queen of Scots to ever manage her kingdom and affairs either, with the baby queen moved to Stirling Castle in July 1543, while her future was decided on her behalf. Mary's primary role, as contemporaries saw it, was to perpetuate the Stewart dynasty by producing heirs. She *had* to marry someone. Henry VIII of England was determined to acquire Mary for his son, the future Edward VI, since her marriage would unite England and Scotland under one male ruler, with the Scottish queen's input in the government likely to be minimal. Unsurprisingly, the Scots were not keen on the English approach, with the lawyer and royal servant Adam Otterburn asking the English diplomat Ralph Sadler, 'If your lad was a lass, and our lass were a lad, would you then be so earnest in this matter?'[65] It was a fair point and very much summed up the downsides of a reigning queen. All the Scots would gain from giving up their 'lass' to Henry was 'an Englishman king of Scotland', something that was hardly an attractive proposition. However, to refuse such a match, when there were few other alternatives at that point, flew in the face of standard practice. With considerable misgivings, the Scots agreed to the Treaty of Greenwich on 1 July 1543, which incorporated the peace terms between the two nations and confirmed the marriage of Mary to Prince Edward, with the young queen due to travel south for her wedding when she turned ten. Although, on the surface, matters had been settled by mid-1543 for Mary's minority, in reality the Scottish nobility were wracked by rivalries into which the English monarch, now calling himself her 'father-in-law', inserted himself.[66]

In all this manoeuvring, little thought was given to Mary's more than capable mother, Marie of Guise, who would later prove herself to be as able as her descendant Emma of the Netherlands centuries later.******
Indeed, Henry VIII, perhaps anxious about the Frenchwoman's loyalties, actively wanted to separate mother and child, informing his

---

****** Marie of Guise's descendant Augusta, a granddaughter of George II, married into the Brunswick ducal family from whom Queen Emma descended.

ambassador that Marie should 'be in no wise permitted to continue in the castle where the queen is, but to be appointed to remain in the town in some convenient place for her, and to have liberty now and then with two or three in her company, such as both the barons being keepers for the time shall think meet, to come in to the castle to visit the queen'.[67]

Understandably Marie, who had left her son by her first marriage in France when she was forced marry James V, was aggrieved by attempts to remove her from her daughter's life. Cardinal Beaton, Scotland's leading churchman, as well as Arran himself, were also infuriated by the insertion of Henry VIII, the little queen's far from loving great-uncle, into the kingdom's politics. This six-times married king was hardly an advert for stable family life, while his failure to fill the English royal nursery meant that – after his own three children – little Mary was actually heiress to his crown.******** Neither of the British kingdoms had succeeded in crowning a woman as monarch before, with Mary's coronation on 9 September 1543 therefore a landmark event, although the child, over whose head the crown must have been held, would have remembered nothing of a ceremony that was, as Ralph Sadler snarkily put it, 'not very costly'.[68] Alliances were shifting too, with no effective monarch to guide policy, and with the Earl of Arran soon shifting from a pro-English to a pro-French stance. On hearing this, Henry VIII, as one of Mary's biographers Antonia Fraser puts it, decided that he 'would no longer woo the Scots with gifts, but attempt to constrain them by force'.[69] This 'Rough Wooing' would come to dominate Mary's early childhood.

The question of marriage also dominated Isabella II of Jerusalem's childhood, with the crown that she wore a potentially enticing

---

******** On her father's death she was technically second in line, after Edward, as Henry's daughters were declared illegitimate and barred from the succession under the terms of the First and Second Acts of Succession (1533 and 1536 respectively).

dowry for suitors, even if little remained of her kingdom. In March 1223, her father, who was then living mostly in Italy, negotiated a marriage for her with the Holy Roman Emperor, Frederick II, a widower who was eighteen years her senior.[70] With the marriage brokered by the Pope himself as a means of ensuring Frederick's continuing support for the reconquest of the Holy Land, the emperor agreed to respect Jean of Brienne's claims to be King of Jerusalem for the remainder of his life.[71] Satisfied, in July 1225, Jean permitted Frederick to marry Isabella at once, in exchange for a promise that the emperor would pay him 100,000 ounces of gold (an astronomical sum, which he never received) and join a new Crusade by August 1227.[72] Once married by proxy, the twelve-year-old Isabella was crowned in the cathedral at Acre in the only example of a sole coronation accorded to any of Jerusalem's reigning queens. She would spend two further weeks in her kingdom, before sailing away in a fleet of twenty galleys to her future in Europe. Weeping 'hot tears', it would later be claimed that, as she embarked, Isabella prophesied that she would never see her kingdom again, something that would indeed prove to be correct and, at the time, was not an unreasonable assumption.[73] On 9 November 1225, Isabella was formally married to Frederick at Brindisi. With this *fait accompli,* the trap was sprung, with Frederick immediately declaring himself King of Jerusalem and divesting his father-in-law of his authority. Isabella was spirited away to Sicily, where she was kept isolated and closely watched. With the chronicles giving strong hints of the abuse that the young queen suffered at the hands of her new husband, Frederick left for Jerusalem without her: once he had secured his position as her husband, he had little need of the kingdom's reigning queen.[74]

Like Isabella, the child Queen Mary of Scotland played nothing more than the role of figurehead in the battles for control of both her person and her marriage during the early years of her reign. She was a symbol of monarchy, but her youth and sex rendered any active role non-existent: she was treated as a pawn when she should have been revered as a queen. The gameboard further shifted when, in January 1544, Catherine de Medici, the wife of the future King Henri II of France, gave birth to a healthy son after more than a decade of childless marriage. Suddenly, there was a French prince to rival England's, a fact of which Mary's English 'father-in-law' was acutely aware. Mary need not marry Edward of England when there was an alternative candidate sleeping in his cradle in Paris.

In spite of the still-lingering English hopes that the Scots would send their queen south to marry Edward, in May 1544 Henry VIII's brother-in-law, Edward Seymour, Earl of Hertford, set out with an army to Scotland, burning Edinburgh on the seventh of the month, although he was unable to take the city's castle. Beautiful Holyrood Palace, too, which lay just outside the city was sacked, while the important port of Leith was badly damaged and the ships captured. It was a blitzkrieg, designed to inflict the most damage on the Scots, with repeated waves of violence over the next few years, to ensure that they were menaced into keeping their side of a bargain agreed under duress. The little queen's safety was, of course, the paramount consideration, while in the face of so many disasters, the political acumen of her mother, Marie of Guise, became more apparent, with calls made for her to share in her daughter's regency.

Henry VIII had been captivated by Mary's glittering crown, but his death in January 1547 changed little for the child, with the Earl of Hertford, who was promoted to Duke of Somerset and Lord Protector of England, merely continuing the war in his stead. On 10 September 1547, he crushed the Scottish army at the Battle of Pinkie, leading to so much bloodshed that an eyewitness reported that 'the river ran all red with blood', while 'the dead bodies lay as thick as a man may note cattle grazing in a full replenished pasture'.[75] With Somerset effectively the master of southern Scotland and the four-year-old queen a fugitive in her own realm hunted by her kingdom's invaders, drastic action was required.

On 29 July 1548, Mary, after leaving her weeping mother's arms, embarked on the King of France's own ship to begin her childhood anew. The now five-year-old queen was accompanied by many familiar faces, including two of her father's illegitimate sons. Yet, she would not see her mother, who would soon wrest the regency from Arran, again for four years (and then, after that visit, never again). She would not see her kingdom for another fourteen years, with the Protestant Reformation, so far removed from her Catholic upbringing, occurring in her absence. England's 'Rough Wooing' had succeeded only in divorcing Mary from her kingdom and driving her into the arms of the French. It was a war that was fought entirely due to the sex and age of Scotland's monarch: child queens were very much seen as fair game by predatory neighbours due largely to the expendability of girls in the European royal marriage market. It was normal for princesses to marry and leave their homes in the hope of building alliances, so why shouldn't the same be true for girls whose dowry happened to be a crown?

It was the same for Isabella II of Jerusalem, who was used first by her father and then by her husband as the basis of their claims to rule her kingdom. Like her mother, Maria, her life is a vague one. It was also similarly short. Isabella became pregnant not long after her marriage, losing a child to miscarriage or stillbirth when she cannot have been more than thirteen or fourteen.[76] She died in childbirth in May 1228 aged only fifteen, having 'reigned' but never ruled Jerusalem for the entirety of her brief life. In fact, she never even visited the city from which her kingdom was named.[77] Isabella's child was a boy, bringing the kingdom's run of queens to an end.[78] Frederick II would continue to claim the title of King of Jerusalem, which he held in right of his long-dead wife, for the remainder of his life. As Natasha R. Hodgson in her study of women in the Crusader states notes, 'Maria and Isabella II did not live long enough to mature into the political life of the Latin East.' Indeed, they were given no opportunity to do so.[79] The double disadvantage of being both female and a child at their accession proved to be insurmountable.

Mary Queen of Scots was also destined for a foreign marriage far from her kingdom. She was betrothed to the Dauphin Francois following her arrival in France and was raised amongst the steadily increasing number of children in the royal nursery. Although, as a reigning queen she was given precedence over all her young sisters-in-law (to the chagrin of their mother, Catherine de Medici, who never warmed to the girl), Scotland had become little more than her dowry, to be passed over to her husband on their marriage. With her absence from Scotland the political situation calmed down, although the young King Edward VI did send ambassadors to France in June 1551 to demand Mary's return so that he could marry her in accordance with the Treaty of Greenwich.[80] In a somewhat awkward interview with Henri II, they were told this was impossible, since Mary was engaged to his son. They immediately asked for the hand of the French king's eldest daughter, Elisabeth, instead, which had been the true purpose of their embassy and which was readily granted (although not without some considerable haggling over the dowry). For a period, it seemed that the former betrothed monarchs of the kingdoms of the island of Britain would become siblings-in-law.

Mary, who grew into a notably attractive girl with auburn hair and a pronounced nose, towered above her fiancé (she would eventually stand at five feet eleven inches tall). She finally married Francois in April 1558 when she was fifteen and the groom fourteen. Just under three weeks before she had signed a secret agreement in which she ceded Scotland to her husband and his heirs, in default of any of hers:

only Francois' early death the following year stopped the kingdom becoming subsumed by France. One right that Mary did not cede to her French husband were her claims in relation to the English throne. Infuriated by Scotland's defiance, Henry VIII had responded by cutting Mary out of his will and leaving the throne to the heirs of his younger sister, should his own descent fail. Regardless, there were a great many people in England and the wider world who, on the accession of Henry's final child, Elizabeth I, to the English throne in 1558, viewed Mary as heir to the throne. One of these was Mary herself, with her desire for the richer of the two British kingdoms dominating her adult life, just as the English desire for her crown had overshadowed her childhood. It was a cause for which she would, ultimately, meet a bloody end and it is a story to which we shall return in Chapter 7.

Louis VII of France, who was blessed with a son in 1165, after three marriages and nearly three decades of trying, wrote of his relief, since he had been 'terrified by a multitude of daughters'.[81] A child monarch tended to throw a kingdom into chaos the world over in any period, with the accession of a female increasing the problem. The acquisition of their crowns in childhood brought little joy to Maria and Isabella II of Jerusalem, Mary Queen of Scots, Teri'imaevarua II of Bora Bora or Wilhelmina of the Netherlands, with the children disparaged, fought over and, in some cases, even spirited away. Wilhelmina endured a childhood not so very different from the little girls who had gone before her. She found no joy in the loneliness and uncertainty of her position, while her mother was forced to fight for the girl's very right to rule. Well schooled in world history by her English governess, she would undoubtedly have been familiar with her ill-fated ancestress, Mary Queen of Scots, while she might have known the stories of her Jerusalemite counterparts or her near-contemporary in Bora Bora. In a way, the specifics hardly matter. James V, King of Scots, dying of uncertain causes in the cold December of

1542 lamented the advent of an heir who was both female and a child. While his prediction that his daughter would prove to be the end of his dynasty was incorrect, the path of a child queen across the world and across history was strewn with obstacles and disparagement. In name and title, they were queens, but they moved as pawns on the chessboards of their kingdoms. Adult queens could sometimes fare rather better.

CHAPTER 5:
A LION'S CUBS ARE LIONS ALL

Tamar of Georgia, Jeanne of France (alias Juana II of Navarre) and Maria Theresia of Austria-Hungary

News of the queen's death spread fast through the mountainous border of Europe and Asia. 'The tints of happiness faded from the countenance of the Georgians,' lamented one chronicler, 'for they had had no name but Tamar's on their lips.'[1] All people could talk about was Tamar, with ploughmen singing verses in her honour as they prepared their land for planting and musicians strumming sad laments on their zithers. It was 1213 and a woman who had dominated the politics of this sizeable state for thirty-five years was gone.

Tamar is little known in the West, though she is still much revered in Georgia, with the adoration in which she has been held posthumously swaying depictions of her life and reign.[2] Such adoration was not in evidence when she became sole monarch of Georgia in 1184, with a female '*mepe*' (king) unlooked for and unwanted. This 'king of kings' or 'queen of kings' was initially a highly unwelcome addition to the mighty Caucasian kingdom's royal pantheon.

Unsurprisingly, given the near-universal cultural prejudices against female rule, most reigning queens have been undesired and unwanted figures. They tend to succeed only when there really are no other candidates, with women grudgingly preferred to chaos or dynastic change, even if they were far from welcomed. They were, effectively, seen as the lesser of two evils. This was something that Tamar's father, Giorgi III of Georgia, recognised when he decided to publicly declare her his heir at a great court, which gathered in 1178 when Tamar was around eighteen years old. His daughter was, he assured those assembled, 'the radiant light of their eyes, the crown and necklace of all monarchs and sovereigns'. Tamar then appeared, dressed in a floor-length robe of cloth of gold and gold brocade and was sat beside her father as queen. As everyone watched, Giorgi then did something extraordinary – he placed the crown on her head himself. All of those assembled bowed before her, swearing oaths of loyalty, with the most conspicuous of the oath takers the king himself.[3]

Giorgi was a strong and adamant ruler who had recently defeated a rebellion and had his own nephew blinded and castrated, making overt opposition to Tamar's appointment unsurprisingly muted. His plan was, however, a radical one. In the 300 years since the kingdom's unification, the crown of Georgia had always passed through the male line. It was far from certain that his noblemen, even as they bowed before the new queen, would accept Tamar as their ruler. She was, however, the dynasty's only hope.

In fourteenth-century France, King Louis X accepted a petition by his younger brother Philippe to allow his daughters to succeed to his lands in Poitiers in the event that he had no sons. Louis considered, 'Reason and natural law instruct us that in default of male heirs females should inherit and have succession to the goods and possessions of the fathers of whom they are procreated and descended in legal marriage, the same as do the males.'[4] It had been widely established across Europe that women could have inheritance rights, although only in the event that they had no brothers and, often, other close male relatives. Could this inheritance and succession extend to females when the possession in question was the French throne?

Louis X was the latest monarch in a French dynasty that had been remarkably stable since the reign of Hugh Capet in the tenth century: each French king had, in turn, managed to produce a son to succeed them (albeit sometimes with considerable difficulty and multiple successive wives). As a result, the kingdom had never really formalised its succession system or explored the possibility of female rule. Only the obscure King Raoul, who in 923 succeeded his father-in-law, Robert I, claimed through a woman, with his strident wife Emma pushing for her husband's election over that of her younger brother, reputedly declaring (in a sentiment recognisable to big sisters the world over) that she would rather embrace her husband's knees as a vassal than her brother's.[5] She was a powerfully ambitious woman, but she cannot be said to have reigned.[6]

The question of female succession became suddenly and unexpectedly very pressing when the still-youthful Louis X died without warning in 1316. His wife was pregnant at the time. Would the child be the hoped-for boy, thereby resolving any doubt over who should succeed him? For five months, while everyone waited to find out, Louis' brother Philippe of Poitiers, who had petitioned for the inheritance rights of his daughters, was made regent. The child was born – a boy, but he lived only days. This left only one surviving child of the late king – a four-year-old girl.

Little Jeanne's childhood had already been troubled. Her mother, the king's first wife, had been accused of adultery in 1314, before being imprisoned and found dead in conveniently short order. Louis never questioned his daughter's parentage, but the circumstances of her mother's arrest and death were a major hinderance to the child's claims.[7] It is perhaps unsurprising that a four-year-old possible bastard, who was also female, found few allies when the time came to dispute the succession. That she did find some support is a testament to a sense of natural justice, but it was still a relatively straightforward matter for her paternal uncle Philippe of Poitiers to secure his coronation at Reims in 1316, in spite of opposition both from within the royal family and outside.[8] Philippe's position became insurmountable on 2 February 1317 when an assembly of the grandees of France declared that no woman could wear its crown. They did not supply any legal basis for this.

The birth of a new royal baby into the House of Habsburg in Austria in 1717 caused consternation rather than delight, with the parents, Holy Roman Emperor Karl VI and Elisabeth Christine of Brunswick-Wolfenbüttel, almost immediately attempting to conceive again in an attempt to produce a son. They did not succeed. Maria Theresia would be joined in the royal nursery by only two further girls, with her mother's health eventually wrecked by quack fertility treatments that left her unable to stand. The lack of a male heir drove the couple apart, with widespread rumours that Karl hoped his wife would die so that he could remarry.

The Austrian Habsburgs had been facing a succession crisis for years before Maria Theresia's birth in a situation not unlike that faced by Jeanne in fourteenth-century France. Maria Theresia's grandfather, the Holy Roman Emperor Leopold I, had brokered a scheme between his two sons, Josef and Karl in 1703, at a time when they three were the last remaining male Habsburgs. With the dynasty under threat, the brothers agreed that the elder, Josef, would inherit the Austrian Habsburg lands, while the younger, Karl, should make an (ultimately unsuccessful) attempt on the Spanish crown, which had, until recently, been held by another branch of the family which had recently died out in the male line.[9] Each was to be the other's successor if no male heirs were produced before, crucially, the inheritance was to pass to the brothers' daughters, with Josef's ahead in the line of succession.

Josef, a notoriously licentious man who infected his wife with a sexually transmitted disease that destroyed her health and fertility, was then the father of two young daughters, but unlikely to sire more heirs.[10] On Josef's death from smallpox in 1711 Karl hurried back from Barcelona to claim the Habsburg inheritance. In accordance with tradition, he was duly elected as Holy Roman Emperor.

Two years later (and still childless after five years of marriage), Karl issued his 'Pragmatic Sanction', which confirmed the possibility of female succession to the Habsburg lands and titles while, crucially, settling the thrones on his own yet-to-be-conceived daughters over those of his elder brother, Maria Josefa, the future Electress of Saxony and Maria Amalia, future Electress of Bavaria. 'A truly revolutionary document', according to one historian, its importance lay in the fact that it was enacted at a point where female inheritance looked to be almost certain, naming a woman as heiress to the Habsburg kingdoms and territories.[11] It also went further than the 1703 settlement, since Karl intended his new regulation to be eternal and binding. Whether the estates of the different portions of the realm would accept it, was another matter.[12]

Karl, as head of the Austrian house of Habsburg, ruled over an enormous collection of kingdoms, principalities, archduchies and counties in Central and Eastern Europe, which were tied only by their common ruler rather than any formal unification. Most of these territories had been acquired over the centuries through advantageous marriages, with the Habsburgs famed for marrying well (at least until they narrowed the gene pool by largely only wedding each other). Overlying this loose assortment of lands was the elected title of Holy Roman Emperor, which – since the late fifteenth century – had always been held by a Habsburg and effectively made them overlords of Germany and much of northern Italy, although their actual power in these lands was often negligible.

Emperor Karl knew full well that his daughter would never be elected as Holy Roman Empress. None of the electors, who were primarily the heads of ancient German princely families, were going to cast their vote for a woman, even if technically they could.[13] She could, however, succeed to almost all the Habsburg lands, including the Archduchy of Austria, the Kingdom of Bohemia and the Kingdom of Hungary. Karl therefore spent the final thirty years of his life attempting to ensure that Maria Theresia was accepted in the underlying realms and territories: the kingdoms, dukedoms and counties that made up the vast Habsburg Empire. There would inevitably be a non-Habsburg Holy Roman Emperor after his death, but he hoped that the family's power would endure under the rule of his daughter.

In spite of her position as heiress to three crowns and numerous independent duchies and estates, Maria Theresia was given no political grounding: after her marriage to Francois Etienne of Lorraine in 1736, it was her male consort who was permitted to attend council meetings, not her. 'It never pleased my father to involve me when he attended to foreign or domestic affairs, nor to inform me about them' she later complained.[14] She was intelligent and her education was not lacking: she learned French, Italian, Spanish and Latin, as well as her native German, all of which she would need to rule her diverse lands, but such an education was not out of the ordinary for any Habsburg princess of her time. Maria Theresia herself produced three children in quick succession following her marriage in 1736, but they were all girls. Had they been boys, they would have pushed their mother down in the line of succession. By the terms of the Pragmatic Sanction, Maria Theresia was heir to the vast Habsburg inheritance when her father died unexpectedly in October 1740, but it was another matter to claim it.

King Giorgi III died in 1184. Tamar was already in possession of Georgia's crown on her father's death, thanks to her coronation at the great court some six years earlier. She undoubtedly saw herself as a ruler, but she was a young woman at the head of an old and fiercely independent kingdom; to hold on to power, in defiance of those who would take it from her, was to walk a difficult and precarious path.[15] Tamar received a second coronation and initially had some success in establishing her rule, though she was very soon facing opposition from almost all of her nobility and the members of her court. Most viewed her only as a continuator of her dynasty and the future wife and mother of kings.

According to local myth, Georgia was God's own country, gifted soon after the Creation to the Georgian people who wined and dined Him, while the reigning family claimed descent from the Biblical King David.[16] Tamar's kingdom was deep within the Caucasus mountains and its subjects spoke a language unrelated to its Indo-European neighbours, close in form to almost no languages in current usage, and yet it was far from isolated. The country lay on the division between the Christian world of the west and the Muslim world of the east, with Christianity ubiquitous by the third or fourth century CE, giving the national church, which had initially been subordinate to Constantinople, time to develop its own unique flavour by Tamar's day.[17] Common faith naturally inclined the Georgians to look westwards, although they also traded widely with the cities and settlements of the east, with good caravan roads running to Iran, Egypt, Russia, China and beyond.

Tamar, like her great-grandfather, King Davit the Builder (reigned 1089–1125), whose nickname spells out his importance to Georgia's development, spent time and effort in ensuring that these roads were kept in good repair, as well as building inns and bridges.[18] Artisans in Tbilisi, the principal city, as well as other settlements, made fine saddles, bridles and bow cases for export, while beaver and otter skins, cotton and wool were also sold. Primarily, though, Georgia was an agricultural society, with serfs as rooted to the land as their crops. In theory, one peasant family occupied a *'pudze'*, which was a plot of land approximately 15 acres in size on which they carried out subsistence level agriculture, as well as growing crops to pay their taxes to the crown, their lord and the church.[19] These serfs lived in single storey stone or wooden houses alongside their livestock, and undoubtedly the highly stratified society, frequent invasion and high taxes caused social unrest. Davit the Builder had pushed the Seljuk Turks out of Georgia and curbed the power of the hitherto highly independent church by combining the most important secular office – that of *Mtsignobartukhutsesi* (effectively, High Chancellor) – with prominent church office and then appointing his closest supporter to the role.[20] Tamar's father, Giorgi III, had placed similar constraints on the power of the nobility, but they were quietly furious and merely waiting for a change from a powerful regime to one that they perceived would be weak. Giorgi, by the force of his dominant personality and fearsome reputation, deterred invasion and rebellion in the latter years of his reign, but much of the tension was simply bubbling under the surface.

Tamar's first step was to secure the recognition of her rule by the church, but this was at considerable cost – she was forced to backtrack considerably from her great-grandfather's church reforms and accept the Georgian Church patriarch, Mikel Marianisdze, who was a cunning and highly political figure as *mtsignobartukhutsesi*, high chancellor. In return, she received only his lukewarm support. Through this, she kept her throne, but Marianisdze became the power behind it.[21]

This in turn emboldened the already rebellious nobles at Tamar's court, many of whom had held grievances against the monarchy since her father's day, but used the accession of a woman to make them public. Their first target was the middlemen (lower status administrators and men outside the traditional nobility), whom her father had appointed to high office and who remained her staunchest supporters. With regret, she was forced to remove her vizier and the commander in chief of the royal army who were amongst such men, further weakening the crown.

The earliest known representation of Tamar, painted onto the walls of the church in the rock-cut monastery at Vardzia, seems to date from this uncertain period immediately after King Giorgi's death. It shows the father followed by his daughter adorned in Byzantine imperial robes and wearing identical crowns. Both are referred to as 'king of kings of all the East', but Tamar occupies the subordinate position. Such imagery could be highly active in denoting the queen as ruler and situating her within a traditionally male dominated position of power and is a clear attempt by Tamar at controlling the narrative. In the depiction, she is tied to her father, whose blood made her eligible to rule, while at the same time presenting herself in the guise of a virtuous woman.[22] It appears almost as a desperate attempt to affix her rule to the bedrock of her kingdom. Studies of Tamar's reign have so often been blinded by her gilded reputation as one of Georgia's greatest monarchs, but this came later. At her accession, her power was shaky and she was viewed as a colossal liability.[23]

When Emperor Karl died in 1740, Maria Theresia immediately became – on paper – the most powerful woman in the world, ruling over an unofficial empire that encompassed Austria, Hungary (including modern Slovakia), Bohemia (now Czechia), Croatia, parts of Italy and the Netherlands, to name but a few. As with Tamar, the reality was more complicated.

Even before her father had been buried, Maria Theresia's status was being questioned. She received the homage of the estates of Lower Austria on 22 November 1740, effectively a coronation for the archduchy, against the backdrop of riots, the noise of smashing windows and the marching feet of her dragoons, called out to calm the streets. It must have hammered home to Maria Theresia just how difficult her attempt to assert her rule over six million fragmented and diverse people, spread over more than 700,000 square miles, was likely to be.

Despite her impressive education in languages, Maria Theresia had received little schooling in rulership. And yet she knew the workings of the vast Habsburg court in Vienna, which was home to 2000 people and was notable for its rigid ritual. She had maids whose sole role was to iron her undergarments, as well as a dedicated bonnet stitcher, who would attach and remove her headwear when required.[24] This was the world in which she grew up. Maria Theresia's first appearance in court dress was not long after her eleventh birthday, so she was a native in this world: she understood how it worked considerably more than her foreign-born husband, Francois Etienne.

Their relationship was an interesting one. It was to be expected that a husband would rule on behalf of his wife as, effectively, the power behind the throne, something which Maria Theresia's father had acknowledged when he allowed his son-in-law to attend his councils. Francois Etienne was lazy and weak willed, but seemingly well meaning; he certainly showed remarkable equanimity for an eighteenth-century husband, playing the role of consort rather than rival, and Maria Theresia loved him for it. Years later, after his death, she carefully noted the exact length of their marriage, right down to the hours ('29 years, 335 months, 1540 weeks, 10,781 days, 258,744 hours') in her personal prayer book, in an extraordinary exhibition of devotion and grief.[25] In a letter to one of her newly married daughters on the secret to marital success, she wrote: 'What happiness to find always at home a pleasant wife, busy in creating the happiness of her husband, amusing, consoling, and being useful to him: who never presumes to thwart him, lets him always come, is content with his attentions and considers herself happy in being occupied with them!'[26] In reality, it could hardly be said that Maria Theresia practiced what she preached, but it was undoubtedly a difficult balancing act given the couple's disparity in rank. As Maria Theresia further acknowledged to her daughter, who had also married somewhat beneath herself: 'Your position in this respect is as delicate as mine was. Never let him feel your superiority; nothing is too much, when one loves well and reasonably: I am at peace on that point.' Although she would always attempt to portray herself as a submissive spouse, cautioning another daughter against showing a craving for power ('do not forget that we women may show nothing of all that towards our husbands: that is our duty before God and Man'), Maria Theresia saw her succession as a ruler in her own right as ordained by God.[27]

The driving force behind the Pragmatic Sanction had been to ensure that the hard-won Habsburg monarchy remained intact. Maintaining the lands of her ancestors also propelled Maria Theresia forwards, but not everyone recognised her right to rule. Most notably, her two cousins, Maria Josefa and Maria Amalia. The daughters of the Emperor Josef I had married the Electors of Saxony (and, by 1740, King of Poland) and Bavaria respectively, and were aggrieved at their relegation.[28] As such, not all of the opposition to Maria Theresia's claim was directed specifically at female succession, although there were no attempts made to actually crown either cousin in her place. When voices were raised against Maria Theresia in Vienna following her father's death, most spoke in favour of Karl Albrecht, Elector of Bavaria and a son-in-law of the Emperor Josef I. These voices were also almost entirely focussed on Maria Theresia's sex.

Jeanne of France's sex made her succession to any kingdom unlikely, although her supporters continued to press for her rights. Her uncle, Philippe V, was forced back to the negotiating table in 1318, with a settlement reached on 27 March that year in which six-year-old Jeanne was to renounce her title to France in return for marriage to a cousin

– Philippe of Evreux, who was himself a male-line contender for the crown – a sizeable pension and potentially favourable inheritance rights to the counties of Champagne and Brie, should the king die without male heirs.[29] It was hardly spectacular compensation for the loss of France, which was then the intellectual and cultural capital of Europe and whose language was, quite literally, the *lingua franca*. According to the settlement, when Jeanne reached what was then regarded as adulthood at the age of twelve, she would need to ratify its terms, something which does not seem to have been done.[30] As such, the agreement – and Jeanne's renunciation of her inherited right to rule – was almost certainly voidable. She likely understood very little of it, however. And, either way, in 1318, the idea that an adult Jeanne could ever mount a successful claim to France was laughable. She was hampered by her youth and her questionable birth, but mostly, she was hampered simply by her sex. Only the most devoted of Jeanne's supporters considered her a better candidate that her adult uncle who was obviously dynastically preferable to the people of her time, while her rejection set a firm present against female rule. She was quietly stepped over again in 1322 when Philippe died and was succeeded by his younger brother, Charles IV. However, when he too died in 1328, the direct male line of the House of Capet came to an end. Sixteen-year-old Jeanne, along with a smattering of younger female cousins, was now the last survivor of this once-great dynasty, which threw her claim into sharp focus.

She was not the only claimant, though she viewed herself as the rightful ruler. In France, a kinsman, Philippe of Valois, who was a paternal grandson of Philippe III, emerged as the strongest contender, while over the channel in England, the young King Edward III (Jeanne's first cousin) had a very strong claim as her grandfather Philippe IV's only surviving grandson.* It was Philippe of Valois, as

---

* Edward did have a younger brother, John of Eltham, but he would die in 1336.

an adult Frenchman, who was successful, securing his coronation as Philippe VI. As a compensation, Jeanne was permitted to become queen of the smaller kingdom of Navarre, which had belonged to her paternal grandmother and over which the new Philippe VI of France had no hereditary claim.[31] If he had, her rights there would almost certainly have been overstepped too. Jeanne's son, Carlos II of Navarre, would later be rumoured to have asserted that 'if he ever wished to lay claim to the French crown, he could show that he had a better right to it than the King of England', but he never backed his claim with muscle.[32] It was, instead, left to Edward III of England, claiming in right of his very much still living mother Isabella, daughter of Philippe IV, to raise the issue of female inheritance in France with force, although he intended to ignore his mother and reign himself. Unsurprisingly, as war broke out, the French became much more entrenched in their unwillingness to accept either female rule or female inheritance. They would fight for over a century to assert this principle, while a legal rationale would soon be found to underpin it.

Though she had been conciliatory in the early days of her reign, Tamar of Georgia soon went on the attack. The final straw was a 'Magna Carta moment' only a few months into her sole rule when Kutlu Arslani, Tamar's *mechurchletukhutsesi*, or finance minister, demanded major constitutional concessions. His requirements, which proposed a new government building in which matters of justice could be decided without input from the queen, looks very much like a parliament, with a constitutional monarch at its head. Unsurprisingly, Tamar viewed the proposals as 'the end of my reign' and she had Arslani arrested.[33] When his supporters threatened to storm the palace and remove her, she agreed to enter into negotiations, using two women of her court as her go-betweens.[34] This gave her the time she needed to sow discord between Arslani and his supporters, with the nobility backing down on the proviso that they suffered no harm. It was a major achievement for Tamar, but she was still far from secure. She was also forced to agree to take her *Darbazi* (royal council) into account in the decisions that she made, something which undoubtedly decreased the power of the sovereign. Her bold attempt in calling a Church Synod in order to remove Mikel Marianisdze from his high secular office also failed and she was saddled with his unwelcome presence until his death some years later.

An even more unwelcome presence was provided by the arrival of Yuri Bogolyubsky, son of the Grand Prince of Rostov-Suzdal (to the Georgians he is always 'Giorgi the Russian'). As an unmarried woman, Tamar was ostensibly under the guardianship of her father's sister, Queen Rusudan, with this widowed princess providing a strong example of female rule to her niece. Rusudan, along with the nobility, agreed on the need for Tamar to marry, to supply Georgia with a king, with those about the young queen 'making a concerted effort to choose a bridegroom'.[35] For unknown reasons, their choice fell on Yuri, whose foreign birth may suggest that he was a compromise candidate, hinting at further discord at the centre of Tamar's reign. This was ominous, since (as a contemporary chronicle notes) 'they knew nothing about the man he [the Georgian emissary] was to bring back'. He was good-looking but Tamar had her doubts, asking for time to consider the matter since, 'How can it be right to do this without deliberation? We know nothing about this foreigner, his behaviour, his actions or his qualities as a warrior, his character or manner of life. Let us take time to acquaint ourselves with his qualities and defects in every respect.'[36] In this, as in so much else of the early days of her reign, Tamar was overruled, with Yuri crowned king shortly after the marriage in 1185. She remained, ostensibly, the senior monarch, but she was still unable to fully assert her authority over a year after her accession to the throne.

Tamar's foisted first marriage proved to be a disaster, with complaints soon voiced by contemporaries of Yuri's drunkenness, as well as dark hints of other personal shortcomings: 'When he was in his cups he committed various abominable and unnatural acts, not worthy of mention or fit to be recorded here at length.'[37] The couple were entirely incompatible, but it took Tamar two years to build up a strong enough powerbase to take action, divorcing her Russian husband and exiling him to Constantinople in 1187. This was a seminal moment for Tamar as a ruler. Three years after she had come to the throne, it was now entirely clear just who ruled Georgia. She would crush a rebellion by the returning Yuri not long afterwards, permanently ending his hopes of retaking the throne. Then, her hated Patriarch, Mikel Marianisdze, died shortly afterwards 'and was mourned by none great or humble, for everyone detested him', according at least to Tamar's tame historian who recorded the major events of her reign.[38]

She was finally an independent ruler and could chose her own second husband. This was Davit Soslani, an Ossetian prince who was the foster son of her beloved aunt, Rusudan, and 'a fine figure of a youth as became his lineage and well-bred in all other respects, a strong and courageous soldier, unrivalled as a horseman and supreme in archery, well built, and endowed with every virtue'.[39] They apparently made a good-looking couple, since 'people swooned at the sight of' Tamar, whose 'face captivated men's hearts'.[40] She bore a son and a daughter a few years after the marriage, but for her the primary satisfaction was likely to have been the fact that Davit – like Maria Theresia's husband – showed no interest in usurping her position. Happiest when he was leading an army of conquest, he left the government to Tamar, with coins minted by the couple always depicting the queen as the dominant party.[41]

Maria Theresia, too, did not include her husband on any of the at least 2000 types of coin issued throughout her inherited territories during the early years of her reign, with her profile on the coins soon well-known there too.'**42 The people spending the coins in the market or squirreling them away as savings could be in no doubt as to the sex of their sovereign, while she made it clear from the first that she intended to wear the crowns and ducal-hats of her domains herself. This was not necessarily a foregone conclusion, with both the Electors of Bavaria and Saxony registering protests against her accession to the Habsburg states immediately after the death of Emperor Karl. As the claimed monarch of Bohemia (one of the many titles she had inherited), Maria Theresia was entitled to a vote in the forthcoming election to replace her father as Holy Roman Emperor, but there were doubts about whether a woman could actually take part in the election. As a result, she attempted to transfer her vote to Francois Etienne, but this raised protests too. Maria Theresia's husband was the relatively insignificant Grand Duke of Tuscany (a title that he had acquired through the efforts of his father-in-law) and not a grandee of the empire, casting his ability to vote on her behalf in doubt. As such, when she sent an emissary to the Imperial Diet in Frankfurt where the contest was to be held, the other electors refused to speak to him: 'an unprecedented public affront'.[43]

While Maria Theresia faced immediate opposition to her accession within the empire, it was also soon apparent that she faced threats from without, with the new King Frederick II of Prussia marching his troops into her territory of Silesia on 16 December 1740, less than two months after her father's death.[44] Frederick, who was highly ambitious and, crucially, immensely wealthy, certainly meant to benefit from the chaos that a woman's accession was already looking likely to cause, assuring Maria Theresia that he occupied this wealthy part of her inheritance only to prevent other neighbouring powers from taking it from her. Unsurprisingly, she was unconvinced, viewing this as a

---

** She did order that some coins be minted for Francois Etienne after he became emperor, but these were not numerous, while her gold ceremonial coins weighed twice as much as his.

naked threat and extortion but it took time to martial her troops.[45] In late April 1741, Maria Theresia's forces were soundly defeated at the Battle of Mollwitz. Significantly, at the service of thanksgiving that the victorious Prussian king ordered, the minister read from St Paul's first epistle to Timothy, declaring: 'But I suffer not a woman to teach, nor to usurp authority over the man.' There was Biblical precedent to refute Maria Theresia's claims to rule and, while Frederick was motivated more by opportunism than hostility to female succession, it was a useful stick with which to beat his opponent.

As news of Mollwitz spread, the war expanded with the Spanish attacking the Habsburg Empire in Italy and the French attaching themselves strongly to the Elector of Bavaria. On 24 January 1742, Karl Albrecht of Bavaria was elected as Holy Roman Emperor – the first non-Habsburg in more than 300 years. With everyone aware just how ruinously expensive and destructive the War of the Spanish Succession had been in the early years of the century (a conflict in which Maria Theresia's father had been a major participant), Maria Theresia's usual allies Britain and Russia both separately advised her to make peace with Prussia. The queen refused but, as 1741 progressed and French and Bavarian troops entered Austria, she was slowly pushed backwards deeper into her territories.

The Sultan of Rum was in no doubt that Tamar's sex made her deficient as a ruler, sending a message to inform her that since 'every woman is feeble of mind' her kingdom was ripe for the picking. Only her immediate conversion to Islam and submission to life in his harem would be enough to spare her.[46] In 1205, Sultan Rukn-ad-Din decided to launch an invasion.

Georgia's success on the world stage was provoking envy from a number of its neighbours. For Tamar presided over a golden age of Georgian culture and expansion, with the kingdom reaching its greatest territorial extent with the conquests made during her reign. She was charitable, building and restoring religious buildings both in her kingdom and abroad (in this, she was 'a second Constantine', her chronicler gushed), as well as acting as a patron of literature.[47] She even improved the country's agriculture, ordering significant irrigation systems, one over twelve miles long to be built during her reign.[48]

The Sultanate of Rum was a Muslim state whose relationship with Christian Georgia was a complex one.[49] And yet it is inconceivable that Sultan Rukn-ad-Din would write on such terms to a male ruler, particularly one of Tamar's reputation and calibre. She wept on receiving the letter, before showing her mettle and, particularly, her lack of 'womenly weakness' (a phrase that damns her with faint praise and shows that even her own pet historian underestimated her). Tamar did not lead her troops personally, but she did march with them to the Basiani Valley in what is now modern-day Turkey. There, her troops surprised the enemy while they were in their camp, inflicting huge losses and bringing Tamar a victory that is still celebrated in Georgia today. She rode into her capital, Tbilisi, to crowds and acclaim.[50] As the leading Georgian historian Kalistrat Salia noted, this merely inspired Tamar to undertake more conquests, with the queen ruling over a multi-national empire by the time of her death in 1213.[51]

Internationally, she was a force, being instrumental in the creation of the Trebizond Empire, which acted as a buffer state between Georgia and a Byzantine Empire that was in the process of falling to the Latin Crusaders from Western Europe. The first two Trebizond emperors, Alexios I and his brother, David, were offshoots of the Byzantine royal family, but owed their new throne to Tamar, who was their relative. They may have been the sons of her younger sister, also named Rusudan, but the relationship is not entirely clear. Regardless, it would have seemed remarkable at the start of Tamar's reign that she would ever have been in a position to become a kingmaker.

A LION'S CUBS ARE LIONS ALL

By the end of 1741, one year into her reign, the chances of Maria Theresia maintaining control of her own multi-national empire must have seemed unlikely, with the estates of Austria recognising Karl Albrecht of Bavaria – now Emperor Karl VII – as their archduke that October and Bohemia following suit and naming him as their king in November. Although he ostensibly claimed through a woman – his wife, Maria Amalia – it seems impossible that the Habsburg inheritance would have fragmented so easily if his opponent had been male. Most had serious doubts about the ability of a woman to rule over a territory so large and diverse, while they also saw this apparent inherent weakness in the queen as an opportunity to break up the ancient empire.

It was only with considerable difficulty that Maria Theresia, dressed in Hungarian fashion, was able to secure her coronation in that kingdom on 25 June 1741. Hungary crowned her as king rather than queen, with the new monarch happy to embrace this ritualised change of gender in return for the support of at least one of her realms. It was certainly a neat way of overcoming the perceived problem in being ruled by a woman: the Hungarians simply declared their monarch to be male.

With Hungarian support the tide of the war turned, but it would still be some years before Maria Theresia could be confident that the Habsburg inheritance was hers. She was able to recapture Prague, the ancient capital of Bohemia, in late 1742 and entered the city in May 1743 to finally secure her coronation – also as 'king' – there. Significantly, Maria Theresia, unlike her Bavarian rival, Karl VII, was invested with the crown of St Wenceslas, Bohemia's famous 'good king' (actually a duke), whose bones were (and still are) reverentially interred in the Gothic masterpiece of St Vitus's Cathedral where the ceremony occurred. Maria Theresia had, prudently, kept the crown in her possession following the death of her father, ensuring that even when Karl was calling himself the 'King of Bohemia', he could not support his claims with a crowning in the name of the kingdom's most important saint. While she was in Prague, Maria Theresia heard that the 'Pragmatic Army', an international coalition consisting of Dutch, British, Hanoverian and Hessian troops, which had formed in her support and was named for the instrument that had named her as Habsburg heiress, had won a great victory over the French at Dettingen.

The tide turned for Maria Theresia with the sudden death of Emperor Karl VII on 20 January 1745, with his teenaged son coming to terms with her four months later. She was single minded, resolutely refusing to agree to anything that would diminish her inheritance. But as a woman, she had been forced to fight for every foot of land that she claimed. It may have seemed a bitter irony to her that, had her short-lived elder brother survived, he would have simply been handed everything for which she battled.

Only the cunning and highly capable Frederick II of Prussia now remained. He had changed sides repeatedly throughout the war but still held Silesia. While Maria Theresia could, by that stage count on the troops of Empress Elizaveta of Russia, who threw in her support behind a fellow female monarch, as well as the British, Frederick still won a substantial victory against the Austrians at Hohenfriedberg on 4 June 1745, while the month before the French had defeated the Pragmatic Army at Fontenoy.

Nonetheless, on 13 September 1745 at an Electoral Diet in which Maria Theresia was invited to attend as Queen of Bohemia (with doubts about her right to vote quietly swept aside), Francois Etienne was elected as Holy Roman Emperor. It has, rightly, been demonstrated that there was 'no credible alternative' to Maria Theresia's beloved husband, but the election was still both an important political coup and a personal triumph for the queen.[52] Maria Theresia clearly did not entirely practice what she preached to her daughters in demanding that they be subservient to their husbands and home loving, but she did truly adore the somewhat ineffectual man that she had married.

In order not to overshadow him, she refused his urging that she be crowned as empress beside him on 4 October 1745.

The War of the Austrian Succession was formally ended by the Peace of Aachen in October 1748, leaving Maria Theresia as undisputed mistress of all her father's territories, save Silesia, Glaz and three small Italian duchies. On the whole, she had been vindicated, albeit at great cost. A woman was the undoubted mistress of the Habsburg's great empire. She had done so, too, while almost continually pregnant, a hazard not faced by her male counterparts: Maria Theresa bore sixteen children in the nearly twenty years between February 1737 and December 1756. She attributed her victory to God's favour, but her own political skill and determination undoubtedly played a significant role. So too, in the end, was the decision of the estates of most of her realms to back her succession. They preferred a Habsburg, albeit a female one, to the Bavarian House of Wittelsbach.[53] The Pragmatic Sanction, which had looked so shaky in the face of internal and external opposition, held.[54]

While Maria Theresia's ultimate success was no doubt down to her strength of mind and ambition, it was founded on a strong claim to rulership. Jeanne of France had no such opportunity, regardless of the strength of her hereditary claim. Students of medieval European history will doubtless have heard of the Salic Law, which was used as the basis for a ban on female succession, or even the succession of a female line claimant in various states across the continent. Its roots were undoubtedly ancient, going back to the fifth century and King Clovis, the founder of France's Merovingian dynasty. His Salic Law was a 'synthesis of Frankish custom, Roman law and the new law that Clovis had himself brought into being' and dealt with a range of issues that were important at the time. Its provisions concerning the presumably pressing matters of theft of cattle, sheep and even bees were treated as more important than the inheritance provisions buried within the code.[55]

At first glance, these were not even obviously helpful to those seeking to bar female inheritance, since at least part of a deceased's lands were expressly noted to be inheritable by women.[56] Only one final provision, which stated 'but concerning Salic land, no portion or inheritance is for a woman but all the land belongs to members of the male sex who are brothers' suggests a contrary position, but it was seized upon by the French, in spite of it apparently having nothing to do with the crown of France itself.[57] The law code, too, which was rediscovered in the fourteenth century amongst forgotten manuscripts, only applied to the northern portion of France, making it even more inexplicable that it came to be adopted as the basis on which several of the crowns of Europe refused to admit women as one of their number. While not expressly used to bar Jeanne's inheritance in 1316 or 1328, her exclusion, followed by that of Edward III of England who claimed through his French mother, set a precedent that would later be backed by claims of the ancient Salic Law. It was a retrofitting, but a highly successful one, standing as 'a fundamental law of the monarchy' by the end of the fifteenth century.[58] Indeed, it became so synonymous with the French monarchy that no woman ever mounted as serious a claim to the throne as Jeanne of France: the prohibition had forever been enshrined in a dusty law that had been wilfully manipulated and misinterpreted.

The accession of Philippe of Valois to the French throne in 1328 ended any residual hopes that Jeanne might have of finally wearing the kingdom's ancient crown. Although an almost entirely unwanted monarch in the land of her birth, she was a surprisingly welcome female sovereign when, accompanied by her husband, she made the journey to Pamplona, high in the Pyrenees, to rule her paternal grandmother's kingdom. As we saw in Chapter 2, Navarre had no problem with the

A LION'S CUBS ARE LIONS ALL

idea of female rule (although they still preferred a male heir where possible), and so Jeanne morphed seamlessly into Queen Juana II. She was an active and successful ruler, celebrated as the foundress of a new dynasty that freed the kingdom from nearly fifty years of absentee monarchs and French rule. The Navarrese, in particular, were keen to limit the authority of Juana's spouse, Philippe of Evreux, but the couple have been characterised as 'an effective partnership'.[59]

Juana II of Navarre, who had once been Jeanne of France, never forgot the land of her birth, nor her claim to its crown. Dying in 1349 of the terrifying Black Death, she requested burial in the church of St Denis in Paris. Jeanne's tomb, in the traditional burial place of the kings of France, makes a statement more pointed than any she dared to make in her lifetime. She had proved herself as a monarch in Navarre, but it still was not enough. Her descendant, Maria Theresia, could look back on Jeanne/Juana as both a cautionary tale illustrating the difficulties that a royal woman could face when she came to claim a throne, but also as an example of a successful reigning queen. Juana II of Navarre truly reigned.

So, too, did Maria Theresia, who remains one of the most well-known of the world's reigning queens. While denied the title of Holy Roman Empress, she was the undoubted mistress of the crowns, duchies and territories which made up the Habsburg inheritance, reigning until her death in 1780. She was a progressive ruler, carrying out considerable administrative and constitutional reforms as she sought to modernise the unwieldy states that she had inherited.[60] Maria Theresia was no proto-feminist – her letters to her youngest daughter, the unfortunate Marie Antoinette, in which she all but orders the girl to share her new husband's bed and earn his confidence, make that clear: it was the new French queen's 'one task'.[61] Yet, she had an all-encompassing belief in the ability of at least one woman to rule: herself. She might, ostensibly share power, first with her husband and then, after his death, with her eldest son, Josef, but it was Maria Theresia who continued to reign, even if she protested to her son to 'have no fear that I should trouble you, in either your military or your political activities; you know that I have given them up to you entirely, and enter into them only to know them'.[62] Josef, who was himself strong-willed, must have grimaced when he read this, but his mother almost always held sway on important issues.[63]

Tamar's death brought Georgia's golden age to an end. She was succeeded by her short-lived son, before her daughter Rusudan became Georgia's second reigning queen in 1223. Rusudan, who reigned for twelve years during the turmoil of the Mongol invasions, might mint coins declaring that she was 'Queen of Queens, Glory of the World and the Faith, Daughter of Tamar and Champion of the Messiah', but circumstances ensured that she never did live up to her mother.[64] Queen Tamar of Georgia – since referred to as Tamar the Great – is her kingdom's King Arthur, providing a final gasp of medieval glory before the kingdom bent under the weight of conquest. She, like Arthur, is a once and future monarch, sleeping in a golden coffin hidden in a cave beneath the mountains of her homeland.[65] It has been declared that one day – it is not entirely clear when – she will rise from this sleep of the almost-dead to 'fling the gates of her cave wide open' and 'that shall be the day of happiness and the great revival for Georgian people'. It is hard to reconcile this queen with the reviled young woman who used her wiles, luck and excellent judgment to cling on to her throne, before slowly manoeuvring herself into a position in which she thrived.

It is difficult, now, to unpick Tamar the human from Tamar the glorious myth, but it is a task worth doing. Her achievements are surely all the more remarkable precisely because her reign was so unwelcome to her subjects. As we saw, the young Tamar had herself depicted as a secondary and subservient monarch on the church walls at Vardzia, standing behind her father. In her final representation, which was painted onto a wall in the Monastery of Bertubani, she had stepped out from behind her father's shadow. Here, it is Tamar who is the dominant of the two crowned figures depicted, with her adult and bearded son, Giorgi Lasa, following in her wake.[66]

A famous line from *The Knight in the Panther Skin*, an epic poem dedicated to Tamar and one of the glories of medieval literature, famously declared: 'A lion's cubs are lions all, male and female alike.'[67] This is surely the pertinent point in the stories of Tamar and, centuries later, Maria Theresia: their sex was a disadvantage, but they were their dynasty's last hopes. Both women believed themselves born to rule regardless of their sex and their people eventually came to agree. It was likely the view of Jeanne of France, who thrived in Navarre although she never did acquire her French crown. It was a lesson long in the learning, when history shows that most female succession was unwelcome and unwanted. All three of these queens struggled to maintain their authority in the face of misogyny. Each was, at least to some extent successful. Maria Theresia, while forced to share power with the men in her life, undoubtedly reigned, while Jeanne, as Juana II, governed in Navarre. Cutting through the extravagant myth of Tamar the Great, or the warrior queen Tamara, Georgia's first reigning queen was undoubtedly a great success. Almost no reigning queens were desired or wanted by their people, but in the face of considerable opposition, many still thrived.

CHAPTER 6:

THE PHOENIX'S CHOICE

Wu Zetian of China and Elizabeth I of England and Ireland

There was a new, wild horse in the palace stables, which no one could control. This both angered and confused the emperor, Taizong, who saw himself as lord of the world and, certainly, master of the men and beasts in his household. The 'Palace Girl', more than thirty years his junior and barely in her teens, stood with him to watch the horse with interest. Bravely (or brazenly, since opinions vary), she turned to the near-stranger who was, in some way, her husband. 'I can control him, but I shall need three things: first, an iron whip; second, an iron mace; and third, a dagger'. She continued, 'If the iron whip does not bring him to obedience I will use the iron mace to beat his head, and if that does not do it I will use the dagger and cut his throat.'[1] Taizong, the girl proudly related years later, 'understood my meaning'. He was perhaps startled by the fierceness shown in a teenager who, only shortly before, in 638 CE, had been brought to him from the arms of her weeping mother, but it may also have amused him. Young Wu Zhao, who is better known today as Wu Zetian or, simply, Empress Wu, was there as an ornament, to entertain and to serve. What need could she ever have for an iron whip, a mace and a dagger? Yet, she would use all three to control Taizong's empire – one day to be hers – which was then the most powerful realm on the planet. She was as untameable and unconventional as the wild horse.

Empress Wu, China's sole example of a female head of state, is the most controversial figure to ever sit on the country's ancient imperial throne. Her reputation is both complex and bloody, but she stands like a beacon in China's past and the history of world queenship: here is a female monarch that succeeded. She is Catherine the Great of Russia or Isabel I of Castile. Even more so, she is Elizabeth I, the final monarch of England's famous Tudor dynasty, which won the crown on the battlefield in 1485, witnessed the ogrish Henry VIII and his doomed six wives, as well as the Protestant Reformation, rebellions and the first attempts to create permanent European settlements in continental North America.

At first glance, Wu and Elizabeth have little in common, save for their sex, their political dominance and the inscrutable faces they display in contemporary depictions of the rulers: they give nothing of their thoughts away, something that is largely the result of their impressive ability to control their own images. Elizabeth I had almost certainly never heard of Wu, while her Chinese counterpart, reigning all those centuries before her, cannot have been expected to have been aware of distant Europe, let alone a small cultural backwater on the edge of the Atlantic Ocean, whose citizens had buried the famous Sutton Hoo treasure, complete with its glorious ship and ornate iron and bronze helmet, at around the time she was born. England as a political entity was still two centuries from existing when Wu died.* Elizabeth's

---

* The kingdom of Wessex, one of the small Anglo-Saxon kingdoms that made up England in the period had a reigning queen, Seaxburh, during Wu's lifetime. She reigned for two years after her husband's death in 672. Nothing else is known about her.

kingdom, 900 years later, was only just catching up in comparison to the culturally and technologically advanced seventh-century China. Elizabeth's was the age of William Shakespeare, Christopher Marlowe and Sir Walter Raleigh; her reign saw the expansion of ocean-going travel, growing state organisation and the development of the theatre and the arts – all putting this Northern European island finally on the map. Whereas Wu lived in the most inventive, innovative society ever known, with fine porcelain, paper money, gunpowder and even lavatory paper (although Elizabethan England would witness the invention of the flushing toilet), all products of the Tang dynasty or before.[2] Culturally, Wu and Elizabeth were diverse, yet the shared fact of their success and some of the methods they used to achieve it draw them together. Peel away the layers of time, geography and culture and there are similarities that serve as a model of how to win a throne and how to flourish on it. They were not, by any means, the only reigning queens to dominate the eras in which they lived, but they are two of the most remarkable. That they reigned at all was startling.

In the Confucian tradition of Wu's realm and court, the idea that a woman could rule over the greatest empire on earth was an abomination and a violation, while Elizabeth's entire life was dominated by notions of women's innate inferiority.**[3] It is therefore unsurprising that the two women played up to this by stressing their own exceptional qualities and the God-given nature of their rule. In this, Elizabeth I was assisted by the divine right of kings, which held that the monarch was directly appointed by God as His representative on Earth. Since she *was* monarch, then it must be God's will. As she said herself, on being informed of her accession to the throne, 'This

---

** Keith McMahon, *Women Shall Not Rule: Imperial Wives and Concubines in China from Han to Liao* (Lanham: Rowman and Littlefield, 2013) also notes the informal access to power Imperial women could achieve. Royal women – most notably Empress Dowager Cixi – also sometimes ruled through weaker male members of the dynasty.

is the Lord's doing and it is marvellous in our eyes.' For Wu, it was even more necessary to stress the religious element of her rule since the circumstances of her reign were highly controversial. A few days before she finally decided to take the throne for herself, a phoenix was spotted, perched in the palace gardens.[4] This could only be taken as an omen prophesying success. The blood-red sparrows who flocked in great numbers to perch on the roof of her palace similarly soothsaid fortuitous change.

Wu Zetian had, on paper (which was, incidentally, a Chinese invention), no business coming anywhere near the throne of China. Her ascent remains astonishing, leading to countless depictions of her in film, novels and histories of her native country. At first glance, she is a 'Cinderella' figure, a story which she may actually have known, since it was first written down in Tang Dynasty China, with a talking dead fish in place of the fairy godmother and a golden, rather than glass, slipper.[5] The future Wu Zetian was born in 625, the daughter of a well-born but lowly lumber merchant and his ambitious second wife, Lady Yang.[6] Wu's father, Wu Shihou (a man 'rather fond of social intercourse'), had a connection with Li Yuan, the founding emperor of the Tang Dynasty, who came to power through a rebellion in 618.[7] This was a stroke of fortune for the Wu family, with their prospects improving still further when Wu Shihou was appointed governor of Lizhou, a long-established but somewhat insignificant city in south-eastern China on the banks of the River Liu. It was there that Lady Yang raised her three daughters, who were each at their births a disappointment. Tang Dynasty China valued sons who would continue the family lineage; girls were seen as merely visitors in the family home, there until claimed by their future husband.[8] For Lady Yang, too, who loathed her husband's first family, the position was even more humiliating since Wu Shihou's first wife had succeeded in producing at least two surviving sons. In her infancy, Wu was dressed as a boy, but it was not a charade that could be maintained when she reached puberty. The girls were reared for marriage, hopefully to minor imperial officials or governors, although their lowly position and lack of wealth made this uncertain.

Wu, the middle child, was notably attractive, but no marriage had been arranged for her by 635 when her father died. Later accounts would mythologise her childhood, claiming that a travelling fortune teller had once prophesied that she would rule China, but this is highly unlikely.[9] Using her family connections, Lady Yang sent her teenaged daughter to the imperial palace to become a concubine to the Emperor Taizong, an acknowledgement that she could not find her daughter a husband of her own. Technically, this was akin to marriage, but Taizong had over one hundred other wives and is unlikely to have spent much, if any, time with his new spouse, who was assigned to the fifth grade of his hierarchically arranged concubines (with the ranks going down to a lowly eighth grade).[10] Finding herself in a lavish but cloistered environment inhabited by women and the palace eunuchs who were trusted to attend them, Wu was effectively a palace servant. She was assigned to work in the royal wardrobe, while also called on for dancing and entertaining the emperor and his guests on occasion.[***]

Emperor Taizong, who was famous for his 'curly whiskers', had been a charming and energetic young man who ordered his officials to sleep in shifts so that they were available for business day and night.[11] But, by the time of Wu's arrival, he had become fixated on the image that he would project to future generations, seeing himself as 'an actor on a stage', as one historian has suggested. He was also visibly ailing.[12] This was a problem for the newly arrived Wu, who knew that when their 'husband' died, imperial widows were sent to Buddhist convents to live out their lives in seclusion, something that alarmed her.

[***] Incidentally, Wu's feet would not have been bound, since this was not practiced in the Tang Dynasty.

She was still only in her mid-teens and far from ready for her life to be, effectively, over.

In 649, she snatched her chance and flirted (according to one early source) at the bedside of the dying emperor with his son and heir. It had the desired effect and, following Emperor Gaozong's accession, she was recruited as one of his concubines.[13] This was a breach of protocol so severe, since Gaozong was effectively her stepson, that the new emperor can only have been motivated by love or lust. She was still only a lowly figure, ranking far below Gaozong's empress, Wang, and his chief concubine, Xiao Liangdi, but it was with Wu that the emperor spent his nights.

There is nothing in Wu Zetian's early life to suggest that she would one day wear China's imperial crown and certainly no precedent for her accession. Elizabeth I, too, had unpromising origins. Her father, Henry VIII, had become King of England as a teenager in 1509, but had still not produced a surviving son as he eagerly anticipated the birth of his first child with his second wife, Anne Boleyn. Henry, who by September 1533, was not quite the monstrous tyrant of his later years, would probably have envied the polygamy of China's emperors. He had spent nearly seven years attempting to exchange one wife, Catherine of Aragon, for a younger model, finally breaking the English Church away from the Pope in Rome to allow him to annul the marriage himself. Anne Boleyn had, during the long days of their courtship, promised 'to be to you both loving and kind', which she inscribed beneath a picture of the Annunciation in her prayerbook. The implication was clear: she would succeed where her predecessor had failed and bear England an heir. Apparently not entirely convinced, Henry paid fortune tellers to confirm the child would be male. It was a crushing blow for the king when, on 7 September 1533 in the comfortable riverside palace of Greenwich, Anne Boleyn gave birth to a daughter. The preprepared birth announcements were amended to change 'prince' to 'princess' and the celebratory tournament was cancelled. Less than three years later, Anne was beheaded and Elizabeth declared a bastard, although she was later reinstated in the succession behind more legitimate children.[14]

With her red hair, so characteristic of the highly interrelated dynasties of Europe, Elizabeth was clearly a Tudor, although whispers about her paternity continued. It was to be a difficult adolescence and early adulthood, with the princess molested by her stepmother's new husband in the late 1540s and disinherited by her younger half-brother, Edward VI, on his deathbed in July 1553 on the grounds that she was related to him only in the 'half-blood' and also illegitimate. When Elizabeth's elder half-sister, the equally bastardised Mary I, became England's first crowned reigning queen, she imprisoned Elizabeth in the Tower of London, with the princess living in fear of execution or murder. The fact that she survived at all to take the crown on Mary's death in November 1558 must have seemed miraculous, but it was down to Elizabeth's drive and determination. Elizabeth seems to have been spurred on by adversity, something that is common amongst the most successful of reigning queens. It was the same for Empress Wu in the distant past. Having to fight for their position made these women stronger. Neither Wu nor Elizabeth had any desire to return from whence they came.

Wu Zetian and Elizabeth I are shining examples of women who made a success of reigning, but sometimes at the expense of reputation and popularity. As we have seen time and again, no world culture found the juxtaposition of political power and femininity an easy one to navigate. Both are now, to some extent, admired figures, but there was undoubtedly a ruthlessness to Wu and Elizabeth in the way that they sought, grasped and maintained power that made their contemporaries shudder. A female ruler will always have rivals and the removal of these rivals was absolutely crucial to both women.

WOMEN WHO RULED THE WORLD

By a quirk of fate, Wu and Elizabeth had an advantage in the sense that while women were strongly disenfranchised in both their eras, they lived in times of somewhat ineffective royal men. In Elizabeth's case, there simply were no adult male members of the royal family to challenge her succession in 1558, legitimate or illegitimate. She had no surviving siblings, no nephews, no uncles, no male cousins. Part of Elizabeth's success was that she had no male rivals.

This was the same for Wu, who was propelled to power due to the weakness of the men in her life. Her husband, Gaozong, who adored her, had been a late selection as crown prince, only coming to prominence after his father had murdered or pushed out the older sons that displeased him. (One, allegedly, for daring to favour Turkish dress over Han Chinese, possibly causing offence due to his father's sensitivity over the mixed ethnic origins of the Tang imperial family – or perhaps a euphemistic way of expressing contemporary concern over his homosexuality.) Gaozong therefore had only limited training and little aptitude for his new role, particularly since he was increasingly affected from a chronic, debilitating condition that can perhaps be identified as the effects of a stroke or epilepsy.[15] He retreated into his palace, relying so heavily on Wu that she became his mouthpiece. Everything the emperor said was mitigated through her, until there came a point – she claimed – when he did not need to say anything at all.

Wu and Elizabeth may have been lucky with the ineffectual men in their lives, but they had powerful female rivals that needed to be eliminated. The major political problem of Elizabeth's reign was her cousin Mary Queen of Scots, who had made the fatal error of declaring herself Queen of England in preference to Elizabeth in 1558. We will hear more of Mary's fate in Chapter 7, but she was undoubtedly a victim of Elizabeth's need for security. The English queen was also deeply ruthless in her treatment of Catherine and Mary Grey, two English sisters who had a strong claim to the throne by virtue of their descent from King Henry VII. Although she loathed them, Elizabeth kept them at her court, even once going so far as to claim that she intended to adopt Catherine as her daughter. When both sisters dared to make secret marriages, Elizabeth had them imprisoned for the rest of their lives, intent on ensuring that they could not pass their claims on to a younger generation.[16] She invalidated Catherine's marriage and declared her children illegitimate, for good measure.

Elizabeth's ruthlessness pales into insignificance when set against the legend of Wu Zetian's grip on the Chinese throne. It began in the rivalry over who would become Emperor Gaozong's chief wife. Empress Wang, who was herself an ambitious woman, had no children, leaving her open to attacks from within the emperor's harem. It was, of course, expected that an emperor would be polygamous, with regular sexual intercourse considered necessary for a man's continuing vigour and health.[17] As such, skill in the bedroom was prized. Gaozong, had he so wished, could consult works on the art of the bedchamber in the imperial library which often focussed on maintaining the male partner's stamina (something that was likely necessary for a man with more than one hundred wives).[18] Such works were often highly explicit, right down to the number and intensity of the thrusts that he should make, although it is not entirely clear how closely these manuals were followed in practice. Royal women were expected to be faithful to their shared husband, although this did not preclude same sex relationships and sexual experimentation (known as 'mirror rubbing') amongst the women of the harem, which were likely common.[19]

Although women could have some expectation of pleasure in the bedroom (since it was believed that this improved a man's vigour), female rulers were routinely castigated for perceived sexual immorality. Late dynastic China's most powerful woman, Empress Dowager Cixi, who ruled through a series of inadequate emperors in the late nineteenth and early twentieth centuries, was baselessly accused of soliciting young men for sex before ordering their murders. Wu, it was widely whispered, was similarly promiscuous in her final years, something that scandalised her contemporaries and further blackened her reputation.

The sex lives of prominent women have always been a powerful means of denigrating them, with few more pawed over than that of Elizabeth I, which is surprising since she expressed an early (and apparently sincere) desire to remain a virgin. In her lifetime, her ministers would bribe her ladies in waiting for a monthly sight of her blood-stained sheets, while scurrilous stories delighted in tales of her bawdy behaviour. Elizabeth, who kept good-looking male favourites, was undoubtedly attracted to men, but there is no indication that anything 'improper' ever occurred between them (as she herself claimed in relation to her particular favourite, Lord Robert Dudley). If it did, then she was highly discreet, just as Wu's likely love affairs during her later years as a widow were conducted with circumspection. She certainly did not invite ten sexual partners into her chamber, one after another, as male emperors were cautioned to do in the sex manuals of her time, taking care not to exhaust themselves too early. What was normal sexual behaviour for a male monarch was rarely considered acceptable in a female one.

It was to the advantage of the emperor's harem wives that they please him sexually, to enhance their opportunities to conceive. Officially, only the children of the emperor's chief wife were eligible for succession to the throne, although there was nuance to this, with minor wives jostling for position and keen to bear their shared husband a son. The childlessness of Empress Wang, Gaozong's chief wife, left her vulnerable as she and her chief rival, Xiao Liangdi, who was the second-ranked wife and mother of the emperor's favourite son, 'slandered each other' in their competition for Gaozong's favour.[20] It was with the empress's blessing that Wu, with her fashionable long hair, beautiful features and sharp intelligence, captured the emperor. There was something magnetic, even hypnotic about her as she cemented her place as the only woman to hold Gaozong's heart. Unlike Empress Wang, she bore him children, too. First a son, Li Hong in 652, and then a daughter, Princess Anding in 654, with younger children following.

The empress, who as the chief wife was the nominal mother of all Gaozong's children, came to visit Wu after the births. It was shortly after her visit to Princess Anding that the women's quarters, which were separate to the main palace and reached by a courtyard, suddenly rang with screams. Wu, on discovering her daughter dead in her cradle, angrily cried that Empress Wang had been the last person to see her alive.

It is a tragic fact of life before the mid-twentieth century that infant mortality rates across the world were high. If you visit the collection of the Science Museum in South Kensington today, you may see a plaster cast of a Roman infant's face, from where the cement of their sarcophagus seal had leached to form a mould, with the chubby cheeks and tightly closed eyes looking as though they were sleeping.[21] In Egypt, you can see the two little daughters of King Tutankhamen, both premature and likely stillborn, who were provided with their own golden coffins and gilded mummy masks. Britain's Queen Anne, who reigned from 1702 until 1714 and was debilitated by near-constant pregnancies, failed to leave an heir: all eighteen of her children died. Before the advent of modern medicines children died with some frequency. As such, Princess Anding's death, which is so often attributed to murder, may well have been natural. The leading source for the period, *Jiu Tang shu* (*The Old Book of Tang*), remains silent on the matter. What is certain, however, is that Wu undoubtedly benefitted from it, accusing Empress Wang of murder by sorcery.

Not everyone was convinced, with Wu's ascent bitterly resented.

WOMEN WHO RULED THE WORLD

The emperor's closest advisors possibly spoke for many when they cautioned him against marrying a woman who had 'once served in the inner palace of your late lamented father' and was, thus, effectively his stepmother. The breakthrough came during a tense meeting in the summer of 655, when the trusted statesman Li Zhi declared that 'this is a family matter, others should not interfere'.[22] This lukewarm support was all Gaozong, who even at this early stage in the relationship was largely at his fiancée's bidding, and Wu needed. In November 655, Wu was declared Empress Consort. The demoted Empress Wang, along with Gaozong's former chief concubine Xiao Liangdi, were stripped of their rank and imprisoned in the palace grounds under strict orders that they be permitted no contact with the outside world.

Their continuing presence likely made the new Empress Wu nervous, particularly when she discovered that Gaozong had visited them and used their old titles, suggesting that they might be rehabilitated. She ordered that they be subjected to 100 lashes, before having their hands and feet cut off. The two women were then placed in vats of wine to slowly die over several days.[23] It is a mark of Wu's dominance that she had the authority to order these deaths and that Gaozong muttered no word to prevent it. Xiao Liangdi, on hearing of her fate, cursed her rival, declaring that, 'Wu is a treacherous fox, who has bewitched the Emperor and now sits on the throne. I hope I shall be reborn as a cat, and the bitch Wu as a rat, that I may bite out her throat.'[24] It was later rumoured that Wu banned cats from the palace after hearing of this curse, while she admitted to being troubled by bad dreams. Interestingly, Elizabeth I's main rival, Mary Queen of Scots, who spent long years at her embroidery to pass the time of her imprisonment at her English cousin's hands, would create a piece depicting Elizabeth as a great ginger cat with a mouse in her paws. Both women lived in dangerous times and, to be a queen, often meant that brutal acts were required. It was the price of power.

THE PHOENIX'S CHOICE

There is a remarkable similarity in the length of time in which Wu and Elizabeth dominated their respective nations, with their periods of rule stretching longer than four decades each, although Wu would only officially hold the throne for fifteen. Wu and Elizabeth present a masterclass in female power, something that was largely achieved through the use of image and the ways in which they displayed themselves to their subjects. Wu ruled over a vast land, mainly occupied by agricultural workers, but with a substantial civil service involved in a state administration that was efficient and far reaching. China had independently invented its own writing system around 2000 years before Wu's birth, and it provided her with an effective means of spreading her message to the distant edges of her realm. Around May 655, only six months before she removed Empress Wang to take her place as Empress Consort, 'Concubine Wu' published *Nei xun*, which was a short volume of rules and guidance for the women of the palace.[25] Clearly, she already saw herself as the leader of the feminine world of the emperor's harem.

Nei xun was just the beginning for Wu, with the written word a potent outlet for her propaganda. In the 660s, while still ostensibly acting as Gaozong's mouthpiece, she recruited a group of educated men, known as 'The Scholars of the Northern Gate' to act both as her advisors and as the writers of a series of political tracts that were sent out in her name.[26] These were ostensibly written by her, although most were not. The majority of these works have not survived, possibly due to a deliberate suppression of her writings after her death. However, we do have a sense of the contents of some. A collection of her prayers was held by a Japanese temple library as late as the eleventh century, while two secular collections – a work of music composed for her and another titled *Chen gui*, effectively a conduct manual on the role of royal ministers – survived in Japan, likely having been taken there by a Japanese embassy to Wu's court towards the end of her reign.[27]

Chen gui was largely composed by the Scholars of the Northern Gate, although Wu's input can be seen in the book's line of argument. In the preface, Wu spoke of her role as empress and in being 'the supreme female power in the empire'. She praised the 'Heavenly Emperor' Gaozong, which by implication glorified his 'Heavenly Empress', unique titles that the couple had first adopted in 674. Wu saw *Chen gui* as part of a larger scheme of works, which defined and directed the roles of members of the royal family, women and, in particular, the heir apparent. Once she had become reigning empress, Wu ordered that *Chen gui* be used as a set text in the state examination system for the civil service – exams that could make or break the lives of her educated and ambitious young subjects. As such, it became widely known, with even those who failed the exam and lurked in the cities afraid to return home to their parents aware of its contents and message.**** It was unusual for a woman to be so open and so bold in her attempt to control the political narrative, while it was completely unprecedented for a new, non-canonical work to be inserted into the conservative state examination system. This success did Wu's Scholars of the Northern Gate little good, though – by 690 she had purged them all.[28] Wu's dissemination of political writings as justification for her rule continued after she took the throne for herself, with her chief minister Yao Shou, giving orders that a record of what was said in the palace should be noted down, 'since the emperor's [i.e Wu's] instructions cannot go unrecorded'.[29]

Much of what Wu achieved was later dismantled or removed, but some of her more subtle actions proved to be lasting. During her reign she cultivated the peony as a symbol of wealth and rank, and this

---

**** This was not Wu's only foray into China's education system. She also changed some of the characters used in Chinese script and adopted her own, often for propaganda purposes (J-P Drége, 'Les caractéres de l'impératrice Wu Zetian dans les manuscrits de Dunhuang et Turfan', *Bulletin de Ecole Francaise d'Extreme-Orient*, vol. 73 (1984), pp339–354.)

connotation, in the delicate spherical spring flowers, would remain for centuries.[30] Wu also showed an interest in women's rights at various points in her life, as can be seen from a programme of reforms that she dictated in 675. These included increasing agricultural productivity and the reduction of taxes among other measures, but she also ordered the increase in the status of women, specifying that the mourning period for a mother should be made equal to that of a father: a significant change for the patriarchal world in which she lived. She employed female assistants and secretaries and sponsored the compilation of biographies of famous women.[31] It can be difficult to pick through the sources for Wu's life, however, since she is known to have altered them retrospectively.[32] On becoming Gaozong's empress, she expressly denied that she had been his father's concubine, instead claiming to have served her new husband's mother (a woman who was dead before Wu entered the palace). The obfuscation was deliberate and lasting.

If Wu was astute at self-aggrandisement, Elizabeth was its master and perhaps should be recognised as one of the greatest propagandists in history. Even today, as historians have evaluated and re-evaluated her achievements, she is seen popularly through the prism of her own myth-making.[33] We view Elizabeth as she portrayed herself. This is evident in the unchanging, unageing face that she presents to us from surviving portraits, with artists forbidden from painting her as she truly appeared. It is also visible in the iconography of her paintings, which would have been all too clear to contemporary viewers. Elizabeth was depicted wearing pearls to symbolise chastity, with one dress covered in eyes and ears to demonstrate her all-seeing, godlike qualities. The allusions could be subtle. In one painting she carries a sieve, referencing the Roman legend that a virgin could carry water in such an implement.

It is particularly interesting that Elizabeth's virginity, arguably a negative factor in a ruler who needed an heir to perpetuate her dynasty, was used by her as a strength. This is all the more remarkable since she faced considerable pressure to marry and procreate, with a stream of male suitors – both English and foreign – seeking her as a wife and deputations regularly setting out from parliament to beg her to wed. Very few royal women, certainly not reigning queens, in any period had any choice over their marriage partners and they were unsurprisingly not free to remain single. Elizabeth managed to reframe celibacy as a virtue. Countless references were made to her purity or comparing her to the chaste goddess Diana. She was the fairy queen, an otherworldly figure. She was Gloriana, too, reigning over a kingdom at the peak of its achievements. None of this was, of course, by chance – she deliberately sought to portray herself as a magical, unchanging figure. The myth of her eternal youth continued until her death in 1603, although it became more difficult to hide the passage of time. As one visitor to her court ungallantly noted in 1602, 'She did not look ugly, when seen from a distance', while contemporaries remarked on her toothlessness, a product of an upper-class addiction to sugar (she would have benefitted from tooth fillings – another invention of Tang Dynasty China).

Elizabeth 'managed' her potentially vulnerable position as a female ruler with great skill, too. She stressed the exceptional nature of her rule, even while admitting that, as a woman, she was the weaker vessel (as contemporaries believed). In her famous speech to her troops at Tilbury in Essex while expecting a Spanish invasion in 1588, she declared, 'I know I have the body but of a weak and feeble woman; but I have the heart and stomach of a king and of a king of England too.' Like Hatshepsut of Egypt, she accepted her sex but also blurred the lines of gender. She *was* a woman, but she was also a *very* special one. When the Spanish Armada was defeated by the English fleet, it was Elizabeth who took the credit. In the great Armada portrait displayed today in the Queen's Gallery at Greenwich on the site of Elizabeth's birthplace, she sits confident as the enemy ships are driven to ruin in the background, while her hands rests on a globe: Britannia, as personified by Elizabeth, surely ruled the waves.

But behind Elizabeth's myth-making, and despite the shoring up of her power by events like the defeat of the Armada, lay the truth that it was no easy feat ruling as an independent queen in the sixteenth century. Elizabeth lived in a world where her ministers and those around her routinely threw in misogynistic comments, while she remembered the marginalisation suffered by her fellow reigning queens, Mary Queen of Scots and Mary I of England, when they married. She likely knew of the example of poor Juana of Castile, too, who died only three years before Elizabeth accepted her own throne, having spent half a century imprisoned by male relatives who coveted her crown.

Perhaps, though, it was easier than ruling in seventh-century China, where the political system did not even conceive of a female taking the throne as 'Son of Heaven'.[34] Wu herself initially heeded this. She remained the power behind Gaozong's throne until his death in 683 after years of illness and incapacitation, though she could never be complacent. Even her own eldest son, Li Hong, who rashly suggested in public in 675 that the daughters of the murdered concubine Xiao Liangdi should be permitted to wed, would meet a mysterious death shortly afterwards, something that was blamed on Wu. Gaozong was devastated, ordering that his son should be buried with the honours of an emperor rather than merely a crown prince, but Wu's feelings are harder to unpick: Li Hong had begun to show signs of being a dangerously competent heir to the throne.[35]

Following his death, Gaozong's heir was his eldest surviving son by Wu, who was enthroned as Emperor Zhongzong. Wu, however, quickly found her son not to be as amenable as she had hoped. When he attempted to assert himself by promoting the father of his forthright wife, Empress Wei, to imperial office, Wu had him removed from power. He was replaced by her much more pliable youngest son, Ruizong, after only five weeks. Ruizong made no decisions, took no action without his mother's express permission, and was entirely under her control, but within a few years of his accession Wu was looking to take her role further.

By the late 680s, prophecies and new sacred texts were being identified on a regular basis, such as a carved stone 'discovered' in a river by Wu's nephew, which stated that, 'The Sage Mother comes among men – an imperium of eternal prosperity.'[36] Of even more importance was the propitious revelation of a sacred Buddhist scripture called the *Great Cloud Sutra*. In one passage, towards the end of a work that must have seemed sent from Heaven by Wu, the Buddha prophesied that, in his final incarnation, he would come back as a woman. So perfect was this text for Wu that for centuries it has largely been regarded as a forgery, created by her supporters. In recent years, a more ancient example has been discovered in a cave in Dunhuang, indicating that it was indeed genuine, but it was also just what Wu required. Almost immediately, she ordered copies to be sent out across China, while from 690 Great Cloud temples were founded with more than 1000 monks tasked with chanting the sutra in the streets of the empire. It was, considered R.W.L. Guisso, whose 1978 work on Wu remains the most extensive in English, 'one of the most ambitious attempts in medieval China to mould men's minds, to use religious feeling to justify the very existence of a regime and even to rationalise its most unpopular acts'.[37] The continuing stream of prophecies and predictions that were 'found' were enough to plant the idea that China was at last ready for a female emperor. When a phoenix was spotted perching in the palace gardens, Emperor Ruizong begged his mother to depose him and taken the throne. As with Elizabeth I, Wu's accession to the throne in 690 was, effectively, endorsed by heaven.

THE PHOENIX'S CHOICE

This was a sensible strategy for a woman to take, because it provided divine authority for an individual who, by virtue of their sex, would usually be considered inferior to the men around them. Elizabeth, who also made use of the phoenix motif, which symbolised her chastity and the rebirth of England under her reign, was born into the most profound spiritual turmoil in Europe. She was, quite literally, the child of the English Reformation: born not due to her father's desire to follow Martin Luther (the founder of Protestantism, who had lit the spark of reform in 1515 and always loathed Henry VIII), but of his passion for Anne Boleyn. Henry did make changes to the traditional Catholic church, most notably by questioning the key doctrine of Purgatory.***** However, his own last will, made on his deathbed in December 1546, made elaborate provision for the good of his soul, indicating that he had a healthy Catholic fear of this terrifying waiting room for Heaven. It was only *after* Henry's death that England underwent a full Protestant Reformation, with the churches whitewashed and the rood screens torn down. These were hurriedly returned and the churches repaired after 1553, with the reign of the Catholic Mary I, at a time when the faith of the state was indistinguishable from the religion of the monarch.

The question of the state religion was therefore the most pressing item on the agenda when Elizabeth rode south from Hatfield in late November 1558 to take up residence in her capital. Attractive, with fashionably pale skin (which she would later lighten with toxic white lead) and red hair, she drew huge crowds, calling out and waving to them as they cheered for her. Elizabeth, who had conformed to the Catholicism of her half-sister's reign, was widely known to be a

---

***** This is, of course, a simplification of the Reformation. Even the terms used are contentious. 'Protestant' began life as an insult, while both 'Protestants' and 'Catholics' would vie for the right to call themselves Catholic, which means 'universal church'. Evangelical and traditionalist might be more appropriate terms to use.

Protestant. Her religious settlement, born from the parliamentary Acts of Supremacy and Uniformity in 1559, confirmed this, reinstating Protestantism as the faith of the state and naming Elizabeth as the Church of England's Supreme Governor (a demotion from her father and half-brother's Supreme Headship which was not deemed appropriate for a woman). Elizabeth, who apparently did not wish to make windows into men's souls (and, thus, look too deeply at their faith – she merely wanted conformity), intended her religious settlement as a middle way. She would frequently offend the Puritans at her court, who were the 'hotter sort of Protestant', for example, by keeping a silver crucifix on her altar. Elizabeth may have summed her own faith up best when she said, 'There is only one Christ, Jesus, one faith. All else is a dispute over trifles.' In an era where many people would rather burn than accept the transubstantiation of the Mass, this was not a sentiment that most at her court would agree with, forcing her to tread a fine line with religion throughout her reign. Puritans found much to dislike in her settlement but preferred it to a 'popish' alternative. For Catholics, whose faith was forced underground, it was a disaster, with the queen implementing increasingly harsh penalties against priests and the people who protected them. Nonetheless, the modern Church of England very much owes its birth to Elizabeth's settlement of 1559.

As Supreme Governor of the Church of England, Elizabeth I was considered, effectively, to have a special relationship with the Christian God whom she worshipped, with this religious association an important element of the propaganda of her reign. For her spymaster Sir Francis Walsingham, maintaining Elizabeth on the throne was essentially a pious act, keeping the kingdom out of the hands of an antichrist (as he and many other English Puritans saw it) in Rome. Many of the men with whom Elizabeth governed, such as the father and son duo William and Robert Cecil, viewed protecting the queen as essential to maintaining the faith. She was, effectively, *the* Church of England. Wu, too, recognised the value in associating herself with religious beliefs as we have seen in relation to the *Great Cloud Sutra*.[38] She at times promoted Taoism, which was both a philosophy and a religion, accepting the bestowal of the Taoist title 'Queen of Heaven' by her husband, while in 665 she participated in the important imperial ceremony of the feng-shan, in which a ruler's achievements were pronounced to Heaven, with a request for further blessings. This was the only time a woman would ever participate in this ritual, which was considered so sacred that neither Gaozong's father nor grandfather had felt worthy of performing it.

Wu's main religious focus, though, was always Buddhism, with the empress creating an institutional form of the religion through a new network of monasteries, which helped to spread Buddhist teachings in China. She encouraged monks to visit her court, something which both promoted her faith and, when the monks returned to their monasteries in the provinces, promoted the empress.[39] She has even been credited with promoting printing as a means of disseminating this state-sponsored Buddhist teaching. While the origins of wood block printing are obscure, there is evidence that she, and those around her, were aware of the technique.[40] It was a laborious process, with each page of a manuscript carefully carved back to front onto blocks of wood before being covered in ink and pressed onto a page. Blocks would frequently wear out or require repairs, but it was still possible to produce multiple copies of a manuscript in a considerably shorter time than copying by hand. It was not until the invention of moveable type in the tenth century in China and the fifteenth century in Europe that printing became a world-changing technology. So, while Elizabeth in sixteenth-century England might benefit from a goddess-like adulation as 'Gloriana' or the 'Virgin Queen', Wu was able to portray herself as, effectively, an actual goddess. In *Great Spells of Unsullied Pure Light*, a Buddhist text that she had translated into Chinese and disseminated across her empire, she identified herself as the living embodiment of the goddess Pure Light.[41] It would certainly prove to have lasting influence, with copies of this Indian text circulating long after her death. It spoke to a later female ruler who we will meet in Chapter 9, Empress Shōtoku of Japan who, as reigning empress between 764 and 770, distributed a million excerpts from the text. Wu had set a lasting precedent: female monarchs across the world frequently sought to attract worship and, thus, help consolidate their thrones.

Both Wu and Elizabeth viewed themselves as acting in the best interests of their countries, in spite of the cultural preferences against their reigns, with one of Wu's recent biographers considering that she saw herself as 'the mortar which held together the state structure'.[42] Elizabeth I made similar allusions, referring to herself as being married to her people or as the mother of the state. And yet in both these cases of powerful reigning queens, they primarily acted in their own best interests rather than their country's in the fact that they showed no interest in establishing lasting dynasties. Wu's Zhou Dynasty, which she established on her accession, lasted only for the fourteen and a half years of her official reign before the return of the Tang Dynasty that had preceded it.

Even the markers of dynastic change, which were so important in the strictly ordered life of the Chinese court, were largely absent at the start of Wu's Zhou Dynasty. She changed the Tang's yellow banners to red and replaced Tang with Wu in some of the placenames across China, but there was little other obvious change to suggest that she considered herself the foundress of a lasting dynasty. In truth, as she was sixty-six years old when it was founded, she must have known that it could not endure for long (although she did tell one official that she hoped her dynasty's reputation would equal that of the Han, suggesting that she was hopeful).[43] Her remaining children were members of the Tang Dynasty, while she was lukewarm towards her half-brothers and their heirs, who would have been the obvious inheritors of her throne had she chosen to pass it through her family. Indeed, one of her nephews, Wu Youxo, was so alarmed at the prospect of succession that he became a hermit, living in a simple peasant's hut in the summer and retreating to a cave in winter. He did all he could to stay away from the dangers of his aunt's court (something that was probably sensible – Wu had earlier had two of her half-brothers' sons executed on trumped up charges of poisoning).[44]

The Tudor dynasty died with Elizabeth I's decision to remain unmarried. Dynastically, the birth of an heir was imperative, but she knew full well that the husband of a queen became a king. As Elizabeth is reported to have said, 'I will have but one mistress here, and no master.' That ambition, as with Wu's decision to form a dynasty at all, placed the queen's independence and welfare above the welfare of the state. Again, we see that to successfully reign a queen had to be ruthless.

Queens have always reigned only when necessity required it and then they did so on sufferance of their subjects. Neither Wu Zetian nor Elizabeth I seemed like particularly plausible rulers when they ascended to power. Their stories show clearly that queens could face similar difficulties on different sides of the world and in vastly different eras, something that has its roots in the patriarchal society that is pervasive to human civilisation. Their success was seen as an afront by the men of their realms and of their governments. Why else did the people flock to Elizabeth's successor, James VI of Scotland in 1603, revelling in the return to the normality of male government? Why else did the stelae that marks Wu Zetian's tomb remain uninscribed and her great achievements left unrecorded? Removed from power when finally brought low by ill health and old age, she was relegated once again to Empress Dowager, dying a few months later on 16 December 705.

Visit the Tang burial place close to Xi'an City in Shaanxi on the northern bank of the Weishui River and you will find only eighteen mausoleums for the period's nineteen rulers. Wu and Gaozong share one, with Wu being posthumously readopted into a dynasty that she had rejected in favour of her own. Elizabeth also shares a grave with another sovereign – her hated sister, Mary I. She has a fine tomb in Westminster Abbey, paid for – reluctantly – by her successor, James VI, who made his feelings plain in building a similar, but larger, monument for his own mother, Mary Queen of Scots. Elizabeth, like Wu, was commemorated perfunctorily and more for form's sake than for any desire to do her honour.

Such dismissal was far from uncommon with queens all over the world; their very success – in holding the throne and governing – was often seen as a threat in itself. These two women found a way to reign independently and, despite societal pressures to the contrary, they flourished. Elizabeth is remembered as presiding over a golden age – a rare achievement for a sixteenth-century woman. Wu, whose family name means 'martial' or 'strong', is a much more ambiguous figure, but still a titan in the history of dynastic China. A ninth-century Japanese visitor to her empire would hear her referred to, somewhat respectfully, as 'Granny Strong'.[45] More than an empress, of whom there were many in China, she should correctly be referred to as 'Emperor Wu'. Elizabeth, too, understood the limitations of merely being a queen in a man's world, referring to herself in masculine terms as a 'prince'. Beneath the gloss, and the gilded finery of their dress they were, however, women. And they were both triumphant. Many reigning queens were not so fortunate.

CHAPTER 7:
MONSTROUS REGIMENTS

*Athaliah of Judah, Arsinoë IV of Egypt and
Mary Queen of Scots*

The English House of Commons was not, in the sixteenth century, noted for its diversity, something that would have been apparent to anyone who watched its members shuffling into their seats amongst the choir stalls of the old Chapel of St Stephen in Westminster. The all-male assembly consisted primarily of the younger sons of the nobility, country gentlemen and ambitious merchants. They were a largely homogenous grouping of Protestant worthies far removed from the great unwashed whom they supposedly represented.

In November 1586, the chatter as they came to order was all about Mary, the former Queen of Scots, who was kept closely watched at the ancient castle of Fotheringhay in Northamptonshire, well away from the eyes of prying observers. Their hearts 'quaked and trembled' at the threat that Mary posed to their own queen's security.[1] To sign her fellow monarch's death warrant would be, reasoned the House of Commons in their debate, almost a pious act, since it would mirror the Old Testament accounts of the glorious putting to death of 'those mischievous and wicked Queens Jezebel and Athaliah!'. There was Biblical precedent for the righteousness of their cause, something that helped salve worried consciences, while well-thumbed copies of Plutarch, which detailed the untimely deaths of Egypt's last Ptolemaic queens, gave further historical support. Queen regnants could sometimes be too dangerous to be allowed to live.

In late sixteenth-century England everyone knew the Bible, either from reading it themselves (the Bible had been available in English since 1539 and literacy rates were high thanks to free parish schools), or through the stories told in the sermons in the parish churches or at family members' knees on Sundays. The Gospels remained – to English Protestants – the precise word of God and a manual for how they should seek to live their lives. The Old Testament, however, with its tales of giant-slaying, ghostly kings and women turning into pillars of salt, was a particular favourite and people looked for parallels between their own time and the Holy Book's story of the early history of the Jewish people: the Bible was the bedrock on which the citizens of sixteenth-century England built their lives.

The Old Testament is not, at first glance, an obviously historical document. Few would now take seriously the calculation of the seventeenth-century Archbishop Ussher that the world began in the late evening of 22 October 4004 BCE (a date, based on intensive study of the Old Testament which leaves no room for dinosaurs or, indeed, early hominins). Some parts may not even be original, with Noah's Flood remarkably similar to the flood of Utnapishtim detailed in the (at least) 4000-year-old Babylonian *Gilgamesh* narrative in which both men built a heavenly-ordained boat and filled it with breeding stock to repopulate the animal kingdom. Yet, although most would agree today that the Old Testament is shrouded in myth as its early compilers sought to understand the world around them, it was not seriously questioned as an historical source until the start of the nineteenth century when a young German scholar, Wilhelm Martin Leberecht de Wette, stuck his head above the parapet and declared that the Old Testament could not be taken at face value. It took time, but almost everyone would now agree with him. There is, however, some history buried in its ancient pages, which is sometimes corroborated by other ancient texts and archaeology.

The Old Testament is more about kings than queens, with women in general portrayed as inferior and less visible than their male counterparts. It has been calculated that the word 'king' appears over 2000 times in the Old Testament, but queen only on around 50 occasions, showing a sense of the inequality.[2] It is, therefore, hardly surprising that when sixteenth-century commentators looked for a Biblical precedent to justify their actions, as they did for Mary Queen of Scots and the other reigning queens of the period, they tended to land on the same handful of women. Mostly, that was Jezebel, queen consort of Israel, and her relative Athaliah, reigning Queen of Judah.

Jezebel, the wife of the Bible's irreligious and weak-willed King Ahab, is by far the most well-known of the two women, whose kingdoms covered ground that broadly approximates to modern-day Israel and Palestine.[3] Israel claimed the famously wise King Solomon as its founder, while Judah, whose capital city was Jerusalem, gave that honour to David, the shepherd-turned-king who reputedly slayed the giant Goliath with a slingshot. Evidence for the existence of either woman outside the Bible is sketchy, although an opal seal matrix inscribed with Jezebel's name is displayed in the Israel Museum in Jerusalem and may be the only archaeological proof of her existence. For Athaliah, there is nothing, although some of the men in her life are independently corroborated by Assyrian annals and surviving inscriptions.[4]

Jezebel was (according to the Old Testament) a Samarian princess, from modern-day Lebanon.[5] A polytheist in a kingdom where Yahweh, the 'jealous god' of Abraham held sway and a powerful woman in a time when women were fiercely subjugated, it is perhaps unsurprising that she was portrayed negatively.[6] The bare facts of Jezebel's life, as we know them, are brief. She was the daughter of a king and was given in marriage to Ahab where she drew the opprobrium of the holy men of Israel for her promotion of the Samarian god, Baal. She dominated her husband and then her son before being thrown to her death and fed to the dogs by Israel's conqueror, King Jehu, having first taunted him from a window dressed in all her finery as queen. As Helena Zlotnick has noted in her insightful work on the images of the queens in the Old Testament, 'the hostility of biblical narrators to queens who, like Jezebel, usurp the role of kings in a manner that highlights the limitations of kingly power and the breakdown of male authority within the home is undisguised.'[7]

Most portrayals of her have been less nuanced. The respected Scottish Biblical scholar Herbert Lockyer, who was prolific in the mid-twentieth century in his works on the Old Testament, considered that: 'Jezebel, a devil incarnate, comes before us as the most infamous queen in history. She was the female counterpart of Adolph Hitler who, in hell, is forever tortured by the cries of the millions he maimed and massacred.'[8] Even the Biblical portrayal hardly goes so far, making this comparison an outrageously misogynist stretch. According to the *Oxford English Dictionary*, a jezebel is 'an immoral, impudent, or sexually promiscuous woman', which sums up the one-sided portrayal of this powerful queen consort and queen mother. 'Jezebel' is not used as a noun in other European languages, although the name has frequently been applied to women considered to be too politically active or promiscuous in some way across the continent.

Athaliah, the Old Testament's only reigning queen, was raised by Jezebel and was probably her daughter by Ahab. She is less well known but still draws outrageously overstated criticism. Lockyer, again writing in the 1960s, thought that she loved blood, which 'flowed at the door of her palace'.[9] The blood did undoubtedly flow, but much of it, ultimately, would be Athaliah's.

Around 865 BCE, Athaliah was sent to marry Jehoram, who would become King of Judah in 848 BCE.[10] The couple were probably teenagers, although nothing is known of their relationship, save that Jehoram had children by other women, while the Jewish chronicler, Flavius Josephus, writing in Roman times, concluded that it was Athaliah 'who taught him to be a bad man in other respects, and also to worship foreign gods'.[11] Jehoram killed his six younger brothers on taking the throne to ensure that he had no rivals, something for which Athaliah has, right up to the twentieth century, been blamed.[12] His reign was otherwise of little note. He was succeeded by his son by Athaliah, Ahaziah, who was murdered by the rebellious military commander Jehu, who killed Jezebel and took the throne of Israel.[13] In Judah, the result was different: Athaliah defied convention and claimed Judah's crown for herself, beginning her reign in 841 BCE, or thereabouts.

Living in the largely secular twentieth century, it is hard to conceive of just how well-versed pre-modern Europeans were in the Bible. Athaliah, far removed from her ancient Middle Eastern setting, was a familiar figure. To John Knox, the sixteenth-century Scottish religious reformer and the principal architect of the Church of Scotland, she was evidence of the dangers of allowing women too much power. He seethed at the idea of two Catholic queens, Mary I of England and Scotland's regent, Marie of Guise, heading their respective governments in the 1550s. 'In them,' he ranted, 'we also find the spirit of Jezebel and Athaliah; under them we find the simple people oppressed, the true religion extinguished, and the blood of Christ's members most cruelly shed.'[14] At best, they were God's instruments, sent to punish their nations by their very existence. ('But, alas, he hath raised up these Jezebels to be the uttermost of his plagues, the which man's unthankfulness hath long deserved. But his secret and most just judgment shall neither excuse them, neither their retainers, because their counsels be diverse.')

In this opprobrium, he was not alone – although undoubtedly the loudest voice to shout against female rule; a Protestant polemicist named Christopher Goodman, for example, also wrote a tract against England's Mary I, explaining that, since women were created inferior to men, it was a breach of divine law to permit them to rule.[15] Any voices raised in support of female rule (and there were not many) were decidedly lukewarm in comparison. The English scholar John Aylmer, who had links to the royal family, wrote in defence of the accession of Elizabeth I to the English throne noting that, while uncommon, there were well-known historical examples of female rulers, rendering the argument that they were monstrous invalid.[16] He compared female rule to twins and triplets, which are rare, but not impossible: 'In like manner, though it be for the most part seen that men and not women do rule commonwealths: yet when it happens some time by the ordinance of God, and course of inheritance, that they bear rule: it is not to be concluded, that it repugneth against nature.' He noted that this had happened 'in the commonwealth of the Jews, more than once or twice', which was almost certainly an oblique reference to Athaliah and, perhaps, also Jezebel, providing a rare positive assessment of their positions. He probably deliberately did not refer to them by name, however.

It was John Knox's bad luck that, only a few months after he had published his 'First Blast of the Trumpet Against the Monstrous Regiment of Women', which mounted an indiscriminate attack on the idea of women as rulers, Mary I (the 'cursed Jezebel of England') died from influenza, with her Protestant half-sister, Elizabeth I, taking the throne.[17] Although a woman, she was a ruler who was religiously more palatable to Knox, but his contention that the very idea of a female ruler was 'repugnant to nature' understandably made Elizabeth furious.[18] Marie of Guise died two years later in 1560, but Knox had no sympathy to spare for her teenaged daughter. Grieving, Mary Queen of Scots was equally outraged to hear 'that it is more than a monster in nature that a Woman shall reign and have empire above Man'. Since Mary was a Catholic queen, the identification of her with Jezebel or Athaliah held firm with Knox, one of her most troublesome subjects.

At around nine o'clock in the morning of 19 August 1561, the people of the port of Leith on the east coast of Scotland watched as a tall and stately young woman stepped confidently out onto the shore, still dressed in deepest mourning black.[19] She was a little early, with a local dignitary named Andrew Lamb offering her dinner and the use of his house while the leading lords of the kingdom hurriedly assembled to meet her. Mary had been absent from Scotland for over thirteen years, effectively missing the turmoil of the Protestant Reformation which, like a wall of water, her Catholic mother, the regent Marie of Guise, had attempted (and failed) to hold back. Initially, none of this seemed to matter. Mary was welcomed to her capital with great rejoicing: bonfires were lit in the street and she heard cheers and acclamations wherever she went. They were glad to have her back, in spite of her sex, since she was the last of the Stewart Dynasty, who had sat on Scotland's throne for nearly two hundred years and was the only person with an undoubted claim to the throne.

When she had left, aged only six, she had been a fugitive child; now she returned as an exotic, Frenchified teenager, poised and confident and ready to finally rule her kingdom. The sudden death of her young husband, Francois II of France, nine months earlier had ended her hopes of remaining in the country that she very much considered to be home. There was no place at the French court for a childless dowager, while she clashed with her mother-in-law, Catherine de Medici, who made it very clear that she wanted her gone. Mary, who had never been expected to rule her kingdom herself, had been wary of journeying to a land that she had been informed was small, poor and wild. She possibly never truly appreciated her windswept homeland, which stood at the northern boundary of the known world and was peopled by outward-looking and ambitious men and women.[20] Scottish pride and a sense of their own self-worth made her subjects an important force in the politics of Europe, but Mary simply could not see it. She had no choice but to return, hazarding a sea voyage when her cousin, Elizabeth I, shockingly refused to grant her safe passage through the southern British kingdom.

Mary and Elizabeth, who were 'dear sisters' in correspondence, eyed each other warily across their border after Mary's return. They were each the other's closest relative and Mary undoubtedly the hereditary heiress to her cousin's English throne. This was a sore subject, since the Scottish queen had actually claimed the English crown on the death of Mary I in November 1558, on the grounds of Elizabeth's illegitimacy.* It was something that Elizabeth did not forgive, and she certainly did not forget. Mary understood just one heartbeat stood between her and the crown of the richer southern kingdom. Even as she established herself as an independent monarch of her own kingdom, she kept one eye firmly on England.

Initially, Mary did rather well, installing herself at Edinburgh's Holyrood Palace, which had been built by her father, James V. The Scottish court was far from the scale and sophistication of its counterpart in Paris, but Mary was able to bring a touch of glamour, dazzling her subjects with her charm and tact and displaying, as one of her biographers, Antonia Fraser, has noted, 'heroic enthusiasm' in the face of her kingdom's evident shortcomings when compared to

---

* Legally, Elizabeth had been declared illegitimate in the Second Act of Succession of 1536, with this confirmed in the Third Act of Succession of 1545. Her illegitimacy was never overturned although her father had reinstated her in the succession in the Third Act of Succession behind his legitimate offspring. This was reconfirmed in his will.

France.[21] Bands of locals serenaded her at night from beneath the palace walls, while people flocked to see her, including Mary's half-brother, James Stewart, who was the product of one of her father's youthful indiscretions. The siblings, who had first met in France, differed in religion, but at first this hardly seemed to matter. Anxious for family support, Mary created him Earl of Moray and appointed him as her leading councillor. Mary, who had promised before her arrival not to turn Scotland away from its Protestant 'kirk', remained steadfast to her word, despite frequent assaults on her chaplains and chapel when she attempted to hear Mass privately. She even faced down John Knox during several interviews and, while the two would never see eye to eye (a considerable understatement), he did at least agree to accept female rule, noting with his acid tongue that, after all, St Paul had lived under Nero.[22] It was a rapprochement, at least, for the time being. She was not quite a Jezebel or an Athaliah, but perhaps a pagan Cleopatra.

Elizabeth I was fascinated by her Scottish counterpart, whose early successes doubtless infuriated her. Initially, the two remained estranged, with Mary's refusal to ratify the Treaty of Edinburgh, which had been made by her regents, filling the English queen with fury. To Mary, the treaty, which required her to abandon any pretensions towards the English crown, was prejudicial to her succession rights and she continued to push for recognition as heiress, something that Elizabeth, who was nine years older than her Scottish cousin, would never grant. When Mary sent Sir James Melville, a young man who had served her as a page in France, to England as her ambassador in 1564, the English queen took the opportunity to quiz him on her rival at their very first meeting. On being told, diplomatically, that 'she was the fairest queen in England and ours the fairest queen in Scotland', Elizabeth pressed further, with Melville answering that, 'They were both the fairest ladies of their courts and that Her Majesty was whiter, but our queen was very lovely.'[23] Who was taller, asked the English queen? Since this was a more objective question, Melville admitted that this was Mary, who towered above almost everyone. To this, Elizabeth responded, 'She is too high and that herself was neither too high nor too low.'

This personal rivalry was so well known that William Shakespeare 'shadows' it in *Antony and Cleopatra*, which was first performed only a few years after the English queen's death. In one of the few scenes not derived from Plutarch (the go-to Classical source for all educated Elizabethans), his Cleopatra, on hearing of Antony's marriage to Octavia, sends a messenger to 'Report the feature of Octavia, her years, Her inclination; let him not leave out The colour of her hair ... Bring me word how tall she is.'[24] On being told later that Octavia was shorter than she, her rival dismissed her as 'dwarfish'.[25] The parallel between the Cleopatra of Shakespeare's conception and the Elizabeth that Sir James Melville encountered is obvious.[26]

It has long been acknowledged that the extravagant Cleopatra VII of Egypt in William Shakespeare's *Antony and Cleopatra* bears more than a passing resemblance to Elizabeth. While the comparison between Elizabeth and Cleopatra was less explicit than sixteenth-century attempts to portray Britain's reigning queens as Jezebels and Athaliahs, Cleopatra was undoubtedly the historic reigning queen with whom the Elizabethans were most familiar.** Through the pages of Plutarch, they could view her as a highly intelligent woman, able to speak several languages (as, indeed, both Mary and Elizabeth could), but also a figure who was highly morally ambiguous and who, for her assumption of a 'male' political role drew ire, just as the 'monstrous regiment' of female rule in sixteenth century Britain sent tempers flaring. If Elizabeth was Cleopatra then Mary was Arsinoë, a queen who attempted to snatch Cleopatra's throne.

** For the avoidance of doubt, the reference to 'Britain's reigning queens' means the island of Britain and, thus, the queens of Scotland and England. It is not a premature reference to the Kingdom of Great Britain, which was created in 1707.

MONSTROUS REGIMENTS

Arsinoë IV is a much more intangible figure than her elder sister, Cleopatra VII, existing only in the shadow of this rival. She was likely very young when her father, Ptolemy XII, died in 51 BCE and was succeeded by Cleopatra ruling jointly with her younger brother, Ptolemy XIII.[27] Within a few brief years, this uneasy co-rule had broken down, with both monarchs raising an army against each other. With four siblings all vying for power, an attempt was made to appoint Arsinoë and her younger brother, Ptolemy XIV, as King and Queen of Cyprus. On the face of it, this was a generous solution, since the wealthy Mediterranean island, which had only recently been taken from the Ptolemies by Rome, was a fine prize, but it was obviously intended as a means of clearing the field for Cleopatra.[28] It was also not received well in Rome, with Cassius Dio, writing around 200 years later recalling that Caesar was so in thrall to Cleopatra 'that he not only laid hold on none of the Egyptian domain, but actually gave them some of his own besides'.[29] It would become a common trope for Caesar's missteps and, later, Mark Antony's, to be blamed on their desire to please Cleopatra. For the moment, however, Caesar and Cleopatra found themselves in dire straits. Facing an army of around 20,000 strong bearing down on the city, they barricaded themselves into the palace district, as the city burned around them and Alexandria's great library blazed. Amidst the chaos, Arsinoë, in the company of her eunuch tutor Ganymedes fled from the royal residence.[30] On joining the army outside the city she was proclaimed as Queen of Egypt in Cleopatra's stead. There were two queens in one city, just as in the middle years of sixteenth-century Britain there were two queens in one isle.

Mary Queen of Scots surprised many with the effectiveness of her governance. Knox, in the parliament of 1563 had taken it upon himself to insert his views into the question of Mary's second marriage, with the queen granting him a personal meeting in which he was so impertinent that she wept. Almost everyone thought that they had the right to an opinion on who her second husband should be. Even Elizabeth, an avowed and vocal virgin, suggested her favourite, Robert Dudley, Earl of Leicester, and almost immediately regretted it. Mary, who had previously scoffed at Dudley as the Queen of England's 'horsekeeper, who has murdered his wife to make room for her', was prepared to consider him, but only if the English queen acknowledged her as heir.

In any event, Mary likely had her own candidate in mind, appearing infatuated with the vapid teenager Henry, Lord Darnley ('yonder long lad' as Elizabeth I dismissively referred to him), when he arrived at her court in 1565.[31] Darnley, whose portraits make clear that he was spectacularly handsome, could also be charming. But, for Mary, the main attraction was the fact that he was 'nearest prince of the blood' to the English throne. Like her, he was a grandchild of Margaret Tudor, elder sister of Henry VIII, and, thus, a rare Tudor male. That he was petulant, jealous and easily led would later become all too clear. The match, which was celebrated only five months after the couple met, was undoubtedly hasty and ill-conceived. It alienated Mary's half-brother, James Stewart, Earl of Moray, who had hitherto been a loyal, if somewhat overbearing, counsellor to his father's only legitimate surviving child.

With the marriage, Scotland had a new monarch. 'King Henry' appeared on coins beside his wife while, as the male partner, his image and titles were given the place of honour. Initially, Mary appeared content, with the English ambassador, Thomas Randolph, considering her so blinded by love that she had abandoned herself, with 'all care of common wealth set apart, to the utter contempt of her best subjects'. Behind the scenes, the royal marriage disintegrated rapidly, with the couple publicly arguing at court by October. In November 1565, when Darnley was away yet again hunting, Mary ordered a stamp of his signature to be made so that she could dispatch state documents even in his absence. The following month she changed the order of their names to 'Mary and Henry' on the coins, while the English ambassador noted at Christmas that 'a while ago there was nothing but King and Queen, now the Queen's husband is the common word. He was wont in all writings to be first named: now he is placed second'. When Darnley was very openly involved in the murder of the queen's personal secretary, David Rizzio, with whom he believed she was having an affair, it was clear that the relationship was doomed. Mary, to whose skirts the doomed man had clung before he was dragged away to his death, believed that she was also in danger, particularly since she been threatened with a pistol pressed to her belly by one of the murderers. She gave birth to her only child, a son, three months later to great rejoicing.

By the time of the birth, Mary and Darnley were almost entirely estranged, with the queen looking for a way to end her marriage. This came explosively when, at around two o'clock in the morning of 10 February 1567, a blast rocked the peace in Edinburgh, causing the citizens, including the queen, to rise 'from their beds at the noise'.[32] This great 'crack' had come from Darnley's house in Kirk o'Field, which was found to be a smouldering ruin. Citizens rushed to the rubble, from which cries for help could be heard, but Darnley was found in the garden, lying beside his servant. Still in their nightclothes, they appeared unharmed, save for their necks, which were bruised purple and red. On hearing of the stranglings, Mary quaked with terror, apparently genuinely believing that she had been the plot's target, since she had initially intended to spend the night with her husband before instead returning to Holyrood, a decision which, she declared, 'we believe it was not chance but God that put it in our head'.[33] She was apparently completely oblivious to the possibility that whoever had carried out the murder had been closely acquainted with her movements and had timed the attack perfectly to ensure that she was in no way harmed. It all looked very suspicious. It *was* very suspicious. There were many, then and now, who thought that the queen was involved in Darnley's death.

Over 300 miles to the south, Elizabeth plunged her court into mourning, but her thoughts turned to Mary rather than her murdered cousin, advising her in the strongest possible terms to be seen to bring the killers to justice. The Scottish queen, who was probably suffering from shock, was, however, strangely passive, weeping when her half-brother, Moray, left for London at the start of April, despite their recent estrangement. The English envoy, who came to offer Elizabeth's condolences, found her 'very doleful' on 8 March, while around that time placards began appearing in Edinburgh depicting her as a mermaid, the symbol of prostitution.[34] Alarmingly, alongside this Marian mermaid appeared a hare – the symbol of James Hepburn, Earl of Bothwell, to whom Mary had begun to turn for all her support. Given the fact that Bothwell, a staunchly loyal but highly turbulent figure, was widely (and with good reason) reputed as Darnley's murderer, this was a colossal mistake. So, too, was Mary's failure to bring anyone to justice for the crime. With around 4000 of Bothwell's men present in the capital city, she may have had little choice, but her inactivity was disastrous.

In late April 1567, Mary left her capital to spend a few days with her baby son, arriving at Stirling on the 21 April. She spent the whole of the next day there, before setting out to return to Edinburgh on the 23rd, entirely unaware that she would never see her child again. Staying the night at Linlithgow, Mary was six miles from Edinburgh the following morning when Bothwell appeared, accompanied by some 800 men. He took the queen's bridle into his hands, before leading her back down the road to Dunbar Castle where he raped her.

Astoundingly, over the centuries Mary has been implied to have been somehow complicit in this attack, with the suggestion being that it was a pretext, designed to justify what was otherwise an unjustifiable marriage. Yet, Mary herself writing later confirmed that 'we found his doings rude, but were his answer and words but gentle', while he also apparently 'asked pardon of the badness', all of which makes very clear the non-consensual nature of the encounter.[35] Bothwell may well have approached the rape almost as a business arrangement, something which in many ways makes it all the more horrific: he knew, as all his contemporaries knew, that any extramarital sexual activity in a woman was considered shameful. As Sir James Melville, who was himself imprisoned at Dunbar during the rape recorded: 'The Queen could not but marry him, seeing he had ravished her and laid with her against her will.'[36] To compound matters, Mary may even have been aware that she was in the early stages of pregnancy by the time of her marriage at Holyrood on 15 May 1567. This pregnancy, of twins, would end in miscarriage, but it was taken as another sign by Mary's enemies of her moral degeneracy. She had, as far as her contemporaries were concerned, become the mermaid of the placards.

In the ensuing rebellion and civil war, led by twenty-six Scottish lords who were furious at the queen's marriage to Darnley's likely murderer, Mary was forced to abdicate in favour of her son and was imprisoned on the island of Loch Leven. Bothwell fled to Scandinavia, where, in an apt twist of fate, he was recognised and denounced by his abandoned first wife who had him arrested for desertion. Proving too valuable a hostage to the Danish king to be released, he ended his life insane and imprisoned, chained to a pillar that can still be seen in Dragsholm Castle in Denmark. It is encircled by a groove in the floor said to have been the product of ten years of aimless shuffling.

Mary, too, would never truly regain her liberty. On 2 May 1568 she escaped from Loch Leven, but after suffering yet another defeat in battle, she took the fateful decision to escape to England, sure that her 'dear sister' would support her in her bid to be restored to her throne. As Retha Warnicke notes in her scholarly account of this much romanticised figure, 'with hindsight it is clear that the flight to England was a blunder, but Mary had few options'.[37] France, where she had been raised and where she was an extensive landowner, may well have been the Scottish queen's first choice of refuge, but it would have been impossible to get there in a fishing boat. Remaining in Scotland would, perhaps, have been a better long-term solution too, since she could likely expect some level of sympathy from her child and supplanter as he grew. While she was in Scotland Elizabeth could safely (and probably genuinely) rail against the Scots' treatment of their reigning queen, a subject close to her own heart. In England, Mary became a different beast entirely.

There are similarities here to Arsinoë in far-distant Alexandria attempting to establish her own legitimate rule in the face of her sister's presence in the city. Arsinoë was still a young teenager, raising the very real possibility that she was more puppet to her tutor, Ganymedes, than independent ruler. Certainly, a good deal of her worth lay in the fact that the army 'now had as leader a representative of the family of the Ptolemies', suggesting that she acted largely as a figurehead.[38] While Ganymedes took charge of Arsinoë's forces and attempted to flush out her rival, Cleopatra VII, by poisoning the palace's water supply, it was the young queen that was the face of a regime which complained that 'they were irritated at the rule of the eunuch and of the woman'.[39] To complicate matters, Julius Caesar also released the imprisoned Ptolemy XIII, seeing 'no source of strength in the lad', in the hope that this gesture would secure peace, but instead the king rejoined his army.[40]

Soon, he and Arsinoë had agreed to rule Egypt jointly, in the Ptolomeic tradition, but Cleopatra – newly pregnant by Julius Caesar – was a formidable enemy. In a decisive battle at the start of 47 BCE, Ptolemy XIII drowned attempting to flee and Arsinoë was captured, while Cleopatra VII, now ruling with the only surviving brother, Ptolemy XIV, returned to the throne. Arsinoë IV had proved all too clearly that she was a threat to Cleopatra, with her sister too shrewd a politician to show mercy. Arsinoë would never regain her freedom.

Mary Queen of Scots, stepping out of the boat that had brought her to England in 1568, would also never taste liberty again. Elizabeth could never bring herself to set eyes on her. She would be imprisoned in locations across the north of England and the midlands for the next nineteen years, frustrated and unfulfilled and increasingly aware that all that stood between her and the English crown was Elizabeth.

This 'daughter of debate' was, in the eyes of almost everyone, heir to the crown while, in the highly charged sectarian politics of the day, she was a Catholic queen to Elizabeth's Protestant. As early as 1572, only four years after Mary had begun what would be nearly two decades of English imprisonment, the English parliament were clamouring for Mary's execution, noting that, 'We find also in the Scriptures that in this Zeal of Justice two wicked Queens, Jesabel and Athaliah, both inferior in mischief to this late Queen [Mary], have been by Gods Magistrats Executed, and the same Execution commended in Scripture.'[41]

For Arsinoë, the defining event of her life was almost certainly not her queenship, brief and contested at it was. Perhaps it was her last sight of Alexandria, as her ship moved slowly out of the charred port. The mighty lighthouse, possibly over 300 feet tall and one of the seven wonders of the ancient world, loomed as she was carried away from Egypt. It was built by her ancestor, Ptolemy II Philadelphus and would stand for another 1000 years until earthquakes swept it away. By winning the support of mighty Rome, Cleopatra had created another earthquake, which swept her sister away from her homeland and towards that distant city which was then at the height of its powers. Cleopatra would visit Rome twice as an honoured guest, riding in triumph through the streets and monuments of the capital of the world. For Arsinoë, as a captive and defeated queen, the welcome was different. Forced to walk in chains as the symbol of Rome's victory over Egypt, the teenager was the centre-point of a pageant intended to humiliate her.[42] The greatest mortification must have been her sister's presence, yet Arsinoë drew the sympathy of the crowd, with the sight of this mere child ('once considered a queen') arousing 'very great pity'.[43] Surprisingly, and probably against her sister's wishes, she was permitted to live, perhaps as a spare Egyptian heir, should this ever prove useful to Rome.[44] Even exiled to far distant Ephesus in modern Türkiye, Arsinoë retained her political importance. Cleopatra could never be safe on her throne while her sister breathed.

Sixteen centuries later, Elizabeth I (who appeared to one contemporary 'as if Cleopatra had been resuscitated') could easily be forgiven a similar sentiment.[45] Plots, naturally enough, attached themselves to Mary, with the queen both an active and a passive figure in attempts to free her from captivity and place her, as a Catholic queen, on Elizabeth's throne, just as Arsinoë had been in her uprising in Alexandria. It was always illegal to attend Catholic worship in England during Elizabeth's reign, with her excommunication by the Pope in 1570 raising the stakes since it positively encouraged her Catholic subjects to rise up against her. Mary was the obvious figurehead as heir to the throne, with the state faith in the sixteenth century tied to the beliefs of the monarch. Elizabeth's Protestant ministers were haunted by the threat Mary posed, with Sir Francis Walsingham, the English queen's famed and zealous spymaster, particularly determined to bring about her ruin. Walsingham had been in Paris during the St Bartholomew's Massacre in 1572 when the mighty queen mother of France, Catherine de Medici, presided over an orgy of violence in which thousands of her Protestant subjects were killed. His terror of a similar occurrence in England drove him to build a network of spies so good that even today historians struggle to determine just who was working for him. Running a spy school, Walsingham trained and employed cryptographers and other agents, adept at spotting invisible ink, cracking codes and, crucially, as it would prove, resealing a letter without damaging its wax seal. He was rumoured to have kept his own torture chamber in the basement of one of his houses, ensuring that he knew what was happening almost before the participants themselves. Implacably opposed to Mary and everything she represented, he was determined to find evidence to prove to Elizabeth that, once and for all, the Scottish queen must die.

The opportunity came in 1586, eighteen years into Mary's English imprisonment, via a young Catholic gentleman, Anthony Babington. Addressing Mary as 'his most mighty, most excellent, my dread sovereign Lady and Queen, unto whom only I owe all fidelity and obedience', Babington succeeded in getting a letter through to the Scottish queen in July.[46] Mary, who was still smarting from the arrival of a new Puritan gaoler, Sir Amyas Paulet, who in his zeal and strictness had ripped down her cloth of estate – a rare remaining symbol of her monarchy – was prepared to listen.

Babington, who was more zealous than capable, promised to free Mary from her imprisonment himself, while 'for the dispatch of the usurper', as he called Elizabeth, six of his friends were ready to 'undertake that tragical execution'.[47] He held out the tangible promise of both freedom and the English crown and had contacted Mary at a fortuitous moment. For the first time in months she had contact with the outside world, thanks to an ingenious scheme whereby the letters, first wrapped in a waterproof cover, were carefully inserted into the bungs of beer barrels.

Since the water in England was widely not regarded as safe to drink, every great household needed a steady supply of ale. The system meant that, along with Babington's letter, Mary could receive a stream of correspondence from friends in France and supporters in

England and Scotland. Mary likely devised the cipher that she used in her correspondence herself, with symbols representing key words and leading figures in Europe. Sadly, since the cipher was not easy to decode, she sent the key out early in the correspondence. Sir Francis Walsingham, who had bribed the brewer, copied the key and the letters, before carefully resealing them and sending them on their way. There is a dark comedy to the whole affair in that the brewer, who realised at once that he now had a monopoly in his supply at Chartley Castle where the queen was kept, immediately put his prices up, to the annoyance of Sir Amyas Paulet. In late July, Mary sealed her fate when she replied to Babington in cipher giving her consent to Elizabeth's murder.[48] Recognising this, Thomas Phelippes, the linguist and forger employed by Francis Walsingham to decipher the correspondence, drew a little gallows on the copy that he gave to his master. Finally, Mary had given them enough rope to hang her.

Having spent most of her adult life in prison, Mary Queen of Scots was weary and depressed by the time of the Babington Plot. Only a few months before she had been rejected by the son she had not seen since his infancy (and whom she very pointedly referred to as 'the prince of Scotland' in her cipher key) when he refused to countenance the possibility of sharing the Scottish throne with her.[49] James merely commented on hearing of his mother's arrest in the Babington Plot that she should 'drink the ale she had brewed', presumably referring to the means by which her correspondence reached her.[50]

Finally, and almost against her better judgment, Elizabeth permitted Mary to be tried for treason. The Scottish queen was taken to the more secure prison of Fotheringhay Castle, a bleak and foreboding fortress that is now little more than a romantic ruin in Northamptonshire. As the proceedings began, Mary was defiant, declaring that, 'I am myself a Queen, the daughter of a King, a stranger, and the true kinswoman of the Queen of England. I came to England on my cousin's promise of assistance against my enemies and rebel subjects and was at once imprisoned.' On being informed bluntly that she would be condemned in her absence if she refused to attend the proceedings, Mary came. The trial of a queen regnant (even if she had been forced to abdicate) was an unprecedented one, with Elizabeth later admitting that she would have preferred Mary to be quietly murdered. Undoubtedly, as Mary herself had realised, one of the two queens had to die. It took Elizabeth, who was often squeamish about ordering the deaths of her kinsfolk, somewhat longer, but she eventually signed the death warrant.

On the morning of 8 February 1587, Mary, sometime Queen of Scotland and heir to the throne of England, stepped out onto a scaffold in the great hall of Fotheringhay Castle. She was no longer the attractive young woman who had drawn so much attention in her carefree early days in France or during the years of her personal rule in Scotland. Yet, despite ill health and years of disappointment and boredom, she stood tall, removing her black dress to reveal a red bodice and petticoat beneath: the colour of martyrdom. Forgiving the executioner, as was customary, Mary kneeled and placed her head on the block, praying as she waited for the end. It took two brutal strokes to sever her head, before the executioner held it up to those assembled, crying out 'God save the Queen'. As he did so Mary's severed head, tumbled from her wig to the floor before him. It was only at that moment that Elizabeth finally felt safe on her throne.

Arsinoë's forced retirement in the Temple of Artemis in Ephesus would prove far briefer than Mary's long years of incarceration and uncertainty. In 41 BCE, only five years after she had so piteously walked in chains through Rome, she was dragged out of her temple and murdered on its steps. While the Roman triumvir Mark Antony may have been the man who gave the orders for this execution, it was widely recognised that the sentiment came from his lover, Cleopatra:

Arsinoë, like Mary Queen of Scots, by virtue of who she was, was far too dangerous to be allowed to live.'***[51]

The English government had been well aware of historical precedent when they finally decided to take action against Mary, citing the example of another execution ordered by Mark Antony – that of Antigonus II, last King of Judea, whom they believed to be the first example of a monarch being put to death by an axe.[52] They turned, too, to Athaliah, using her as proof that it could be legal and even God-sanctioned to take extreme action against a monarch. Even more than two millennia after her death, this Biblical queen, who dared to subvert the submissive status of women of her time, was used as a model for the illegitimacy of female rule.[53] We know almost nothing about her reign, save that she drew the Scripture compilers' opprobrium for building a temple to honour the god Baal, just as her kinswoman Jezebel had done. She reigned for seven years, which suggests some measure of acceptance and success.

There was much whispering amongst the palace staff and temple guards in the final months of Athaliah's rule, which she must have heard. As those who should have served her assembled in the temple of Yahweh (the god of Judaism and, later, Christianity), the priest Jehoiada produced the now seven-year-old Prince Jehoash, Athaliah's grandson, crowning and anointing him as Judah's legitimate king. On hearing the news, Athaliah rushed to the temple, crying 'Treason! Treason!'[54] Guards moved at once to restrain her. She was then carried outside and executed by sword. With Athaliah's death her temple of Baal was torn down, restoring the monotheistic, patriarchal *status quo*. It is hard to resist the conclusion that Athaliah failed and died due to attitudes to her sex, with the Books of Kings treating her reign as an

---

*** Arsinoë may have been provided with a splendid tomb known as the Octagon, which has been suggested as hers due to its resemblance to the lighthouse of Alexandria. The identification remains contested. See Hilke Thür, 'Arsinoe IV, eine Schwester Kleopatras VII, Grabinhabeirin des Oktogons von Ephesos? Ein Vorschlag', *Jahreshefte des Österreichischen Archäologischen Institutes*, vol. 60 (1990).

interregnum.[55] Like the murdered Jezebel, there is an abiding sense in the Biblical narrative that the presumptive Athaliah, who usurped the arenas of men, got exactly what was coming to her.[56] The trumpet had blasted even this early in history against the monstrous regiment of women and she would be used as an example of the dangers of female rule ever afterwards.

T.S. Eliot, in the opening lines of part II of *The Waste Land*, paraphrased Shakespeare's description of Cleopatra, which was itself based on Elizabeth I: 'The Chair she sat in, like a burnished throne, / Glowed on the marble, where the glass / Held up by standards wrought with fruited vines / From which a golden Cupidon peeped out / (Another hid his eyes behind his wing).' In his monument to desolation, emptiness and futility composed in the wake of the First World War, Eliot could have been writing about the careers of any of the reigning queens who died for their ambition, or their hopes of a throne. The title of this – the second part of his epic poem – 'A Game of Chess' is particularly apt; chess begins with two queens on the board but one is, ultimately, doomed to fail.

Athaliah, Arsinoë and Mary died for the crowns which they wore. So, too, did Cleopatra, locked in her struggles in a changing world. Elizabeth, who recognised in her final address to her parliament a year and a half before her death that 'to be a king and wear a crown is a thing more glorious to them that see it than it is pleasant to them that bear it', understood the struggle too. She was fortunate to die in her bed. Athaliah, Arsinoë and Mary struggled, vied and, ultimately, lost, but they were far from the monstrous regiment of John Knox's vicious imagination or of the violent misogyny of the anonymous Books of Kings. While they may have regretted their ends, it seems unlikely that they regretted how they lived. They died for their thrones.

CHAPTER 8:
WARRIOR QUEENS

The Kandakes of Kush, Zenobia of Palmyra, Isabel I of Castile and Juana 'la Beltraneja'

Push through the crowds filling the Ancient Egyptian galleries on the first floor in the British Museum, past hi-vis-wearing school children, tourists and a smattering of scholars, and you will find yourself in the Nubian gallery, its far wall dominated by a huge stone relief, hacked from the wall of a pyramid. Staring down is the depiction of a warrior monarch, who presided over the second great African civilisation of antiquity, a land of pyramid builders, goldsmiths and warriors, overshadowed only by the seemingly eternal Egypt of the pharaohs.

Sitting, preserved in carved relief, the Kandake (queen) of Kush uses bound prisoners as a footrest as they cower beneath her throne. Beside her sits a smaller figure. He is probably her son, but few eyes linger on him. It is the woman who commands attention. The figure is aeons old and looks it, dating to around 170–160 BCE, but the idea that it conveys is timeless.[*1] The Kandake and the female successors to her mighty

---
* The relief most likely depicts Queen Shanakdahete. See Necia Desiree Harkless, *Nubian Pharaohs and Meroitic Kings* (Bloomington: AuthorHouse, 2006) p146.

throne are the ancestresses of the concept of warrior queens across the world who, by their very existence, transgress the gender norms of a patriarchal planet.[2]

When we imagine a warrior queen, we think of Boudicca, Queen of the Iceni in eastern England, famous for her attempt to overthrow the yoke of Rome as she stormed through the battle lines in her bladed chariot. She burned the Roman cities of St Albans, Colchester and London in 60 or 61 CE, with her statue – installed centuries later – looming over tourist kiosks on Westminster Bridge. Although Boudicca was ultimately defeated and committed suicide to avoid being paraded in the streets of Rome, it is a mark of her might that, when archaeologists dig down to the Roman levels of London, they frequently come across a burned layer in the soil indicative of the queen's destruction. She was far from the only woman to earn the epithet of 'warrior queen', although it is a label which we must treat with caution lest we land on the stereotype of the barbarian queen in bikini top breastplate of many a computer game or fantasy depiction.

Given how pervasive warfare has been, and is, to human societies, however, there is much to be said about considering the role of reigning queens in war and how they mediated their involvement in what was, mostly, considered to be a wholly male sphere. For most of recorded history, to be a monarch meant riding into battle and this is something that reigning queens have been forced to negotiate, in spite of their almost universal lack of military training. To be a warrior queen was to exist outside the norm for women – but it was to exist within the norm for a monarch. No wonder warrior queens are viewed with such interest today.

Like Boudicca, it is as a warrior that Zenobia, Queen of Palmyra, now modern Syria, is remembered.[3] Born around 240 CE, she was always an active figure, renowned for bringing down lions, panthers, bears 'and other beasts of the forest' while hunting in the woods and mountains of Syria in her youth.[4] She was a consort initially, having been married young to Odanaith, the ruler of what was then one of the greatest cities in the world, at the crossroads where east met west and, by that time, a part of a Roman Empire that was still very much in its prime.[5]

As a young wife, Zenobia used to stroll in markets bustling with wares from Han Dynasty China, Parthian Persia or thrusting Rome. They came on camel caravans criss-crossing the desert, with glass and jade unloaded and glorious silks and fine muslins unravelled and cut. Her world was scented with spices from the east and fragranced with exotic perfumes and incense. There was a dark side, too, with the human cargoes of slaves destined for household work or the brothels of the west unloaded and displayed before being carried far from their homelands. Their voices rarely survive, while even those of the silk-clad elites are indistinct over the passing of years. We initially catch only glimpses of Zenobia, but she was soon to emerge out of the shadows and into legend.[6]

Unlike her stepson, Herodianus, whom she disliked and who was described as 'the most effeminate of men', no one ever accused Zenobia of being overly feminine, with the queen frequently described in masculine terms both during and after her lifetime. If the *Historia Augusta* can be believed (and it possibly cannot), she presented herself in her later career as a warrior queen 'in the manner of a Roman emperor', in mannish dress and wearing a military helmet in public. The writer of the anonymous source was fascinated by this exotic, eastern queen, with eyes 'black and powerful beyond the usual wont, her spirit divinely great, and her beauty incredible'.[7] He admired her white teeth that resembled pearls and her strong, bare arms. She had a clear, manly voice, he said, while she could be both tyrannically stern and righteously fair. Zenobia was a paragon whose legend echoes down the centuries. In the fourteenth century, Geoffrey Chaucer recorded that she was so chaste she lay only with her husband for the purposes of procreation.

WOMEN WHO RULED THE WORLD

In his *Canterbury Tales,* culturally so distinct from her own times and experience, she was recalled as an Amazonian, or Diana-like being. She became a popular subject of the Pre-Raphaelite painters of the nineteenth and twentieth centuries: there is a sense of their fetishisation in the buttoned-up days of Victorian Britain.[8] However, it is frequently difficult to pick through the sources for Zenobia. Myth clings to her like the drapes of her scanty dress, as sketched by the great Michelangelo centuries after her death.

Zenobia's husband, Odanaith, was loyal to his imperial masters, but he claimed significant political power, calling himself 'Chief Magistrate of the Whole World' and 'King of Kings' on the coins that he minted.[9] The Romans effectively accepted him as a client-king, ruling on their behalf, with his assassination in late 267 CE, along with his eldest son, Herodianus, sending shockwaves through the Classical world. There were whispers, now impossible to substantiate, that Zenobia was herself involved in the plot.[10] She undoubtedly benefitted from it. With both her husband and her eldest son out of the way she was able to rapidly secure Palmyra. She was initially a regent, ruling on behalf of her son Wahballath as the 'most illustrious queen, mother of the king of kings', but it soon became apparent that she had other ambitions.[11]

Isabel I of Castile would reign well over 1000 years after Zenobia in Castile, the largest and wealthiest kingdom in the Iberian Peninsula and the point from which (thanks to Isabel's vision, funds and a seven-year lobbying campaign by Christopher Columbus) Europe's discovery of the New World of America would be launched in 1492. Like Zenobia, Isabel is presented as both a masculine woman and a chaste, virginal being, portrayals that make sense in the context of a warrior queen: they were, by their very nature, considered to be exceptional women by the men of their kingdoms, their allies and their rivals, since they adopted very obviously the trappings of male kingship. Isabel had the 'heart of a man dressed as a woman' and was 'the epitome of queens, model for all women, and for all men a subject to write about' according to one contemporary, currying favour.[12] She was vigorous and active, as only a man could be (according to the contemporary viewpoint), but she was simultaneously hyper-feminine – an echo of the Virgin Mary returned from Heaven. This dual conception, notes the historian Barbara F. Weissberger, 'share the misogynist belief that the worthy woman can only be one who transcends the limitations of her gender'.[13] Yet 'plasticity of gender' could also be useful to a female monarch actively seeking to fix herself to a throne.[14] It is a story centuries old: one Kandake of Kush, who ruled in the first century BCE, would be described as a 'masculine sort of woman'.[15]

Reigning queens have, until very recent times, been seen and portrayed as exceptional, unwomanly figures, and nowhere is this more true than with a woman who took to the battlefield or sent her troops to war, an arena that was, arguably, the ultimate male domain. There were powerful women in the Rome of Zenobia's time, of course, who defied the stereotyping of their society, but they usually hid behind a male figure. The female kin of the Emperor Elagabalus (reigned 218–222 CE), for example, were responsible for placing him on the throne and removing him when he proved less amenable than hoped. North Hertfordshire Museum, which displays one of the emperor's coins, decided in November 2023 to use female pronouns for Elagabalus, whom they consider to be a transwoman. It remains to be seen whether other institutions will follow suit, although there is considerable evidence of gender fluidity in accounts of a ruler who directed a follower to 'call me not Lord, for I am a Lady' and reputedly requested gender reassignment surgery.[16] Elagabalus' biological sex was, however, male.

For the most part, there was a tension in the role of upper-class women of the Roman Empire, as Zenobia, as one of its citizens, doubtless observed. They might be highly political, but they were also expected 'to spin and weave', which is akin, in modern times, to Hillary Clinton being required to submit a cookie recipe in a 'bake off' with Barbara Bush, during the 1992 US presidential election.[17] In law, Roman women of all classes were usually under the guardianship of their male relatives and, ideally, confined to their homes, although there was a good deal of nuance in practice. Emancipation was possible. The *jus trium liberorum* decreed that freeborn women who bore three children and freedwomen who bore four, would be exempt from guardianship.[18] This was done to incentivise childbearing in a world that required more Romans, in much the same way that the little municipality of Lesijärvi in modern-day Finland has paid each new mother a 10,000 Euro 'baby-bonus' since 2013.[19] But many Roman women who proudly asserted that they had acquired the *jus trium liberorum* still required the assistance of male relatives in relation to their own legal business, suggesting a continuing degree of control. Usually, the *pater familias* held the power of life and death over his daughters. The position in Palmyra was more liberal: women could own property and, in some cases, exercise authority over their households, but the general principles held true: Zenobia's assumption of authority was greatly at odds from her expected role as a virtuous Roman widow.[20]

The assassination of her husband and stepson led Zenobia to power. First as regent for her own young son and, later, in her own right. She ruled Palmyra and the east through her own cunning and the sword but, most importantly as far as contemporaries were concerned, 'with the vigour of a man'.[21] In the Roman world, the idea of a woman ruler was anathema but Zenobia, with her Hellenistic and Arabic background, was aware of precedents from outside the empire.[22] She could look to Dido, the mythical foundress of mighty Carthage or Cleopatra VII of Egypt, from whom she claimed descent.[23] She may only have been distantly aware (if at all) of the reigning Kandakes of Kush, who arguably provided the most immediate precedent to her rule.

WARRIOR QUEENS

The Kandakes of Kush are the earliest known examples of monarchs who can be described as 'warrior queens', with their examples (perhaps subconsciously) resonating down the centuries. Their kingdom, in modern-day Sudan and Ethiopia, was once the rival to its neighbour, Egypt, with its culture of pyramids and pharaohs (after unexpectedly conquering its northern neighbour it actually provided Egypt's Twenty-fifth Dynasty of kings, who reigned for just under a century).[24] Significantly, succession to the throne was most likely matrilineal, with kings passing their crowns to the sons of their sisters, something that gave royal women influence although, not initially, direct power.

The title Kandake was applied to queen mothers, before it was adopted by women who began to reign themselves.** [25] The Biblical Queen of Sheba was probably a Kandake, with Ethiopian tradition recalling that she bore King Solomon a son.[26] The Classical geographer Strabo would recall that Kushite women were fierce, arming themselves with wooden bows, hardened by fire.[27] The power achieved by Kush's royal women was, nonetheless, remarkable, since cooking, baking, food processing, weaving and other household tasks remained the preserve of women in ancient Kush.[28] Unlike their men, who are usually represented like pharaohs in Egyptian depictions, the Kandakes had a style distinctly their own, appearing with their natural, tight curls (instead of the wigs worn by Egyptian women), while their dress was unique with shawls wrapped around their bodies either at the hips or breasts and a fringed or striped second shawl on top. Most notably, they are almost always depicted with a little tail, hanging down to their feet from beneath their dresses.[29] Possibly intended as a fertility symbol, these fox tails make Kushite women immediately identifiable as they stare sideways out of the walls of Egyptian tombs or from contemporary monuments. It could, of course, be a symbol of their power.

** The title of Kandake confused foreigners, who tended to think it referred to one particular woman named Candace.

The Kingdom of Kush is little remembered today, but it was once well known to the powers of the Classical world. It was a place where explorers, sent by Rome's Emperor Nero (whose regime Boudicca rebelled against) in the first century AD could marvel at the parrots soaring through the air, or the forests close to Meroë's pyramids (around a four-hour drive from modern-day Khartoum) in which 'the tracks of rhinoceroses and elephants were seen'.[30] The people, who were universally referred to as Ethiopians by Roman writers, fascinated them and were viewed as warlike and 'other'.[31] They lived (according to the Greek geographer Strabo) on the 'extremities of the inhabited world' as pastoral farmers, almost naked in the heat, while the city houses were thatched and constructed of palm wood or bricks.[32] The people whom at least one Roman writer considered 'scorched by the heat through the closeness of the sun' were renowned for being 'wise' due to 'the mobility of the air', which apparently stimulated the mind.[33] Nubians were contrasted favourably with the barbarians of Northern Europe with their 'ice-like skin and long blond hair' since 'the freezing cold' makes them 'savage'.

Female power in Kush appears to have developed over time, although since their script remains undeciphered, they are veiled in silence. They likely would have known of at least some of the handful of women who ruled as pharaoh of Egypt, including the powerful Hatshepsut.[34] We also know, from Egyptian hieroglyphics, of a Kushite Queen Katimala who was described as the 'great wife of the king', 'daughter of the king' and, significantly, 'king of Upper and Lower Egypt', as well as a military leader and politician in an inscription in the fortress of Semna, on the edge of Egypt, but nothing else is known of her save that she likely lived at the very beginning of the first millennium BCE.[35] This was an early flourishing of reigning queenship, but a flood was to follow. In the 500 years between 260 BCE and 320 CE, there were at least ten reigning Kandakes, and an astounding six in the period between 60 BCE and 80 CE. Kush cannot merely have tolerated reigning queens: it actively encouraged them.

Unlike Kush and the growing power of its Kandakes, fifteenth-century Castile had scant tradition of reigning queens.*** Isabel would not have remembered her ineffectual father, Juan II, who died in 1454 when she was only three. Her childhood was troubled due both to her mother's severe and debilitating depression and the difficulties faced by the royal family, which was headed by her much older half-brother, Enrique IV, 'el Impotente' (whom we met in Chapter 2), who was both unpopular and ill-equipped to reign. He was increasingly suspicious of his half-siblings, with Castile's rebellious nobility turning to the youngest, Alfonso, in 1464 when they ceremonially deposed an effigy of the king. Alfonso was named as heir to the throne in preference to Enrique's infant daughter, Juana, but his sudden death in 1468 changed everything. Now, both rival heirs were female, and Isabel craved the throne.

She covertly arranged her own marriage to Fernando, heir to the neighbouring kingdom of Aragon, beginning a partnership that would endure for more than thirty years. In 1474, on Enrique's death, she seized the throne, a move that could only lead to war. She most likely recognised this: as she left her coronation the sword of state was unsheathed and held aloft before her, a gesture that attracted criticism from some of her contemporaries. Her candidacy for the throne was born from the fact that there were no other male candidates, but she had to become a war leader to defeat her female rival. By July 1475 she had an army of 30,000 men.

Unlike Zenobia or the Kandakes of Kush, Isabel survives in a wealth of documentary evidence, from accounts to petitions, to letters to chronicles and, even, the books she read. We know a lot about Isabel, or at least we think we do, although there can be no doubt that we

---

*** Castile had two earlier reigning queens. Urraca in the twelfth century and Berenguela, who abdicated mere weeks after succeeding.

view her through a particular lens, frequently her own.[36] This was, of course, not unusual amongst reigning queens who, if they wanted to be successful, needed to take control of their own image – just as Wu Zetian did in China and Elizabeth I achieved in sixteenth-century England. Isabel *knew* how to present herself. She was the consummate propagandist, employing historians at her court and raising their status through salary increases and royal favours.[37] She waged much of the war against her niece, Juana, in the pages of her chronicles, particularly Alfonso de Palencia's *Cronica de Enrique IV,* which has remained highly influential and which Isabel commissioned.[38] In it, Enrique IV was painted as both homosexual and sexually impotent, casting doubt (by contemporary standards) on the potency of his kingship and – crucially – Juana's legitimacy. There were even rumours that Juana had been conceived by artificial insemination, when Enrique was assisted in the filling of a golden vial that was then hurriedly passed to his queen.[39] Neither Enrique nor his second wife, Juana of Portugal, whom he wed after the annulment of his marriage to Blanca II of Navarre, ever suggested that their daughter was illegitimate. Queen Juana's later very open affair which resulted in the birth of two children out of wedlock did not, however, help.[40] Young Juana was cast as the daughter of Enrique's favourite, Beltran de la Cueva, leading to the enduring nickname of 'la Beltraneja'.

These rumours were not entirely the work of Isabel, or even necessarily her supporters, but she very much worked to ensure that they stuck. We know that Isabel ordered chronicles to be revised to present a more damning picture of her half-brother and his daughter, while it has also been suggested that she falsified documents.[41] It is, of course, interesting that a female ruler would present a male ruler as effeminate as a means of discrediting him, reminding us of the 'Persian' tastes of Zenobia's hated stepson centuries before, which had been used to discredit him as a lover of luxury and other 'unmanly' pursuits.

WARRIOR QUEENS

Unlike Boudicca, who is recalled riding through battle in a bladed chariot, there is little evidence that Zenobia fought, although she travelled with her army. As it became increasingly apparent that the Emperor Claudius II and his successor, Aurelian, had no intention of allowing her or her son to rule the Roman east as Ordanaith had done, she went on the offensive. In early 270, she secured control of Arabia, becoming 'Al-Zabba' in Arab sources, an almost mythical reigning queen who built fortresses and tunnels, was duplicitous, treacherous and crafty, and who eventually died by the sword.[42, 43] Later works would credit her with founding a city on the Euphrates named in her honour.[44] She presided over a scholarly court, taking instruction from the great Sophist scholar Cassius Longinus, who also became her chief counsellor. Longinus was much admired in his day, instructing his queenly pupil in the works of Homer and Plato, as well as writing his own celebrated volumes, which unfortunately have not survived.

We can see from the coins that she minted that Zenobia was initially cautious in assuming control. Relations between her and Emperor Claudius II, who died suddenly of plague in 270, were difficult, but they were immeasurably worse with Aurelian (r.270-275), who assumed control of the empire later that year. That October, Zenobia ordered her general, Zabdas, into Egypt at the head of 70,000 troops (according to the chronicler Zosimus, who was probably exaggerating). One 'sharp engagement' and the province was conquered, leaving Zenobia mistress of Egypt and the Roman East, something that was considered a stunning achievement then and now.[45] When Aurelian began an advance across Asia Minor to confront her in the spring of 272, Zenobia started to issue coins in her own name for the first time, calling herself both queen and, significantly, 'Augusta' (the title used by Roman empresses).[46] She was finally an independent monarch, but the writing was already on the wall for Palmyra's warrior-empress and, by

June 272, Rome had reconquered Egypt. Zenobia's attempts to portray herself as the heir of Cleopatra proved an unhappy precedent.

Zenobia's short-lived Palmyran Empire disintegrated under her reign. Following the loss of Egypt, she retreated to Palmyra before fleeing the city by camel (a female one, according to the Greek chronicler, Zosimus, 'which is the swiftest of that kind of animals').[47] She was captured as she boarded a boat and taken to Rome, where she and her son were exhibited in Aurelian's triumphal procession, being led before his chariot in chains.[48] After this, their fate is uncertain. Even the *Historia Augusta* was unsure: 'Many maintain that they were killed by Aurelian, and many that they died a natural death, since Zenobia's descendants still remain among the nobles of Rome.' For its author, her role was, in any event, over. She was, for him, a cautionary tale, a vehicle for attacking male emperors perceived of as weak or inadequate since, 'While Gallienus [the emperor when Zenobia's husband was assassinated] conducted himself in the most evil fashion, even women ruled most excellently.' Aurelian, according to this (most likely apocryphal) account, was forced to defend himself in a letter to the senate for being so staunchly resisted by a mere woman. 'I have heard, Conscript Fathers, that men are reproaching me for having performed an unmanly deed in leading Zenobia in triumph. But in truth these very persons who find fault with me now would accord me praise in abundance, did they but know what manner of woman she is.'[49] It suited her opponents to view Zenobia as a most unusual kind of woman: a warrior. With the end of her reign, we lose sight of her. One account has her retiring to Tivoli, close to Rome, where she married a senator and lived out her days in retirement. The warrior queen became just another Roman matron. She most likely never returned home.

Isabel I of Castile worked hard to portray herself as the legitimate heir to her half-brother, Enrique IV, who had favoured the succession of his disparaged daughter. The legitimacy or illegitimacy of Juana la Beltraneja is as impossible now as it was in the fifteenth century to prove. Enrique is spending eternity beneath a grand tomb in the monastery of Santa Maria de Guadalupe, making his body at least identifiable for DNA testing (should permission ever be granted), but Juana is well and truly lost. Her grave was destroyed during the Portuguese earthquake of 1755, which all but flattened her resting place in the monastery of Santa Clara while, for good measure, any remnants were razed in 1828 before new construction work was placed on top.[50] As such, whether she was truly Castile's legitimate sovereign is a question of faith. Many were prepared to take up the twelve-year-old's cause, most notably her uncle, Afonso V of Portugal, to whom she was hurriedly betrothed.[51]

As a child and as a female, she was labouring under a double disadvantage, with Juana playing little direct role in the War of the Castilian Succession, which would rage for the next four years as a conflict of sieges, skirmishes, naval encounters and the occupation of territory rather than pitched battles. Afonso, who probably considered Juana's role to be more akin to that of consort than ruler, called himself King of Castile, as did his rival Fernando although, thanks to Isabel's successful bargaining in the negotiations before their wedding, she remained the supreme authority in the parts of the kingdom occupied by her. She was, however, not trained in fighting and, while she prepared reinforcements and advice, it was Fernando who was expected to lead her troops, with the queen remaining close to her army throughout. Of the two, though, it is Isabel who is remembered as a warrior, again highlighting the focus that has always been given to women who subverted gender roles in this way. Following the only major pitched battle of the war at Toro on 1 March 1476, it was Isabel who snatched victory from an inconclusive engagement, securing the acknowledgement of her own daughter, Infanta Isabel, as heiress to the crown of Castile shortly afterwards. The war would drag on, but it was from this moment that it turned in Isabel's favour.

Unlike Zenobia, Isabel was victorious in her struggle to secure the crown of Castile, but the cost of this was the loss of the authority and liberty of another reigning queen. The pathos of the life of Juana la Beltraneja echoes through the centuries. Raised with strong hopes of becoming Castile's monarch, she was outmanoeuvred by her aunt and vanquished in war. When Isabel met with Juana's ambassadors in the ancient Roman town of Alcantara in Castile in 1479 they agreed peace terms. Both sides would return all castles, towns and prisoners without ransoms, while Afonso V of Portugal would abandon his marriage to Juana.[52] The title of Queen of Castile was to belong to Isabel alone, while Juana could not even use the title of Princess, with the Portuguese eventually granting her the vague, but impressive, name of 'Excellente Senhora'. Her future was in the hands of Isabel, whose preference was for her niece to marry her infant son, with the betrothal to occur when he reached the age of seven and consummation when he was fourteen. It is at this moment that we get a glimpse of just how impressive Juana could have been. Even in the face of such powerful opposition, she resisted Isabel, refusing a marriage that could eventually have returned her to the throne as a consort. She chose, instead, immurement in the convent of Santa Clara in Coimbra, north of Lisbon. 'With painful lamentations', her hair was shorn with shears as she tearfully took her vows as a nun, but everyone knew that she was not freely dedicated to god.[53] Juana would sign her name as queen for the rest of what would prove to be a long life – she always believed that she was Castile's reigning queen, even if no one else did.

Isabel entirely emerged from the shadow cast by Juana la Beltraneja. Her reputation is an ambiguous one. Thanks in large part to her gift for self-fashioning, she remains central to conceptions of the birth and history of Spain.[54] While to many she is a saintly figure (and, in fact, there exists a long lasting but, so far, unsuccessful campaign for her canonisation), twenty-first century sensibilities have introduced nuance particularly due to the association of her legend with General Franco's dictatorship from 1939 until 1975. While Isabel added a codicil to her will requiring that her new subjects in the Americas be treated justly and fairly, the people of the New World undoubtedly suffered under her rule and the reigns of her successors (as we saw with poor Tecuichpotzin 'Isabel Moctezuma' in Chapter 1). She was a woman of great faith, but the Spanish Inquisition which she and her husband gave licence in 1479 to proceed against 'infidels and bad Christians and heretics' remains a complex legacy and one that was criticised even in her lifetime.[55] Unsurprisingly, she is a wholly negative figure in Jewish and Muslim sources from her reign, with Rabbi Eliyahu Capsali, who wrote from Crete in the early sixteenth century, punningly referring to her as 'Jezebel' rather than 'Isabel', highlighting once again the parallels that were commonly drawn between reigning queens and their Biblical counterparts.[56] From 1492 she began expelling her Jewish subjects from Castile, fragmenting what had once been the largest Jewish community in Europe and causing untold personal hardship.

In her zeal to Christianise her realm, Isabel also conquered the ancient Muslim kingdom of Granada at Spain's southernmost tip, cementing her reputation as a warrior queen, but leading to further dislocations and tragedies.[57] She likely believed that she was doing God's work, although her conscience could be a flexible one.[58] She became more ostentatiously pious in the final years of her life, after the deaths of her only son, her eldest daughter and her eldest grandson caused 'knives of pain' stabbing into her heart.[59] We can see Isabel, dour and serious, staring out at us from her many portraits, but it is difficult to view the real Isabel through the lens of her propaganda. In large part, this was necessary. Like Elizabeth I gazing out from behind layers of the toxic white lead with which she plastered her skin – a female ruler in the fifteenth and sixteenth centuries could not present their true face to public inspection since, as a woman, she would always be found wanting. This was a sentiment that would echo through the eras.

Like Isabel, the Kandakes of Kush presented themselves as warriors, but is this how we should view them? They lived their lives along the banks of the Nile, on which millet, cotton and other grain crops were cultivated and cattle reared.[60] Theirs was a wealthy, stable and long-lasting culture, although since Meroitic script remains undeciphered we must view the Kandakes through the eyes of others.[61] Through Greek and Roman sources we know of Kandake Amanirenas, who reigned at around the time of the birth of Christ. This 'masculine sort of woman, and blind in one eye' (according to her contemporary, the Greek Strabo), launched an invasion of southern Egypt while the Roman prefect was absent in Arabia, taking the city of Syene, decapitating statues and enslaving the inhabitants.[62] The Kandake's forces were heavily defeated when she returned to Kush, with the Romans sacking her capital of Napata. Raising an army of 'many thousands of men', she sent ambassadors again to the Emperor Augustus, who – perhaps recognising that he could never hope to defend a border so far into Kush – agreed to her terms. Her depictions are martial, with a surviving wall painting showing her armed with bow, arrows and a spear while leading a tethered group of seven captives.

Another Kandake, who reigned in the middle of the first century CE, was shown with her husband holding a sword with which she smote her enemies, while at the same time she had loosed her pet lion to attack.[63] Being a war leader was intrinsic to a Kandake, although what limited evidence survives hints at a rich peacetime life – this Kandake and her husband restored and built temples. Kandake Amanirenas' martial reputation secured Kush as a queendom for centuries to come, but she was also a shrewd negotiator. In 2023 there was considerable controversy over the casting of a Black actor as the Graeco-Egyptian

Cleopatra in a Netflix drama, yet here we have a succession of strong, undoubtedly Black African women doing stunningly impressive things.

The Kandakes of Kush reveal themselves most frequently in their monuments in the royal cemeteries at Meroë, where men and women of the royal family and the elite were buried over a period that spanned more than one thousand years, from the early ninth century BCE to the mid-fourth century CE.[64] They are astoundingly remote, requiring a long drive across the Sudanese desert, through dunes, scrub vegetation and sand as far as the eye can see.[65] It is a beautiful, desolate, remote place, which perhaps partly accounts for the fact that an area that has twice as many pyramids as the whole of Egypt has been so neglected by scholars. Nubia's pyramids have a flavour all of their own, standing as compact structures, rarely more than 100 feet high, reaching upwards towards the sky at an angle so much steeper than anything that can be seen at Giza, Dahshur or the pyramid field at Saqqara in Egypt. Even Egypt's famously inept 'Bent Pyramid' initially rose at a shallower angle, before tapering off at a gentler incline. Peaking upwards like square-based witch's hats, those at Meroë are deliberately lofty. They have been described as tombstones, which is apt. The pyramids are solid and contain no chambers, with the burial cut into the rock below.

Meroë's pyramids tell the stories of Kandake after Kandake, although what they can provide is patchy since they have been subject to sporadic, and often destructive, excavation from the early nineteenth century. The worst of these grave robbers was the Italian physician and adventurer, Giuseppe Ferlini, who was stationed in Meroë while in the service of the Ottoman army in 1834. Bored, he set out on a treasure hunt, hiring 500 men for 'excavations' so destructive that several small pyramids were completely destroyed. He struck lucky with the more substantial pyramid No. 6, finding a fabulous treasures of bracelets, necklaces and other rich jewellery belonging to Amanishakheto, a Kandake who reigned shortly before the birth of Christ.[66] Carrying off his treasure, Ferlini failed initially to sell his booty, due to racist doubts in Europe that a Black African civilisation could have produced such marvels. Eventually, and only with some persuasion, they were purchased by the King of Bavaria, with the Kandake's treasures now on display in Berlin, glittering and golden. Her body was already missing from her burial chamber when Ferlini plundered it, although we can see her in the walls of her mortuary chapel: armed and ready to strike down four bound prisoners with her spear. She was a fighter, prepared to defend her people and her throne, but we know almost nothing else about her. Ferlini almost certainly penetrated the burial chamber cut into the rock beneath the monument but, to cover his tracks, claimed that he had discovered it in a chamber at the top of her steep-sided pyramid. It is for this reason that most of Meroë's pyramids are now topless, as vulture-like treasure-hunters descended on the pyramid-fields looking for further bejewelled warrior-queens.

The Kandakes of Kush are a story that demands considerably more airtime. They endured until the civilisation's vanishment. The last known ruler of Kush was Kandake Amanipilade, who reigned in the middle of the fourth century CE.[67] With her, the ancient kingdom simply melted away.

When the strapping Scottish adventurer James Bruce made his way down the Nile searching for its source, he was initially unimpressed with the small town of Shendi, which he reached in October 1772 and which lay close to the pyramid fields of Meroë.[68] Walking around its collection of 250 scattered houses, most built of clay and reeds and (in Bruce's view) 'miserable hovels', he found the people in a state of alarm as, for the whole month he stayed there, Venus 'appeared shining with undiminished light all day, in defiance of the brightest sun'. This may have been an astronomical phenomenon connected to the transit of Venus that Captain Cook had been sent to observe in the Pacific in

1769, a decade before his death in Hawaii, but to the people of Shendi – and to Bruce – it gave an eery timbre to his visit.[69]

On 12 October, he was invited to meet Sittina, the ruler of the local area, whom he found concealed behind a screen in her house half a mile outside the town. He was permitted to see the queen the following day, finding an attractive woman of around forty, with (as he related) red lips and the finest teeth that he had ever seen. She was tall, too, which given the fact Bruce stood himself at six foot, suggests a stately, prepossessing woman. Sittina was 'magnificently dressed' in a purple silk stole wrapped around her shoulders, a gold crown on her head and rich jewels covering her body. Her dark hair was tightly plaited, with the braids, swinging as she moved, hanging down to her waist. He kissed her hand, later having to assure her that he did so as a mark of respect: he would do so to Europe's kings 'and the queens, too, always on the knee'.

Perhaps it was the strange light in the sky, or the pyramids pointed like the ears of the fennec foxes that darted amongst the desert dunes, but the queen brought to Bruce's mind Candace, the mythical amalgam of Kush's Kandakes from so long ago who appears in the Bible. Their deeds may be largely lost to time, but the Kandakes of Kush, to some extent, live on. So, too, do Zenobia and Isabel and even poor Juana la Beltraneja, who continued to defy her detractors even from behind the walls of her convent. To be a warrior queen, a virago, was to be an exception, but also something that was acceptable. To the men of their time, these were something more than *mere* women. This constructed exceptionalism made them – just – the acceptable face of female power. Reigning queens would, however, continue to be dismissed and diminished almost the world over.

CHAPTER 9:

QUEEN HIMIKO'S MIRRORS

The Eight Reigning Empresses of Japan

Crowds gathered outside the Imperial Household Agency Hospital on the eastern edge of Tokyo's royal palace, waiting for news. It was December 2001 and, despite the biting cold, they were expectant, fervently hoping that a new generation would spring from a family tree at least 1500 years old.[1] No other reigning family comes close to the ancientness of Japan's imperial line. Denmark's royal family – the oldest in Europe – reaches only a comparatively short-lived 1100 years. China's imperial tradition, until its removal in the twentieth century, is admittedly older, but dynasties came and went.

Yet, at the turn of the twenty-first century, Japan's royal family was hovering close to extinction: no royal heir had been born into the family for thirty-six years. Considerable media pressure was placed on thirty-eight-year-old Crown Princess Masako, an intelligent, well-educated woman who had worked for many years as a diplomat before her marriage. She and her husband, Crown Prince Naruhito, and her husband's parents had made love matches with commoners (retired Emperor Akihito had romantically met his future wife on a tennis court in 1957, something which very much captured the public's imagination). But despite this seeming modernity of the current members of the country's royal family, Princess Masako's miscarriage two years before had been blamed on the stress of her desperate desire to fulfil that ancient duty of providing an heir.[2] For myriad reasons this was unfair.

Beaming with happiness, the Crown Prince and Princess of Japan left the hospital early in December 2001, giving the world a first glimpse of the dark haired, sleeping baby who had been born more than eight years after their wedding. The infant, whose name, 'Aiko', means 'child of love', was perfect in all ways except for one: she was a girl.

Japan's imperial family today perform a largely ceremonial role, but they remain central to the country's sense of identity and as a symbol of the state that has endured for more than a millennium and a half. Japan famously cut itself off from the wider world in the seventeenth century, expelling foreigners and limiting its contacts for outside trade. With the accession of the reforming Emperor Meiji in 1867 this abruptly changed, with the country re-establishing contact with the people outside its borders. Meiji, who transformed his inward-looking nation into a global power, was a moderniser in many respects and, in 1889 he turned his attention to formalising the succession rules for the first time in Japan's long imperial history.

As the 122nd sovereign in Japan's official list of monarchs, Meiji came from a long line of emperors, with the throne always passing down the male line, right back to the mythical Jimmu whose seventy-five-year reign reputedly began the dynasty more than 600 years before the birth of Christ. This, as far as Meiji was concerned, was all right and proper, but one thing troubled him: if all that was required of a sovereign was male descent from Jimmu then this could apply to women just as well as men, although they could not then transmit their claim to their children. Addressing this, Meiji established the Imperial Household Law which banned women sitting on Japan's chrysanthemum throne and limited the succession to the males of the royal family only. It caused no comment.

Nor, too, did the reiteration of this prohibition in 1947 during the years of turmoil that followed World War Two. In fact, as well as restating the bar on female inheritance, the then-Emperor Shōwa (better known by his name during his lifetime, Hirohito) also excluded the sons of concubines from the throne, as well as demoting many of the subsidiary branches of the royal family to commoner status.[3] Since at least half of Japan's historic emperors, including Shōwa's own father, had been born to secondary wives, this was shortsighted and almost guaranteed to cause a succession crisis further down the line. It is difficult not to credit the view of one historian, writing in the 1980s, that there has traditionally been a 'fear of female power' in Japan.[4]

Yet, while being born of the male line conferred royal status, it is not widely appreciated that eight of Japan's emperors in this long list were women. By the end of the nineteenth century and throughout many of the years of the twentieth, it became commonplace for historians to denigrate the reigns of Japan's ruling empresses, referring to them as mere regents until the true heir emerged. This denigration can be linked to the influence of Confucianism from China, which became highly important from the eighth century onwards and which viewed the idea of female rule as aberrant.[5] Emperor Meiji in his reforms of the late nineteenth century certainly showed himself influenced by this all-encompassing social philosophy, although he sometimes found it at odds with his efforts at modernisation.[6] To remove the idea of female succession is to ignore the undisputed fact of these earlier female emperors who (as one modern historian forcefully puts it) 'stride through the pages of the earliest extant Japanese chronicles'.[7]

★

According to a fifth-century Chinese source, in the third century CE the Japanese archipelago, then known to their mighty neighbours as the 'Kingdom of Wa', was ruled by the shaman-queen Himiko, who enchanted her people from a palace in which she was served by one thousand female servants and only one male.[8] Himiko was considered important enough to receive an embassy from China, who supplied her with 100 bronze mirrors amongst other riches. When she died in 239, she was so beloved that her thirteen-year-old niece was selected as queen, in opposition to a male candidate.

Did Himiko exist? Possibly. Some of her mirrors may have been found in archaeological excavations from the period, with their tarnished faces reflecting back the idea of reigning queenship through the millennia.[9] Japanese histories make no mention of either Himiko or her mirrors, but the country did not have its own script until the fifth century, when Chinese (kanji) script began to be, somewhat awkwardly, adapted to fit the language. And so, its early history is clouded in myth and obscurity. One legend has it that the Japanese dynasty is descended from the sun goddess, the pre-eminent deity in Shintoism, the origins of its power coming from a female divine source.

Shintoism, Japan's native belief system, translating to 'the way of the gods', was challenged in the sixth century by the arrival of Buddhism from neighbouring Korea. Emperor Kinmei, who had happily worshipped the gods and goddesses of Shintoism all his life, was uncertain how to respond, although since Japan's native faith was both polytheistic and animistic, there was no real bar to the adoption of Buddhism alongside it. The emperor's chief minister, who was also one of the polygamous emperor's many fathers-in-law, Soga no Iname, was ordered to worship a statue of the Buddha to see what would happen.[10] With no signs of divine displeasure, Soga no Iname became the country's leading proponent of Buddhism. His granddaughter,

Princess Suiko, was exposed to the faith as it slowly began to creep into the country, creating religious turbulence*[11].

On her father's death in 571, Suiko followed the convention of the time and wed her older half-brother, the new emperor, Bidatsu. She was probably still a teenager, but quickly became the most prominent consort, renowned for her beauty and conduct which was 'marked by propriety'.[12] She was politically active, too, retaining her considerable influence after her husband's death in 585 when her full brother Yomei took power. Two years later, he was succeeded by Suiko's half-brother Sushun, who also favoured Suiko, with their shared devotion to Buddhism binding the powerful siblings together. However, Sushun unwisely quarrelled with the then chief minister, Soga no Umako, who had succeeded his father, Soga no Iname, in this role. In 592, Emperor Sushun was assassinated. There were plenty of males in the sizeable royal family but Suiko, who was approaching forty – a venerable age for the time – unexpectedly emerged as the leading candidate.

Suiko was clearly the choice of her powerful maternal uncle, Soga no Umako, who was accustomed to playing the kingmaker. Six centuries later, one chronicler, writing in very different times, would attempt to make sense of this election, considering that she was Umako's puppet, who intended to rule through her.[13] There is, however, no evidence of contemporary concern over the fitness of a woman to rule, although a crown prince – Suiko's nephew Prince Shōtoku – was appointed to assist her.** Like his aunt, Shōtoku was a passionate Buddhist, but he died before Suiko in 621 and she took no steps to replace him with a new heir. As one historian has suggested, Shōtoku may 'simply have furnished

---

*   Suiko is a posthumous name, bestowed long after her death. During her reign she was Empress Toyo-mike Kashiki-ya-hime. Earlier, she was Princess Nukada-be. Posthumous names are used here for simplicity and also for recognition. Few people would be able to identify Suiko by the names she used for herself.

** Shōtoku is a posthumous name. His birth name was Umayado.

male cover for the awkwardness of having a female in a customarily male position'.[14] One early Japanese chronicler, who was clearly nonplussed by the idea of a reigning woman, considered, grudgingly, that 'the state was well governed under Suiko', while he credited her with preserving Buddhist and imperial law in a period of turmoil.[15]

Suiko was the first person to adopt the title of Tenno, which has been applied to all Japanese sovereigns, male or female, since her accession. We know she was an active and powerful ruler as she held the imperial seal, which was used to finalise or confirm important decrees, and received embassies from China, Korea and even India during her reign, graciously accepting diplomatic gifts of deer, peacocks, sheep, camels and, somewhat randomly it seems, magpies, which she allowed to nest freely in woods close to her palace.[16] The decision to go to war or to remain at peace rested on the empress's command. It was also down to Suiko to decide whether or not to punish Imoko no Omi, her ambassador to China, when, in 608, he admitted that he had lost a letter sent to her by the Chinese emperor while travelling through Korea.***

Her council was keen to punish the diplomat but, anxious not to cause a diplomatic incident, Suiko decided to overrule them. She declared: 'Although Imoko is guilty of losing the letter, We cannot easily punish him, for in that case the guest of the Great Country [China's ambassador to Japan] would hear of it, and this is undesirable.'[17] They would, she considered, be diminished on the world stage if word of the incompetence got out. She feted the Chinese embassy, before sending them home with a message of her own, addressed to the 'Emperor of the West' from the 'Emperor of the East' and enquiring about her counterpart's health since 'we', as she claimed, 'are in our usual health'. Showing that small talk has changed very little in the centuries that

---

*** There may be more to this incident. Suiko offended China's emperor by writing to him as an equal and it has been suggested that his reply contained a rebuke, which the Japanese ambassador did not dare give to his empress.

separate us from Suiko, she moved on to discuss the weather, noting that 'the last month of autumn is somewhat chilly'.

We know so much about Suiko because she was the first person in Japan to see the value of writing their own history, bringing her country's heritage to life in its own language. 'Suiko', her posthumously conferred name, and the moniker by which she is most familiar, can be translated as 'conjecture of the past'.[18] The first book known to have been written in Japanese (albeit using Chinese characters phonetically) dates from 620, late in Suiko's reign, although sadly this chronicle no longer exists.[19] There was soon delicate love poetry, written by the educated aristocracy, as well as scholars dutifully copying and recopying Buddhist scriptures.

Suiko, as a patroness of the written word, acted as a beacon to the women of Japan, who went on to trailblaze Japanese autobiographical literature.[20] While the noblemen, who were routinely educated in Chinese, often chose to write in that language, the women of the imperial court turned to their native language. Thanks in a large part to Suiko's legacy as a pioneer of Japanese literature, by the medieval period upper-middle-class women were often recording their thoughts and experiences. Even centuries later, their voices – telling the facts of their lives and, often, their innermost thoughts – explode off the page. And so we are able to know that, 1000 years ago, while Aethelred the Unready was sitting anxiously on the English throne harried by Vikings, one little girl, on a journey from the provinces to Japan's then-capital, Kyoto, spent a restless night as ripe persimmons hammered down onto the roof of her hut from a tree above (the servants were sent out to collect them for breakfast).[21] She saw Mount Fuji for the first time, which was then still a highly active volcano, and recorded that she thought it 'has a most unusual shape and seems to have been painted deep blue; its thick cover of unmelting snow gives the impression that the mountain is wearing a white jacket over a dress of deep violet'.[22]

As is so often the case, we do not know the name of this girl – simply nicknamed 'Lady Sarashina' – or much beyond the facts that she grew up to become a royal attendant and then, at the advanced age (for the time) of thirty-six, a wife. And yet, we know her hopes, her dreams, her fears, her griefs, her love for romance novels as a teenager (she 'took out the books one by one and enjoyed them to my heart's content. I wouldn't have changed places with the Empress herself'), as well as so much mundane detail about her life.[23]

The books that Lady Sarashina so enjoyed were volumes of the *Tale of Genji,* which, when translated into modern English runs at more than 1100 pages of text.[24] That work, an early novel of unparalleled brilliance, was also created by a woman, 'Lady Murasaki' (a descriptive name – again, her own is unknown), who was born around 973 and who was, like Lady Sarashina, the daughter of a minor official.[25] While in the service of the then-emperor's second ranked wife, she kept a diary, which allows us an intimate view of Japanese court life at this time. She loved her mistress, a woman with the power to 'make me quite forget my troubles'. Many of the scenes she relates are so jarringly modern, such as the preparations that were made for an imperial visit to the empress's residence. 'Rare chrysanthemums were ordered and transplanted. As I gazed out at them through the wraiths of morning mist – some fading to various hues, others yellow and in their prime, all arranged in various ways – it seemed to me that old age might indeed be conquered'.[26] Hurried gardening in the face of a royal visit could be a scene right out of the twenty-first century, not just the tenth. Certainly, the gardeners out on the Mall in front of Buckingham Palace worked feverishly in the run up to Charles III's coronation in 2023.

Lady Murasaki was surrounded by educated and accomplished women at the royal court, although there were clearly rivalries.[27] Murasaki's fellow lady-in-waiting, Sei Shōnagon, author of the famous *Pillow Book* (a journal that she kept amongst her bedsheets to allow her to record her innermost thoughts), was 'dreadfully conceited', apparently thinking herself 'so clever and littered her writings with Chinese characters; but if you examined them closely, they left a great deal to be desired.'[28] Most scholars today would consider Sei a titan of early literature, with her biting but on-the-nose observations: 'It breaks my heart to think of parents sending a beloved son into the priesthood. Poor priests, they're not the unfeeling lumps of wood that people take them for,' she wrote, before forgiving them the 'forbidden urge to peep into a room, especially if there's a woman in there'.[29]

These autobiographies and diaries, which appear so modern and unlikely to us, are almost unknown in the West. Is it because they were written by women and about the realities of their domestic lives rather than the politics of their day?

Although she lived nearly four centuries before, we have Suiko to thank for this early flourishing of women's literature and pertinent self-analysis. Like these unnamed but expressive women, centuries earlier, Suiko had joys and despairs of her own, which echo down the centuries. Throughout her reign, her passion for Buddhism remained and was hugely influential. Almost immediately after taking the throne she laid the foundation stone for a great temple, while in 605 she ordered the construction of two sixteen-foot-tall statues of the Buddha, one of copper and one of rich embroidered fabric. Unfortunately, no one had taken the measurements of the entrance to the Golden Hall of the Gangoji temple, where the statues were to be placed. The following year, the court assembled to watch their installation but the copper statue proved impossible to squeeze through the doors. Eventually, with great ingenuity, the Buddha was prised inside, to the relief of the empress and the assembled crowds. Suiko also welcomed Korean missionaries, promoted the sutras and ordered the inspection of Japan's monasteries amidst concerns about their orthodoxy. However, wisely hedging her bets, she did not neglect the traditional deities, ordering hurried prayers to the earthquake god after a devastating tremor in 599.

Suiko knew what it meant to be a ruler. On her deathbed in 628, she informed one of her many nephews as they crowded around her: 'To ascend to the Celestial Dignity, and therewith to regulate the vast foundation, to direct the manifold machinery of government, and thereby to nourish the people – this is not a matter to be lightly spoken of, but one which demands constant and serious attention. Do thou therefore be careful and observant, and let no hasty words escape thee.' She was in her seventies when she died and venerable, having reigned considerably longer than any of the men in her immediate family, while her reign, which had seen the population rise to more than five million, was a prosperous one.[30] She was, as one historian has forcefully stated, 'no passive figurehead'.[31] It is hard to disagree with this statement.

Japan's second reigning empress, Kōgyoku, ascended to the throne on the death of her husband and cousin in 641, only thirteen years after Suiko's death. She was probably the choice of the mighty Soga clan, who feared the enemies they had made, including the new empress's two adult sons.[32] Soga no Iruka, who served as Kōgyoku's chief minister, wore 'a sword day and night', but on 10 July 645 he was persuaded to leave his weapon at the door of the empress's audience chamber. He was therefore helpless when the empress's eldest son, the future Emperor Tenji ordered the guards to lock the gates behind him. Taking out a spear that he had hidden in the hall, Tenji and his supporters crowded around with weapons drawn. It was a brutal, shocking sight, with at least one of the assassins recorded as 'moist with streaming sweat, his voice was indistinct, and his hands shook'.[33] To Kōgyoku's evident horror, the wounded Iruka 'rolled over' to her as she sat on the throne, crying out that 'she who occupies the hereditary Dignity is the Child of Heaven. I, Her Servant, am conscious of no crime, and beseech Her to deign to make examination into this.' Visibly shocked, the Empress called out to her son 'I know not what has been done. What is the meaning of this?' On being told that Iruka had aspired to become emperor himself, something that was likely untrue, she simply got to her feet and left the room, leaving her minister to his fate.

As Iruka died, rain fell heavily, beating down on the palace roof and flooding the building with puddles of water, something which was considered an ill omen. It was enough to bring down the empress and her sons. Kōgyoku abdicated in favour of her younger brother, Kōtoku, who announced the beginning of the Taika (Great Reform) era and set about improving the government, including the important clarification that it was for the emperor to rule, not their advisors.

However, when Kōtoku died in 654, somewhat surprisingly, Kōgyoku retook the throne, posthumously being given a new regnal name of Empress Saimei.[34] Her second reign was rather less eventful than her first, with the empress dying in 661 at the age of sixty.

The troubles of her reign were clearly not prejudicial to other women wearing the imperial crown, since her granddaughter (and daughter-in-law), Jitō, claimed the throne on the death of her husband, Emperor Tenmu, in 686. Jitō had been raised by Kōgyoku and had been more than a consort during the reign of her uncle-husband, with this period characterised as 'joint rule'.[35] Her advice to the government was 'of the greatest assistance'.[36] She was not afraid to ride amongst her soldiers and address them as she 'mingled with the throng'. As reigning empress from 686 until 697, she has been described as a woman 'who gave the finishing touches to the consolidation of the centralised imperial regime', effectively meaning that she held almost all the power in Japan in her own hands.[37]

Few sovereigns were as active as Jitō, with the empress presiding over a period of almost unparalleled power for the imperial house. However, she abdicated in favour of her teenaged grandson Emperor

Monmu (and nephew, since he was also the son of her half-sister) when he came of age, which is what has allowed her to be interpreted as a temporary guardian of male power rather than a ruler in her own right. In reality, she continued to dominate the reign of her grandson, remaining prominent as a literary patron and avid traveller.[38] She died unexpectedly in 703, not long after she had returned from an arduous tour of her country's neglected eastern provinces. In the words of one of her biographers, Michiko Y. Aoki, 'All in all, Jitō is a brilliant exemplar testifying to the ability of Japanese women to occupy positions of power and shape the course of the nation's history.'[39] If only the Imperial Diet in 1947, or in 1889, had taken her example more seriously.

Jitō's reign came in the midst of a fascinating time of female power in Asia. At the same time as she became Empress of Japan, in China, Wu Zetian was powering her way to the throne with the force of her will (and the threat of force). A few decades earlier, the kingdom of Silla, in the south-east corner of the Korean peninsula, was under the rule of two consecutive queens: Sŏndŏk, who became queen in 632, succeeded by her kinswoman Chindŏk in 647.[40] Though they were not exactly welcomed, being selected only when there were no male candidates, these women were accepted unreservedly as rulers. Their kingdom's knowledge of the example of Empress Suiko may have helped, but their position was largely down to their top status as members of the *sŏnggol* or 'Holy Bone' class – reserved for royal family members – of the Silla dynasty's hereditary *kolp'um* ('bone-rank') system. This was essential for a ruler in early Silla, just as male line descent from the imperial royal family was crucial in the elevation of Japan's reigning empresses.

Sŏndŏk's legend presents her as an almost supernaturally gifted being, with the queen predicting an invasion from neighbouring Paekche when she spotted a huge gathering of frogs. ('The bull frogs have anger in their eyes looking like that of soldiers,' she observed).[41]

Left: An original photograph from the 1902 excavation in which Flinders Petrie discovered Merneith's tomb. The stelae contains the queen's name in hieroglyphics, although the image is reversed due to the nature of early photography.

Below left: Empress Matilda from a gospel book belonging to her granddaughter's husband. She is identified in the text as a queen – a title that was largely denied to her during her lifetime.

Above right: Margrete I of Denmark, Sweden and Norway depicted as a queen in a late fifteenth-century portrait. As the 'husband' of her kingdoms, she was not included in regnal lists until the twentieth century.

Top: Atotoztli depicted in a sixteenth-century genealogy. Although there is evidence that she reigned in Tenochtitlan, she is usually credited only as the daughter and mother of rulers.

Below left: Cleopatra depicted as a red-haired Roman matron in a first-century CE wall painting from Herculaneum which has been identified as her.

Below right: Catherine the Great on horseback in the uniform of the Preobrazhensky Life Guards, whose support was crucial in her coup. This painting depicts Catherine in male dress as a means of stressing her power and authority.

Above left: Irene of Byzantium, depicted in a twelfth-century mosaic from Hagia Sofia, now one of Istanbul's grand mosques. Now little remembered, Irene was the most powerful woman the Byzantine Empire would witness.

Above right: Teri'imaevarua II, who became queen of Bora Bora in her infancy thanks to the political maneuverings of her grandmother, Pomare IV of Tahiti. Never permitted to rule alone, she was removed from her throne following the French annexation of her kingdom.

Below left: Tamar of Georgia from a fresco in the Betania Monastery. Her rule was initially staunchly resisted, although she would go on to become Georgia's most important ruler.

Below right: The Habsburg heiress, Maria Theresia, had to fight for almost every inch of her inheritance, but is now arguably the most well-known member of the dynasty

Right: Wu Zetian, China's only reigning empress. Her rise to power was both bloody and remarkable, with Wu continuing to evoke strong opinions today.

Below: Elizabeth I depicted in her famous Armada Portrait, which was painted to celebrate her victory over the Spanish in 1588. In the background, we can see the Armada being scattered while Elizabeth's hand rests on a globe depicting the Americas.

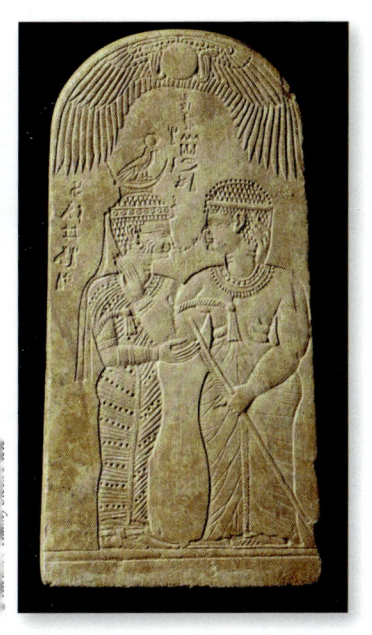

Top left: A stele depicting Queen Amanishakheto (on the right) being embraced by the goddess Amesemi. The Kandake is depicted as a strong figure, far removed from the lithe female figures of neighbouring Egypt.

Top right: Suiko, the first reigning empress of Japan, who set a precedent for strong female rule. She would be followed by seven other empresses, although female succession is currently outlawed.

Bottom: A nineteenth-century depiction of Isabel I of Castile accepting the surrender of Granada. Isabel, who is depicted riding with her army, viewed the conquest of Spain's last Islamic kingdom as a crusade.

Right: Liliʻuokalani, the last monarch of Hawaii. Highly cultured and well-travelled, Liliʻuokalani attempted to resist the annexation of her kingdom by the United States of America.

Below right: Queen Victoria, whose sixty-three-year reign witnessed Britain build the largest empire the world has ever seen. While there were initially concerns over the accession of a teenaged girl, she came to personify the age in which she lived.

Below left: A one-rupee coin minted for India in 1862. Victoria's dress, plaited hair and straightened nose have been deliberately designed to imitate an Indian ruler.

Left: The final nawab begum of Bhopal, Sultan Jehan, attending the Delhi Durbar in 1911. Observing purdah, she appeared in public only in her burka.

Below right: One of Cora Gooseberry's two surviving breastplates, which were awarded to her by the British authorities in New South Wales and were intended to symbolise her 'queenship' and authority within the Aboriginal community of Sydney.

© Mitchell Library, State Library of New South Wales, SAFE/R 251b

Below: Sālote Tupou III of Tonga made headlines around the world when she kept the roof of her carriage lowered during the coronation procession for Elizabeth II in 1953, in spite of torrential rain.

Above: The Commonwealth leaders and prime ministers posed for this photograph in Buckingham Palace in 1962. Elizabeth II was, unsurprisingly, the only woman in the room.

Below: Ngā Wai hono i te po Paki, the Maori Queen who is, at the time of writing, the world's only reigning queen. She was photographed at the funeral ceremony of her father in September 2024 in which she was also inaugurated.

She 'by nature was generous, humane, and intelligent', apparently seeking out details of poor widows and orphans to ensure their support, while she also directed her kingdom's foreign policy.[42] The succession of another woman after her death indicates that Holy Bone rank was more important than sex in early medieval Silla, but it was apparently a close-run thing.

There was considerable contact between Japan, China and the kingdoms of Korea in this early period, with the stories of the female rulers of all three passed backwards and forwards, just as the Sutras and lavish statues of the Buddha crossed national lines.[43] Certainly, surviving annals of the reigns of Sŏndŏk and Chindŏk in Silla speak of close contact with Wu Zetian's two emperor husbands, Taizong and Gaozong, who claimed the kingdom as a tributary state, with knowledge of these two reigning queens likely to have reached Wu's ears during her political apprenticeship.[44] It is unlikely to have escaped Wu's notice that her husband ordered official mourning for Queen Chindŏk on her death in 654, conferring on her the posthumous title of *Gaifu yidong sansi* or 'Commander unequalled in honour'.

Silla had become the dominant polity in Korea by the time of Wu and Jitō's reigns, effectively uniting the peninsula into a political, cultural and geographical entity that would remain until the division of the country in 1945 into the warring and suspicious neighbours of North and South Korea. At present, the likely heir to the ruling Kim family in North Korea is Kim Ju-ae, daughter of the country's 'Dear Leader'. If she does succeed, she will be the first female leader of a Korean polity since the ninth-century reign of Queen Jinseong, the third of Silla's reigning queens. Clearly, as in Japan, female rule has not been historically welcome.

Jitō's grandson, Emperor Monmu, did not long survive his elevation to power, with his mother, Genmei (both daughter-in-law and half-sister to Jitō), stepping forward to take the throne in 707.[45] In order to regularise her rule, she seems to have asserted that her father, Emperor Tenji, on his deathbed, ordained that his two daughters, Jitō and Genmei, should reign after him.[46] While Genmei undoubtedly took the throne with the ultimate aim of passing it on to her young grandson, Shōmu, there is plenty that testifies to Genmei's power. In particular, she was responsible for the establishment of the country's first capital city, settling upon Nara in what was then Yamato Province, some 200 miles south-west of Tokyo.[47] This city, which was laid out in streets of wide boulevards, with Chinese-style palaces and temples, marked a significant move away from the model of the peripatetic court.[48] Much about her new regime was based on China, with court dress, etiquette, political doctrines and even the law codes 'enthusiastically adopted' from Japan's sizeable neighbour.[49] Nara was soon home to more than 200,000 people, making it one of the largest cities in the world at its time, as people flocked both to the power of the court and for the opportunities afforded by this rapid programme of building work. The woman who conceived all this was surely no mere placeholder, marking time before the awaited ascension of her grandson.

Like that of Suiko, Genmei's reign is also notable for its literary achievements and focus on recording the country's history. The empress commissioned a young scholar, Ōno Yasumaro, to write the first work of Japanese history that still survives. It is probably significant that this monumental work, the *Kojiki,* ended with the reign of Empress Suiko, while its author sang Genmei's praises. Her 'virtue' he considered, laying it on thick, 'reaches to the utmost limits of the horse's hoof-marks: dwelling amid the Sombre Retinue', while their 'influence illumines the furthest distance attained to by vessels' prows'.[50] This illustrious monarch, who (according to her chronicler) 'having obtained Unity, illuminates the empire' abdicated in 715 in favour of her eldest daughter, Genshō, in the only instance in Japanese imperial history of female to female succession. Genshō, who was also a male-line descendant of the royal house through her father, would herself abdicate in 724, after a nine-year reign, finally placing her nephew Shōmu on the throne.

The obvious interpretation of the abdications of first Jitō in favour of her grandson, and then Genmei and Genshō for, respectively, their grandson and nephew, is that these female emperors were merely holding the throne until the male heir was able to rule. This is certainly how they have been interpreted in more recent centuries, and it has very much been used as a way to dismiss, diminish and overlook their power. Yet, can they really be said only to be temporary monarchs?

In reality, a great many Japanese sovereigns have abdicated, including Emperor Shōmu, the beneficiary of his aunt Genshō's abdication. It is a recurring phenomenon in Japanese imperial history. Shōmu retired in 749 after a twenty-five-year reign, passing the throne to his daughter, Empress Kōken. Yet, nobody says he was merely keeping the throne warm for her. In the eleventh century, the 'Insei' system of government developed, whereby Japanese emperors routinely abdicated but continued to wield power from their seclusion.[51] While there is no cohesive evidence of this arrangement as early as the seventh and eighth centuries, some of the abdicated sovereigns did retain authority. Genshō issued at least one edict from her retirement, while she also spent her time travelling and visiting the temples and palaces of her former realm. Abdication is very much not a measure of a sovereign's power, reign or status in Japan.

Emperor Shōmu – who was the nephew, grandson, great-grandson and great-great-great-grandson of reigning empresses – saw nothing unusual in women ruling. When he passed the throne to his daughter, Kōken, in 749, he retired to a monastery, with both father and daughter exhibiting a strong desire to unite the faiths of Japan. Early in Kōken's reign she announced that the statue of the ancient Shinto god Hachiman in his shrine at Usa, in the far south of Japan, was to be installed in the Todai-ji Temple in Nara, to be worshipped alongside the great Buddha there as a Great Bodhisattva (a figure travelling the path to Buddhahood).[52] Kōken, along with her monk father and nun mother attended a great ceremony in the mighty temple, which had only recently been built on her father's orders, to watch as the Shinto god became firmly identified with Buddhism. As 5000 monks recited the sutras, the court assembled to dance and worship, while it was later noticed that the characters for 'world peace' had appeared miraculously on the palace walls. It is an opaque incident, suggesting that both the reigning empress and her retired father were attempting a policy of amalgamating the two religions, and demonstrates clearly the empress's power and her ambition.

That it was not universally popular is suggested by the fact that, in 757, a Shinto priest and priestess who had been involved in the translation of the god tried to assassinate the empress.[53] It seems reasonable enough to assume that Kōken was placed under mounting political opposition at court, perhaps due to her religious policies. She abdicated the following year, taking her vows as a Buddhist nun, but she did not retire quietly to a nunnery, retaining her own powerbase and, significantly, armed retainers. Meanwhile, the new emperor, who was only a distant cousin of Kōken's, owed his elevation to the support of the powerful minister Fujiwara no Nakamaro. He aimed to be the power behind the throne and married his daughter to this new puppet emperor.

The still-powerful Kōken had fallen under the influence of a monk named Dōkyō, who may, or may not, have become her lover. (He 'shared her couch as well as directing her conscience' according to one modern historian.)[54] By 762, she was powerful enough to declare that she would rule Japan from her convent, while the disenfranchised emperor would carry out the ceremonial function of monarchy. Fujiwara no Nakamaro revolted against this edict in 764, providing Kōken with the excuse needed to resume the throne. Sending her troops to arrest the emperor, she had him exiled to Awaji Island where he could be kept under strict watch. The 'deposed Emperor of Awaji', as he would be known for the next millennium, died under suspicious circumstances the following year, only receiving his posthumous name – Emperor Junnin – 1100 years after his death on the orders of the same Emperor Meiji who removed women from the line of succession to the imperial throne. In reinstating the 'deposed Emperor of Awaji' into the line of legitimate emperors, Meiji was almost certainly making a point about his opinion of female rule.

In accordance with Japanese tradition, the nun-empress is known by the posthumous name of Empress Shōtoku during her second reign, which began in 764. The first matter she had to deal with was, understandably, her status, since Japan had never had an emperor who had taken holy orders before ('this was indeed the most unusual of developments' notes one early chronicler).[55] As a result, she issued an edict, declaring that 'although our head has been shaven and we wear Buddhist robes, we feel obliged to consult the government of the nation. As Buddha declared in the [Bommo] Sutra, "Kings, ye who take up a throne, receive the ordination of the bodisattvas."'[56] Her reappointment, essentially, had been divinely approved.

Evidently so too was Dōkyō's elevation at the side of his empress. 'Having fallen in love' with Dōkyō, as a thirteenth-century source later relates, Kōken-Shōtoku could deny him nothing, appointing him to the unprecedented position of 'Hoo', which is commonly translated into English as 'pope' or 'priest emperor', with the lowborn monk now outranking almost everyone at court.[57] He served as Kōken-Shōtoku's 'great minister of the council of state' as well as holding his religious office. 'Since,' as one chronicler relates, 'Dōkyō had his way in all things, there seems to have been no one to oppose these advancements.'[58] He did eventually fall from grace, however, when he declared to the empress that the recently enthroned god Hachiman had appeared to him in a dream and desired that he become emperor. Kōken-Shōtoku sent an emissary all the way to the god's emptied shrine in Usa more than 400 miles away, where the god's presence was still felt, to consult him herself through his priests. On hearing a report that the god had said no such thing Dōkyō's hold over her began to fade. Kōken-Shōtoku's reputation has been irrevocably damaged by her association with the ambitious monk, but her actions do at least demonstrate that it was she who remained ultimately in charge until her death in 770.

The power of Japan's emperors has always ebbed and flowed, with the Soga of Suiko and Kōgyoku's day giving way to the Fujiwara who all but reigned as perennial regents, although the same family has remained on the imperial throne throughout. Many emperors carried out the important ceremonial functions of what was a semi-divine role but had no real access to power. By the seventeenth century, the emperor had become a mere figurehead.[59] The shogun of the day, a hereditary but non-royal military title, was the undoubted power, with visitors to the country frequently mistaking them for the emperor. The cosmopolitan Roderigo de Vivero was one when he was shipwrecked in Japan in 1609 while attempting an arduous sea voyage to Mexico from the Philippines.[60] Vivero, who had been raised in the palaces of Felipe II of Spain, was well versed in the formality of the stiffest court in Europe, but even he did not recognise that the 'emperor' to whom he was taken was no such thing. Watching servants approach prostrate on their knees, he marvelled at the throne room in which he found himself, admiring the opulence and the deference shown to the richly dressed old man seated there, 'with a venerable yet lively face'.[61] The actual emperor, Go-Yōzei, was far away in the imperial capital of Kyoto, while Edo (modern Tokyo), as the seat of the shoguns, had become the *de facto* capital of Japan.

The Japan of the shoguns was very different to the world that Suiko, Jitō or the other reigning empresses had known centuries before. It had opened up (although that was soon to change), with Vivero able to speak through the translations of a Japanese Christian 'who was one of his company'. In Edo, where he was honourably escorted, he found a monastery dedicated to St Francis, which the shogun's son, Tokugawa Hidetada ('the prince' according to Vivero) had agreed to tolerate.[62] There were around 300,000 Japanese Christians according to Vivero's estimate, although their churches tended to be discrete. Edo, with its long, wide and straight streets ('much more so than those of our own Spain') was a surprisingly cosmopolitan place, while even the wooden houses, which Vivero considered inferior to Spanish dwellings when viewed from the outside, were 'perfection' once he stepped over the threshold. The streets were so clean that it was 'such that one would say that no one ever walks there'. As well as Portuguese missionaries and merchants from China and Korea, there were also a handful of other foreigners who had found themselves in Japan for a variety of reasons. These included the English shipwright, William Adams, who had been shipwrecked there in 1600 and who would rise, in the favour of the shogun, to the rank of samurai. Jan Joosten, a Dutchman who arrived with Adams, became an advisor and interpreter to the shogun, with the *Yaesu* district of central Tokyo taken from the Japanese version of his name. A hard to find memorial to him has been placed in the Yaesu Underground Shopping Mall beneath Tokyo Station.

'The prince' who Vivero met was Tokugawa Hidetada, the second of the Edo-period Tokugawa shoguns, who succeeded his famous father Tokugawa Ieyasu (Vivero's 'emperor') and was 'a man thirty-five years old, dark skinned but with a fine face and of a fair height'.[63] Although princely in appearance, Tokugawa Hidetada was not of royal blood. He aspired to majesty, wedding his daughter, Kazuko, to the unwilling Emperor Go-Mizunoo. This was an outrageous breach of protocol, with it clear that the commoner shogun was looking to place a grandson on the throne. Seeking to outplay him, Go-Mizunoo abruptly abdicated in December 1629. With only daughters surviving from the union between the emperor and Kazuko, Hidetada was forced to support the succession of his five-year-old granddaughter, Meisho, as Japan's seventh reigning empress, resurrecting the idea of female rule after more than eight centuries. Meisho, whose posthumous moniker is made up of the final characters of the names of her illustrious predecessors Genmei and Genshō, had no power. But, then, neither did the male emperors in the period. On the instructions of her father, she abdicated in 1643 at the age of nineteen and spent the next fifty-three years immured in a convent. Go-Mizunoo had proved his point and quelled the shoguns' imperial ambitions.

Meisho's reign did, however, re-establish a precedent for female rule, with Go-Sakuramachi succeeding to the throne in 1762 following the sudden death of her brother, Emperor Momozono. She reigned for nine years before abdicating in favour of her brother's then thirteen-year-old son. However, with the imperial house still required to delegate their powers to the shoguns, Go-Sakuramachi, who was Japan's last reigning empress, had little to do by way of actually ruling. Nonetheless, she was highly educated and very cultured, remaining active in Kyoto society in the decades after her reign.

Only two years after her daughter's birth in 2001, Princess Masako was hospitalised and cancelled all appearances. In the face of her continued absence from public life, the palace confirmed vaguely that she was suffering from an 'adjustment disorder' the following July.[64] The Crown Prince, who was supportive of his wife's position and furious at her treatment by both palace officials and the media, openly complained that they had moved 'to negate Masako's career and her personality', while she had 'totally exhausted herself' in her attempts to adapt to imperial life.[65] Little Princess Aiko, growing up in the tranquillity of Tokyo's Imperial Palace amongst the cherry blossom and water gardens, was likely oblivious to the controversy surrounding her birth, as well as her parents' continued failure to add a male heir to the royal nursery.

By the time Princess Aiko started kindergarten at the famous Gakushūin School in Tokyo, there were only six people in the entire world who had a claim to the Japanese throne. The youngest of these was thirty-nine, while the eldest was eighty-nine, with an average age of nearly sixty between them. It was clear to everyone that if the royal house was not to become extinct, something had to be done. Perhaps recalling the extraordinary run of 178 years between 592 and 770 CE when half of the rulers had been female, eyes began to turn towards Princess Aiko. In a poll taken just one week after Princess Aiko's birth, 86 per cent of the Japanese people were in favour of rule by an empress.[66] Even the ninety-year-old Princess Takamatsu, who was the baby's great-great-aunt and a relic from a more conservative era, was open to the idea. She published an article declaring: 'It is possible that an imperial princess will ascend the throne as the 127th emperor. Considering the long history of Japan, such an outcome should not be ruled out.' Though it had largely been overlooked or actively denied in subsequent centuries, there was, after all, very strong precedent for women taking this most venerable of thrones.

In January 2005, the Prime Minister of Japan instituted an Advisory Council, charging them to consider the future of an imperial family tree that seemingly had no buds. They sat seventeen times over the course of the year, examining the past and considering the future, acutely aware of the distinct possibility that, as they later reported, 'A situation may sooner or later arise in which there is no eligible candidate for the Imperial Throne.'[67] One option was to bring male line descendants who had been removed from the royal family in 1947 back into the imperial fold, but this seemed unfeasible. Too much time had passed and, in some cases, their closest common ancestor to the reigning emperor dated back 600 years or more. Should they permit illegitimate lines to succeed? As the Advisory Council noted, 'The present system of Imperial succession is the most stringent in history.' In fact, there really was only one solution.

Faced with 'biological extinction', the answer seemed clear to the Advisory Council writing their report in November 2005.[68] They came down firmly on the side of female succession. Such a decision, which flew in the face of the historically politically subjugated position of women in Japanese society (and in world society in general), was not lightly taken, with the precedent of the eight reigning empresses a powerful one in this tradition-led society. But then, on 6 September 2006, less than a year after the report was made, Princess Kiko, the forty-year-old wife of the Crown Prince's brother, gave birth to a son. With that, attention shifted away from Princess Aiko and towards her little cousin.

The matter has been rested for now, but it is impossible not to think that Prince Hisahito's birth has merely kicked the can down the road. Placed on pause, Japan will likely witness a reigning empress again in the not-too-distant future. Gazing back into the furthest reaches of Japan's history and its ancient royal dynasty, it is not the mythical founder Emperor Jimmu that we see but the shaman-queen Himiko, staring back at us from her bronze mirrors. Japan, the world's only remaining empire, might well add a ninth empress to its existing tally before the century is out.

CHAPTER 10:

QUEENSHIP AND COLONISATION

Victoria of the United Kingdom, Liliʻuokalani of Hawaii and the Rain Queens of the Balobedu

It was a beautiful warm morning as Queen Victoria eased herself into her chair at her writing desk at Windsor Castle on Wednesday 8 March 1893.[1] She had written millions of words and tens of thousands of letters since succeeding to the throne nearly fifty-six years before, yet it was rare for her to take up her pen in support of a fellow reigning queen. 'Victoria by the Grace of God, of the United Kingdom of Great Britain and Ireland, Queen, Defender of the Faith, Empress of India, &c, &c, &c, To Her Majesty Queen Liliuokalani, Sendeth Greeting!' The words were neat and well-formed on paper lightly lined. 'We have,' she assured her addressee, 'received and referred to our advisers the letter which you addressed to us informing us of the revolt which has taken place in your kingdom. We wish you a happy issue from your present difficulties, and We take this opportunity of renewing to your Majesty the assurance of our highest consideration and regard, and so we recommend you to the Protection of the Almighty.' The Queen almost certainly meant it when she signed, 'Your Good Friend Victoria R', but it would have been clear to Liliʻuokalani, on receiving the missive, that she could expect no help from her fellow monarch.[2]

The fact that Liliʻuokalani, a woman who would write almost as many words as Victoria over the course of her lifetime, had appealed to Britain's powerful monarch was very much a sign of her times. While Japan had spent much of the 250 years before the 1860s in self-imposed isolation, shutting out the wider world, the rest of the globe had opened up. Liliʻuokalani was born fifty years after the British Captain James Cook sailed into Hawaii in 1778, his arrival changing everything for the inhabitants of the oceanic labyrinth of eight main islands and innumerable smaller ones. Suddenly, Hawaii's cool, comfortable grass huts and fertile, volcanic landscape, were pushed into an increasingly globalised world, opening the floodgates of contact with Europe and North America. These visitors, with their alien diseases, brought tragedy. Cook had found a population of around 500,000 people living in the Hawaiian Islands. By the 1890s, there were only 35,000: an almost unfathomable calamity. Workers from China and plantation owners from Europe and America, as well as a steady stream of Christian missionaries bolstered the population, but the residents of the islands remained overwhelmingly Hawaiian by the late nineteenth century. In spite of their disproportionate political clout, white settlers made up only around 3 per cent of the population by the 1890s.

The incomers were fascinated by Hawaii, viewing it through their own cultural lens. The hula enthralled, but attempts were made to ban this traditional and sacred dance on moral grounds. The national pastime of 'surf-bathing' garnered admiration, although it was much harder that the Hawaiians made it look, with one visitor at least who tried it returning to the surface without his board and 'with a couple of barrels of water in me'.[3] Pele, goddess of fire, who had looked down from her volcano tops for eons, was replaced with the distant and paternalistic God of Abraham.

QUEENSHIP AND COLONISATION

Liliʻuokalani had an almost dual identity. Born Liliʻu Kamakaʻeha into a chiefly family, her parents immediately handed her to their distant relatives Abner Paki and his wife, Laura Konia, to raise in accordance with the Hawaiian custom of 'hanai', where children were fostered in order to create closer bonds of kinship, while still retaining ties to their birth families. Raised as their daughter, she became Lydia Kamakaʻeha Paki through a combination of baptism and adoption. She was proud of her distant kinship to the reigning dynasty, who descended from Kamehameha the Great ('a sort of Napoleon in military genius'), who had conquered the islands in 1795, just as the wider world was becoming aware of their existence.[4]

Hawaii's ruling Kamehameha dynasty, which dominated the kingdom's elective throne for nearly eighty years, produced no queens and nor did it particularly want to. This was made very clear in 1874 with the death of the short-lived King Lunalilo, who had attempted to name his relative, Emma Rooke, as his successor. Amidst much political turmoil, Emma, who was herself the widow of a previous monarch, was passed over in an assembly of the islands' chiefs in favour of a distant relative, David Kalākaua, Liliʻuokalani's brother. She was now theoretically much closer to the throne of Hawaii than she could have expected to be, but it seemed unlikely that she would ever be the nation's figurehead.

Politically, Hawaii's royal, or chiefly class, bridged the gap between the 'heathen' native population (who were by this point, in fact, mostly Christian) and the white settlers. Liliʻuokalani understood the need to keep a foot in both camps. Her native language was Hawaiian, and she would retire to her grass hut in the countryside in periods of relaxation. Yet, even in the home there could be appalling racial tensions. Liliʻuokalani's marriage to her childhood friend, the American John Owen Dominis in 1862, evoked the hostility of his mother who despised the inter-racial union, regardless of her daughter-in-law's undoubted social superiority. Lili'uokalani was devoutly patriotic, composing Hawaii's first national anthem in 1866, which pointedly replaced the British 'God Save the King' that had hitherto been used.[5] Yet the world into which she was born, on islands that sat strategically in the centre of the Pacific Ocean, were buffeted by the forces of colonisation.[6]

The nineteenth century saw the rise of industrialisation, the invention of the telegram, photography and the revolutionary installation of cross-continental railways. Yet it also witnessed the fast-expanding colonising desires of the European powers, alongside the notions of European superiority that this engendered. The era saw many crushed under the boot of oppression. As a royal woman in the nineteenth century, Lili'uokalani confronted, or engaged, with change at every moment of her life. The same was true for the Rain Queens of the Balobedu tribe, who lived in the picturesque foothills of South Africa's Drakensberg Mountains.

Maselekwane Modjadji I was renowned as 'the greatest magician of the north', with her powers so great that it persuaded her people to abandon their traditional kingship when she took the throne in 1800.[7] She was both monarch and deity, with her individual identity subsumed by a role that required her to keep the fields wet.[8] Modjadji I was an elusive figure, rarely seen. Was she, as rumours claimed, born of an incestuous relationship between a king and his daughter, a coupling that gave their offspring magical powers?[9] Were her powers darker still, with the rain summoned in the blood of human sacrificial victims? Such slanderous claims would still be recorded as fact in the 1980s.[10] There were other local rainmakers, but Modjadji I, who reputedly never experienced a day's illness in her life, was supreme in the skill. As a result, her people followed her and obeyed her, while members of neighbouring tribes or even those further afield would seek her approval. As a queen, she transgressed traditional gender roles, taking brides as tributes from her neighbours, with her wives moving into the complex of huts that she occupied in her village.[11] The Rain Queen had no peers, bypassing the usual submissive position of women in her society.

The girl born to the fourth son of George III of the United Kingdom in May 1819 was a remote prospect as a reigning monarch. Only with the death of her father, grandfather, uncles and cousins did she find herself in line to succeed to the British throne. The princess, who was forced by her strict mother to keep a daily record of her behaviour (once 'very very very very horribly naughty!!!'), was raised far from the royal court and not initially told of her royal prospects, which had become almost a certainty by the mid-1820s. Unsurprisingly, there were concerns that Victoria, who was eighteen when her uncle King William IV died, still played with dolls and shared a bedroom with her mother, and would not be up to the task ahead. The queen, on hearing of her accession on 20 June 1837, immediately insisted on her own bedroom for the first time in her life, but she still had to take her overbearing parent with her to Buckingham Palace, for propriety's sake.

When Victoria was five years into her reign, in 1843, the British flag was raised over Hawaii by Captain Lord George Paulet of the HMS *Carysfort*. It was soon realised that Paulet had grossly overstepped his orders, with the British somewhat sheepishly forced to restate the islands' independence five months later. The American novelist Mark Twain would mock Hawaii as a 'play-house "kingdom"' by infantilising an entire political system and poking fun at the king's small-scale 'drawing-rooms' and the grand titles given to the officers of state, yet the United States, Britain and Japan, amongst other world powers, watched the kingdom closely.[12] Twain, as were so many other European or American visitors, was guilty of viewing Hawaii through the prism of their own cultural convictions.

We are fortunate to know so much about the reigning queens of the nineteenth century thanks to the reams of words that were written about what was still an anomalous role. While the lives of the Rain Queens survive through the accounts of others, in the case of Victoria, we can read her journals. She kept these diligently almost every day from the age of thirteen until only nine days before her death at the age of eighty-one, with the originals surviving in the Royal Collection. Victoria, who spent her final days still active in the business of government, survives in the words that she wrote. We can see her passions and her desires, as well as her troubles and her successes through her own eyes.

The same can be said for Lili'uokalani who, like Victoria, was encouraged in her childhood to write her diary, something which later became a habit. Many of her volumes from later in her life survive, written in her neat hand in brown leather-covered pocket diaries produced by the Bancroft Company of San Francisco, which also (as they proudly proclaimed in printed text) contained 'useful memoranda, and tables for reference', such as the festivals and feasts of the church, a list of San Francisco fire alarm stations and the respective values of foreign coins, something that may have come in handy for Lili'uokalani during her travels.[13]

It is a thrill to pull out a day, sometimes at random, and read the mundane or the extraordinary events in the lives of these powerful women. Their words, however, have not reached us entirely unredacted. Victoria's youngest daughter would butcher her mother's journals after her death based on her own sense of propriety, robbing us of her most strident voice. Lili'uokalani herself likely burned some of her more controversial diaries, with the surviving volumes those in which the Hawaiian queen felt she had nothing to hide.

Queen Masalanabo Modjadji II succeeded as Rain Queen in 1854, following the ritual suicide of her mother, Modjadji I, who could not be permitted to suffer from illness or the rigours of old age. She was an elusive figure to the few Europeans who visited her realm. Friedrich Reuter, a persistent German gentleman who had become a missionary in spite of fierce parental opposition, arrived amongst the Balobedu in 1881 but seems never to have actually seen her, instead conducting tense negotiations through intermediaries.[14] His journals, which survive in the archives of the Berlin Missionary Society, paint Modjadji II as a villain, suspicious of this 'white intruder' – though by his own reckoning, he knew nothing of the Balobedu's customs, manners and conditions and did not speak their language. She attempted to turn him away four times, but eventually grudgingly relented, only to become openly hostile when he convinced one of her chiefs, Khasane, to convert. Modjadji II tried to persuade Khasane to leave the mission by enticing him to take a second bride, but when this failed war erupted between the pair, lasting on and off for some years. There was likely an added political dimension to the conflict, with Khasane telling Reuter that he viewed himself as heir to the throne due to his royal blood and his own rainmaking ability, but Modjadji was also understandably hostile to Europeans and Christianity, which she denounced (according to Reuter) as a 'lie by white people'.[15]

Modjadji II would be immortalised as 'She-Who-Must-Be-Obeyed' by the British novelist H. Ridger Haggard when he struck literary gold in his depiction of a mysterious, white-skinned, immortal and highly sexualised African queen in his story *She: A History of Adventure*. He picked up the scent of the Rain Queen during his time living in South Africa, as the British and the Dutch-descended Boers – both tiny percentages of the population – vied for control of what had never before been a unified country. There was something about the idea of a woman reigning deep in the Transvaal that captured the European imaginations. Indeed, despite considerable evidence to the contrary, Europeans were determined to depict the Rain Queens as white skinned. Jan Christian Smuts, Apartheid-era Prime Minister of South Africa in the first half of the twentieth century, when invited to write a foreword to his nephew and niece-in-laws' study of the Balobedu people, mused on whether the queens were the descendants of fabled Dutch girls lost in the mountains and forests of South Africa.[16] Even his nephew and nephew's wife, the Kriges, who had lived amongst the Balobedu as anthropologists, bought into this to some extent, explaining, 'That Mujaji [Modjadji] II, who died in 1894, was fair cannot be disputed. Fairness is a feature of many Lovedu [Balobedu]; it is a highly prized quality.'[17] The idea of her whiteness made her an acceptable figure of fascination, but it cannot be supported by the evidence. As Smuts, a firm adherent of South Africa's racist system of government, noted, 'For at least half a century the Rain-Queen and her people and the curious stories about them have interested me.' To feed his curiosity, it was essential that, in his mind, she was white. This was not, however, true.

It is a strange thing to note that Victoria, whose reign saw an expansion of the British Empire so large that it was boasted that the sun never set on the lands over which she ruled, rarely set foot outside Britain. She journeyed little farther than her annual summer holidays to the south of France, where she enjoyed the sights of the Riviera, receiving visitors, admiring gardens and soaking up the sunshine.[18] Victoria expected the empire to come to her. To a very great extent, it did, leading to encounters – all too frequently painfully one-sided – with fellow monarchs, different political systems and diverse (from a Western European perspective) ways of life.

In geographically isolated Hawaii, there was a curiosity about the European world that they knew to be so dominant, with more than one Hawaiian monarch watching from their ship as Honolulu, with its neat white cottages and green window shutters, disappeared from view. In 1823, only forty-five years after the nation received its unasked for first visit from Captain Cook on the HMS *Resolution*, King Kamehameha II and his wife, Queen Kamāmalu, began the trend, boarding a whaling ship, which took them to the newly declared empire of Brazil before the wind drove them purposefully across the Atlantic to Britain. They caused a sensation when they were spotted in the royal box at the Theatre Royal in London, but they died from measles, to which Hawaiians had no immunity, less than two months after their arrival.

It was an inauspicious start, although relations between the royal families of both nations were always cordial. Queen Victoria welcomed a small but steady stream of royal Hawaiian visitors to her court, including Lili'uokalani's foster sister, Bernice Pauahi Bishop in 1876, who was presented to the queen exquisitely dressed in a Parisian silk gown augmented by a train nearly four yards long.[19] Queen Emma Rooke, the widow of King Kamehameha IV, proved a particular favourite, although her charming manners surprised the British queen, who noted on meeting her at Windsor on 9 September 1865 that 'the lady looks like an uncivilised savage', before adding her surprise that she 'is, on the contrary peculiarly civilised & well mannered, very pleasing & clever'. Such prejudice says much more about insular, sheltered Victoria than it does about cultured Emma Rooke. The British queen never questioned Emma's royal status, rank or right to meet her on a personal level, inviting her to sit on the sofa between her and her daughter, the Crown Princess of Germany. Yet, it is very clear that she was surprised by Emma, noting approvingly that the Hawaiian dowager 'was dressed in just the same widow's weeds as I wear'. The pair struck up a close friendship, with Victoria admiring her 'fine features & splendid soft eyes', while also noting that she was 'dark, but not more so than an Indian'.

Lili'uokalani's brother, King Kalākaua, also made an excellent impression during his world tour of 1881, in which he was feted by governments globally, presenting (as he said himself in a souvenir booklet distributed in Hawaii on his orders) 'the style and manner of a highly cultivated gentleman'. It was during his absence that his equally cultured sister Lili'uokalani received her first taste of royal authority, ruling as regent.

On meeting King Kalākaua, Victoria compared this bewhiskered giant of a man to her friend, observing that he was 'darker than Queen Emma, but with the same cast of features, black but not woolly hair, more like a New Zealander, but without their thick lips'. Victoria was fascinated by remote parts of the world that she would never visit, but she was oblivious to the fact that she presided over an empire that caused lasting harm to race relations across the world. Emma was, in fact, mixed race. Having a white British grandfather had counted against her when she vied for the crown against Kalākaua in 1874.

While the Hawaiian monarchs travelled frequently, the world of the Rain Queen was smaller and shrinking. The queens could not leave their territories for fear that the rains would cease, something that was of real concern to the agricultural Balobedu, who remain renowned for their extensive knowledge of plants and trees, growing their crops in the reddish, loamy soils of their scattered fields. As the nineteenth century progressed, the 30,000 Balobedu people were increasingly encircled. Their lands encompassed mountains and flat country, with magnificent cycad trees abundant in the forests, but the boundaries drawn by the newly arrived Europeans meant that it was densely populated, with villages of small, round thatched huts pressing up to each other.[20] Masalanabo Modjadji II lived in a complex of huts such as these.

While Victoria remains the personification of almost an entire century, there was a time when the continuation of her reign had seemed less certain. During her long lifetime she faced eight assassination attempts, mostly when she was out driving in her carriage. Her early days as queen, too, had been floundering, with Victoria becoming entirely dependent on the advice of her first prime minister, Lord Melbourne,

QUEENSHIP AND COLONISATION

('dear Lord M'), whom she looked upon as a father figure, but whom the press suggested was a paramour. 'Mrs Melbourne' compounded her unpopularity by insinuating that her mother's unmarried lady-in-waiting, Lady Flora Hastings, was pregnant, only for her to die from liver cancer (the true cause of her distended belly) in 1839.*

The deepest crisis of Victoria's reign came later when she retreated from public view following her husband Prince Albert's early death in 1861, becoming introspective in her misery.[21] The 1860s saw a growing republican movement. Victorian widows were expected to mourn openly, but the queen's mourning for Albert, which would last for nearly forty years, was particularly extravagant, with the queen requiring her newlywed children to pose miserably with a bust of the late Prince Consort as a means of including him in what should have been happy occasions. Her dear friend and sometime prime minister, Benjamin Disraeli, declined a proffered visit from the queen when it became clear that he was dying in 1881: 'She would only ask me to take a message to Albert.'

But by 1887 – her fiftieth year on the throne – Victoria's widow's weeds, which she would wear for the remainder of her life, belied the fact that she had left her husband behind. She was nearly seventy and about to surpass all previous British reigning queens, as well as most of its kings, in her longevity and her hold on her throne. The celebrations that were planned for the occasion of her Golden Jubilee were intended as a way of demonstrating a Britain at the peak of its powers. As such, Victoria wanted the world to attend.

Unlike her British counterpart, Lili'uokalani did not find domestic happiness in her marriage, although she too would appoint her spouse

---

* Victoria wrote in her journal on 2 February 1839 that 'Lady Flora had not been above 2 days in the house, before Lehzen [Victoria's old governess] and I discovered how exceedingly suspicious her figure looked,- more have since observed this, and we have no doubt that she is – to use the plain words – with child!!'.

233

as prince consort following her accession. John Owen Dominis had been reluctant initially to wed; following the marriage, the two quickly realised that they were sexually incompatible (she was 'frigid', complained her husband who consoled himself with mistresses).[22] Liliʻuokalani had received no training in how to run a household, earning rebuke after rebuke from her mother-in-law, who resented her son's marriage and 'Lydia's' (as she always called her daughter-in-law) inadequacies in the home. Frustrated domestically, Liliʻuokalani channelled her energies into her political ambitions, willingly accepting her brother, King Kalākaua's, request that she accompany his wife Queen Kapiolani to Britian to attend Queen Victoria's Golden Jubilee celebrations. She embraced the opportunity, devoting a considerable portion of her autobiography to the trip.

It was a long journey to London and an exciting one, with the royal Hawaiian party taking a ship to San Francisco before being feted as they crossed the US overland, visiting the White House and seeing the sights, including the famous mummies of New York's Metropolitan Museum. This in fact, somewhat unnerved Liliʻuokalani, finding one – a long dead royal woman – too lifelike for comfort, with 'the curiosity almost too startling for enjoyment', since 'it spoke too plainly of death and burial'.[23] Queen Victoria, who coincidentally spent a portion of that same day – Monday 16 May 1887 – in contemplation in the Frogmore Mausoleum, which was the final resting place of her beloved Albert, would likely have found the sight less disturbing. She presided over an age still renowned for its morbidity, with postmortem photography and jewellery made from a deceased's hair common.

The Hawaiian party arrived in good time for the Jubilee, landing in Liverpool where they were met by curious crowds that Liliʻuokalani, watching from the deck, estimated to be in their thousands.[24] They were well received, with her sister-in-law, Queen Kapiolani, obligingly taking up a silver spade to plant a tree at Rackheath Hall in Norfolk as

QUEENSHIP AND COLONISATION

they made their way towards London (a surprisingly commonplace royal requirement). A stone plaque on a folly, Thorpe Tower close to Norwich, also proudly declares that 'Queen Kapiolani ascended this tower 6 June 1887'.[25] They made something of a triumphal progress, escorted by a troop of 100 British soldiers and lodged comfortably in the Alexandra Hotel in London at Queen Victoria's expense. Lili'uokalani spent the next days shopping, sightseeing and attending a concert at the Royal Albert Hall, where she and the rest of her party heard the great Madame Adelina Patti sing. Finally, on 20 June Queen Victoria arrived from Scotland and Queen Kapiolani, accompanied by Lili'uokalani and the rest of the party, went that afternoon to call on her at Buckingham Palace. They were far from the only royals to do so, joining a throng of visitors, including close family of the queen and those that had come from further afield, including Thailand, Japan and Persia.

Lili'uokalani would remember her first interaction with a reigning queen for the rest of her life, recalling in her autobiography that she was greeted by Prime Minister Lord Salisbury. While she waited, she noticed some of the ladies of the court peeping through the cracks in the door, curious to see the visitors from Hawaii. They soon entered a moderate sized room, furnished only by a sofa and two chairs. Victoria stood to receive them, while Lili'uokalani recalled that she greeted 'her sister sovereign, Kapiolani' with a kiss on each cheek and 'then, turning to me, she kissed me once on the forehead', something which differs from the simple handshake of Lili'uokalani's contemporary diary and suggests that she may have subconsciously embellished her encounter with Victoria when she herself had become a reigning queen – an equal.[26] While Victoria and Kapiolani chatted through interpreters, Lili'uokalani spoke amiably in English with Victoria's children, Prince Arthur and Princess Beatrice. She wrote, 'Queen Victoria then entered into a little conversation with me, confining her remarks chiefly to educational matters, and asked me some detail about the schools of the Hawaiian Islands.' It was all very polite, very genteel, before the British queen 'again kissed me on the forehead; then she took my hand, as though she had just thought of something which she had been in danger of forgetting, and said "I want to introduce to you my children."'[27] Lili'uokalani may have later remembered the meeting as more intimate, more significant, than it was, although Colonel Curtis Iaukea, an important Hawaiian court official, who was also present, recorded that Victoria spoke happily of King Kalākaua's visit a few years before.[28] Lili'uokalani was thrilled to meet the queen recalling that 'thus terminated my first interview with one of the best of women and greatest of monarchs'.[29]

The days following Lili'uokalani and Victoria's meeting passed in a whirl of social events and public engagements for both monarchs, culminating in the jubilee service itself in Westminster Abbey, in which Lili'uokalani was seated next to the elderly Duchess of Mecklenburg-Strelitz. She spent the day amongst fellow royalty, being escorted into Buckingham Palace by Victoria's son, Prince Alfred, whom Lili'uokalani had earlier met in Hawaii, and speaking animatedly with the future Kaiser Wilhem II ('who proved to be a most sociable neighbour') throughout the celebratory banquet.[30] They went together to view the gifts presented to Queen Victoria, with Lili'uokalani certain that the 'unique frame placed on an easel, in the centre of which was an embroidered piece, with the letters "V.R." worked in rare royal feathers, while the frame itself was studded with diamonds', was the most impressive. Victoria's journal suggests that it was less well received than Hawaii might have hoped, with the queen describing it as 'a present, of very rare feathers, but very strangely arranged'.[31] It was, however, one of a select number of jubilee presents displayed to the public in St James's Palace. In 1888, the gift was taken to the Bethnal Green Museum but, sadly, this is where the trail grows cold. Victoria's monogram, wreathed in royal yellow feathers from the ʻŌʻō bird, perhaps languishes unrecognised in a museum storeroom or, more likely, the precious feathers simply faded and perished with time. The small bird which provided the feathers was known as the Royal Bird, with its gradual extinction over the course of the nineteenth century echoing that of many of the monarchs who so valued its feathers.

Like their royal bird, the days of the Hawaiian royal family were numbered even before Liliʻuokalani could ascend to her throne. Theirs was an independent sovereign state, something that was recognised in treaty after treaty with the United States, Britain and the rest of the world, but this did not stop greedy eyes gazing upon them. A visitor to Hawaii in the late nineteenth century, while intrigued by the islands' volcanoes, palm trees and sandy bays, would also have noted substantial sugar plantations; a considerable change from the pre-contact islands which did not even have a concept of landownership.

A visitor could gaze at the 1000-acre plantation of the American James Makee on Maui, a whaleboat captain turned entrepreneur whose $1 million investment yielded him around 800 tons of sugar a year and was amongst the biggest on the islands. Native Hawaiians were not entirely excluded from the sugar business – King Kalākaua went into partnership with the slender, severe-looking Makee on another estate – but it was like an unstoppable freight train of colonial greed rolling towards the archipelago. In 1879 the sugar estates in Hawaii were worth less than $10 million per year. By 1900 the business was worth $40 million and 10 per cent of the sugar consumed in the United States was Hawaiian.[32] It drove immigration. It drew the attention of ambitious foreigners and, to the minds of the sugar planters and many consumers of their products, if they thought about Hawaii at all, it made the islands too economically important to remain solely in the hands of a Westernised, but still (in their view) dangerously native, elite. Conflict was inevitable since, although Hawaii had been greatly depopulated, native-born Hawaiians were still a vast majority, a fact that Kalākaua, and later, Lili'uokalani, understood well.

The Hawaiian monarchy was a constitutional monarchy when the Kalākaua dynasty took the throne, with the written constitution of 1864 providing for the establishment of a cabinet, whose appointments were owed entirely to the monarch's pleasure. Kalākaua's reign provided much of the blueprint for Lili'uokalani's, with the king seeking to push and protect Hawaiian culture. At the same time, he very much sought to present the Hawaiian monarchy as a Westernised one, with one recent historian considering that 'he also worked to frame Hawaii as a sovereign nation within a global market': with the building of his Florentine residence, the Iolani ('bird of heaven') Palace, as well as the installation of electricity and the telephone, he intended to signal Hawaii's civility to a world that was often highly uncivilised to those that it sought to dominate or conquer. On 12 February 1883, nine years after his accession to the throne, Kalākaua also staged a Western-style coronation with a ball, regatta and fireworks displays.

None of this was enough. Lili'uokalani was just returning to her hotel from a final garden party staged by Queen Victoria when she learned that a group of US settlers had staged a coup against her brother, forcing him to agree to a new constitution. Under this new 'Bayonet Constitution', power was placed in the hands of a cabinet over whom the king could exercise no control, while property ownership became a requirement for voters and the residency required to vote was lowered to only three years. This, unsurprisingly, disenfranchised most ordinary Hawaiians, placing the power firmly in the hands of the US and European settlers, with the king a nominal figurehead. News of this disaster hung over Lili'uokalani as she made her slow return to Hawaii shortly afterwards. Kalākaua, who railed against the limits placed on his authority, sought aid from the US, but his health was in tatters. He died in San Francisco on 20 January 1891.[33]

QUEENSHIP AND COLONISATION

Since his successor was a woman, and a middle aged one at that, the king's opponents had no doubts that they could bully her into submission. Alarmed, Lili'uokalani, who refused to spend the night in the Iolani Palace for fear of another coup, was forced to immediately swear an oath to uphold the hated Bayonet Constitution.

As she recalled a few years later, 'few persons have ever been placed without a word of warning in such a trying situation, and I doubt if there was any other woman in the city who could have borne with passable equanimity what I had to endure that day'.[34] While Lili'uokalani's opponents, who viewed themselves as superior to the native Hawaiians amongst whom they lived, would have bullied any monarch, there is no doubt that they believed the new queen's sex would make her all the more pliable. The role envisaged for Hawaii's first reigning queen was that of figurehead. 'I doubt,' wrote Lili'uokalani, 'if many men could have passed successfully through such an ordeal.' She had been underestimated, making that clear at her first cabinet meeting, held the day after King Kalākaua's funeral. In contravention of the Bayonet Constitution, Lili'uokalani refused to sign her cabinet ministers' commissions unless they first resigned and were reappointed by her. It was an early victory for Hawaii's new queen, but one that marked her out to her opponents as a stubborn and dangerously independent monarch.

Lili'uokalani's diaries frustratingly do not survive for the first year of her queenship. It is likely she destroyed them herself. She involved herself in the ceremony of monarchy, staging a grand costume ball at her brother's lavish Iolani Palace in Honolulu and undertaking a tour of her islands with her husband, the new Prince Consort, at her side. While her guests dined on fine French plates, embossed with her monogram and used napkins held in place with silver napkin rings, she was a surprisingly isolated figure. John Dominis, Lili'uokalani's husband, died suddenly only eight months into the reign, while her niece, the new Crown Princess Kaʻiulani, was attending school in Britain. Most of the queen's old friends from Hawaii's Royal School were dead. She was, effectively, the last of her generation.

Rain Queen Modjadji II also found her rule severely tested due to the forces of expansion. By the 1890s, she had reigned over the Balobedu for four decades and, while her people would admit no signs of weakness in her, to outsiders she appeared ancient and was so shaky that she had to be carried in a chair.[35] Modjadji II remained a political force to be reckoned with as she 'played a game of cat and mouse' with the Boer Commandant General, Piet Joubert – a political rival to the more famous Paul Kruger and a man bent on expanding the Boer Transvaal state in South Africa in 1894 by the use of military force against the local tribes. According to the memoirs of one of his officers, they arrived at a difficult battleground, flanked by mountains and rivers and amidst heavy forests which rendered their 1200 mounted troops somewhat redundant.[36] Reading these memoirs, one is left with the sense that the Boers found the Rain Queen rather unsporting, since her men weaved in and out of crevasses and other hiding spots and were found to have old, but perfectly serviceable, firearms loaded with homemade bullets made by mixing fine pebbles with lead. Those that did not have guns were armed with bows and arrows.

Modjadji II also played for time, sending one of her advisors down into Joubert's camp. He (the Commandant-General's Officer recalled) 'explained that she wants peace and wishes to prevent all bloodshed', making 'pious speeches' and asserting that his mistress would rather surrender than go to war. The Rain Queen was able to string out negotiations over some weeks as she continued to promise to surrender, sometimes sending five or seven men down to give themselves up as a sign of willingness, but declining to come down from the mountains herself. Finally, amidst Joubert's obviously growing frustration, he was promised that she was on her way, halting his orders to advance once more. The Boers were in a state of excitement as they waited for 'her majesty, the old witch', having heard that she could strike them blind with just one glance at her face, as well as other supernatural powers that she enjoyed.

The woman who finally arrived, carried in an old armchair was, therefore, something of a disappointment. Joubert's officer had been told by another soldier, who had claimed to have seen her, that she was 'white, pure white!', but the woman who was presented to them was 'slightly yellow in complexion' and very elderly ('a decayed, cane-horned old creature').[37] As she sat facing the general, her lower jaw snapped up and down as if she was speaking, leaving Joubert constantly questioning the interpreter over what she was saying. Nonetheless, as a surrendered war leader, she was promptly arrested, but she was not badly treated. Joubert's wife Hendrina provided her with her own clothes, as well as assisting the Rain Queen in dressing. Having effectively demonstrated their dominance, the Boers ransomed the queen for 5000 cattle although, as Joubert's officer noted grumpily, the Balobedu promptly recaptured 1500 of them, so that she was able to return to her people with very little loss and still wearing the general's wife's finery. Later, some of the Balobedu people present would quietly inform two white anthropologists that a substitute had been employed: no European was permitted to see the queen, adding to the mystique of this most elusive of monarchs.

Although Modjadji II had likely fared as well as possible and spared her people prolonged and futile bloodshed, it was the beginning of the end for the second Rain Queen: she had died by her own hand before the end of that year, as tradition required. She appointed her successor – the daughter of one of her wives (who were permitted to take male lovers with the aim of conceiving children for the queen) – and took leave of her all-male council before retiring to her hut. Once alone, she took a poison containing the brain and spinal fluid of a crocodile, guaranteed to cause a slow, lingering death, as her people – oblivious – continued as normal. She was buried standing up beneath the place where the sacred drums of her rituals were stored. There, it was hoped, she could continue to take care of her country from beyond the grave, but it was remembered decades later that her death ushered in three years of droughts that caused the death of a third of the population.

Pushed from their lands and, for decades, politically disenfranchised, against the odds, the Balobedu and their Rain Queens endured. Up until the death of the last undisputed Rain Queen in 2005, the queens remained subjects of fascination, though, even while usually secluded from the Western gaze, they were increasingly expected to navigate an increasingly Westernised world. Modjadji III, who had reigned since 1895, disappointed a German visitor in 1953 for wearing 'a cheap European dress made, moreover, for a stouter woman', but her jewels were traditional and stunning.[38] She sat on a carpet, where only a few years before there had been a lion skin. For the enthronement of Modjadji IV six years later, more than twenty oxen were slaughtered for a feast that also included sandwiches, tomatoes and fruit salad. In an echo of the formal courts of Europe, Queen Modjadji IV was escorted to her enthronement by one of her ladies of honour. The ceremony drew huge crowds, with Balobedu boys climbing trees in order to view the proceedings, just as British boys on 28 June 1838 had climbed the trees in the Mall to watch the young Queen Victoria travel by coach to her coronation. The Rain Queen's inauguration was of national importance to South Africa, with even Michiel de Wet Nel, the Minister for Bantu Administration and Development for South Africa's racist Apartheid government, there to present the ceremonial mace, crowned with a wooden bush pig.[39] Seated on a carved wooden throne in her leopard skin robes, the queen received the mace to signify her accession. For Victoria at Westminster Abbey 121 years earlier, it was St Edward's Crown ('which hurt me a good deal'), then nearly

200 years old. For both women, these ceremonial items – one a mace, the other a crown – imbued them with the authority to rule. Victoria understood this all too well, writing in her journal that night, 'I really cannot say how proud I feel to be the Queen of such a Nation.'[40]

Lili'uokalani received no coronation, although it is likely that she would have done, had she reigned longer, with her brother's crowning a fusion of Hawaiian and European. On taking her place as queen, Lili'uokalani's overarching desire was, understandably, to overturn the Bayonet Constitution and 'restore some of the ancient rights of my people', as she later contended. In the Hawaiian State Archives today there survives a draft constitution and other documents relating to it, some in Lili'uokalani's own hand.[41] While she returned the power to appoint cabinet ministers to the monarch, she also made provision for the legislature to remove a cabinet minister without her assent if so required, belying claims that she was power hungry.[42] Found amongst her papers, her draft constitution declared that 'God hath endowed all men with certain inalienable rights; among which are life, liberty, and the right of acquiring, possessing, and protecting property, and of pursuing and obtaining safety and happiness'. She permitted freedom of worship, free speech, freedom to assemble and protest and the writ of habeas corpus, as well as the right to a fair trial. The judiciary was to be impartial, while she also barred slavery.[43] Although moderate and reasonable in tone, in the end it amounted to nothing.

Queen Lili'uokalani did not foresee the end of her reign or the cessation of Hawaiian independence – a blindness that is understandable although, to a certain extent, somewhat culpable. She finally decided to bring in her new constitution on 14 January 1893, six days short of the second anniversary of her reign. She dissolved the legislature and was immediately met with rebellion from the white settlers.[44] On 16 January 1893, quite without orders and certainly in defiance of international law that recognised Hawaii as a sovereign state, John L. Stevens, the US Minister to the Hawaiian Kingdom, ordered 150 men of the USS *Boston* to go ashore to protect the rights of the rebels. They captured the kingdom and deposed the queen. In her formal protest she noted furiously, 'I yield to the superior force of the United States of America.'[45, 46]

While there had long been talk of the United States, which had shown such an interest in this distant archipelago, taking over control of Hawaii, the government in Washington was taken just as much by surprise as the Hawaiians. Liliʻuokalani would fight for the return of her throne all her life, railing against the new Republic of Hawaii and, later, in 1899, the formal secession of Hawaii to the United States. She had friends in high places, including President Grover Cleveland, who would entertain her in her exile when she journeyed to Washington, and even Queen Victoria, who wrote her such a friendly, but empty, letter of commiseration.[47] Liliʻuokalani sought to make use of these worldwide contacts, with letters of appeal to the President of France and that entertaining dinner party companion Kaiser Wilhelm, found during a search of her papers. She would later be convicted of misprision of treason and sentenced to imprisonment in the Iolani Palace, where she had once reigned supreme and where she was now taken at gunpoint.[48] In the splendour of the beautiful house her brother had built, Liliʻuokalani occupied a simple, uncarpeted room, furnished with a single bed, a sofa, a small table and chair and a few other items of furniture. It was, at least (as she recalled) light and airy and she would write her autobiography there, calling it provocatively, but accurately, 'Hawaii's Story'. With her deposition died Hawaii's independence.[49] She formally signed the act of abdication, in her prison, on 22 January 1894, bringing the kingdom of Hawaii to an end.

Part of her legacy is that, in her later life she carefully translated and published that most sacred of oral records, the 'Kumulipo', an 'ancient chant' that gave a history of Hawaii through its chiefs all the way back to 'the slime which established the earth'.[50] In her preface, Lili'uokalani spoke of the chant's value 'to genealogists and scientists', but she also recognised its importance as folklore since 'language itself changes, and there are terms and allusions herein to the natural history of Hawaii, which might be forgotten in future years without some such history as this to preserve them to prosperity'. The 'Kumulipo' belonged to her family: it was their genealogy, their history, and to publish it in English was both to preserve it and, most pertinently, raise awareness of Hawaii's plight in the final years of the nineteenth century, as well as the continuing legitimacy of her dynasty.

Lili'uokalani would end her life in 1917, an old woman who had long since retired from the political arena. Her counterpart, Victoria of the United Kingdom, lived to an even grander age, dying peacefully in her bed in Osborne House in 1901, one of her most private residences. The two women, who knew and liked each other, belonged to different arenas, living out the daily events of their life far away. Yet, when we read their journals, their letters or other literary remains of their lives, there is a remarkable synchronicity. What it meant to be a queen in nineteenth-century Hawaii was not so different to that of nineteenth-century Britain; they also shared some of the experiences and hurdles of the many women who had gone before them or claimed thrones since their times.

The end of both reigns marked the passing of an era. Victoria's line and legacy endures, while Hawaii will almost certainly never have another monarch, let alone a reigning queen. In Victoria, we see the personification of the nineteenth century ('the Victorian Age'), while in Lili'uokalani, we witness 'Hawaii's Story', with 7000 marching to the Iolani Palace on the hundredth anniversary of her overthrow, in protest. The Rain Queens of the Balobedu tell a similar story: enduring through the turmoil of the past few centuries. The world opened up in the colonial era, bringing opportunities but also despair. Hawaii was, as Liliʻuokalani wrote, 'crushed under the weight of a social order and prejudice with which even another century of preparation would hardly fit it to cope'.[51] It was a change with which she, and so many of her reigning counterparts, failed to navigate.

CHAPTER 11:
AGE OF EMPRESSES

The Nawab Begums of Bhopal, Victoria of India, Cora Gooseberry of Sydney, Ranavalona I of Madagascar

Nazar Mohammad Khan was sleeping in his palace gardens on a sunny day in November 1819 when the peace was shattered by a pistol shot.[1] As attendants came running, they discovered Nazar, the nawab (or princely ruler) of Bhopal dead, his eight-year-old brother-in-law, Fajudar Mohammad Khan, standing over him with a gun. Amidst recriminations and suspicions that the shooting may have been less accidental than the young 'assassin' would admit, it was unclear who was to succeed. At the funeral, Nazar's teenaged widow, Qudsia Begum, stepped forward. Removing her veil, she declared that she intended to reign.[*] Qudsia Begum's actions were audacious, but no one liked to object lest suspicion for Nazar's death be laid on them.

---

[*] Surprisingly, claims that this was an accidental death were largely accepted at the time. For example, Major William Hough, who wrote a history of Bhopal, considered it an 'unhappy accident' since 'the child always appeared very fond of the Nuwub [sic]' (William Hough, *A Brief History of the Bhopal Principality in Central* India (Calcutta: Baptist Mission Press, 1845), p115). Nazar's granddaughter, Shah Jehan Begum, considered assassination more likely (Shah Jahan Begum of Bhopal, *The Taj-Ul Ikbal Tarikh Bhopal or, The History of Bhopal*, trans. H.C. Barstow (Calcutta, 1876), p41.

WOMEN WHO RULED THE WORLD

When seeking to establish her rule, Qudsia Begum could look towards precedent for Muslim women taking up the reins of power, both as regent or (occasionally) as monarch in their own right, as Fatima Mernissi's illuminating *The Forgotten Queens of Islam* makes clear.[2] In the second half of the eighteenth century, Bhopal was ruled by the powerful regent Mamola Bai.[3] In the Mughal Empire, too, whose monarchs ruled as overlords over all the kingdoms and principalities of India, there had been mighty female figures, in spite of the strict Purdah under which the women of the imperial harems were expected to live. Empress Nur Jahan (c.1577–1645), superseded them all, rising to dominance over her cultured, but somewhat ineffectual spouse, Jahangir.[4] She effectively established a form of co-rule, but failed to secure her own independent regime in widowhood. Finding herself forcibly retired, the woman who had ridden into battle and hunted tigers alongside the men of her court devoted herself to planning gardens and supervising the building of the exquisite tomb of I'timād-ud-Daulah, nicknamed the 'Baby Taj', in Agra.

Most of these examples would have been unknown to Qudsia, although she may have heard of Sultana Radiyya, who had reigned in Delhi between 1236 and 1240.[5] Qudsia certainly did not see her elevation to power as at odds with her faith, while she also raised her daughter as a future ruler. She was pragmatic, taking the decision to abandon purdah around 1832, which had required her to wear a veil in public and screen herself off from unrelated men in her palace, to better facilitate her rule. She also knew that she would need to negotiate with the East India Company who had effectively superseded the Mughal Empire and which, by 1819 was almost synonymous with the British state.

The subcontinent, rich in its centuries of history, had long fallen under the greedy gaze of Britain. The East India Company, founded by merchants and seafarers, received its royal charter in 1600 to 'venture' to the East, something that it did tentatively at first and then with a forcefulness that astounded those who witnessed this colonisation by a joint stock company. The East India Company changed the rulers of India from the famed Mughal emperors to the aristocrats, merchants and tradesmen of Britain, whose shares in the company entitled them to the dividends of the spoils.

Bhopal's independence had been born at the start of the eighteenth century when its ruler the Afghan Dost Muhammad Khan broke away from the weakened Mughal Empire. The British, who, by a treaty made with the former nawab in 1818 held Bhopal's 7000 square miles as a dependency and made plain their dislike of female rule, accepted Qudsia's fait accompli, provided that she abided by the system of 'subordinate cooperation' and the stationing of a garrison of red-coated troops within her borders.[6]

In order to rule, Qudsia and her female successors in Bhopal had to learn to do business with the small North Atlantic island of Britain, a position that would have been unthinkable to Bhopal's nawabs in earlier centuries. She was not the only one. It is a strange fact – perhaps a coincidence, but probably not – that the nineteenth century witnessed a dramatic rise in the number of reigning queens, from Victoria, Liliʻuokalani, the Rain Queens of the Balobedu and Pomare IV, to Isabel II of Spain, Maria of Portugal and Brazil, Cora Gooseberry of Sydney and the reigning queens of Madagascar, to name but a few. It is highly singular that in this time of exploration and increasing global contact, but also asset-stripping and atrocities, that across the world a very high number of reigning queens emerged to rule. Undoubtedly, even over vast oceans, they looked to each other for precedents but they also faced challenges unknown to their predecessors: the way in which Victoria, as Empress of India, and the other reigning queens of her dominions and the wider earth negotiated an empire and the opening up of the world seems a story worth telling.[7]

WOMEN WHO RULED THE WORLD

The era, which is commonly personified as Victorian for the most powerful of all its women, was a time of queens or, perhaps more aptly, an age of empresses. That is not to say that these women found the establishment of their rules and then their reigns easy. They were still subject to all the old pressures, from male relatives to domineering courtiers, while at the same time they often also faced an encroachment to their rule by remote colonial powers. While ostensibly independent, Qudsia was under considerable pressure from the British Governor-General in 1835 to marry her daughter, Sikandar, to 'a very close relative' as stipulated in her husband's will. Even Victoria found her power contested and questioned in various parts of her realm.

Qudsia Begum quickly established herself as a popular ruler in Bhopal, which lies almost in the centre of India and is romantically known as the City of Lakes, while its mosques and palaces still dominating the skyline.** She made frequent visits to the houses of her poor subjects and dispensed charity. Inspired by the technological wonders of her age, she was determined to modernise Bhopal, employing a British engineer to design a water pipe system so that clean, free water could be made available to her citizens. (Something that was not necessarily the case across Britain at the time – in 1854 the physician John Snow would famously bring a cholera outbreak in Soho to an end by removing the handle of the public pump.) Qudsia would later bring the railway to Bhopal, too, funded in part from her private income.[8] No image of this dynamic ruler survives from her youth, but we can see her, white haired and steely eyed, staring directly at us from a portrait taken during her final years. She was (as one writer has put it) 'brave and ahead of her times' and with 'such

---

** Now most well-known as the site of the world's worst industrial disaster (with the Union Carbide gas leak of December 1984 still casting a horrendous pall over the area), this surprisingly green city was once more famous for its 107 years of female rule.

a strong personality that none of the male members in the family or royal household dared to challenge her'.[9] Since a nawab had to lead their forces into battle, she learned to ride an elephant and a horse. As a devout Muslim, she used her knowledge of the Qur'an and Islamic history to counter the widespread criticism of female rule that she encountered. She was, as her biographer and descendant Shaharyar M. Khan has noted, 'the first protagonist in favour of recognising a Muslim woman's legal right to rule a state'.[10] Would Qudsia have done all this without her knowledge of the wider world that colonialism, for all its faults, had engendered? Perhaps, but there is no doubt that she, like many of her peers, bought into the benefits of globalisation, while also being all too aware of the downsides.

Yet, while she embraced modernity, Qudsia also had to contend with the ages old suspicion of female rule throughout her reign. In 1837, eighteen years after she had announced she would be taking her husband's place as head of state, Qudsia finally relinquished power to her son-in-law. That Jahangir, an alcoholic and capricious young man who forced his educated and accomplished wife into the role of consort, was selected as nawab above the experienced Qudsia demonstrates just how strong the pressures remained against female rule both in Bhopal and in Britain. Qudsia's was an honourable, but disenfranchised retirement. However, she did not go quietly, with the British political agent Lancelot Wilkinson noting that the nawab begum (a female title of respect commonly accorded to princely women in the region) 'now begins to manifest frequent symptoms of furious passion approaching insanity. She rides and walks about in public, and betrays her determination to maintain herself in power by learning the use of the spear and other manly accomplishments'.[11] She was, he considered, a 'tigress', although whether he would have made a similar assessment of a male ruler in the same circumstances is open to question (Qudsia's great-granddaughter, Sultan Jehan, who had known her, attributed Wilkinson's behaviour towards the nawab begum to a heavy dose of misogyny). Certainly, ascribing female independence to insanity was a common enough trope in the nineteenth century to need little introduction. *The Woman in White,* which was written in Qudsia's lifetime, centred on the fate of an escaped – and entirely sane – female asylum inmate, for example. And the teenaged Victoria faced opposition to her rule on the grounds of the old trope of female hysteria and mental instability. However, Major William Hough, a British colonial officer in Bhopal assessed Qudsia in 1845, as 'perfectly mistress of the art of Government'.[12]

Victoria, who succeeded to the throne a year before Qudsia was forced to step aside, 'personified British rule in India for almost half a century', as she did the myriad other parts of the largest empire the world has ever seen.[13] As such, her role as Empress of India, a title that she formally acquired in 1876, although used intermittently earlier, is a difficult story to tell since it was a relationship always mitigated by distance and the need for intermediaries. Miles Taylor took up the challenge in *Empress: Queen Victoria and India,* identifying her as active in the rule of her imperial nation and a ruler who left a lasting mark, even after train stations were renamed and statues removed. Victoria would never visit India, but it was a land for which she felt an intense sense of longing. There is a dark irony that Victoria, in grey-skied Windsor or taking to the choppy Solent in her yacht, fell in love with an idea of a sun-baked, spice-scented India that her own empire was exploiting and rapidly dismantling. The India of its nineteenth century empress did not exist – perhaps it had never existed – but it informed the ways in which she interacted with this, the largest of her realms.

Victoria was determined to be a hands-on empress, even if she would stop short of visiting this part of her realm. In 1858, when the initial bill authorising the transfer of power from the East India Company to the British government was drafted she asked 'is this absolute power?', demanding of her government that she see all dispatches regarding India, as well as making all appointments in the Indian civil service and its military.[14] The Government of India Act, which was passed in 1858 and in which Victoria played an important and active role, was a 'remarkable achievement' for a woman whose position in Britain was mediated through its unwritten constitution and centuries of precedent. In India, the queen-empress was an absolute monarch.

Although backed by her red-coated forces, Victoria's sex placed her at a disadvantage in Indian society, where female rule was far from the norm (the nawab begums of Bhopal notwithstanding). She was, herself, concerned enough about this to insist that her eldest son give precedence to her viceroy during his tour of India over the winter of 1875–6, lest anyone should think that 'Shahzardah' (as the adoring crowds called him) came as ruler. Strenuous efforts were also made to present Victoria in ways acceptable to her Indian subjects: as a loyal widow, devoted to continuing the memory and works of her husband; as 'Bharat Mara' (Mother India) or as a sister monarch to the powerful women of the princely houses. From 1862, an 'Indian version' of the queen appeared on the coinage, banknotes and postage stamps, with her eye colour darkened (on bank notes), her nose straightened, her hair plaited and her dress distinctly more Indian in appearance.[15] In this way Victoria, disadvantaged by her sex, was at least presented to a diverse, enormous and largely illiterate population in familiar terms.

India was the source of many of the jewels with which Victoria is pictured wearing over her long reign, including the famous Koh-i-Noor diamond, which was displayed in the Great Exhibition of 1851. (It has, however, become a source of contention owing to a dispute over which country owns it, and one that is so intense that Queen Camilla elected not to wear the consort's crown in which it was set during her 2023 coronation.) Victoria wore it sparkling 'like a third eye' at a ball in Paris in 1855, with the crown being created for the jewel twelve months before she formally acquired it.[16]

Western imperialists had long since had a similarly romantic view of the island of Madagascar as Victoria had of India, while eyeing it as a potential colonial possession. In the seventeenth century, the British-based Prince Rupert of the Rhine was one who was caught by 'the dream of Madagascar' (as the contemporary diplomat Sir Thomas Roe put it) in 1637 when he vainly attempted to raise funds to found a colony there.[17] Two and a half times the size of the United Kingdom and densely forested, the island was a world in itself, with its unique flora and fauna, including its famous lemurs which are found nowhere else on earth. The island, made up of multiple small kingdoms and polities, already enjoyed strong trading links with eastern Africa and became an important staging post for the European traders who made the long voyage around the Cape of Good Hope and on towards the markets of India and China.

By the late eighteenth century, the British had made contact with the Merina people, whose kingdom lay almost in the centre of the vast island. Warlike and more than a little obsessed with his hero Napoleon, Radama I became King of the Merina in 1810 and almost immediately attempted to conquer the entire island. A slight, handsome and compelling figure, he could raise armies of 40,000 or 50,000 men. In return for abolishing the export of slaves from Madagascar, he agreed a treaty with Britain in which they would supply him with European weapons and his troops with training. Soon, the newly proclaimed King of Madagascar had conquered all but the extremities of the island. He was the Bonaparte of the southern hemisphere, but it could not last.[18] On 27 July 1828, Radama died at the age of only thirty-six, with his widow, Ranavalona, emerging as his successor, to the horror of her husband's British allies.

AGE OF EMPRESSES

No one in Madagascar dared raise a complaint about Ranavalona's accession, with her success characterised as a military coup, or as the victory of tradition over the Westernisation of Radama I's reign. Ranavalona had been the neglected spouse of her royal cousin, bearing her only child, the future King Radama II, twelve months after her husband's (the child's ostensible father's) death. It is difficult now to assess the extent of her power, with at least one historian claiming that 'henceforward, until the end of the monarchy, the real power was in the hands of the oligarchy'.[19] Undoubtedly, her ministers were influential, particularly Andriamihaja, who was appointed to the official role of 'queen's guardian' and who was most likely the father of Ranavalona's son. Nonetheless, few in the nineteenth century disputed Ranavalona's agency, with doubts over her independence likely in part due to the novelty of a female ruler in Madagascar.

Ranavalona I of Madagascar remains controversial, with one biographer entitling his book *Female Caligula* and others making a comparison to the sixteenth-century Bloody Mary, England's first crowned reigning queen whose reputation remains strongly linked to the 280 of her subjects that she had burned at the stake during her five-year-reign.[20] Like Bloody Mary – properly, Mary I of England and Ireland – who had hoped to turn back the tide of religious reform, so too did Ranavalona try to maintain her traditional life in the face of considerable pressure from those who wished to colonise her kingdom. In this, she responded very differently to Qudsia Begum in faraway India, who attempted to work with the colonial officials who sought to impose on her: Ranavalona did almost exactly the opposite.

She certainly felt strongly about the Protestant missionaries, who had been encouraged to come by Radama I.[21] Ranavalona viewed them as the agents of her enemies and as an affront to the traditions with which she had grown up, with the queen expelling them in 1835. Madagascan religion was based on a veneration of the ancestors, who watched over the living and could intervene – where appropriate. It was a religion with few ceremonies and no priests, with even inanimate objects believed to have a spirit.[22] This was the religion in which Ranavalona was raised and she saw no reason to change it for one that, in theory at least, presented her slaves and servants as equal to her. She made many martyrs over the course of her thirty-year reign, but she effectively kept Christianity, and the Western influences that it engendered, small and scattered, to the outrage of the missionaries who returned to London furious.

The final break came in 1837 when six of Ranavalona's ambassadors arrived in Britain, meeting with King William IV at Windsor Castle. With the accession of Victoria, later that year, it seemed only natural to the British press to draw comparisons between the two queens, with Ranavalona (as the historian Arianne Chernock has observed) portrayed 'as an emblem of savage femininity and a terrifying manifestation of what could happen to polities that allowed women to govern in more than a purely ceremonial capacity'.[23] Ranavalona became, in the British press and in publications such as William Ellis's *History of Madagascar*, the emblem of everything a reigning queen should not be, with Victoria ('the great white queen') conversely everything that one should be.[24] In these depictions, the racism of colonialism was writ large. While Ranavalona's regime was undoubtedly often brutal, she saw it as necessary to maintain her kingdom's independence. Beneath the veneer of 'civility', the diamonds, the wealth and the pageants, Victoria too oversaw a regime that was, at times, savage, with the dark heart of empire continuing to cast a long shadow over the globe.

Ranavalona rejected the trappings of European civilisation, yet, somewhat anomalously, she favoured Parisian haute couture in her dress and she was more than happy to use the extensive weaponry that the British had provided to her late husband.[25] In 1845, this was used to great effect against a joint British and French assault on the island, with the attackers leaving twenty of their number on the beach as they retreated to their ships. It did nothing for Ranavalona's reputation in Europe when twenty heads were later observed affixed to poles set up on the coastline. In this, as in everything, Ranavalona was defiant, with Captain William Kelly, who had led the British forces in the attack, later reporting her words to the *Manchester Guardian* newspaper.[26] She had, she said, 'as much right to nail her enemy's head at the end of a pole, as the Queen Victoria to send her prisoners to exile', demonstrating that she was well aware of the British penal colonies in Australia and the hardships they engendered. She later declared that she would correspond only with Victoria, who duly wrote requesting a new treaty of friendship. She may not have been popular in Britain, but Ranavalona was an effective monarch both at home and abroad, with her people largely accepting the reign of Madagascar's first queen.

In Bhopal, the British quickly came to regret pushing Qudsia Begum's abdication in favour of her son-in-law, Jahangir ('not a bright sovereign' according to one contemporary's estimation), with Qudsia, her daughter Sikandar and her six-year-old granddaughter, Shah Jehan, returning triumphantly to power in 1844 with the nawab's little-lamented death.[27] All three were mutually supportive of each other, with Sikandar presenting as such an obedient daughter that she would not even sit in her mother's presence. When Sikandar's beautiful Jama Mosque was built in Bhopal, Qudsia, who lived until the great age of eighty, attended the ceremonial opening. She kept her eyes fixed to the ground, declaring that, had she looked up, 'I was afraid I would be imbued with too much pride.'[28]

Sikandar, the second nawab begum, was perhaps the greatest of them all. She has been called a 'reform-orientated ruler', something which is plainly apt, changing Bhopal's court language from Persian to the Urdu of her subjects and even paying off her kingdom's national debt.[29] She built one of the earliest schools for girls in India, providing religious education in the Qur'an, literacy, arithmetic, languages, handicrafts and trades to her female subjects.[30] This 'Victoria School' was named after Sikandar's far-distant overlord, with whom she exchanged gifts and correspondence.[31] Sikandar was undoubtedly a valuable ally to the British with her fame overseas largely resting on her support for the colonial power during the first Indian War of Independence in 1857 (sometimes called the Indian Mutiny), in which she suppressed rebellion in her own kingdom and offered support to the British in the wider subcontinent.[32] As historian Siobhan Lambert-Hurley has aptly noted, the nawab begum's support for Britain was likely due to a concern about the effects that a reimposition of centralised Muslim rule in India might have on her own sovereignty.[33] It was very much a case of better the devil you know.

The relationship between the nawab begums and their British colonisers was undoubtedly a complex one. In the short term, Sikandar's loyalty gained her international renown, with Lord Lawrence, Governor-General of India, ordering the other Indian princes to emulate her in a speech that he made in the mid-1860s, while she was also finally recognised by the British as a ruler in her own right (rather than as regent for a yet-to-emerge male nawab) in 1860. She received a nineteen-gun salute and was invested with the Exalted Order of the Star of India, which made her one of the British Empire's only two female knights (the other being Queen Victoria). As a female ruler, Sikandar used some aspects of colonisation to her advantage, but the costs to India were high.

Sikandar who, like her mother, combined her religious devotion with her secular role as ruler, was highly politically adept. She built Bhopal's famed *Moti Masjid*, or Pearl Mosque, which remains one of the city's greatest landmarks today, while she is also the first known Indian ruler to have performed the Hajj pilgrimage to Mecca. But she also insisted that her granddaughter, Sultan Jehan, who would reign from 1901, was instructed in Persian, Urdu and (uniquely) English.

While India seemed to interest Victoria immensely, she showed less direct concern for Australia, the farthest distant land in her possession. It was there, on the other side of the globe, that another woman negotiated a queenship that was imposed upon her within the bounds of colonisation.

Unlike in Bhopal or Madagascar, there was little that the occupants of this land could do to negotiate with or resist the arrivals claiming the place in which they had lived for perhaps 50,000 years. Sydney Cove and surrounding areas, which were selected as the site of Britain's first Australian penal colony (on the strength, improbably, of only one visit, some decades before by Captain Cook), was then home to approximately 1500 people according to estimates made by Arthur Phillips, the colony's new governor. That number would soon be decimated by smallpox, carried on the British ships. The Gadigal people of Sydney Cove, who called the illness *gal-galla*, went from around sixty people in 1788 to only three a few years later.[34] They had survived through fishing, hunting and gathering, making tools and weapons and shelters, with signs of their rituals, their art and their daily life everywhere on the rocky shoreline. Within a few years, British observers were noting that where once they had seen many canoes from their ships, now there were none.

The loss of so many people fractured communities, breaking kinship and friendship ties and causing new relationships to be formed.[***]

[***] There is no guarantee that the survivors could understand each other. One Russian observer noted in 1820 that 'their language is not everywhere the same: the natives who live around Sydney understand each other but those who occupy the territories in Newcastle or Port Stephens, or who come from the other bank of the Nepean River, cannot understand the Sydney natives at all. And each man considers his own community to be the best.' G. Barratt, *The Russians at Port Jackson: 1814–1822* (Canberra: Australian Institute of Aboriginal Studies, 1981), p39.

The British, who found Australia a strange new world, marvelling at unfamiliar flora and the fauna (a kangaroo was an 'unparalleled animal', while the sea teamed with 'voracious and monstrous sharks'), struggled initially to establish dialogue with the people that they encountered.[35] As a result, they tended to accord greater status to those who were willing to engage with them, such as Bungaree, a man who has been called an 'unsung Aboriginal hero' by one modern historian, and who had accompanied the British aboard the HMS *Norfolk* in 1799 as it circumnavigated Australia, likely motivated by a sense of adventure and a desire to explore.[36] Recognised by the British as the 'Chief of the Broken Bay tribe', although no such 'tribe' existed, he was honoured with a ceremonial 'king plate' – a breastplate – inscribed with his name and title that he wore around his neck.[****] Bungaree trod a path between two cultures and two worlds, with a famous illustration depicting him in fully European dress with a British officer's coat and wearing his breastplate with his cocked hat held aloft.[37] Yet, even when he presented in European style, he was mocked, with one account noting that 'it must be confessed that his appearance was sometimes grotesque enough'.[38] Most accounts of early contact between the British and Australia's Aboriginal inhabitants make clear that it was the former's view that the latter was badly in need of civilising – and, by that, of course, they meant colonisation. On his death in 1830, he was called by the Europeans 'his Aboriginal Majesty King Boongarie, Supreme chief of the Sydney tribe' in his obituary, with his second wife, Cora Gooseberry, moving into his position as spokesperson and, effectively (as far as the British were concerned), ruler.

[****] A Russian observer noted that 'a copper plate hung from a red copper chain round his neck, with the inscription: 'Bongaree, Chief of the Brocken-Bay Tribe: 1815'' (Barratt, *Russians at Port Jackson*, p29); Bungaree was the first Aboriginal Australian to be appointed as a chief by Governor Macquarie and the first to receive a metal king plate (or gorget) (Keith Vincent Smith, *King Bungaree: A Sydney Aborigine meets the great South Pacific explorers, 1799-1830* (Kenthurst, 1992), p81).

AGE OF EMPRESSES

Caroo, or Cora Gooseberry as she is more well known, was born around a decade or so before the British First Fleet arrived in 1788 to change her life forever. There was clearly something about her that drew the attention of the British authorities of New South Wales, the first European colony in Australia.[39] Away from the sun-bleached busyness of Sydney Harbour is the Rocks, Sydney's oldest neighbourhood, now a series of narrow streets filled with souvenir shops and clothing boutiques. The Rocks Discovery Museum – a treasure of the city which is very much off the usual tourist trail – contains the detritus of colonialism, such as a fascinating assortment of items excavated from a butcher's shop well (delicate bone china, broken bottles and other items of a life that was then on the edge of the world), but also something truly surprising. Beside a copper mug which belonged to Caroo is one of two metal breastplates, which were awarded to her by the British authorities and which she would string around her neck as a mark of her status. 'Cora Gooseberry. Freeman Bungaree. Queen of Sydney & Botany' was crowned and renamed by Australia's colonial authorities.

Cora Gooseberry was acknowledged as a leader and as a monarch in a political system that was not hers. She was not necessarily a leader of her own community, as a perceptive early Russian visitor to Sydney noted, since the Aboriginal people 'live in societies of 30, 40, 50 or more persons, and are ruled by their own elders. Nowadays the English Government itself selects the elders and gives them a special mark to that effect consisting of a copper plate on which their rank is indicated, and which they wear round the neck'.[40] To the British, she was a point of contact with the people of the local area, leading to their acknowledgment of her as a reigning queen, a status she didn't have in her own community, with male elders more dominant and women apparently having no 'specific powers or rights'.[41] As Jakelin Troy has noted in her study of the breastplates with which the British ennobled 'favoured' members of the Aboriginal community, Gooseberry met with considerable prejudice from the Europeans that she encountered.[42] She was, said one, 'an old woman smeared with fish-oil' and 'truly the personification of ugliness – but meeting one in the bush she always asked to be kissed', while Matora – her predecessor as Bungaree's spouse – had been called his 'hideous wife' by a Russian observer.[*****] Matora insisted on being addressed as queen by the Russian visitors, although one recorded after meeting the couple in April 1820, that she 'behaved with even more unseemliness than all the other guests'.[43]

Both Bungaree and Gooseberry struggled with the position they found themselves in, with Bungaree (according to one British observer) drawn to 'the magical allurements of spirits and tobacco', which has been a perennial blight on the Aboriginal communities of Australia since the arrival of Europeans. Gooseberry eked out a living in the new world of Sydney with fishing and with cultural tours, with European visitors paying in kind with rum or tobacco. Nonetheless, Bungaree's and, later, Gooseberry's newly created rank do seem to have been respected by European settlers to some extent. A Russian sailor, Leading Seaman Yegor Kiselyov, who came upon a group of Aboriginal Australians in March 1820, noted that 'there's a king, too: he has a sign on his chest, given by the English king. And our captain gave him a hussar's greatcoat and a bronze medal, and his wife a white blanket and a pair of woman's earrings'.[44] Interestingly, while the visitors criticised Bungaree's lifestyle ('though he called himself king of this place and had the title, Chief of Broken Bay, his palace did not correspond to his high title: it consisted of a single semicircular wall, some four or five feet high, made of fresh branches'), they did not dispute the title.[45] That he did not necessarily command the respect amongst his

---

[*****] Gooseberry and Matora were frequently confused as the same person in European sources, although it is clear that Matora predeceased Bungaree. Barratt, *Russians at Port Jackson*, p49.

community that the British hoped he did was also suggested by the fact that he would sometimes fight, on one occasion being seen with his head split open. On being asked 'Who broke your head?', he replied, 'My people when they were drunk'. To the man he spoke to, 'it was clear enough from this how much power he had over those whom he called his people'.[46] Aboriginal Australian monarchs were sometimes mocked by the British settlers in Sydney, who derided their apparent airs and graces.[47] But, surely that was expected of a monarch?

Though her status was ambiguous, Gooseberry was a prominent figure in the early history of Sydney, frequently drawn or painted as a white-haired woman with a determined and aged face. She undoubtedly served as a conduit of communication between groups, between whom there was sometimes cooperation but often not. In stories of her life, the unspoken details of what she had lost shine through louder than what she had become and the status that she had achieved. When, on being asked in the 1840s to take some Europeans on a tour of the rock art sites of Sydney, which still survive to be seen today, she initially refused, considering them to be 'forbidden ground'.[48] The engravings around Sydney are ancient and Gooseberry, who was eventually prevailed upon to lead her tour, felt a kinship with them, declaring that her father had told her that a 'black fellow made them long ago'. They were places of dances and ceremonies, with powerful spirits believed to reside there and the fact that she was required to share them with the area's new residents cut deep. She could likely remember the hunger that followed the arrival of the First Fleet, with reports made by the British that the people of the area were starving in the winter of 1788 and 1789. Hers was the last generation to truly remember how life had been before the colonisers arrived, when the rivers could be freely accessed and the lands available to forage.[49]

★

Sikandar Begum's life was similarly changed by colonialism – albeit in a very different way – with the British once wary and then supportive of her rule. She had intended to visit Britain, although her death when still only fifty in 1868 had prevented her from making the trip. Following her death, Sikandar was remembered in a book published by a Hindu author as 'the best by far of all the native sovereigns of India of our time, the ablest, wisest, most enlightened, and most fortunate'.[50] She achieved this, as her gushing biographer noted, in spite of the fact that 'her sex is a great trial in every sense; a damper of all genius but the highest even in Europe – in Asia usually an utter disqualifier'.[51] After Sikandar there were no doubts about the fitness of women to reign in Bhopal. She was 'an argument for the social elevation and education of women'. Queen Victoria, in distant Britain was another argument for the advancement of women, although she infamously had little sympathy for women's suffrage anywhere in her empire.

Sikandar's daughter and successor, Shah Jehan, was as cultured a woman as her mother, with the nawab begum requesting in 1870 that she be permitted to write to Victoria every month in order to practice her English (a request that was denied by the queen-empress's officers in India).[52] Nonetheless, she did send books to Victoria in 1874, detailing the history of Bhopal in Urdu and the account of her mother's journey to Mecca. In exchange, Shah Jehan was gifted Victoria's *Highland Journal* (a work of which she was deeply proud) and the *Early Years of the Prince Consort* by Charles Grey. Still young enough to bear sons when she inherited the throne, Shah Jehan nonetheless named her daughter, Sultan Jehan, as her heir on the day of her coronation, suggesting an active desire to continue the line of the nawab begums of Bhopal.[53] The fact that no one complained strongly indicates their popularity.

Shah Jehan did not travel to London for the queen-empress's Golden Jubilee in 1887, though Victoria was undoubtedly thrilled to be feted by many other members of the royal houses of India. Sunity Devee, Maharani of Cooch Behar, noted in her autobiography of 1921 the subcontinent 'was anxious to show her loyalty to the Sovereign whose high ideals and humanity have endeared her to all her people. Many of our princes therefore decided to render their homage in person'.[54] The maharani, who was the only royal woman to make the journey from India, was disappointed to find Britain with its 'damp and gloomy' climate, and the luxurious Grosvenor Hotel, where she and her husband took a suite, surprisingly lacking in bathrooms.

Victoria had sent a personal message to the maharani to request that she wear her Indian clothes for their meeting. For Sunity, who had been raised on the idea of this distant foreign Queen, the meeting was imbued with meaning as she stepped forward to receive a kiss from Victoria: 'To us Indians she was a more or less legendary figure endowed with wonderful attributes, an ideal ruler, and an ideal woman, linked to our hearts across "the black water" by silken chains of love and loyalty.' Victoria was everything that Sunity had hoped for. She was (she later recalled) 'delighted to find that I had not been disappointed in my ideal, and felt eager to go back to India that I might tell my country-women of our wonderful Empress'.[55] A rare female eyewitness to this distant monarch that most in India would never set eyes on, the Maharani of Cooch Behar, who had grown up under British rule in India and who would live her life under its domination, was as fascinated by Victoria as the queen-empress was of her. A few months after her return home, she gave birth to a son, dutifully naming him the distinctively un-Indian Victor in honour of his royal godmother.[56]

The Golden Jubilee celebrations had been a triumph in public relations on Victoria's part. India's Mughal emperors, who had come before Britain's East India Company were not a native dynasty, but the crucial difference was that they, unlike the British, came to settle.[57] While Mughal culture remains quintessentially Indian, the British legacy was a lasting one too, with the English language remaining of commercial importance. For many of the British – not least Queen Victoria – there was a genuine love for India and its culture – but the plundering was already centuries old.

In Bhopal, Shah Jehan at first continued the social and political reforms of her mother and grandmother.[58] The first nawab begum, Qudsia, was by now elderly, but still active. Shah Jehan was highly educated and a strong example of female rule that undoubtedly played a role in its slow acceptance in India and the wider world. No concerns were raised in the province about the sex of the ruler of the new empire when Victoria was formally proclaimed as Empress of India in 1876, which had been something that she had personally solicited. It was rumoured that she had feared being outranked by her eldest daughter, the future Empress of Germany, although it seems more likely that she had aspired to match her Mughal predecessors in dignity.

By the time of Victoria's formal proclamation, Bhopal had been ruled by women for nearly sixty years. It was, writes one modern academic, 'an oasis of female agency and power within India's patriarchal order'.[59] Qudsia's granddaughter was a writer, composing a detailed history of Bhopal (the *Taj al-Iqbal: Tarikh-e Bhopal*), which drew on the earlier archival research of her mother, Sikandar.[60] She corresponded with Queen Victoria, while the two women also had acquaintances in common (although Victoria disliked Shah Jehan's lowborn and highly controversial second husband, Sayvid Siddiq Hasan, something which she made plain in correspondence).[61] Shah Jehan, however, did not enjoy the warmest of relationships with her heir. The nawab begum at least recognised that it was essential that her daughter gain practical experience of ruling, sending her state papers on which to make orders during her lifetime. Victoria, on the other hand, who never thought much of her eldest son's intelligence or behaviour, kept Bertie well away from the dispatch boxes.

Following this second marriage in 1871, Shah Jehan retreated into purdah, marking a very different approach to rule to that of her mother and grandmother. In 1875, she caused consternation in Bhopal when she initially refused to meet the Prince of Wales, with her own daughter forcefully pointing out that 'the laws of Islam do not prohibit a Musalman lady for appearing at public assemblies in a burkha'.[62] Sultan Jehan could not understand her mother's decision to seclude herself. Undoubtedly, Shah Jehan's husband was a baleful influence, with the nawab begum estranged from her grandmother, Qudsia, who was barred from her court, and her own daughter.[63] In some respects, purdah advanced the position of women, since it gave only female subjects and peers direct access to Bhopal's monarch. The charming Sunity, Maharani of Cooch Behar, noted in her autobiography that she once attended a 'strict purdah party' hosted by Shah Jehan, which allowed the female movers and shakers in India, including the wife of Victoria's British Viceroy, to mix freely without the presence of men.[64] There were, however, also major disadvantages to the seclusion.

When Victoria was sixty-eight years old, two Indian servants arrived, handpicked to wait at her table: the elder, Mohammed Buksh, who had been employed as a senior servant back in India, was content with his lot, but the younger, twenty-four-year-old Abdul Karim, was disappointed. He had hoped to serve as an equerry, riding behind the queen, but he would soon receive much more from the queen-empress becoming the eyes through which Victoria glimpsed the domes and temples of the jewel in her empire.

In 1887, Victoria's two new Indian attendants travelled with her to Balmoral in Scotland for the first time. She seemed to enjoy fussing over them – they would need warm tweeds, she knew, but tailored in the Indian fashion. On this trip, Abdul Karim began to teach Victoria Hindustani. While she was famously a diarist, writing an almost daily account of her life from her childhood until her death, what is less well known is that, in thirteen volumes bound in black Morocco leather, Queen Victoria also kept journals in Hindustani under the guidance of Karim.[65] She enjoyed her studies, turning mundane accounts of taking tea with friends or walking in the gardens into the (for her) exotic Urdu script of the Indian subcontinent.

Victoria was soon addressing Abdul Karim as Munshi, or tutor. Convinced that he was 'almost a gentleman who could not be treated like a common servant', she had him moved away from table service to secretarial work, with the Queen noting happily (and, as usual in the third person) in a letter of 12 September 1887 that 'Abdul is most handy in helping when she signs by drying the signatures'.[66] Victoria's family and senior courtiers invariably hated the Munshi, with many of their objections based on racism, something that the queen-empress herself identified. Victoria, who was lonely, adored him. Soon, this 'almost a gentleman' had become a 'thorough gentleman' and, finally, (as Victoria wrote to her eldest daughter, the Empress of Germany) a 'perfect gentleman'.[67] In Nice, during Queen Victoria's summer holiday in 1899, the French press took to calling him *'Le Prince'*, the 'particular secretary to Queen Victoria for Indian affairs'.[68] He was her constant companion.

Victoria was diligent in her Hindustani and was soon able to speak a few words to visitors from India, as well as write simple sentences independently of her Munshi's oversight. As one of Karim's biographer's, Shrabani Basu, has noted, he was essential to the queen who felt 'her discussions with Karim helped her get a feel of the pulse of Indian affairs, as she was getting the native's view of the British administration and its effects'.[69]

In her youth, Cora Gooseberry, along with the other members of her community slept outside, creating a shelter with (as one European observed) 'a semicircular brushwood fence on the side from which the wind blows' and within which a fire would be lit.[70] But hers was a life lived on the edge of a new culture. Bungaree had been given 'a specially built little house with a garden in Broken Bay' by Governor Macquarie, in an attempt to encourage the Aboriginal people of the area to settle, but neither he nor Gooseberry appear to have made much use of it.[71] As an old woman, she frequently slept in the kitchen of the Sydney Arm's Hotel, whose proprietor befriended her. She died there on 30 July 1852, in her seventies, with her death severing a crucial link between the old Sydney Cove and the new.[72] 'Queen' Gooseberry's surviving breastplates remain a testament to the life of a woman subject to the full force of colonial pressures, with the status conferred by them that of the invading culture. Gooseberry likely wore her breastplates with pride: her husband, Bungaree, certainly did. Yet, they were symbols of a system of which she could never fully be part: a negotiation in which she faced a chasm of disadvantage. She was a reigning queen of a 'kingdom' built on the slipping sands of colonisation. Fifty years after her death her grave, marked by a stone erected 'in memory of Gooseberry QUEEN of the Sydney Tribe of Aborigines', was removed to make way for a new railway station.[73]

Ranavalona, in Madagascar, retained her firm grip on her throne until her death in August 1861, resisting any attempts by aspiring colonial powers without or domestic rivals within to dominate her. She was a traditional monarch, albeit on a grand and sometimes terrifying scale, with the 'tangena ordeal', a type of test that aimed to root out witchcraft in her kingdom, purge-like in its ferocity.[74] This longstanding rite required suspects to ingest the poisonous tangena nut. Those that vomited were acquitted, while the unlucky majority perished and were found guilty of witchcraft. The ordeal perhaps killed around 3000 of Ranavalona's subjects per year, totalling nearly 100,000 in a population of 500,000 or 600,000 over the course of her thirty-three-year reign.

Ranavalona used the rite as a means of ridding herself of her political enemies. She probably viewed 'her reign of terror' as the price of Madagascar's continuing independence and her position on the throne, but it was a bloody cost.[75]

After her death, her polygamous son, Radama II, permitted the missionaries to return, with his widow queens, Rasoherina and Ranavalona II, who reigned in turn after him, further Christianising the country. Madagascar's independence would end during the reign of a final queen, Ranavalona III, when, in 1896, the kingdom was formally annexed by the French. It is difficult to argue that the defiant approach of Ranavalona I, who nailed English and French heads to spikes on the beach, was a miscalculation in this context: Madagascar's 'Bloody Mary', 'Caligula' or 'Nero' was the active ruler the island needed to ward off the encroaching forces of colonisation. She understood how to negotiate with the French and the British who swarmed at the edges of her kingdom: at the barrel of a gun. Queen Victoria celebrated Ranavalona I's death by pointedly gifting a Bible to Madagascar's new king.

Shah Jehan's position, as an effectively invisible sovereign, proved so problematic that, in 1885, her husband was stripped by the British of his titles and a minister appointed to run the state on her behalf. When Shah Jehan died in June 1901, her daughter was determined to govern very differently and, crucially, much more actively. Nonetheless, as her descendant and biographer Shaharyar M. Khan notes, Shah Jehan 'left behind a stable, settled and well-governed state', but hers had been a reign in which the men in her life – both her scheming husband and the British authority – had sought to control and stifle her.[76]

Victoria continued to gaze at India in the final years of her reign, finding solace and friendship in the company of her Indian Munshi. When he was ill she fluffed his pillows, and during his infrequent absences, she fretted. Abdul Karim effectively became one of her ministers, with a flurry of telegrams passing between the queen-empress and her officers in India over a pension for his father and preference for his friends in Agra. The queen-empress even once insisted that the viceroy of India pay a social call on Karim's father to tell him how pleased she was with his son. He was, for her, the vital conduit to a realm over which she had shown such an active interest. As she wrote to her daughter in Germany during one of Abdul Karim's leaves of absence: 'I miss him terribly! 4 months is a long time; I have such interesting and instructive conversations with him about India – the people, customs and his religion.'[77] He was, to Victoria, a tangible link to a world that she could only touch through descriptions, despatches and the Indian furnishings and fashions with which she decorated her 'Durbar Room' at Osborne House. Victoria would always remain close to her Munshi, who stayed with her until her death in January 1901 and who, while a controversial figure, does seem to have been genuinely devoted to her. After being forced by the new king, Edward VII (formally Victoria's disappointing son Bertie), to hand over the letters he had received from the queen, he was sent home to Agra.

As Victoria's reign ended, so Sultan Jahan's began. With India now ruled over by an emperor, she became India's only female sovereign. Never doubting the ability of a woman to wear a crown (and, indeed, after over eighty years of nawab begum rule her succession was not challenged), she was a strong supporter of women's education, building on the work of her beloved grandmother, Sikandar. She made basic schooling free to all children in Bhopal – a radical move for the time, as well as leading the way by publishing her own Urdu autobiography. As a mark of the respect in which she was held, she was elected as president of the All India Muslim Ladies' Association in 1914, while from 1920 until her death ten years later she served as the founding (and, so far, only female) chancellor of the Aligarh Muslim University. It is no exaggeration to state, as did one of Sultan Jahan's biographers,

Siobhan Lambert-Hurley, that 'Nawab Sultan Jahan Begam moulded the state of Bhopal into a centre for reform of India's Muslim women, establishing unique social and educational institutions that placed her at the forefront of an India-wide movement to transform women's status'.[78] She did this from behind the veil of a burka.

Sultan Jahan, like her grandmother, Sikandar, to whom she always remained devoted, was a passionate supporter of the British, meeting with the future George V and his family when they visited India in 1906, while she travelled to Britain in 1911 for George's coronation. On landing in Britain, she noted that – here – she felt 'at home', spending her time attending functions, sightseeing and meeting with friends that she had known in India.[79] On the day of the coronation, she appeared dressed in her burka, on which her many awards were pinned.

She returned to Britain in 1925 in an attempt to settle Bhopal's disputed succession on her youngest son rather than the son of her deceased eldest son. During a highly charged meeting with the king, she reminded him that the nawab begums had always ruled with Queen Victoria's support and that female rule had only been made possible through her. This was an over-simplification, with the nawab begums of Bhopal proving themselves generation after generation and making the case for female rule with their every action. Yet, there was also some truth in it. The nawab begums of Bhopal and Queen-Empress Victoria were intrinsically linked, with their stories interwoven: they were anomalies in their own time, but their rare position as female rulers bolstered one another. The same can be said for all the reigning women of the age of empresses.

At her enthronement in 1828, Ranavalona I of Madagascar swore that people should never say 'she is only a feeble and ignorant woman, how can she rule such a vast empire?', promising that she would reign traditionally and not lose one piece of her inheritance.[80] For all their differences, these could have been the vows of the nawab begums of

AGE OF EMPRESSES

Bhopal or India's queen-empress. These women lived disparate lives in geographically separated lands, but they are also linked by the shared nature of their queenship, as well as their lives in this global and colonial age. They were women living in a man's world, but there were intersections between all their lives as a result of the age in which they lived.

When the court was staying at Windsor Castle Abdul Karim, Victoria's Munshi, would travel to Woking in Surrey to worship at the elaborate, Mughal-style mosque that was built there in 1889, as the first purpose-built mosque in Britain. The Shah Jehan Mosque, which is named for the third Nawab Begum of Bhopal who contributed so liberally to its establishment, remains an important symbol of the fact that the cultural transferal went both ways. The Victorians might have thought that they were 'civilising' India, or Australia or Madagascar, but in so doing they brought something of the cultures that they encountered back with them. With its white walls and onion-shaped domes, the Shah Jehan Mosque in Woking makes it quite clear that the reigning queens of the nineteenth century were ambitious, strident and, crucially, in that age of empires, global in their outlook. There were many queens in the nineteenth century, with their success all too frequently hanging on their ability to negotiate the colonising influences of the day: some, such as Ranavalona, achieved this, others, such as Cora Gooseberry, did not, but the recognition of this need is an important one in itself and defines the queenship of them all. It was truly an age of empresses.

CHAPTER 12:

QUEENS OF THE TWENTIETH CENTURY

Wilhelmina of the Netherlands, Sālote Tupou III of Tonga, Elizabeth II of the United Kingdom and Margarethe II of Denmark

The first twentieth-century royal to become a true media celebrity and sensation in their own right was born at the start of the new century on the tiny Pacific island of Tonga, just nine months before the death of Victoria, the queen who had dominated the old.

Tonga was, legend had it, formed by the great god Maui raising the islands from the Pacific Ocean with his magical fishhook. It was by the turn of the twentieth century the only Pacific kingdom still in existence and remained, surprisingly, uncolonised, although under the somewhat compulsory 'protection' of Britain. According to the terms of a 1900 Treaty of Friendship, Tonga was left to manage its own internal affairs while the British managed its foreign relations. The island had a tradition of monarchy stretching back to at least the tenth century, throughout which time it had only been ruled by male sovereigns.[1] The modern royal dynasty had been founded by King George I Tupou (Siaosi I Tupou in Tongan), a monumental figure to his 20,000 subjects who lived until well into his nineties,[2] King George had allowed in missionaries, converted to Methodism and overseen his isolated nation's increasing contact with the wider world. He cast a long shadow, not least over his great-grandson, namesake and successor, George II (Siaosi II), whose first months on the throne witnessed an outbreak of measles that killed over 5 per cent of the population.[3]

In 1899, George II abandoned his fiancé to marry the comparatively lowly Lavinia Veiongo, in a love match so controversial that supporters of his jilted bride almost ousted him from his throne. Their daughter was christened Sālote – the Tongan version of the European name, Charlotte.* A British civil servant, Sir Basil Thomson, was invited to coo over the new royal baby and later recorded, somewhat dismissively, that he found Lavinia 'not ill looking, but she was far from justifying the King's infatuation with her which had nearly cost him his throne'.[4]

Two years later, Lavina died. Sālote's father married the sister of his former fiancé as a gesture of reconciliation and the union produced another daughter, but no son. Sālote grew up between her island paradise of Tonga and New Zealand, where she was sent for an education befitting a future queen – though her succession was never entirely certain. Tonga had never had a reigning queen before, while the country's constitution, drafted in 1875, prioritised male heirs over female.[5] Her stepmother, who had loathed Sālote's upstart mother Lavinia, not unnaturally favoured the inheritance of her own little daughter, the impeccably royal Fusipala. Despite these barriers, Sālote slowly came to be recognised as the heir to Tonga's throne.

Over 15,000 miles away from Sālote's birthplace, Wilhelmina, Queen of the Netherlands, was twenty years old when the days of the old century segued into those of the new. She had inherited the throne at ten on the death of her father, Wilhelm III, with her mother acting as regent during her childhood. During this time, her residence

---

* Sālote was named after her great-great-grandmother, Queen Sālote, wife of George I Tupou, who had been named after Charlotte of Mecklenburg-Strelitz, wife of George III of Britain.

was the staid and isolated Baroque Het Loo Palace, around an hour's drive by car from Amsterdam. Here, Wilhelmina had felt increasingly cooped up, existing in her 'cage' as she called it, and wanting to break out.[6]

However, she was acutely aware that she was on the cusp of change. Both personally – since she had recently announced her engagement – and as a queen. Wilhelmina's wedding to the minor German princeling Duke Heinrich of Mecklenburg-Schwerin was a wintry one, but the sun shone on the February day and Wilhelmina certainly believed herself to be in love with her blond and blue-eyed ('a real Germanic') prince.[7] She even had to be persuaded not to change the dynasty's name from Oranje-Nassau to Oranje-Mecklenburg. Wilhemina and Heinrich had spent little time together before their wedding, and nor had they considered what the first Dutch male consort's role was to be. One biographer has described Wilhelmina's marriage as 'a fairytale wedding that didn't last', with the inequality of the couple's positions stark.[8] 'She licks the dust of his shoes', said Emma, Wilhelmina's mother and former regent, who resented being pushed aside and abhorred her daughter's submissiveness.[9] Initially, at least, the Dutch queen presented a picture of wifely obedience, with her worried parent complaining in a private letter that 'he is at the bottom of every thing'. And also, 'I have heard her behave in so silly a manner to him when a question was discussed, telling him only to consult his wish, the people had to approve of everything etc. that I only find it sensible (but _very_ sad) that he attaches little value to her opinion.'[10] Notoriously and extravagantly unfaithful, Heinrich despised being outranked by his wife, something that was compounded by the Dutch government's decision not to grant him an income. Instead, Wilhelmina paid him 100,000 guilders per year from her personal income, which was a generous sum, but one that left him dependent on her financially. In contrast, by the late 1940s, his wife would be regarded as the richest woman in the world, with a personal fortune of around $1 billion.[11]

While Wilhelmina had been accepted as monarch, she lived in an era where women rarely had the vote (women gained equal suffrage in 1919 in the Netherlands, quite early amongst European nations), were not expected to take employment and remained very much second-class citizens worldwide. At the same time, increasingly, the relevance of a monarch – and the role itself – was being called into question. The monarchies of China, Russia, Austria-Hungary and Germany would not endure past the second decade of the twentieth century, for example.

In 1917, six months after her seventeenth birthday, Sālote married Prince Uiliami Tupoulahi Tungi, an Australian-educated scion of Tonga's ancient royal line. Prince Tungi, who was thirteen years older than his wife, would prove 'a veritable Polynesian Prince Albert', according to Sir Harry Luke, the British High Commissioner for the Western Pacific, who served in this high-sounding role between 1938 and 1942. Since Prince Albert had deliberately set out to belittle and dominate his spouse, Queen Victoria, until he had cowed her into a form of co-monarchy, this was not exactly a reassuring assessment. It was also largely not a fair one. While it did take Tungi some time to find his place as Tonga's first male royal consort, which involved his wife appointing him as, effectively, her prime minister in 1923, unlike Heinrich, the Dutch prince consort, he accepted his subordinate position.

George II died on 5 April 1918 and was succeeded smoothly by his first wife's daughter. Sālote's position was further secured by her grand coronation later that year in which she wore the heaviest royal crown then in existence. Her far from loving stepmother died from the devastating outbreak of Spanish Flu, which swept around the world that year, wiping out around 8 per cent of Tonga's already tiny population. Sālote, who assumed her little half-sister's guardianship was unopposed. She secured the monarchy's future with the birth of a son on 4 July 1918.[12]

Despite living at the beginning of a new century with increasing calls for equal rights for women being heard around the globe, the purpose of all royal marriages remained, unavoidably, to shore up the dynasty with a nursery filled with (preferably) princes. In this, Sālote was a great success, with two further sons added to her brood in 1919 and 1922. However, Wilhelmina's unpopular marriage in the far away Netherlands was initially less dynastically successful. When – after a series of devastating miscarriages – she bore a child in April 1909, only the baby's father was unhappy with her sex. ('I can assure you,' spoke one cabinet minister, 'that after the nation's wonderful experience with Dowager Queen Emma and with Queen Wilhelmina there is nobody in Holland who is not as delighted with a girl as with a boy.')[13] Heinrich would later sourly inform the visiting former US president Theodore Roosevelt, who politely praised the little princess, that, 'I hope she has a brother; otherwise I pity the man that marries her.' No little brothers joined Juliana in the royal nursery and, by the 1910s the couple lived apart.

The discontent of male royal consorts would become something of a theme as the twentieth century progressed. Nearly sixty years after Wilhelmina's ill-fated marriage, in 1960, Elizabeth II of the United Kingdom would agree that any male line descendants of her marriage to Prince Philip of Greece and Denmark who did not bear a royal title would be surnamed 'Mountbatten-Windsor', in a nod to the surname her husband had taken when he became a British citizen. That Mountbatten was, in actual fact, his mother's Anglicised surname rather than his father's was apparently beside the point, with Philip well known to have complained that, 'I am the only man in the country not allowed to give his name to his children.' Married British women could not even order a sofa on credit without their husband's permission until the late 1970s. In this context, it is unsurprising that some male consorts found their role emasculating.

The future Elizabeth II, or Princess 'Lilibet' of York as she was known to her family, had entered the world via Caesarean section in 1926. Her father, Prince Albert, Duke of York, was a younger son and, while the little girl was third in line to her grandfather's throne, few bets would have been placed on her eventual succession. As a result, the first decade of her life was idyllic, with the little girl's character shining through in the reminiscences of her governess, Marion Crawford, who was later ostracised for making them public. (Wilhelmina's own English governess would receive a similar cold shoulder when she too published her memoirs, although she ultimately remained in the royal fold.) The governess first encountered her charge when she was sitting in her dressing gown driving an imaginary team of horses that she had hitched to the knobs at the end of her bed.

Elizabeth's sheltered world came crashing down in December 1936 when Edward VIII, the glamorous but unstable uncle who had taught her how to make a Nazi salute in disturbing film footage from the early 1930s, abdicated the throne.[14] At a stroke of the pen, Prince Albert became King George VI and his eldest daughter heiress presumptive, since the possibility always remained that her father might sire a son to displace her.

At the start of the twentieth century, Denmark's conservative royal family, which could trace its line of descent all the way back to the semi-legendary Gorm the Old in the tenth century, would not have viewed a reigning queen as any kind of possibility, with women expressly excluded from their line of succession. No woman had ever been acknowledged as reigning queen of Denmark (although, as we saw in Chapter 1 the kingdom did once have a female 'husband'). As such, the birth of a daughter to Crown Prince Frederik and Crown

QUEENS OF THE TWENTIETH CENTURY

Princess Ingrid on 16 April 1940 was more a welcome distraction than a momentous occasion, with the child entering the world only one week after the Nazis began their nearly five-year-occupation of the kingdom.[15] Margrethe was born into the most ancient royal house in Europe at possibly its lowest ebb, with the idea that this 'light in a dark time' would ever succeed to the throne laughable.[16]

Margrethe's liberal and unconventional mother, Crown Princess Ingrid, who, in an attempt at 'maintaining normality in an abnormal world' was regularly observed riding her bicycle in Copenhagen or pushing her daughter in her pram, was expected to quickly produce a male heir.[17] With the births of two further girls, this looked increasingly unlikely.

In 1940, Wilhelmina of the Netherlands, who had been widowed in 1934, reached her sixtieth birthday and the fiftieth anniversary of her accession. She had, by then, already weathered one world war, keeping her small kingdom neutral and free from the tortuous trenches that crisscrossed her neighbours' territories. She had seen this conflict as 'a watershed in all lives' and as 'a new era', but also much remained the same, with Germany's exiled Kaiser Wilhelm II even invited to live out the rest of his life in the Netherlands as his relative's honoured guest. As the 1930s progressed and it became increasingly evident that another great conflict was coming, Wilhelmina again hoped to keep the Netherlands neutral, going so far as to send 'that beast of a Hitler' (as she privately called him) a birthday telegram on 20 April 1940.[18] Less than three weeks later, the recipient of her birthday good wishes invaded her kingdom. As German troops stormed across the border, the queen issued a proclamation, raising 'a fierce protest against the unexampled violation of good faith and outrage upon all that is proper between civilised states'.[19] It was only with great reluctance that the queen was persuaded to embark upon HMS *Hereward* for exile in Britain, with her daughter, son-in-law and grandchildren having fled the day before. The preservation of their monarch and government, albeit in London, was one small consolation for the Dutch people, whom Wilhelmina bitterly regretted leaving. It was, however, to be an awakening for the queen, and the making of a legend.

Princess Elizabeth, along with her parents and younger sister, welcomed the Dutch queen to Britain, with Wilhelmina staying with them at Buckingham Palace before she was able to establish her own base at 82 Eaton Square in London, a grand and dark house, set around a private garden square, with imposing white Classical-style terraces looming above. It was a far cry from the Het Loo Palace and the other royal residences that Wilhelmina had previously occupied, but she liked it. She enjoyed too the more intimate cottage that she moved into close to Richmond Park in South West London, 'where I hope to walk a lot in the wilderness', she confided in a letter to her daughter. On wintry days, she would sit in her pretty living room, looking out of the French doors.[20]

Queen Wilhelmina, who became a familiar figure strolling in the park's long grasses and on its gravel paths, made a great impression on those she met. She was considered by shy, awkward George VI to be 'a remarkable woman and wonderfully courageous'.[21] And one admiring British observer called her 'the greatest man on the throne today', giving undoubtedly heartfelt but all-too predictably paternalistic praise to a woman who had ably headed a government for more than fifty years.[22] She had become, at a stroke, a war leader – in the (modernised) vein of her warrior-queen predecessors. Within weeks she was calling for defiance over the airwaves, with Radio Orange, broadcast from the BBC's studio in London, a major boost to Dutch resistance during the years of occupation.

Wilhelmina was undoubtedly a powerful symbol in the Netherlands' darkest time. Nearly a quarter of a million of her subjects were killed. This included more than three quarters of the 150,000 strong

QUEENS OF THE TWENTIETH CENTURY

Jewish population, with Anne Frank, who was murdered at the age of only fifteen in the Bergen-Belsen concentration camp, becoming a powerful symbol of the horrors of the Holocaust. Wilhelmina has been criticised for her apparent indifference to the plight of her Jewish citizens, having in the spring of 1939 blocked the creation of a camp for German Jewish refugees in the Dutch village of Elspeet. This was, biographer Cees Fasseur has suggested, more 'NIMBYism ('Not in My Back Yard')' than anti-Semitism, since the camp would have been close to the Het Loo Palace.[23] Nevertheless, she made few references to the appalling treatment of the Dutch Jews in her regular broadcasts, although on 17 October 1940 she did condemn the deportations, lamenting 'the inhuman treatment, indeed the systematic extermination of these compatriots, who lived with us for centuries in our blessed homeland.'[24] Wilhelmina perhaps did not distinguish her Jewish subjects from her Christian ones, although it is not in question that Jewish people in the Netherlands, as in most of Europe, experienced anti-Semitism throughout the twentieth century.[25] In Copenhagen, where the future Queen Margrethe was growing up under German occupation, it is to the credit of the Danish resistance that almost the country's entire Jewish population were secretly evacuated to Sweden in 1943 and, thus, survived the war.[26]

The future Elizabeth II of the United Kingdom grew up during the Second World War, turning eighteen in April 1944 when she was presented with a bracelet by her father and a diamond tiara from her mother (who had become as powerful a resistance symbol as Queen Wilhelmina and 'the most dangerous woman in Europe' according to Adolf Hitler, due to her public defiance during the London Blitz).[27] The princess, who remained with her family in the capital throughout the war, had made her first radio broadcast in October 1940, addressed to the children evacuated from Britain's cities as German bombs began to rain down on them. In March 1945, she joined the Auxiliary Territorial Service, where she learned to drive, as well as how to service and strip an engine, effectively giving her own modern take to the eons old concept of a warrior queen. This wartime service emboldened the princess to ask permission from her parents to leave the balcony at Buckingham Palace on VE Day on 9 May 1945 and join the crowds below who had assembled to celebrate the end of the war in Europe. According to an interview that Elizabeth gave forty years later, 'we cheered the King and Queen on the balcony and then walked miles through the streets', while, unrecognised, she and her sister linked arms with strangers and were 'just swept along on a tide of happiness and relief'.[28]

Queen Sālote, too, ordered celebrations to mark the end of a conflict that had impacted even her remote kingdom. Tongan soldiers fought alongside men from the United States, Australia and New Zealand in the Solomon Islands, while the queen raised funds for Britain's Royal Air Force. She experienced a personal tragedy when, in July 1941, Prince Tungi died and was interred in the Tupou Dynasty's royal burial ground ('standing – an unusual juxtaposition – in the middle of the Nukualofa golf-course').[29] While her sudden widowhood threw Sālote into mourning, she remained the cornerstone of her nation. Like Wilhelmina, a national myth attached itself to this figure who was far from contemporary ideas of a wartime ruler. Sālote emerged from World War Two as 'a mother to her people'.[30]

While flags fluttered on London's Mall and people cried with joy, Wilhelmina had already returned to her war-devastated kingdom. Throughout the war she had kept up her efforts, including addressing the United States Congress in a joint session of the Senate and the House of Representatives in August 1942. Speaking, as she said, as 'the spokesman of my country', she asked those assembled: 'Imagine what it means for a liberty-loving country to be in bondage, for a proud country to be subject to harsh alien rule.' She asked what the

American answer would be to such outrages, declaring, 'Having come by first-hand knowledge to know your national character better than ever, I doubt not that your answer would be: resistance, resistance until the end, resistance in every practicable shape or form.'[31]

Resistance was undoubtedly the path that Wilhelmina, who had been a queen for almost all her life, had followed; as she urged on the rebuilding of her country after the war, she 'seemed to be a sixty-five-year-old human dynamo'.[32] The truth was, however, that Wilhelmina was tired. On 4 September 1948, having agonised over her decision for years, she abdicated the throne to her daughter, Juliana.[33] Her Royal Highness Wilhelmina, Princess of the Netherlands, lived for a further fourteen years, making only rare public appearances, writing her autobiography and enjoying her retirement. Juliana, who would follow her mother's precedent in abdicating in 1980, was herself followed by the reign of her daughter, Beatrix, who abdicated in 2013, with all three women creating an accessible and enormously well-liked style of monarchy. It was only in 1983, after nearly a century of female rule, that the Constitution of the Netherlands was amended to allow for equal succession rights for males and females.

There was an air of hope and expectation when Elizabeth II succeeded to the throne unexpectedly early on 6 February 1952. She was then in Kenya, spending the night amongst the branches of the Treetops Hotel.[34] She was twenty-five years old, the same age that her namesake queen had been at her accession, with the press filled with romantic notions of a 'New Elizabethan Age'. There was certainly much to hope for, with British citizens still required to get their ration books out for sugar, confectionary and some meats even six years after the end of the Second World War. The cities bore the scars of the conflict, with gaping holes in the street scenes and piles of rubble where bombed out buildings had once stood. The empire, of which Elizabeth's great-

great-grandmother Victoria had been so proud, was crumbling, with states either taking, or being reluctantly granted, their freedom during the decades of the twentieth century. This process would continue. Elizabeth was queen of South Africa, Pakistan, Ceylon (now Sri Lanka), Ghana, Nigeria, Sierra Leone, Trinidad and Tobago, Uganda, Malawi, Gambia, Guyana, Barbados, Mauritius, Fiji and Kenya at the start of her reign, but not by its end.

Black-clad and sombre, photographs of the new queen stepping out from her plane at London Airport to be greeted by her prime minister, Winston Churchill, as well as the leader of the opposition, featured on all the world's front pages. Young and attractive, her sex made her instantly recognisable and visible. Elizabeth would soon become the most famous face of the twentieth century and, quite possibly, the entire history of the world. She would never again enjoy the anonymity of the jubilant VE Day crowds. Quickly, plans were put in place for her coronation, which, overcoming the queen's own reservations, was to be televised for the first time. Invitees would, of course, include many of the world's crowned heads.

At home in her pleasant timber palace, which stood two storeys high with wonderful views over the ocean, Sālote could already be justly proud of her record as queen by the time she received her invitation to Elizabeth's coronation. She was initially reluctant to travel so far from Tonga, but was soon persuaded to go, making the arduous journey halfway around the world in the early summer of 1953.

By this point, she had reigned for thirty-five years in times of war and of peace, and had proved adept both at fostering tradition and bringing her kingdom into the modern era of televisions and aeroplanes. Strolling through her palace gardens, which were walled only by a low fence and surrounded by tall Norfolk Island pines, she could see her royal standard fluttering above in blue, red and yellow, while the Royal Guard stood warily, presenting a picture of monarchy that was recognisable the world over.[35] Sometimes she walked bare footed, wearing a skirt made from traditional *tapa*, a fabric made from beaten bark and often highly decorated, and covered by a plaited grass apron, other times she wore elaborate European fashions. She was as adept in English, which she spoke with a New Zealand accent, as she was in her native Tongan. She had raised her sons bilingually too, aware that their futures lay in communicating with the wider, outside world. Sālote actively promoted education, particularly for girls, with most of her young subjects literate.

It was a largely agricultural society, and one that was highly stratified with the queen – as a woman – forced to prove herself capable of government time and again in the early years of her reign. By the start of the 1950s Tonga remained a place that was little known outside Polynesia – if the people of Britain knew anything at all of Tonga, it was likely that it was the site of the 1789 Mutiny on the Bounty, when the notorious Captain William Bligh and nineteen companions were unceremoniously dumped into a small rowing boat while the crew made away with the ship. It was, however rather better known and even popular amongst Europe's stamp collectors. Thanks to the 'Tin-Can Mail' system unique to the island of Niuafoʻou where post was thrown to a waiting swimmer in a tin can wrapped in greased paper, a philatelist in London, Liverpool or Edinburgh could send a letter on a remarkable voyage to the end of the earth to have it returned with a Tongan postmark and, perhaps, for it to be a little water damaged around the edges (providing, of course, that they remembered to enclose a stamped addressed return envelope in a missive addressed to the island's postal service). Sālote, who like Wilhelmina of the Netherlands, would prove to be a late bloomer as a truly global reigning queen, could never have expected that, deep into middle age, she was about to emerge as a superstar on the world stage.

Sālote caused a stir of attention when she landed at Southampton, dressed in a mixture of Tongan and European clothing. Standing at well over six foot, she was a statuesque, highly visible figure: 'the tallest Queen of the smallest Kingdom' screamed the headlines, with news reporters shadowing her everywhere she went in Britain.[36] The *Daily Express*, which published a special souvenir edition for the ceremony, even helpfully pointed out Sālote's seat in a diagram indicating the layout of Westminster Abbey so that viewers could try to spot her amongst the crowds.[37] Elizabeth was, of course, the star of the coronation, sitting still and serious in her throne as the crown was placed upon her head, but Sālote stole the show in its aftermath. Gazed at by millions who crowded around television sets and peered at small black and white screens, she beamed out from her carriage, waving to the crowds and, with some regularity, wiping the torrential rain away from her face. With the roofs of all other carriages in the procession resolutely closed against the downpour, Sālote, who sat opposite a drenched and miserable sultan, shone through like the sun, and the British people lining the streets getting similarly wet and watching at home loved her for it. Even now, more than seventy years later, people old enough to remember the coronation invariably recall Sālote.

In the days following, as she attempted to attend functions or see the sights of London, she was mobbed. Her car, which was unmarked, was surrounded at traffic lights. On a visit to an old friend in Kent, she stepped in to admire a fifteenth-century church only to find a group of children, complete with freshly picked bouquets of flowers waiting for her outside. There were practical benefits to the attention, since Qantas reinstated their defunct Tonga aeroplane route from Europe in response to serious demand from the most well-heeled and wealthier of Sālote's fans. In summing up 1953 at the end of that December, one London paper simply wrote: 'dear, dear Queen Sālote'.[38] Sālote, for her part, was moved by the outpouring of love shown to her in Britain, with the Tongans returning the favour when Elizabeth II and Prince Philip paid the islands a visit in December 1953. The Tongan queen met her British counterpart on the wharf at Nukualofa under an arch inscribed simply '*Ofa Atu*' or, 'we love you'. Perhaps fittingly, as the two queens drove away in an open-top car, it began to rain.

King Frederik IX and Queen Ingrid of Denmark had missed the coronation day rain, sending a cousin and his wife to represent them in Westminster Abbey. The accession of a reigning queen was, however, of interest to the royal couple who had long since given up hope of producing a son. To the trailblazing Ingrid, who had always been a modernising force in the royal family and was herself a great-granddaughter of Queen Victoria, it was ridiculous that her husband's younger brother should be heir and not one of the three royal princesses being raised in Copenhagen.

The eldest, Margrethe, who grew into a tall, slim and studious girl was treated as more of a pet by her father's people after his accession in 1947 than as a future leader, with her signature curls copied by countless other young girls and a doll produced with her likeness.[39] Following lobbying from her mother, her position suddenly changed in 1953 with the passing of a new Act of Succession to allow the inheritance of daughters, but only if they had no brothers.** Nineteen years later, for the first time in Danish history, a queen was proclaimed from the balcony of the exquisite Christiansburg Castle, the seat of the country's government, with the prime minister declaring, 'King Frederik IX is dead. Long live Her Majesty, Queen Margrethe II.'[40]

Margrethe, whose choice of the regnal numbering 'II' also upgraded her medieval predecessor, was a constitutional monarch, but her role was highly visible and important: as one Danish biographer noted,

---

** Women only obtained equal inheritance rights in Denmark in 2009.

she 'is with us everywhere', on coins, stamps, the television and in newspapers.[41] Margrethe's position in Denmark was unprecedented, but times were beginning to change. Twelve years before her accession, Ceylon (now Sri Lanka) had stunned the world with the election of Sirimavo Bandaranaike as prime minister, an event that required the invention of a new word: 'stateswoman'.[42] While not head of state – that was Elizabeth II until she was removed in 1972 – she did head the government, something that was absolutely extraordinary for a non-royal woman. Asia, in fact, led the way for female heads of government, with Indira Gandhi following in India in 1966 and Golda Meir in Israel in 1969.[***] None of these appointments were without their critics, with Banadaranaike responding to complaints that her natural place was in the kitchen with the retort that 'a woman's place is everywhere and anywhere duty requires her to be and *also* in her kitchen!'.[43] She would eventually serve three terms as prime minister.

In the first of these early examples there was a sense of dynasty in the elections. Bandaranaike took over as leader of her party following the assassination of her husband, Solomon Bandaranaike. Gandhi, too, was the only child of the highly respected former Prime Minister Jawaharlal Nehru, who had led the country after independence from Britain and was considered to be the 'Father of the Nation'.[44] She was elected, some believed, 'because of the high regard for her father', although those that hoped to be her 'puppet masters' were soon disabused.[45] The US Secretary of State, Henry Kissinger, considered her 'cold-blooded and tough'.[46] Golda Meir was a career politician and one of only two women to sign Israel's Declaration of Independence in 1948. In 1974, Isabel Perón, Vice-President of Argentina, was upgraded to head of state by the sudden death of the country's premier,

---

[***] Central African Republic followed in 1975 with the appointment of Elisabeth Domitien as prime minister. Margaret Thatcher, who became Prime Minister of the United Kingdom in April 1979 was the first woman to head a European government, closely followed by Maria de Lourdes Pintasilgo in Portugal that August.

QUEENS OF THE TWENTIETH CENTURY

Juan Perón. Always overshadowed by her husband's deceased wife 'Evita', Isabel's brief tenure was the first time a non-royal woman served as head of state of an internationally recognised nation. (Sadly, 'The 18-month presidency of Mrs Perón was a disaster,' according to at least one commentator. Most would not disagree.)[47] She had, in fact, been preceded in 1940 by Khertek Anchimaa, who became Chairwoman of the Presidium of the Little Khural in the short-lived Tuvan People's Republic, which sat in the borderlands between the Soviet Union and Mongolia.[48] Technically, the world's first non-royal head of state, her country was almost entirely unrecognised by the wider world, with her presidency ending in 1944 when Tuvan was absorbed into the USSR.

It would not be until 1980 that a woman, Vigdis Finnbogadóttir, was elected to a presidency in her own right, serving as President of Iceland for sixteen years, which remains a record term in her country. At the time of writing, Finnbogadóttir, now in her nineties, remains politically active. She was also the founding chair of the Council of Women World Leaders, which was created in 1996 and, sadly, continues to have a somewhat limited membership. Margaret Thatcher, who became prime minister of the UK in 1979 and was the first woman to head a government in Europe, was heavily criticised by the press in 1989 for seemingly using the 'royal we' in her excitement over becoming a grandparent.[49] Most likely a slip of the tongue, it must be said that the Queen was her only real close example of female rule. In photographs taken at meetings of the leaders of Commonwealth nations throughout her reign, Elizabeth II was usually the only woman present.

The reign of Elizabeth II was a turning point for monarchy in Britain and the wider world. By the second half of the twentieth century there was little real objection to a reigning queen, at least in Europe, although equally there was no real appetite for making changes to the succession. The Queen's second son, Andrew, immediately outranked his nine-year-old sister, Anne, at his birth in 1960, as did the youngest son, Edward, who was born when his sister was thirteen. Despite the long reign of Queen Elizabeth and worldwide recognition of her as a symbol of her country, this patriarchal mode of succession would only be changed in 2013 with the passing of the Succession to the Crown Act, and then only for royal children born after that date. As such, the Queen's great-granddaughter, Princess Charlotte of Wales stands ahead of her younger brother, Prince Louis, in the succession, but Princess Anne remains behind her younger brothers and their children. With queens reigning in Britain for 133 of the past 200 years, the idea of a female monarch was hardly an alien one, but it remained the compromise option.

Elizabeth II's long reign was, inevitably, one that saw setbacks as well as triumphs, with the relevance of her position called into question at times, particularly during the difficult 1990s which witnessed political and family turmoil. How her role was viewed in February 1952 as she climbed down from a tree in Kenya and how it was perceived at the celebrations of her Platinum Jubilee in the summer of 2022 were starkly different, with the person of the Queen herself, and the ancientness of her office, the thread that held the monarchy together. One scratchy recording of Queen Victoria's voice survives on a Graphophone wax cylinder from 1888, in which we can hear almost nothing, but Elizabeth and her fellow twentieth century queens speak to us. That the increasingly insistent demands in the summer of 1997 following the death of Diana, Princess of Wales, requiring the Queen to appear in public and speak to the people were eventually (and reluctantly) heeded shows that the role of a monarch – and, perhaps, especially that of a reigning queen – had changed forever. Already highly visible due to her sex, Elizabeth had nowhere to hide and no right to privacy at a time of national mourning. Queens of the twentieth century and later are the most visible the world has ever known, something that it took the naturally shy Elizabeth II some time to be reconciled with.

Elizabeth II lies beneath a black marble plaque in the royal chapel at Windsor Castle, a place that meant much to her in her lifetime. With her death, Margrethe II of Denmark became the world's only reigning queen. Although still alive, she has already prepared her own tomb, which remains covered and waiting in Denmark's historic Roskilde Cathedral, where her distant predecessor Margrete I of Denmark, Norway and Sweden also lies. Margrethe II's tomb, which was commissioned from the artist Bjorn Norgaard, includes a clear glass sarcophagus with effigies of the queen and her French-born consort, Prince Henrik. It will inadvertently symbolise the still contentious and anomalous position of reigning queens into the twentieth century and beyond, since Henrik, who died in 2018, will not be spending eternity with his wife.

It is interesting that despite the changes to women's rights and increasing parity between the sexes, socially as well as legally, in the late twentieth century and the early years of the twenty-first, it seems that being married to a reigning queen could still be a difficult pill for some male consorts to swallow. Henri Marie Jean André de Laborde de Monpezat, who married Margrethe in 1967, was an intellectual and a poet, but never truly at peace with his role as Henrik, Denmark's prince consort.**** In August 2018 he told the Danish magazine *Se og Hør* that his wife 'is the one who makes a fool of me'.[50] He continued, stating that 'My wife has decided that she wants to be queen, and I am very happy about that. But as a human being, she must know that if a man and wife are married, they are equal.' While the royal couple insisted that their marriage was solid, there was obvious and undoubted tension based squarely on Henrik's status as prince.[51] Indeed, in an interview in 2017 he insisted that he would only agree to burial with his wife if she

---

**** He published his memoirs in his native French, using his birth name rather than his Danish title. Henri de Monpezat, *Destin Oblige* (Plon, 1996).

made him a king consort: neither happened and Henrik was cremated following his death in 2018.[52] His ashes were also scattered, making any chance of a posthumous reunion unlikely. Queen Juliana, daughter of Wilhelmina, who reigned following her abdication in 1948 would find the same, with her husband, Prince Bernhard, informing her during one disagreement: 'in the nation you rule; in the home, I do'.[53] Their marriage was unsurprisingly troubled.

The queens of the twentieth century, like their predecessors, were often unwanted and sometimes underestimated. Take Wilhelmina, who was cruelly summed up by the outdoorsy, bullish Theodore Roosevelt after one lunch in 1910 as appearing as 'a puffed-up wife of some leading grocer proud of her position'. Should you decide to play the sixth instalment of the strategy computer game *Civilisation*, however, where players build and rule a polity led by a real historical world leader, you can choose to play as Wilhelmina.[54] Few female world leaders have been so immortalised, with the queen – in the digital world at least – now taking her place beside the dismissive former US president who so disliked her. Cleopatra VII, Wu Zetian, Tamar, Elizabeth I and Victoria, who are amongst the most well-known of reigning women, stand digitally alongside her. By virtue of her position as a female head of state resisting the invasion of her country, Wilhelmina has become a warrior in the popular imagination, a role that is as constructed as that accorded to the so-called warrior queens of Kush, Zenobia of Palmyra or Isabel I of Castile. Actions and circumstances have changed, but much remains the same in the way that powerful women are perceived and interpreted.

Wilhelmina, Sālote, Elizabeth and Margrethe witnessed great change during their own reigns, as warfare turned to peace and the era in which they lived became truly – and digitally - global. Elizabeth II would see three female prime ministers, while Margrethe's final prime minister was a woman. Sālote became the most popular person in a land a world away from her own, while all were instantly recognisable on television screens across the world. All four live on (or in Margrethe's case, will live on) and their queenships continue in the countless films, photographs and recordings of their lives and deeds. Never before have reigning queens, and powerful women, been so visible.

AFTERWORD:
THE WOMEN WHO WILL RULE THE WORLD

Princess Masalanabo Modjadji turned eighteen on 20 January 2023, celebrating with a party a few months later in Pretoria, one of South Africa's three capital cities. It was a significant moment for the young woman, who had grown up largely away from the spotlight, harbouring schoolgirl dreams of becoming a doctor.[1] Yet, Masalanabo had also been raised to understand that she was different. She knew, her guardian admitted from the quiet Johannesburg suburb where they lived, that to rule was 'her position by birth'.[2] Masalanabo was only a few months old when her mother, the Rain Queen Makobo Modjadji VI, died suddenly in 2005, ending the shortest reign in the Balobedu queendom's 200-year history. Times were already changing, with Modjadji VI the first of her maternal line able to read and write, while she could also speak English, send an email and drive a car. Even as the modern world impinged on her ancient realm, much remained the same. The rain still had to fall and Masalanabo, following her eighteenth birthday, was expected to be crowned.

On 14 January 2024, six days before the still-uncrowned Masalanabo

WOMEN WHO RULED THE WORLD

Modjadji turned nineteen, a fellow reigning queen, the world's only reigning female sovereign, Margrethe II of Denmark, climbed out of her carriage and entered the Christiansborg Palace in central Copenhagen to add her signature to the instrument of abdication. She had astonished her kingdom and the wider world when, two weeks before, on New Year's Eve, she had announced her decision to hand over to her son, Frederik. In doing so, Margrethe joined former Queen Beatrix of the Netherlands as an ex-reigning queen, moving into well-deserved, but likely somewhat daunting, retirement. She had reigned fifty-two years to the day and remained popular in Denmark to the end, with the crowds coming out to wave her goodbye.

The Dutch and the Danes of the early years of the twenty-first century could have been forgiven for viewing themselves as living in a queendom, with Margrethe and Beatrix (along with the Dutch queen's mother and grandmother) making the monarchies their own. Yet, there is only one acknowledged queendom in the world and that is that of the Balobedu. South Africa's Apartheid government had mounted a challenge to this, stripping the Rain Queen, Modjadji IV, of her queenship in 1972. They relegated her, with the stroke of a pen, to the status of a chieftainess, attempting to diminish the mythology and power of her rule.[3] On 26 July 2016, in the midst of a deep and typically dry South African winter, the Minister for Cooperative Governance and Traditional Affairs, Des van Rooyen, and the Deputy Minister responsible for Traditional Affairs, Obed Bapela, were startled by torrential rains, which showered the entire country. Was it an omen? It certainly seemed like it. On the orders of President Jacob Zuma, the dignitaries came to the Balobedu to inform them of official recognition of their queendom once more, in a new section added to the Traditional Leadership and Governance Framework Act of 2003. According to the official government report, 'This important breakthrough of recognising the queenship of the Balobedu is victory to the women and highlights the progress that government has made thus far to ensure equality between men and women.' The Balobedu queenship was, the government report noted, matrilineal and could only pass to women. As such, Masalanabo, the only daughter of the previous Rain Queen, was undoubtedly next in line.

Yet, in November 2021 Masalanabo's uncle and regent during her childhood, Prince Mpapatla Modjadji, declared that 'the rain-making tradition was not attached to the gender of the monarch'.[4] It was, he insisted, a collaborative effort, involving the whole community. As a result, he declared Masalanabo's elder brother, Prince Lekukela, as the queendom's first Rain King. He was, accordingly, installed as king in late 2022, although he remains uncrowned.[5] So, too, does Masalanabo, who may or may not be the seventh Rain Queen and whose supporters and lawyers continue to mount a defence of her rights through South Africa's constitutional courts. At the time of writing, it is still far from clear that the Balobedu will continue as a queendom, or whether, after more than 200 years, they will revert to a kingdom. It is depressing that even in the twenty-first century a woman can be pushed aside and marginalised at the hands of her male kin although, as Blanca II of Navarre, Charlotte of Cyprus and even Cleopatra VII of Egypt (amongst many others) could assert, it was ever thus.

Although the numbers of monarchies have dwindled over the centuries, it remains a prominent and enduring system of government. There are, perhaps, twenty or so monarchs alive today, although the numbers are difficult to quantify with certainty. Charles III, who himself succeeded a reigning queen in 2022, rules over fifteen states, making the number of monarchies considerably higher than the number of monarchs. Conversely, there are seventeen elected female presidents in office today, presiding as heads of state in (at the time of writing) the Marshall Islands, Georgia, Moldova, Greece, Tanzania, Kosovo, Barbados, Honduras, India, Peru, Slovenia, Trinidad and Tobago,

WOMEN WHO RULED THE WORLD

Dominica, Malta, North Macedonia, Iceland and Mexico. Two of India's fifteen presidents have been female, two of Iceland's seven have been women, and so have three of Malta's eleven.* These figures are surprisingly encouraging, although as women make up 50 per cent of the global population, they remain highly underrepresented. Even if female prime ministers are included as heads of government, it is clear that inequality abounds. There are approximately 150 presidencies today – 90 per cent are occupied by men.

What the stories of the world's reigning queens has shown most clearly is that women must often fight to have their voices heard, but they do take up that struggle. This happens at all levels of society, as we have seen with the Japanese noblewomen writing their own autobiographies in the tenth and eleventh centuries as a means of recording thoughts and feelings that would otherwise have remained unspoken. In most cases, the personal names by which they were known have not survived. Nothing similar exists from Europe at such an early date, although the English merchant's wife, Margery Kempe, poured out her soul in her *Book* written at the start of the fifteenth century. In it, she recounted her religious visions alongside more hum-drum facts of her daily life. Kempe also sought out other women, seeking solace and support in a life that was often gruelling. In her *Book* she recounts her meeting with the anchoress Julian of Norwich, who had walled herself up in a cell beside her parish church, devoting her life to spiritual matters, prayer and, crucially, writing.[6] It is astounding that the two earliest known female authors in the English language knew each other, even if only by passing acquaintance.[7]

Christine de Pizan, writing in French in the late fourteenth century, could envisage an allegorical city ruled over and peopled by women.

---

* While the prime minister is the most prominent member of the Indian government and the country's true ruler, the president is the head of state. This is currently Droupadi Murmu, who was sworn in on 25 July 2022.

She was inspired by the realisation that, 'So many men – clerics as well as others – have always been so ready to say and write such abominable and hateful things about women and their nature.'[8] Pizan, a widow who supported herself and her children with her pen, was an evocative writer, with her griefs, frustrations and joys echoing down the centuries. She admitted many reigning queens into her 'City of Ladies', such as the devoted Artemisia II of Caria, who built the Mausoleum of Halicarnassus, one of the Seven Wonders of the Ancient World in honour of her brother-husband.[9] Even 1700 years after her death, Artemisia spoke to Pizan. Just as Pizan, 600 years after her death, speaks to us.

Such writings often survive by chance: Kempe's *Book* was rediscovered at a house party in the 1930s while guests were scouring the cupboards trying to find a table tennis ball. They happened, instead, on the only remaining manuscript of the earliest autobiography written in English. As the Classical historian, Professor Mary Beard, who has herself been the victim of appallingly overt misogyny has noted, 'if there's one thing that bonds women of all backgrounds, of all political colours, in all kinds of business and profession, it is the classic experience of the failed intervention; you're at a meeting, you make a point, then a short silence follows, and after a few awkward seconds some man picks up where he had just left off'.[10] Even successful reigning queens, who often had to fight to achieve and maintain their positions of power faced this. How frustrating must it have been for Elizabeth I to hear that her favourite, the Earl of Essex, had complained that 'they laboured under things at this Court, delay and inconstancy, which proceeded from the sex of the queen'? How exhausting for her that, after voicing an opinion regarding one of her own kingdoms her Lord Deputy in Ireland declared that 'this fiddling woman troubles me out of measure'? Women's voices are frequently dismissed, and their wisdom goes unlistened to. Even where a reigning queen failed to fully make her voice heard (and this is arguably more the fault of the people listening than the woman speaking), her story is still essential. There was power in the attempt to rule: when Atototzli abandoned her spinning and Qudsia Begum her veil. We cannot understand female power, nor build on it, without now listening to what they had to say.

In many ways, the title of this book is a misnomer. Even successful queens, such as the fearsome Wu Zetian, literary Suiko, ambitious Elizabeth I, enlightened and despotic Catherine the Great and dogged and determined Maria Theresia, existed as anomalies in a man's world. There has never been an age where any woman ruled the world, nor an era where women ruled the world (although Victoria made a very strong attempt at it). As we have seen, if they were fortunate, they might – just might – rule a small portion of it. Yet, women keep trying. At the time of writing, Kamela Harris has just become the second female candidate to lose a United States' presidential election. She and Hillary Clinton are the only two women to ever be chosen as candidates for the presidency and both lost to Donald Trump. It is a sobering thought. The United States has never had a female head of state, although Britain's American colonies were once ruled by absentee queens Mary II and Anne at the end of the seventeenth century and in the early years of the eighteenth. Through the vagaries of hereditary monarchy, Anne could rule as head of state in America in the eighteenth century, while Kamala Harris was defeated in the twenty-first. Will the United States ever elect a woman as president? Probably, but we may have a long wait.

Female candidates for election tend to face higher scrutiny of their appearance, lifestyles and demeanour. What are they wearing? What do they look like? Have they had surgery? Kemi Badenoch, who was recently elected as leader of the UK's Conservative Party, faced criticism from Sir Christopher Chope MP, who claimed that she was too preoccupied with her young children to act as party leader.

THE WOMEN WHO WILL RULE THE WORLD

That Sir Christopher's words caused outrage and he apologised is an encouraging sign of the position of women in modern public life. However, it is notable that he did not similarly criticise Badenoch's male opponent who is himself the father of a young family. In the twelfth century, Empress Matilda of England was accused of wrinkling her forehead into a frown and giving a 'grim look'. She was charged by contemporaries with insufferable arrogance when the same conduct would have been lauded in a king. She lost a crown (apparently) for refusing to stand when her lesser ranking supporters entered the room and for trusting in her own counsel. Her father, the still-revered Henry I, ordered the blinding of his own little granddaughters and sentenced his elder brother to decades-long imprisonment.[11] Women are frequently held to very different standards to men.

Women do not rule the world, but they undoubtedly have ruled across the world, with female rule known from every continent and every era.** The examples in this book could have been added to many times over. Instead of Isabel I, the 'warrior queen' of Castile, we could have had Nzinga, seventeenth-century Queen of Ndongo and Matamba in modern-day Angola, who was famed for her generalship. Alternatively, there is Sayyida al-Hurra, Isabel's near contemporary, who menaced Spanish shipping from her coastal kingdom of Tétouan on the southern edge of the Strait of Gibraltar.[12] Isabel I's namesake and descendant, Isabel II of Spain, led an eventful life in the nineteenth century that could have featured in several chapters dealing with, for example, unwanted females, child queens (she was only two when she came to the throne), a queen who lost her throne (although, unlike others, not her head), or a queen during the age of colonisation and empires, an era of change that ultimately contributed to the removal of her crown.

** Well, perhaps not Antarctica...

While reigning queens must be understood in relation to their own cultural context, it is valid to make comparisons between them, not least because their histories help us to build a model for female power.[13] The synchronicity of the role that has been uncovered is amazing. The world is, in the main, subject to patriarchal systems and, as such, highly diverse women have faced analogous circumstances. They recognised this themselves, with Queen Victoria acknowledging the similarity of her position even as she sat down to write to Pomare IV of Tahiti, Liliʻuokalani of Hawaii or Shah Jehan Begum of Bhopal. That she understood her commonality with the far distant Zenobia, too, is suggested by childhood drawings of her romanticised version of the queen (after she had finally become aware of the likelihood of her own accession). In one, completed when she was just thirteen years old and surviving in the Royal Collection, the future British queen depicted her Palmyran counterpart seated and pensive, surrounded by her children.[14] Entering from the right-hand side of the frame is a self-portrait of the artist herself, with the princess inscribing the drawing as 'Zenobia and her sons, Septimia near her, & Odenathus with Victoria entering'. As a future reigning queen herself, Victoria felt qualified to step inside the ancient queen's life and story.

While there is a dearth of queens today, over the next few decades the position should be very rosy indeed. Leonor, Princess of the Asturias, turned eighteen just ten months after Masalanabo Modjadji. All being well, the princess, who is currently undertaking military training, will one day become Queen of Spain. In Sweden, Victoria, the eldest child of King Carl XVI Gustaf, was demoted from heir to the throne in 1979 with the birth of a younger brother. Only a few months later she was promoted when Sweden's succession laws changed to a system of absolute primogeniture. Victoria will likely be Europe's next reigning queen. Others should follow. In Norway, the teenaged Ingrid Alexandra, the eldest child of Crown Prince Haakon will, most likely, reign. Belgians have the reign of Elisabeth, Duchess of Brabant, to look forward to. She is currently in her early twenties and began carrying out official functions in her childhood. The Netherlands, too, which has such a strong tradition of female rule thanks to the powerful example of Wilhelmina, Juliana and Beatrix, will one day see the reign of Catharina-Amalia. In all of these cases, barring Spain, the royal heiresses' position is fixed: they cannot be supplanted by a younger brother. This is considerable progress and, while these young women are subject to greater scrutiny than their brothers or male cousins, a remarkable equality has emerged in many of the world's royal families.*** Often, succession laws allowing for the equal succession of children regardless of sex have been enacted during the reigns of queens. Women still struggle to secure election as heads of state, but amongst the monarchies of Europe we can expect an abundant crop of reigning queens.

In faraway New Zealand, on the opposite side of the world, a queen has just begun to rule. On 5 September 2024, twenty-seven-year-old Ngā Wai hono i te po Paki seated herself on a throne as part of a ceremony known as *Te Whakawahingha* in which the coffin of her father, Kiingi Tuheitia Pōtatau Te Wherowhero VII was carried by canoe to the royal burial ground on Taupiri Mountain.[15] The sixty-nine-year-old king, who had himself succeeded his mother, Queen Te Atairangikaahu, had died the previous week, with tributes pouring in from across the world. Amidst a crowd that numbered in the thousands, the queen, who wore a wreath of leaves on her head, as well as a traditional cloak and whalebone necklace, was acclaimed by chants and prayers. Don Tamihere, Archbishop of New Zealand, placed a Bible that had been used in every coronation ceremony since 1858 on Nga Wai's

---

*** Catharina-Amalia of the Netherlands, for example, has been subject to 'fat shaming' since her childhood. It seems unlikely that a brother would have been labelled as 'plus-sized' on the cover of a magazine.

head, before anointing her with sacred oils. In this, she followed in the tradition of her predecessors, who had been inaugurated in 1858 as part of the 'Kīngitanga', or Māori King Movement.[16] Alarmed by the growing dominance of white settlers from Europe, the Māori tribes had come together to appoint a king to represent them on a more equal footing. Although an elective rather than a hereditary monarchy, the Māori kingship of New Zealand has effectively been passed through one family line, with sons succeeding fathers and, now in two cases, daughters succeeding to the throne. In spite of the element of choice involved in the election of a successor, there was considerable surprise in the world's press that the new queen had been chosen in preference to her two elder brothers.[17] It was ever thus.

As I write, Nga Wai is the only acknowledged reigning queen in the world, although Masalanabo Modjadji may, perhaps, join her. So, too, will Victoria of Sweden, Leonor of Spain, Ingrid Alexandra of Norway, Elisabeth of Belgium and Catharine-Amalia of the Netherlands. By the end of the century there will likely be a Japanese reigning empress, too, as well as women from across the world yet to be born. These women provide visibility and will be given a voice still often denied to other members of their sex. Monarchy is not going anywhere, and reigning queens are as relevant to female power today as they were in the nineteenth century CE and the nineteenth century BCE.

Step inside the Prehistoric Museum of Blaubeuren in Germany and you will be greeted by a small figurine, painstakingly pieced back together by archaeologists after it was discovered deep inside the Hohle Fels cave in 2008.****[18] Large-breasted with wide hips, this highly stylised figure is unmistakeably female and belongs to a tradition of 'Venuses' created by our prehistoric ancestors, almost all of which depict women.[19] Carved from mammoth ivory, these figures

---

**** The Venus was found near a vulture bone flute, which is possibly the oldest known musical instrument in the world. See Bruce Bower, 'Oldest known instruments found', *Science News*, vol. 176, no.2 (2009), p13.

are impossibly ancient, with their precise purpose and meaning lost in the millennia that separates us from their makers. Perhaps they depict powerful queens ruling over the tribal groups of prehistoric Eurasia. Merneith, reigning queen of First Dynasty Egypt, may stand right at the beginning of recorded history, but she was unlikely to have been the first queen to lead a nation. What is certain is that, at approximately 38,000 years old, the Venus of Hohle Fels is the earliest known representation of a human. And she is female.

The fourteenth-century Christine de Pizan created her all-female city as 'a refuge' or 'a bastion' against the enemies of womankind. This women's utopia was universal: 'Ladies from the past, the present, and the future: you may all live here.'[20] As this book has shown, there is no Amazonian idyll in the depths of the past, but throughout human history women have ruled. Through their stories, their successes and their failures, we can see a rich and varied history of female political power at odds with the prevailing narrative. There are no world conquerors here, in the vein of Chinggis Khan, Timur or Napoleon, but what women have done in daring to reign is all the more remarkable. Unwelcome, disparaged and often ignored, we cannot tell the tale of world history without the likes of Catherine the Great, Tamar of Georgia, Queen Victoria, the nawab begums of Bhopal, the queens of Meroë, or even poor, doomed, Arsinoë IV of Egypt. To ignore them gives us only half the story. These women ruled across the world and their lives speak to us and tell us what it is to bear rule.

REFERENCES
BIBLIOGRAPHY

Manuscript Sources

Archives consulted include Archivo General de Simancas, Hawaiian State Archives, The National Archives (UK). Full references are included in the endnotes.

Printed Primary Sources

Al-Tabari, *The History of al-Tabari, vol IV: The Ancient Kingdoms*, ed. Moshe Perlmann (New York, 1987)

Bernice Pauahi Bishop, *The Memoirs of Hon. Bernice Pauahi Bishop*, ed. Mary H. Krout (New York, 1908)

George Boustronios, *A Narrative Chronicle of Cyprus, 1456-1489*, ed. and trans. Nicholas Coureas (Nicosia, 2005)

Delmer M. Brown and Ichiro Ishida, eds., *The Future and the Past: A Translation and Study of the Gukansho, An Interpretative History of Japan Written in 1219* (Berkeley: University of California Press, 1979)

James Bruce, *Travels to Discover the Source of the Nile*, vol IV (London, 1790)

Florio Bustron, *Chronique de L'Ile de Chypre* (Paris, 1886)

Calendar of State Papers Foreign: Elizabeth, vol 8, 1566-1568, ed. Allan James Crosby (London: HMSO, 1871)

Calendar of State Papers, Spain (Simancas), vol 4 1587-1603 (London: HMSO, 1899)

Doctor Lorenzo Galindez de Carvajal, 'La Cronica del rey Don Juan el Segundo' in *Biblioteca de Autores Espanoles, Desde La Formacion del Lenguaje Hasta Nuestros Dias: Cronicas de Los Reyese de Castilla Desde Don Alfonso el Sabio, Hasta Los Catolicos Don Fernando y Dona Isabel*, vol 2, ed. Don Cayetano Rosell (Madrid: M. Rivadeneyra, 1877)

Dio Cassius, *Roman History Books 41-5*, ed. and trans., Earnest Cary (Cambridge: Harvard University Press, 1916)

Catherine the Great, *The Memoirs of Catherine the Great*, eds. Mark Cruse and Hilde Hoogenboom (New York: Random House, 2006)

Catherine the Great, *Selected Letters*, eds. Andrew Kahn and Kelsey Rubin-Detleve (Oxford: Oxford University Press, 2018)

Basil Hall Chamberlain, ed., *A Translation of the "Ko-ji-ki" or Records of Ancient Matters* (Yokohama, 1882)

Kitabatake Chikafusa, *A Chronicle of Gods and Sovereigns: Jinno Shotoki of Kitabatake Chikafusa*, trans. H. Paul Varley (New York, 1980)

The Chronique d'Ernoul and The Colbert-Fontainebleau Continuation of William of Tyre, vol 2: *The Continuation of William of Tyre*, ed. Peter Edbury and Massimiliano Gaggero (2023)

Arthur Clifford, ed., *Sadler State Papers*, 2 vols (Edinburgh, 1809), p87.

Corpus Juris Sueo-Gotorum Antiqui, vol IX, ed. Carl Johan Schlyter, (Lund, 1859)

Hernan Cortes, *Letters from Mexico*, eds. Anthony Pagden and J.H. Elliott (New Haven: Yale Universtiy Press, 1986)

Sunity Devee, Maharani of Cooch Behar, *The Autobiography of an Indian Princess* (London, 1921)

Simonds d'Ewes, 'Journal of the House of Commons: November 1586' in *The Journals of All the Parliaments During the Reign of Queen Elizabeth* (Shannon, 1682)

Bernal Diaz del Castillo, *The True History of the Conquest of Mexico*, Maurice Keating ed. and trans. (London: J. Wright, 1880)

BIBLIOGRAPHY

Diaries and Correspondence of James Harris, First Earl of Malmesbury, vol I, ed. J.H. Harris (London, 1845)

Lori Boornazian Diel, ed., *The Codex Mexicanus: A Guide to Life in Late Sixteenth-Century New Spain* (Austin: University of Texas Press, 2018)

Diplomatarium Norvegicum, vol I, ed. Christian C.A. Lange and Carl R. Unger (Christiana: P.T. Mallings, 1847)

Michael H. Dodgeon and Samuel N.C. Lieu, eds., *The Roman Eastern Frontier and the Persian Wars AD 226-363* (London: Routledge, 1991)

Katherine Fischer Drew, trans. and ed., *The Laws of the Salian Franks* (Philadelphia: University of Pennsylvania Press, 1991)

Tormod Eide, Tomas Hägg, Richard Holton Pierce and Laszlo Török, eds., *Fontes Historiae Nubiorum: Textual Sources for the History of the Middle Nile Region Between the Eighth Century BC and the Sixth Century AD, vol III: From the First to the Sixth Century AD* (Bergen: University of Bergen, 1998)

Elizabeth I, *Elizabeth I Collected Works,* eds Leah S. Marcus, Janel Mueller and Mary Beth Rose (Chicago: University of Chicago Press, 2002)

England Under the Reigns of Edward VI and Mary, with the Contemporary History of Europe, Illustrated with a Series of Original Letters Never Before Published, vol I, ed. Patrick Fraser Tytler (London, Richard Bentley, 1839)

Excerpta Cypria: Materials for a History of Cyprus, ed. Claude Delaval Cobham (Cambridge, 1908)

Carolyn Fluehr-Lobban, 'Nubian Queens in the Nile Valley and Afro-Asiatic Cultural History', *Ninth International Conference for Nubian Studies, Museum of Fine Arts Boston* (1998)

Marie-Henriette Fourmy and Maurice Leroy, eds., 'Laa Vie de S. Philaréte', *Byzantion,* vol 9, (1934), pp113–167

Jean Froissart, *Chronicles,* trans. and ed. Geoffrey Brereton (London: Penguin, 1978)

Indira Gandhi, *My Truth* (New York, 1980)

Paul Gauguin, *Noa Noa: The Tahitian Journal* (New York: Dover Publications, 1985)

The Georgian Chronicle: The Period of Giorgi Lasha, ed. Simon Qaukhchishvili and trans. Katharine Vivian (Amsterdam: Adolf M. Hakkert, 1991)

Gesta Stephani, ed. and trans. K.R. Potter and R.H.C. Davis (Oxford: Clarendon Press, 1976)

Franciso de López de Gómara, *Historia de las Conquistas de Hernando Cortez* (Mexico, 1826)

The Hamilton Papers: Letters and Papers Illustrating the Political Relations of England and Wales in the XVIth Century Formerly in the Possession of the Dukes of Hamilton Now in the British Museum, vol I, ed. Joseph Bain (Edinburgh, 1890)

Hawaiian Islands: Report of the Committee on Foreign Relations, United States Senate, with Accompanying Testimony, and Executive Documents Transmitted to Congress from January 1, 1893, to March 10, 1894, vol II (Washington: Government Printing Office 1894)

Emerentia van Heuvan-van Nes, ed., *Darling Queen, Dear Old Bones: Queen Wilhemlina's Correspondence with her English Governess Miss Saxton Winter 1886-1935* (Amsterdam: Amsterdam University Press, 2017)

Historia Augusta, vol 3, ed. and trans. David Magie and David Rohrbacher (Cambridge: Harvard University Press, 2022)

Historia de los Mexicanos por sus Pinturas, ed. Joaquín García Icazbalceta (Mexico, 1891)

The Holy and Righteous King David the Restorer of Georgia and The Holy and Righteous Queen Tamar of Georgia: Lives Akathists Canons Works, ed. John Townsend and trans. Irakli Beridze (Tbilisi, 2021)

William Hough, *A Brief History of the Bhopal Principality in Central* India (Calcutta: Baptist Mission Press, 1845)

Ilyon, *Samguk Yusa: Legends and History of the Three Kingdoms of Ancient Korea,* trans. Tae-Hung Ha and Grafton K. Mintz (Seoul, 1972)

Geoffrey C. Ingleton, ed., *True Patriots All: Or News from Early Australia as Told in a Collection of Broadsides* (Sydney, 1952)

The International Exhibition of 1862: The Illustrated Catalogue of the Industrial Department, vol 4: Foreign Division (Cambridge: Cambridge University Press, 1862)

BIBLIOGRAPHY

Jorgen Jensen, 'A Danish visit to the Society Islands in 1846: Extracts from the diary of Cornelius Schmidt', *The Journal of Pacific History*, vol 31, no.1 (1996), pp104–107

Flavius Josephus, *The Genuine Works of Flavius Josephus, the Jewish Historian*, ed. and trans. William Whiston (1737)

Julian of Norwich, *Revelations of Divine Love*, trans. Barry Windeatt (Oxford: Oxford University Press, 2015)

King Kalakaua's World Tour (Honolulu, 1881)

Margery Kempe, *The Book of Margery Kempe*, trans. Anthony Bale (Oxford: Oxford University Press, 2015)

John Knox, *The Political Writings of John Knox: The First Blast of the Trumpet Against the Monstrous Regiment of Women and Other Selected Works*, ed. Marvin A. Breslow (Washington: Folger, 1985)

Prince Alexandre Labanoff, ed., *Lettres et Memoires de Marie, Reine d'Ecosse*, vol 2 (London: Charles Dolman, 1844)

Letters from the East: Crusaders, Pilgrims and Settlers in the 12th-13th Centuries, ed. and trans. Malcolm Barber and Keith Bate (Farnham: Routledge, 2013)

Lili'uokalani of Hawaii, *Hawaii's Story by Hawaii's Queen* (1898)

Lili'uokalani of Hawaii, *The Diaries of Queen Liliuokalani of Hawaii*, ed. David W. Forbes (Honolulu: University of Hawai'i Press, 2019)

Lili'uokalani of Hawaii, *The Kumulipo* (2020)

Robert Lindsay of Pitscottie, *The Historie and Cronicles of Scotland from the Slauchter of King James the First to the Ane Thousand Fyve Hundreith Thrie Scoir Fyftein Zeir*, vol 1, ed. A.J.G. MacKay, (Edinburgh: William Blackwood and Sons, 1899)

Die Lübekischen Chroniken in Niederdeutscher Sprache, vol 1, ed. F.H. Grautoff, (Hamburg: Perthes under Besser, 1829)

Manetho, *Manetho*, ed. and trans. W.G. Waddell (1989)

Maria Theresia of Austria, *Letters of an Empress: A Collection of Intimate Letters from Maria Theresia to her Children and Friends*, ed. G. Pusch and trans. Eilee R. Taylor (London: Massie, 1939)

WOMEN WHO RULED THE WORLD

Henry Byam Martin, *The Polynesian Journal of Captain Henry Byam Martin, RN, in Command of HMS Grampus – 50 Guns at Hawaii and on Station in Tahiti and the Society Islands August 1846 to August 1847* (Canberra: Australian National University Press, 1981)

Sir James Melville, *The Memoirs of Sir James Melville of Halhill*, ed. Gordon Donaldson (London: Folio Society, 1969)

Memorias de don Enrique IV de Castilla, vol 2 (Madrid: Establecimiento Tipografico de Fortanet,1835–1913)

Jerónimo de Mendieta, *Historia Eclesiástica Indiana* (Barcelona, 2011)

Michitsuna's Mother, *The Kagero Diary: A Woman's Autobiographical Text from Tenth Century Japan*, ed. and trans. Sonja Arntzen (Michigan: University of Michigan Press, 1997)

Henri de Monpezat, *Destin Oblige* (Plon, 1996)

Garci Rodriguez de Montalvo, *The Labors of the Very Brave Knight Esplandián*, ed. and trans. William Thomas Little (New York: Medieval and Renaissance Texts and Studies, 1992)

Jose Moret and Francois Aleson, *Anales del Reino de Navarra*, vols 6 and 7 (Tolosa, 1890–92)

Sambhu Chandra Mukhopa'dhya'ya, *The Career of An Indian Princess: The Late Begum Secunder of Bhopal, K.S.I.* (Calcutta, 1869)

The New Oxford Annotated Bible, fifth edition, ed. Michael D. Coogan (Oxford: Oxford University Press, 2010)

Nihongi: Chronicles of Japan from the Earliest Times to A.D. 697, vol II, ed. W.G. Aston (London: The Japan Society, 1896)

The Old Book of Tang (published online at https://chinesenotes.com/jiutangshu.html)

'The Old French Continuation of William of Tyre, 1184-97' in *The Conquest of Jerusalem and the Third Crusade: Sources in Translation*, ed. Peter W. Edbury (Aldershot: Routledge, 1998)

Alfonso de Palencia, *Cronica de Enrique IV*, 5 vols, ed. D.A. Paz y Melia (Madrid, 1908)

BIBLIOGRAPHY

William Patten, *The Expedicion into Scotlande (1548) in Fragments of Scottish History*, ed. J.G. Dalyell (Edinburgh, 1798)

H.J.C. Pieterse, ed., *Volksaltare of 'N Veteraan van die Eerste Vryheidsoorlog Persoonlike Herinneringe van P.C. Joubert* (Kaapstad, Tweede Druk, 1948)

Ruy de Pina, *Chronica d'el-Rei D. Affonso V*, vol I (Lisbon, 1901)

Robert Pitcairn, ed., *Ancient Criminal Trials in Scotland*, vol I, part I (Edinburgh, 1829)

Pius II, *Memoirs of a Renaissance Pope: the commentaries of Pius II, an abridgement*, ed. and trans. Florence A. Gragg and Leona C. Gabel (London: Putnam, 1960)

Christine de Pizan, *The Book of the City of Ladies and Other Writings*, ed. Sophie Bourgault and Rebecca Kingston and trans. Ineke Hardy (Indianapolis: Hackett, 2018)

Pliny the Elder, *Pliny Natural History with an English translation in ten volumes*, vol II, ed. H. Rackham (London, 1942)

Plutarch, *Plutarch's Lives*, ed. and trans. Bernadotte Perrin (Cambridge: Harvard University Press, 1919)

John Hungerford Pollen, ed., *Mary Queen of Scots and the Babington Plot. Edited from the Original Documents in the Public Record Office, the Yelverton MSS, and Elsewhere* (Edinburgh, 1922)

Hanns J. Prem, Sabine Dedenbach-Salazar Sáenz, Frauke Sachse and Frank Seeliger, eds., *Relación de la Genealogia y Origen de los Mexicanos: Dos Documentos del Libro de Oro* (Mexico, 2015)

W.T. Pritchard, *Polynesian Reminiscences; or, Life in the South Pacific Islands* (London: Chapman and Hall, 1866)

Kim Pusik (ed.), *The Silla Annals of the Samguk Sagi*, trans. Edward J. Shultz and Hugh H.W. Kang with Daniel C. Kane (Korea, 2012)

Recueil des Historiens des Croisades, Historiens Occidentaux, vol 2 (Paris: Imperiale, 1859)

Carrie E. Reed, ed., *A Tang Miscellany: An Introduction to Youyang Zazu* (New York: Peter Lang, 2003)

M. de Rulhiere, *A History or Anecdotes of the Revolution in Russia, in the Year 1762* (London, 1797)

WOMEN WHO RULED THE WORLD

Shota Rustaveli, *The Knight in Panther Skin*, trans. Katharine Vivian (London, 1977)

Lady Sarashina, *As I Crossed a Bridge of Dreams: Recollections of a Woman in Eleventh-Century Japan*, ed. and trans. Ivan Morris (London: Penguin, 1975)

Scriptores Rerum Suecicarum Medii Aevi, vol 3, ed. Claudius Annerstedt (Uppsala, 1871–1876)

Dénis-François Secousse, ed., *Recueil de Pieces Servant des Preuves aux Mémoires sur les Troubles Excités en France par Charles II, dit le Mauvais, Roi de Navarre et Comte d'Evreux* (Paris, 1755)

Shah Jahan Begum of Bhopal, *The Taj-Ul Ikbal Tarikh Bhopal or, The History of Bhopal*, trans. H.C. Barstow (Calcutta, 1876)

Izumi Shikibu, *Heian Court Heroines: The Izumi Shikibu Nikki*, trans. Annie Shepley Omori and Kochi Doi and ed. William de Lange (TOYO Press: 2019)

Murasaki Shikibu, *The Diary of Lady Murasaki*, ed. and trans. Richard Bowring (London: Penguin, 1996)

Murasaki Shikibu, *The Tale of Genji*, trans. Royall Tyler (London: Penguin, 2003).

Sources for the History of Cyprus, volume IV: Pero Tafur and Cyprus, ed. and trans. Colbert I. Nepaulsingh (New York: Greece and Cyprus Research Centre, 1997)

Sei Shonagon, *The Pillow Book*, ed. and trans. Meredith McKinney (London: Penguin, 2006)

Strabo, *Geography*, trans. Horace Leonard Jones (Loeb, 1932)

Sultan Jahan Begum of Bhopal, *An Account of my Life*, vol 1, trans. C.H. Payne (London, 1910)

Theophanes, *The Chronicle of Theophanes*, ed. and trans. Harry Turtledove ((Philidelphia, 1982)

Isaac Titsingh, *Secret Memoirs of the Shoguns: Isaac Titsingh and Japan, 1779-1822*, ed. Timon Screech (London: Routledge, 2006)

Mark Twain, *Mark Twain in Hawaii: Rouging it in the Sandwich Islands, Hawaii in the 1860s* (Honolulu, Mutual Publishing, 1990)

Roderigo de Vivero, *An Account of Japan, 1609*, ed. and trans. Caroline Stone (Edinburgh, Hardinge Simpole)

Wilhelmina Princess of the Netherlands, *Lonely But Not Alone*, trans. John Peereboom (London, 1960)

BIBLIOGRAPHY

Zosimus, *The History of Count Zosimus, Sometime Advocate and Chancellor of the Roman Empire* (London, 1814)

Secondary Sources

Nwando Achebe, *Female Monarchs and Merchant Queens in Africa* (Ohio University Press, 2020)

Susan Ackerman, 'The Queen Mother and the cult in Ancient Israel', *Journal of Biblical Literature*, vol 112, no.3 (1993), pp385–401

Wendi L. Adamek, 'Robes purple and gold: transmission of the robe in the "Lidai fabao ji" (Record of the Dharm-Jewel through the Ages)', *History of Religions*, vol 40 (2000), pp58–81

Sheila L. Ager, 'Familiarity breeds: incest and the Ptolemaic dynasty', *The Journal of Hellenic Studies*, vol 125 (2005), pp1–34

Imatani Akira, 'The strange survival and its modern significance' in *The Emperors of Modern Japan*, ed. Ben-Ami Shillony (Leiden: Brill, 2008)

John T. Alexander, *Catherine the Great: Life and Legend* (Oxford: Oxford University Press, 1989)

Jacqueline Alio, *Queens of Sicily 1061–1266* (New York: Trinacria, 2018)

Helena G. Allen, *The Betrayal of Liliuokalani: Last Queen of Hawaii 1838-1917* (Honolulu, 1982)

Stefan Amirell, 'Female rule in the Indian Ocean world', *Journal of World History*, vol 26, no.3 (2015), pp443–489

Clare Anderson, *The Indian Uprising of 1857-8: Prisons, Prisoners and Rebellion* (London: Anthem, 2007)

M.S. Anderson, *The War of the Austrian Succession 1740-1748* (London: Routledge, 1995)

Nathanael J. Andrade, *Zenobia: Shooting Star of Palmyra* (Oxford: Oxford University Press, 2018)

Niels-Erik A. Andreasen, 'The role of the queen mother in Israelite Society' in *The Catholic Biblical Quarterly*, vol 45, no.2 (1983), pp179–194

WOMEN WHO RULED THE WORLD

E.V. Anisimov, 'The question of women in power in the eighteenth century' in *Essays in Honor of Gary Marker,* eds. Maria di Salvo, Daniel H. Kaiser and Valerie A. Kivelson (Academic Studies Press)

Michiko Y. Aoki, 'Empress Jingu the Shamaness ruler' in ed. Chieko Irie Mulhern, *Heroic with Grace: Legendary Women of Japan* (Armonk, 1991), pp3–39

Bethany Aram, *Juana the Mad: Sovereignty and Dynasty in Renaissance Europe* (Baltimore: John Hopkins University Press, 2005)

Kelly M. Askew, 'Female circles and males lines: gender dynamics along the Swahili Coast', *Africa Today,* vol 46 (1999), pp67–102

Val Attenbrow, *Sydney's Aboriginal Past* (Sydney: University of New South Wales Press, 2010)

Kenneth Bain, *The Friendly Islanders* (London: Hodder, 1967)

Robert Nisbet Bain, *The Daughter of Peter the Great* (Westminster, 1899)

Julia Baird, *Victoria the Queen* (London: Random House, 2016)

Laura Balletto, 'Ethnic groups, cross-social and cross-cultural contacts on fifteenth-century Cyprus' in *Intercultural Contacts in the Medieval Mediterranean: Studies in Honour of David Jacoby,* ed. Benjamin Arbel (London: Routledge, 1996)

Dominique Barbe, *Irène de Byzance: La Femme Empereur* (Perrin, 1990)

Malcolm Barber, *The Crusader States* (New Haven: Yale University Press, 2012)

Gina L. Barnes, *State Formation in Japan: Emergence of a 4th-Century Ruling Elite* (London: Routledge, 2007)

T.H. Barrett, *The Woman who Discovered Printing* (New Haven: Yale University Press, 2008)

T.H. Barrett, 'The woman who invented notepaper: towards a comparative historiography of paper and print', *Journal of the Royal Asiatic Society,* third series, vol 21 (2011), pp199–210

William Theodore de Bary, *Sources of Japanese Tradition* (London, 1958)

Shrabani Basu, *Victoria and Abdul: The Extraordinary True Story of the Queen's Closest Confidant* (Stroud: The History Press, 2010)

Susan Bazargan, 'Leopold Bloom and William Ellis's Three Visits to Madagascar', *Joyce Studies Annual* (2017), pp65–93

BIBLIOGRAPHY

Mary Beard, *Women and Power: A Manifesto* (London: Profile Books, 2018)

Fay Beauchamp, 'Asian origins of Cinderella: The Zhuang Storyteller of Guangxi', *Oral Tradition*, vol 25, no.2 (2010), pp447–496

Charles Beem, *The Lioness Roared: The Problem of Female Rule in English History* (Basingstoke: Palgrave Macmillan, 2008)

Karen E. Bell, 'Ancient queens of the valley of Mexico' in *Ancient Queens: Archaeological Explorations*, ed. Sarah Milledge Nelson (Walnut Creek, 2003) pp137–150

Roger Bell, *Last Among Equals: Hawaiian Statehood and American Politics* (Honolulu: University of Hawaii Press)

Charles Benn, *China's Golden Age: Everyday Life in the Tang Dynasty* (Oxford: Oxford University Press, 2002)

Chris Bennett, 'Cleopatra V Tryphaena and the genealogy of the later Ptolemies', *Ancient Society*, vol 28 (1997), pp39–66

Chris Bennett, 'The chronology of Berenice II', *Zeitschrift fur Papyrologie und Epigraphik*, vol 139 (2002), pp143–148

Francis F. Berdan and Michael E. Smith, *Everyday Life in the Aztec World* (Cambridge: Cambridge University Press, 2020)

Mary Bergstein, 'Palmyra and Palmyra: Look on these Stones, Ye Mighty, and Despair', *Arion: A Journal of Humanities and the Classics,* vol 24 (2016), pp13–38.

Haraldur Bessason, 'New Light on Vinland from the Sagas', *Mosaic: A Journal for the Interdisciplinary Study of Literature*, vol 1 (1967), p57

Krishan Bhatia, *Indira: A Biography of Prime Minister Gandhi* (New York: Praeger, 1974)

Roger Bland, 'The Coinage of Vabalathus and Zenobia from Antioch and Alexandria', *The Numismatic Chronicle*, vol 171 (2011), pp133–186

Moniek Bloks, *Queen Wilhemina: A Collection of Articles* (2020)

Greg Blyton, 'Harry Brown (c. 1819-1854): Contribution of an Aboriginal guide in Australian Exploration', *Aboriginal History*, vol 39 (2015), pp63–82

David A. Boruchoff, 'Isabel, her Chroniclers, and the Inquisition: Self-fashioning and historical memory' in *A Companion to the Queenship of Isabel la Catolica*, ed. Hilaire Kallendorf (Leiden: Brill, 2023), pp34–71

WOMEN WHO RULED THE WORLD

Bruce Bower, 'Oldest known instruments found', *Science News*, vol 176, no.2 (2009), p13

Jim Bradbury, *The Capetians: Kings of France 987-1328* (London: Bloomsbury, 2007)

Bob Brier, 'The Other Pyramids', *Archaeology*, vol 55 (2002), pp54–58

Mervyn Brown, *A History of Madagascar* (Princeton: Princeton University Press, 2016)

Reed Browning, *The War of the Austrian Succession* (New York: St Martins, 1993)

Andrew Buckser, 'Group identities and the construction of the 1943 rescue of the Danish Jews', *Ethnology*, vol 37 (1998), pp209–226

Ian Buruma, *A Japanese Mirror: Heroes and Villains of Japanese Culture* (London: Jonathan Cape, 1984)

David Carrasco, *Quetzalcoatl and the Irony of Empire: Myths and Prophecies in the Aztec Tradition* (University Press of Colorado, 2001)

Nigel Cawthorne, *Daughter of Heaven: The True Story of the Only Woman to Become Emperor of China* (Sharpe Books, 2017)

Jung Chang, *Empress Dowager Cixi* (London: Vintage, 2013)

Liana De Girolami Cheney, 'Caterina Cornaro, Queen of Cyprus' in *The Emblematic Queen: Extra-Literary Representations of Early Modern Queenship*, ed. Debra Barrett-Graves (New York, 2013)

Arianne Chernock, 'Queen Victoria and the "Bloody Mary of Madagascar"', *Victorian Studies*, vol 55, no.3 (2013), pp425–449

Marjorie Chibnall, *The Empress Matilda: Queen Consort, Queen Mother and Lady of the English* (Oxford: Wiley-Blackwell, 1991)

Chimnabai II, Maharani of Baroda and S.M. Mitra, *The Position of Women in Indian Life* (London, 1911)

Donald Chipman, 'Isabel Moctezuma: Pioneer of Mestizaje' in *Struggle and Survival in Colonial America*, eds. David G. Sweet and Gary B. Nash (Berkeley: University of California Press, 1981)

Donald E. Chipman, *Montezuma's Children: Aztec Royalty Under Spanish Rule, 1520-1700* (Austin: University of Texas Press, 2005)

BIBLIOGRAPHY

Jonathan Clements, *Wu: The Chinese Empress who Schemed, Seduced and Murdered her Way to Become a Living God* (Albert Bridge Books, 2014)

Tom Coffman, *Nation Within: The History of the American Occupation of Hawai'i* (London, 2016)

Nicholas J. Conard, 'A female figurine from the basal Aurignacian of Hohle Fels Cave in southwestern Germany', *Nature*, vol 459 (2009), pp248–252

Kara Cooney, *The Woman Who Would be King: Hatshepsut's Rise to Power in Ancient Egypt* (London: Oneworld, 2014)

Robert Coughlan, *Elizabeth and Catherine: Empresses of all the Russians* (London: Purnell, 1974)

Nicholas Coureas, 'Envoys between Lusignan Cyprus and Mamluk Egypt, 838-78/1435-73: the Accounts of Pero Tafur, George Boustronios and Ibn Taghri Birdi' in *Mamluk Cairo, A Crossroads for Embassies: Studies on Diplomact and Diplomatics*, ed. Frederic Bauden and Malika Dekkiche (Leiden: Brill, 2019), pp725–740

Edward Crankshaw, *Maria Theresa* (London: Constable and Robinson, 1969)

Pearce Paul Creasman, 'Hatshepsut and the politics of Punt', *The African Archaeological Review*, vol 31 (2014), pp395–405

Arnout van Cruyningen, *The Dutch Royal Family* (2013)

H.G. Cummins, 'Tongan society at the time of European contact' in ed. Noel Rutherford, *Friendly Islands: A History of Tonga* (Oxford: Oxford University Press, 1977), pp63–89

Samia Dafa'alla, 'Succession in the Kingdom of Napata, 900–300 BC' *The International Journal of African Historical Studies*, vol 26 (1993), pp167–174

William Dalrymple, *The Anarchy: The Relentless Rise of the East India Company* (London: Bloomsbury, 2019)

William Dalrymple and Anita Anand, *Koh-I-Noor: The History of the World's Most Infamous Diamond* (London: Bloomsbury, 2016)

Paul D'Arcy, *The People of the Sea: Environment, Identity, and History in Oceania* (Honolulu: University of Hawaii Press, 2006)

John Coleman Darnell, *The Inscription of Queen Katimala at Semna: Textual Evidence for the Origins of the Napatan State* (New Haven: Yale University Press, 2006)

Vanessa Davies, 'Hatshepsut's Use of Tuthmosis III in her program of legitimation', *Journal of the American Research Centre in Egypt*, vol 41 (2004), pp55–66

H.W.C. Davis, 'Henry of Blois and Brian Fitz-Count', *English Historical Review*, vol 25 (1910), pp297–303

Gavan Daws, *Shoal of Time: A History of the Hawaiian Islands* (Honolulu: University of Hawaii Press, 1974)

P.K. De, *Bhopal* (New Delhi, 2015)

Michael Dee, David Winfrow, Andrew Shortland, Alice Stevenson, Fiona Brock, Linus Girdland Flink and Christopher Bronk Ramsey, 'An absolute chronology for early Egypt using radiocarbon dating and Bayesian statistical modelling', *Proceedings: Mathematical, Physical and Engineering Sciences*, vol 469, no.2159 (2013), pp1–10

Dora Shu-Fang Dien, *Empress Wu in Fiction and History: Female Defiance in Confucian China* (2003)

Simon Dixon, Catherine the Great (London: Routledge, 2001)

Filippo Donvito, 'The lioness of the Caucasus', *Medieval Warfare*, vol 4, no.2 (2014), pp19–24

Rebecca Doran, *Transgressive Typologies: Constructions of Gender and Power in Early Tang China* (Cambridge: Harvard University Press, 2016)

S.S. Dornan, 'Rainmaking in South Africa', *Bantu Studies*, vol 3 (1927), pp185–195

Michael Dougherty, *To Steal a Kingdom: Probing Hawaiian History* (Waimanalo, 1992)

Jane Draycott, *Cleopatra's Daughter: Egyptian Princess, Roman Prisoner, African Queen* (London: Apollo, 2022)

J-P Drége, 'Les caractéres de l'impératrice Wu Zetian dans les manuscrits de Dunhuang et Turfan', *Bulletin de Ecole Francaise d'Extreme-Orient*, vol 73 (1984), pp339–354

Archibald Alexander McBeth Duncan, *The Kingship of the Scots, 842-1292* (Edinburgh: Edinburgh University Press, 2002)

Sarah Duncan, *Mary I: Gender, Power, and Ceremony in the Reign of England's First Queen* (London: Palgrave Macmillan, 2012)

BIBLIOGRAPHY

Antony Eastmond, 'Gender and Orientalism in Georgia in the age of Queen Tamar' in *Women, Men and Eunuchs: Gender in Byzantium,* ed. Liz James (London: Routledge, 1997), pp100–118

Antony Eastmond, *Royal Imagery in Medieval Georgia* (Pennsylvania: Pennsylvania State University Press, 1998)

Peter W. Edbury, 'Cypriot Society under Lusignan Rule' in *Caterina Cornaro, Queen of Cyprus,* eds. David Hunt and Iro Hunt (London: Trigraph, 1989)

Peter W. Edbury, *The Kingdom of Cyprus and the Crusades 1191-1374* (Cambridge: Cambridge University Press, 1991)

Amelia Blandford Edwards and Patricia O'Neill, 'The social and political position of women in Ancient Egypt' *PMLA,* vol 120 (2005), pp843–857

John Edwards, 'Windows into souls: Isabel, religion, and the Spanish Inquisition' in Kallendorf, *Companion to Queen Isabel,* pp232–253

Elizabeth Ellem, *Queen Salote of Tonga: The Story of an Era 1900-1965* (1999)

Stephen Ellis, 'Witch-hunting in central Madagascar 1828-1861', *Past and Present,* vol 175 (2002), pp90–123

W.B. Emery, *Archaic Egypt* (Edinburgh: Penguin, 1961)

Vivian Etting, *Queen Margrete I (1353-1412) and the Founding of the Nordic Union* (Leiden: Brill, 2004)

Vivian Etting, *Margrete 1. En Regent & Hendes Samtid* (Gyldendal, 2021)

J. Evans, 'On some coins of the Empress Matilda, Queen of England', *The Numismatic Chronicle and Journal of the Numismatic Society,* vol 14 (1851), pp66–71

R.J.W. Evans, 'Communicating Empire: The Habsburgs and their Critics, 1700-1919: The Prothero Lecture', *Transactions of the Royal Historical Society,* sixth series, vol 19 (2009), pp117–138

Jana Everett, 'Indira Gandhi and the Exercise of Power' in ed. Michael A. Genovese, *Women As National Leaders* (Newbury Park: SAGE, 1993), pp103–134

Janet S. Everhart, 'Jezebel: Framed by Eunuchs?', *The Catholic Biblical Quarterly,* vol 72, no.4 (2010), pp688–698

Toyin Falola and Nana Akua Amponsah, *Women's Roles in Sub-Saharan Africa* (Santa Barbara, 2012)

WOMEN WHO RULED THE WORLD

William Wayne Farris, *Japan to 1600: A Social and Economic History* (Honolulu, University of Hawaii Press, 2009)

Cees Fasseur, *Wilhelmina De Jonge Koningin* (Balans, 1998)

Cees Fasseur, *Wilhelmina Sterker Door Strijd* (Balans, 2002)

Susannah Humble Ferreira, 'Juana La Beltraneja, Dynastic Fears, and Threats of Marriage (1475-1506)', *Renaissance and Reformation,* vol 43 (2020) pp79–100

C.P. Fitzgerald, *The Empress Wu* (London: Barrie and Jenkins, 1956)

Gillian B. Fleming, *Juana I: Legitimacy and Conflict in Sixteenth-Century Castile* (London: Palgrave Macmillan, 2018)

Joann Fletcher, *The Story of Egypt* (London: Hodder and Stoughton, 2015)

Lin Foxhall, *Studying Gender in Classical Antiquty* (Cambridge: Cambridge University Press, 2013)

Antonia Fraser, *The Warrior Queens: Boadicea's Chariot* (London, 1988)

Antonia Fraser, *Mary Queen of Scots* (London: Weidenfeld and Nicolson, 2018)

'Eseta Fusitu'a and Noel Rutherford, 'George Tupou II and the British Protectorate' in ed. Noel Rutherford, *Friendly Islands: A History of Tonga* (Oxford: Oxford University Press, 1977), pp173–189

Lynda Garland, *Byzantine Empresses: Women and Power in Byzantium AD 527-1204* (London: Routledge, 1999)

Susan D. Gillespie, *The Aztec Kings* (Tucson: University of Arizona Press, 1989)

Oscar Villarroel Gonzalez, *Juana La Beltraneja: La Construccion de Una Ilegitimidad* (Madrid, 2014)

Bonar A. Gow, 'Independency among the Merina, 1833-1929', *The International Journal of African Historical Studies,* vol 14, no. 2 (1981), pp229–253

Peter Green, 'The last of the Ptolemies', *Grand Street,* vol 4 (1985) pp133–168.

Monika Greenleaf, 'Performing Autobiography: the multiple memoirs of Catherine the Great (1756-96)', *The Russian Review,* vol 63 no.3 (2004)

Eduard Olid Guerrero and Esther Fernandez, eds., *The Image of Elizabeth I in Early Modern Spain* (Nebraska, 2019)

R.W.L. Guisso, *Wu Tse-T'ien and the Politics of Legitimation in T'ang China* (Washington: Western Washington University, 1978)

BIBLIOGRAPHY

Neil Gunson, 'The coming of foreigners' in ed. Noel Rutherford, *Friendly Islands: A History of Tonga* (Oxford: Oxford University Press, 1977), pp90–113

Neil Gunson, *Messengers of Grace: Evangelical Missionaries in the South Seas 1797-1860* (Oxford: Oxford University Press, 1978)

Christopher Haigh, ed., *The Reign of Elizabeth I* (London: Palgrave, 1984)

A. Hamilton, 1987 'Equal to whom? Visions of destiny and the Aboriginal aristocracy', *Mankind*, vol 17, no 2 (1987), pp129–38

Bernard Hamilton, 'Women in the crusader states: the queens of Jerusalem 1100-90' in *Medieval Women*, ed. Derek Baker (Oxford: Wiley Blackwell, 1978), pp143–174

Bernard Hamilton, *The Leper King and his Heirs: Baldwin IV and the Crusader Kingdom of Jerusalem* (Cambridge: Cambridge University Press, 2015)

Michelle M. Hamilton, 'Hostile histories: Isabel and Fernando in Jewish and Muslim narratives' in Kallendorf, *A Companion to Queen Isabel*, pp213–231

Catherine Hanley, *Matilda: Empress, Queen. Warrior* (New Haven: Yale University Press, 2019)

Necia Desiree Harkless, *Nubian Pharaohs and Meroitic Kings* (Bloomington, 2006)

John Hartley, *Accession: The Making of a Queen* (London: Quartet Books, 1992)

Philip Harwood, ed., 'The Queen's Indian Title', *Saturday Review: Politics, Literature, Science and Art*, vol 41 (1876), p396–397

B.G. Haycock, 'The kingship of Cush in the Sudan', *Comparative Studies in Society and History*, vol 7 (1965), pp461–480

Miriam Lopez Hernandez, *Aztec Women and Goddesses*, trans. Rose Vekony (San Pedro de Los Pinos: Fundación Cultural Armella, 2012)

Judith Herrin, *Women in Purple* (Princeton: Princeton University Press, 2001)

Judith Herrup, *Unrivalled Influence: Women and Empire in Byzantium* (Princeton: Princeton University Press, 2013)

Carola Hicks, *The Bayeux Tapestry: The Life Story of a Masterpiece* (London: Random House, 2006)

George Hill, *A History of Cyprus*, vol 3 (Cambridge: Cambridge University Press, 1948)

Mary Hill, *Margaret of Denmark* (London: T. Fisher Unwin, 1893)

Melinda Hinkson, *Aboriginal Sydney: A Guide to Important Places of the Past and Present* (Canberra: Aboriginal Studies Press, 2010)

Bret Hinsch, *Women in Early Imperial China* (Maryland: Rowman and Littlefield, 2011)

Elfriede Höckner, *Die Lobedu Südafrikas: Mythos und Realität der Regenkönigin Modjadji* (Stuttgart: Franz Steiner, 1998)

Ian Hodder, Women and Men at Catalhöyük', *Scientific American*, vol 290, no.1 (2004), pp76–83

Natasha R. Hodgson, *Women, Crusading and the Holy Land in Historical Narrative* (Woodbridge: Boydell, 2007)

William Hoffman, *Queen Juliana: The Story of the Richest Woman in the World* (London, 1980)

Günther Hölbl, *A History of the Ptolemaic Empire* (London: Routledge, 2001)

Lindsey Hughes, 'Catherine I of Russia, Consort to Peter the Great' in *Queenship in Europe 1660-1815: The Role of the Consort*, ed. Clarissa Campbell Orr (Cambridge: Cambridge University Press, 2004)

Holly Hurlburt, 'Body of Empire: Caterina Corner in Venetian History and Iconography', *Early Modern Women*, vol 4 (2009), pp61–99

Holly S. Hurlburt, *Daughter of Venice: Caterina Corner, Queen of Cyprus and Woman of the Renaissance* (New Haven: Yale University Press, 2015)

G. Cameron Hurst III, *Insei: Abdicated Sovereigns in the Politics of Late Heian Japan 1086-1185* (New York: Columbia University Press, 1976)

Steinar Imsen, 'Late Medieval Scandinavian Queenship' in *Queens and Queenship in Medieval Europe*, ed. Anne Duggan (Woodbridge: Boydell and Brewer, 1997)

Tiffany Lani Ing, *Reclaiming Kalakaua: Nineteenth-Century Perspectives on a Hawaiian Sovereign* (Honolulu: University of Hawai'i Press, 2019)

Charles Ingrao, *The Habsburg Monarchy* (Cambridge: Cambridge University Press, 1994)

Charles W. Ingrao and Andrew L. Thomas, 'Piety and patronage: the empresses-consort of the High Baroque', *German History*, vol 20, issue 1 (2002), pp20–43

BIBLIOGRAPHY

Indira Iyengar, *The Bourbons and Begums of Bhopal: The Forgotten History* (New Delhi: Nihyogi Books, 2018)

Guida M. Jackson, *Women Leaders of Africa, Asia, Middle East, and Pacific: A Biographical Reference* (2009)

Trudy Jacobsen, *Lost Goddesses: The Denial of Female Power in Cambodian History* (Copenhagen: NIAS, 2008)

Ann Jones, 'Finding the Lovedu', *The Women's Review of Books*, vol 15, no.5 (1998), pp11–12

Ann Jones, *Looking for Lovedu: A Woman's Journey Through Africa* (New York, Robinson, 2001)

David E. Jones, *Women Warriors: A History* (Washington: Potomac, 1997)

Sargis Kakabadze, *Queen Tamar: Her Significance* (Tbilisi, 1912)

Hilaire Kallendorf, 'Inventing Isabel' in ed. Hilaire Kallendorf, *A Companion to the Queenship of Isabel la Catolica* (Leiden: Brill, 2023), pp1–33

Hossein Kamaly, *A History of Islam in 21 Women* (London; Oneworld, 2019)

Russell H. Kaschula, 'Alice in Wonderland: Translating to Read across Africa', *Journal of African Cultural Studies*, vol 29, no 3 (2017), pp276–291

H.J. Katzenstein, 'Who were the parents of Athaliah?', *Israel Exploration Journal*, vol 5, no.3 (1955), pp194–197

J. Kehaulani Kauanui, 'Hawai'i in and out of America', *Mississippi Review*, vol 32. No.3 (2004), pp145–150

Barry J. Kemp, 'Abydos and the Royal Tombs of the First Dynasty', *The Journal of Egyptian Archaeology*, vol 52 (1966), pp13–22

Shaharyar M. Khan, *The Begums of Bhopal: A Dynasty of Women Rulers in Raj India* (London: I.B. Taurus, 2000)

Yung-Chung Kim, trans. and ed., *Women of Korea: A History from Ancient Times to 1945* (Seoul: Ewha Womans University Press)

Hans Kirchhoff, 'Denmark: A light in the darkness of the Holocaust? A reply to Gunnar S. Paulsson', *Journal of Contemporary History*, vol 30, no.3 (1995), pp465–497

K.A. Kitchen, *On the Reliability of the Old Testament* (William B Eerdmans Publishing, 2006)

Menno Klapwijk, 'Pot- and Pit- Burials from the North-Eastern Transvaal, South Africa', *The South African Archaeological Bulletin*, vol 44 (1989), pp65–69

Eileen Jensen Krige, 'The place of the north-Eastern Transvaal Sotho in the South Bantu Complex', *Africa: Journal of the International African Institute*, vol 11, no.3 (1938), pp265–293

E. Jensen Krige and J.D. Krige, *The Realm of a Rain Queen: A Study of the Pattern of Lovedu Society* (London: Routledge, 2020)

Keith Laidler, *Female Caligula: Ranavalona, the Mad Queen of Madagascar* (Chichester, 2005)

Ruby Lal, *Empress: The Astonishing Reign of Nur Jahan* (London: W.W. Norton, 2018)

Sarah Lambert, 'Queen of Consort: Rulership and Politics in the Latin East, 1118-1228' in *Queens and Queenship in Medieval Europe*, ed. Anne Duggan (Woodbridge: Boydell and Brewer, 1997)

Siobhan Lambert-Hurley, *Muslim Women, Reform and Princely Patronage: Nawab Sultan Jahan Begam of Bhopal* (London: Routledge, 2007)

Elizabeth A. Lehfeldt, 'Ruling Sexuality: The political legitimacy of Isabel of Castile', *Renaissance Quarterly*, vol 53 (2000), pp31–56

Miguel Leon, ed., *The Broken Spears: The Aztec Account of the Conquest of Mexico* (Boston: Beacon Press, 1992)

Carol S. Leonard, *Reform and Regicide: The Reign of Peter III of Russia* (Bloomington, 1993)

Leanda de Lisle, *The Sisters who would be Queen* (London: Ballantine, 2009)

Lloyd Llewellyn-Jones, *The Cleopatras: The Forgotten Queens of Egypt* (London: Wildfire, 2024)

Herbert Lockyer, *All the Kings and Queens of the Bible* (Grand Rapids: Zondervan Publishing House, 1961)

Angelika Lohwasser, 'Queenship in Kush: Status, Role and Ideology of Royal Women', *Journal of the American Research Center in Egypt*, vol 38 (2001), pp61–75

Angelika Lohwasser and Jacke Phillips, 'Women in Ancient Kush' in eds. Geoff Emberling and Bruce Beyer Williams, *The Oxford Handbook of Ancient Nubia* (Oxford: Oxford University Press, 2021), pp1015–1032

BIBLIOGRAPHY

Philip Longworth, *The Three Empresses: Catherine I, Anne and Elizabeth of Russia* (London: Constable, 1972)

Mariam Lordkipanidze, *Georgia in the XI-XII Centuries* (Tbilisi: Ganatleba Publishers, 1987)

Mariam Lordkipanidze, *Essays on Georgian History* (Tbilisi: Mesniereba, 1994)

Harry Luke, *Queen Salote and her Kingdom* (London: Putnam, 1954)

M. Lunenfeld, 'Isabella I of Castile and the company of women in power', *Historical Reflections,* vol 4 (1977), pp57–99

Thomas Lyngby, 'Dronning af Danmark – et essay' in *Dronning of Danmark* (Der Nationalhistoriske Museum Frederiksborg Slot, 2010)

John P. Maarbjerg, '"Regimen Politicum" and "Regimen Regale": Political Change and Continuity in Denmark and Sweden (c.1450-c.1550)', *Scandinavian Studies*, vol 72 (2000), pp141–162

Simon MacLean, *Ottonian Queenship* (Oxford: Oxford University Press, 2017)

John Man, *Amazons: The Real Warrior Women of the Ancient World* (London: Corgi, 2018)

Cyril Mango, 'Introduction', in *The Oxford History of Byzantium*, ed. Cyril Mango (Oxford: Oxford University Press, 2002) pp1–18

Edward L. Margetts, 'The masculine character of Hatshepsut, Queen of Egypt', *Bulletin of the History of Medicine,* vol 25 (1951) pp559–562

Henry L. Mason, 'Testing Human Bonds within Nations: Jews in the Occupied Netherlands', *Political Scient Quarterly*, vol 99, no. 2 (1984), pp315–343

Robert K. Massie, *Catherine the Great: Portrait of a Woman* (London: Apollo, 2019)

Uros Matic, 'Gender in Ancient Egypt: Norms, Ambiguities, and Sensualities' *Near Eastern Archaeology,* vol 79 (2016) pp174–183

Adrienne Mayor, *The Amazons: Lives and Legends of Warrior Women Across the World* (Princeton: Princeton University Press, 2014)

Richard D. McBride II, *The Three Kingdoms of Korea: Lost Civilisations* (London: Reaktion Books, 2024)

Peter McClure and Robin Headlam Wells, 'Elizabeth I as a second Virgin Mary', *Renaissance Studies,* vol 4, no.1 (1990), pp38–70

WOMEN WHO RULED THE WORLD

Keith McMahon, *Women Shall Not Rule: Imperial Wives and Concubines in China from Han to Liao* (Lanham: Rowman and Littlefield, 2013)

Brenda Meehan-Waters, 'Catherine the Great and the Problem of Female Rule' *The Russian Review*, vol 34 (1975) pp293–307

Johannes Meintjes, *The Commandant General: The Life and Times of Petrus Jacobus Joubert of the South African Republic 1831-1900* (Cape Town, 1971)

Fatima Mernissi, *The Forgotten Queens of Islam*, trans. Mary Jo Lakeland (Cambridge: Polity, 1993)

Townsend Miller, *Henry IV of Castile, 1425-1474* (London: Littlehampton Book Services, 1972)

Simon Sebag Montefiore, *The Romanovs: 1613-1918* (London: Orion, 2016)

William Monter, 'Gendered Sovereignty: Numismatics and female monarchs in Europe, 1300-1800', *The Journal of Interdisciplinary History,* vol 41, no.4 (2011) pp533–564

William Monter, *The Rise of Female Kings in Europe, 1300-1800* (New Haven: Yale University Press, 2012)

Charles Moore, *Margaret Thatcher: The Authorised Biography*, vol 3 (London: Penguin, 2020)

Alan Moorehead, *The Blue Nile* (New York, 1962)

Helen Morris, 'Queen Elizabeth I "Shadowed" in Cleopatra' *Huntington Library Quarterly*, vol 32, no.3 (1969), pp271–278

Andrew Morton, *The Queen* (London: Michael O'Mara, 2022)

Toribio Motolinía, *Relaciones de la Nueva España* (Mexico, 1964)

Barbara E. Mundy, *The Death of Aztec Tenochtitlan, The Life of Mexico City* (Austin: University of Texas Press, 2015)

Michael Nelson, *Queen Victoria and the Discovery of the Riviera* (London: I.B. Taurus, 2001)

Richard Nelson, *Interpretation, A Bible Commentary for Teaching and Preaching: First and Second Kings* (Louisville, 1987)

Sarah Milledge Nelson, 'Ancient Queens: an introduction' in ed. Sarah Milledge Nelson, *Ancient Queens: Archaeological Explorations* (Walnut Creek: Altamira, 2003), pp1–18

BIBLIOGRAPHY

Sarah Milledge Nelson, 'The Queens of Silla: power and connections to the spirit world' in Sarah Milledge Nelson, ed., *Ancient Queens: Archaeological Explorations* (Walnut Creek: Altamira, 2003), pp77–92

Colin Newbury and Adam J. Darling, 'Te Hau Pahu Rahi: Pomare II and the Concept of Inter-Island Government in Eastern Polynesia', *The Journal of the Polynesian Society,* vol 76 no.4 (1967)

Colin Newbury, *Tahiti Nui: Change and Survival in French Polynesia 1767-1945* (Honolulu: University of Hawaii Press, 1980)

Reynold A. Nicholson, *A Literary History of the Arabs* (London, 1907)

Elizabeth Norton, *Elfrida, The First Crowned Queen of England* (Stroud: Amberley, 2013)

Elizabeth Norton, *The Temptation of Elizabeth Tudor* (London: Head of Zeus, 2015)

Patty O'Brien, "Think of me as a woman': Queen Pomare of Tahiti and Anglo-French Imperial Contest in the 1840s Pacific', *Gender and History*, vol 18, no.1 (2006) pp108–129

Gary Y. Okihiro, *Island World: A History of Hawai'i and the United States* (Berkeley: University of California Press, 2008)

Douglas L. Oliver, *Ancient Tahitian Society, vol 3: Rise of the Pomares* (Honolulu: University of Hawaii Press, 1974)

Uwe A. Oster, *Die Frauen Kaiser Friedrichs II* (Munich: Piper Verlag, 2008)

Katherine Pangonis, *Queens of Jerusalem: The Women who Dared to Rule* (London: Weidenfeld & Nicholson, 2021)

Jean-Pierre Patznick, 'Merit-Neith: in the footsteps of the first woman pharaoh in history' in *Egypt 2015: Perspectives of Research: Proceedings of the Seventh European Conference of Egyptologists,* eds. Mladen Tomorad and Joanna Popielska-Grzybowska (Oxford: Archaeopress, 2017)

A.C.S. Peacock, 'Georgia and the Anatolian Turks in the 12th and 13th Centuries', *Anatolian Studies,* vol 56 (2006), pp127–146

Guy Perry, *John of Brienne: King of Jerusalem, Emperor of Constantinople c.1175-1237* (Cambridge: Cambridge University Press, 2013)

Robert Pick, *Empress Maria Theresa: The Earlier Years, 1717-1757* (New York: Harper and Row, 1966)

Joan R. Piggott, *The Emergence of Japanese Kingship* (Stanford: Stanford University Press, 1997)

Dora Beale Polk, *The Island of California: A History of the Myth* (Spokane: Arthur H. Clark, 1991)

Sarah B. Pomeroy, *Goddesses, Whores, Wives & Slaves* (London: Bodley Head, 1975)

Richard Ponsonby-Fane, *The Imperial House of Japan* (Kyoto, 1959)

John Milton Potter, 'The development and significance of the Salic Law of the French', *The English Historical Review*, vol 52, no.206 (1937), pp235–253

Vera Proskurina, *Creating the Empress* (Academic Studies Press)

Jocelyn Rabeson, 'Jesuits and Protestants in Nineteenth Century Madagascar' in eds. Robert Aleksander Maryks and Festo Mkenda, *Encounters Between Jesuits and Protestants in Africa* (Leiden: Brill, 2018)

Marc Raeff (ed.), *Peter the Great Changes Russia* (Lexington: Heath, 1972)

Jessica Rawson, 'Ornament as System: Chinese bird-and-flower design', *The Burlington Magazine*, vol 148 (2006) pp380–389

Andre Raymond, 'Cairo's area and population in the early fifteenth century' *Muqarnas*, vol 2 (1984) pp21–31

R.H.W. Reece, 'Feasts and Blankets: The History of Some Early Attempts to Establish Relations with the Aborigines of New South Wales, 1814-1846', *Archaeology & Physical Anthropology in Oceania*, vol 2, no.3 (1967), pp190–206

Bernard F. Reilly, *The Kingdom of León-Castilla under Queen Urraca, 1109-1126* (Princeton: Princeton University Press, 1982)

Matthew Restall, *When Montezuma Met Cortés: The True Story of the Meeting that Changed History* (New York: Ecco, 2018)

Tamara Talbot Rice, *Elizabeth Empress of Russia* (London: Weidenfeld and Nicholson, 1970)

Linda M. Ricketts, 'A dual queenship in the reign of Berenice IV', *The Bulletin of the American Society of Papyrologists*, vol 27 (1990) pp49–60

Jonathan Riley-Smith, *The Feudal Nobility and the Kingdom of Jerusalem, 1174-1277* (1973)

BIBLIOGRAPHY

Keith Rinehart, 'Shakespeare's Cleopatra and England's Elizabeth', *Shakespeare Quarterly*, vol 23, no.1 (1972), pp81–86

Enrique Rodriguez-Picavea, 'The military orders and the war of Granada', *Mediterranean Studies*, vol 19 (2010), pp 14–42

John Rogerson, *Chronicles of the Old Testament Kings* (London: Thames and Hudson, 1997)

Duane W. Roller, *Cleopatra: A Biography* (Oxford: Oxford University Press, 2011)

John Romer, *A History of Ancient Egypt, From the First Farmers to the Great Pyramid* (London: Penguin, 2013)

Deborah Root, 'Speaking Christian: Orthodoxy and Difference in Sixteenth-Century Spain', *Representations*, vol 23 (1988), pp118–134

N. Harry Rothschild, *Emperor Wu Zhao and her Pantheon of Devis, Divinities, and Dynastic Mothers* (New York: Columbia University Press, 2015)

Branko Van Oppen De Ruiter, 'The marriage of Ptolemy I and Berenice I', *Ancient Society*, vol 41 (2011) pp83–92

Kalistrat Salia, *History of the Georgian Nation*, trans. Katharine Vivian (Paris, 1983)

Tati Salmon, *The History of the Island of Borabora and Genealogy of our Family from Marae Vaiotaha* (1904)

Anne Salmond, *Aphrodite's Island: The European Discovery of Tahiti* (Berkeley: University of California Press, 2009)

Tracey R. Sands, 'Saints and Politics During the Kalmar Union Period: The Case of Saint Margaret of Tentsa', *Scandinavian Studies*, vol 80 (2008), pp141–166

G.B. Sanson, *Japan: A Short Cultural History* (Stanford: Stanford University Press, 1976)

Peter Sarris, 'The Eastern Roman Empire from Constantine to Heraclius (306-641) in *The Oxford History of Byzantium*, ed. Cyril Mango (Oxford, Oxford University Press, 2002) pp19–70

Katesa Schlosser, *Rain-Queens and Python Dance* (Kiel: Universitat Kiel, 2002)

Susan Schroeder, *Tlacaelel Remembered* (Norman: University of Oklahoma Press, 2016

Maureen Seneviratne, *Sirimavo Bandaranaike: The World's First Woman Prime Minister* (Colombo, 1975)

Simphiwe Sesanti, 'Decolonized and Afrocentric Education' in *Journal of Black Studies*, vol 50 (2019), pp431–449

Sudha Sharma's *The Status of Muslim Women in Medieval India* (New Delhi: Sage, 2016)

Ben-Ami Shillony, *Enigma of the Emperors: Sacred Subservience in Japanese History* (Leiden: Brill, 2005)

P.L. Shinnie, *Meroe: A Civilisation of the Sudan* (London, 1967)

P.L. Shinnie, 'The Nilotic Sudan and Ethiopia, c.660 BC to c. AD 600' in *The Cambridge History of Africa*, vol 2, eds. J.D. Fage and Roland Oliver (Cambridge: Cambridge University Press, 1978), pp210–671

Shashi Shukla and Sashi Shukla, 'Political Participation of Muslim Women', *The Indian Journal of Political Science*, vol 57 no.1 (1996,) pp1–13

Nuria Silleras-Fernandez, 'Isabel's years of sorrow: consoling the Catholic Queen' in Kallendorf, *Companion to Queen Isabel*, pp254–278

C. Hale Sipe, *The Indian Chiefs of Pennsylvania* (Butler: Ziegler, 1927)

Torid Skard, *Women of Power: Half a Century of Female Presidents and Prime Ministers Worldwide* (Bristol: Policy Press, 2015)

Matthew L. Skuse, 'Coregency in the reign of Ptolemy II', *The Journal of Egyptian Archaeology*, vol 103 (2017) pp89–101

Keith Vincent Smith, *King Bungaree: A Sydney Aborigine meets the great South Pacific explorers, 1799-1830* (Kenthurst, 1992)

Frank M. Snowden, Jr., *Blacks in Antiquity* (Cambridge: Cambridge University Press, 1970)

J. Alberto Soggin, *An Introduction to the History of Israel and Judah* (London: SCM Press, 1999)

Anne Somerset, *Elizabeth I* (London: Weidenfeld & Nicolson, 1991)

Karen Stevenson, "Aimata, Queen Pomare IV: thwarting adversity in early 19th century Tahiti', *The Journal of Polynesian Society*, vol 123, no.2 (2014) pp129–144

Barbara Stollberg-Rilinger, *Maria Theresa: The Habsburg Empress in her Time* (Princeton: Princeton University Press, 2021)

Richard Stoneman, *Palmyra and its Empire: Zenobia's Revolt Against Rome* (Michigan: University of Michigan Press, 1992)

BIBLIOGRAPHY

Barbara Freyer Stowasser, *Women in the Qur'an, Traditions and Interpretations* (Oxford: Oxford University Press, 1997)

Lawrence Guy Straus, 'The human occupation of southwestern Europe during the last glacial maximum: Solutrean cultural adaptations in France and Iberia', *Journal of Anthropological Research*, vol 71, no.4 (2015), pp465–492

Ronald Grigor Suny, *The Making of the Georgian Nation* (Bloomington: Indiana University Press, 1994)

David Sweetman, *Women Leaders in African History* (London: Heinemann, 1984)

Craig Taylor, 'The Salic Law and the Valois succession to the French Crown', *French History*, vol 15, issue 4 (2001), pp358–377

Miles Taylor, *Empress: Queen Victoria in India* (New Haven: Yale University Press, 2018)

Shashi Tharoor, *Inglorious Empire: What the British Did to India* (London: Penguin, 2016)

Edwin R. Thiele, *The Mysterious Numbers of the Hebrew Kings* (Grand Rapids: Zondervan, 1983)

Basil Thomson, *The Scene Changes* (London: Collins, 1939)

Peter Thorley, 'Self-Representation and Aboriginal Communities in the Northern Territory: Implications for Archaeological Research', *Australian Archaeology*, no.43 (1996), pp7–12

Hilke Thür, 'Arsinoë IV, eine Schwester Kleopatras VII, Grabinhabeirin des Oktogons von Ephesos? Ein Vorschlag', *Jahreshefte des Österreichischen Archäologischen Institutes*, vol 60 (1990)

Conrad Totman, *A History of Japan* (Oxford: Oxford University Press, 2005)

Warren G. Treadgold, 'The unpublished saint's life of the Empress Irene (BHG 2205)' in *Byzantinische Forschungen*, vol 8 (1982) pp237–251

Warren Treadgold, *A History of the Byzantine State and Society* (Stanford: Stanford University Press, 1997)

Giles Tremlett, *Isabella of Castile: Europe's First Great Queen* (London: Bloomsbury, 2017)

Jakelin Troy, *King Plates: A History of Aboriginal Gorgets* (The National Museum and the Australian Institute of Aboriginal and Torres Strait Islander Studies

(AIATSIS, 1993). Published online at https://www.nma.gov.au/explore/features/aboriginal-breastplates/about

E. Patricia Tsurumi, 'The male present versus the female past: historians and Japan's ancient female emperors', *Bulletin of Concerned Asian Scholars*, vol 14, no.4 (1982), pp71–78

Denis Twitchett, *The Writing of Official History under the T'ang* (Cambridge: Cambridge University Press, 1992)

Denis Twitchett, '"Chen gui" and Other works attributed to Empress Wu Zetian', *Asia Major*, third series, vol 16, no.1 (2003), pp33–109

Joyce Tyldesley, *Hatchepsut, The Female Pharaoh* (London: Viking, 1996)

Joyce Tyldesley, *Chronicles of the Queens of Egypt* (London: Thames and Hudson, 2006)

Joyce Tyldesley, *Cleopatra: Last Queen of Egypt* (London: Profile Books, 2008)

Joyce Tyldesley, 'Foremost of Women: The Female Pharaoh of Ancient Egypt' in *Tausret: Forgotten Queen and Pharaoh of Egypt*, ed. Richard H. Wilkinson (Oxford: Oxford University Press, 2012)

Eric R. Varner, Transcending Gender: Assimilation, Identity, and Roman Imperial Portraits' *Memoirs of the American Academy in Rome*, volume 7 (2008), pp185–205

Alberton A. Vela-Rodrigo, 'The sacred treasure of Queen Amanishakheto', *Ancient Egypt Magazine*, vol 21 (2021), pp20–26

J. Vicens Vives, *Juan II de Aragon (1398-1479): Monarquia Y Revolucion en la Espana del Siglo XV* (Barcelona, 1953)

Retha M. Warnicke, *Mary Queen of Scots* (London: Routledge, 2006)

Clifford Weber, 'Intimations of Dido and Cleopatra in Some Contemporary Portrayals of Elizabeth I', *Studies in Philology*, vol 96, no.2 (1999), pp127–143

Howard J. Wechsler, *Mirror to the Son of Heaven: Wei Cheng at the Court of T'ang T'ai-tsung* (New Haven: Yale University Press, 1974)

Sara J. Weir, 'Peronisma: Isabel Peron and the Politics of Argentina' in *Women As National Leaders*, pp161–176

Barbara F. Weissberger, *Isabel Rules: Constructing Queenship, Wielding Power* (University of Minnesota Press, 2003)

BIBLIOGRAPHY

Barbara F. Weissberger, 'Questioning the Queen, Now and Then', in ed. Barbara F. Weissberger, *Queen Isabel I of Castile: Power, Patronage, Persona* (Woodbridge: Tamesis, 2008)

John Whitehorne, *Cleopatras* (London: Routledge, 1994)

Cynthia H. Whittaker, 'The reforming Tsar: the redefinition of autocratic duty in Eighteenth-century Russia', *Slavic Review*, vol 51, no.1 (1992) pp77–98

David Harris Willson, *King James VI and I* (London: Jonathan Cape, 1956)

X.L. Woo, *Empress Wu the Great* (New York: Algora, 2008)

A.H. Wood and Elizabeth Wood Ellem, 'Queen Salote Tupou III' in ed. Noel Rutherford, *Friendly Islands: A History of Tonga* (Oxford: Oxford University Press, 1977), pp190–209

Elizabeth Wood-Ellem, 'Researching (w)riting, releasing, and responses to a biography of Queen Salote of Tonga' in eds. Brij V. Lal and Vicki Luker, *Telling Pacific Lives: Prisms of Process* (Canberra, 2008), pp139–148

Elena Woodacre, 'Blanca, Queen of Sicily and Queen of Navarre: Connecting the Pyrenees and the Mediterranean via an Aragonese alliance' in *Queenship in the Mediterranean: Negotiating the Role of the Queen in the Medieval and Early Modern Eras*, ed. Elena Woodacre (London: Palgrave Macmillan, 2013)

Elena Woodacre, 'Leonor of Navarre: The Price of Ambition', in *Queenship, Gender, and Reputation in the Medieval and Early Modern West, 1060-1600*, eds. Zita Eva Rohr and Lisa Benz (London, Palgrave Macmillan, 2016) pp161–182

Elena Woodacre, *The Queens Regnant of Navarre: Succession, Politics, and Partnership, 1274-1512* (New York: Routledge, 2013)

Jenny Wormald, *Mary Queen of Scots* (Edinburgh: Hamlyn, 1988)

Rosemary Muir Wright, *Sacred Distance: Representing the Virgin* (Manchester: Manchester University Press, 2006)

Janice W. Yellin, 'The royal and elite cemeteries at Meroe' in eds. Geoff Emberling and Bruce Beyer Williams, *The Oxford Handbook of Ancient Nubia* (Oxford: Oxford University Press, 2021), pp562–588

Leni Yahil, *The Rescue of Danish Jewry* (Philadelphia: Jewish Publication Society of America, 1969)

Helena Zlotnick, 'From Jezebel to Esther: Fashioning images of queenship in the Hebrew Bible', *Biblica*, vol 82 no.4 (2001), pp477–495

ENDNOTES

PREFACE

1   John Man, *Amazons: The Real Warrior Women of the Ancient World* (London: Corgi, 2018); Adrienne Mayor, *The Amazons: Lives and Legends of Warrior Women Across the World* (Princeton: Princeton University Press, 2014).

2   Dora Beale Polk, *The Island of California: A History of the Myth* (Spokane: Arthur H. Clark, 1991).

3   Garci Rodriguez de Montalvo, *The Labors of the Very Brave Knight Esplandián*, ed. and trans. William Thomas Little (New York: Medieval and Renaissance Texts and Studies, 1992), pp457–8.

4   Montalvo, *Labors of the Very Brave Knight Esplandián*, p459.

5   Royal Collection Trust RCIN 404710.

6   C. Hale Sipe, *The Indian Chiefs of Pennsylvania* (Butler: Ziegler, 1927), pp256–257.

7   Hale Sipe, *Indian Chiefs of Pennsylvania*, pp256–257.

8   Trudy Jacobsen, *Lost Goddesses: The Denial of Female Power in Cambodian History* (Copenhagen: NIAS, 2008), p115.

9   Stefan Amirell, 'Female rule in the Indian Ocean World (1300–1900)', *Journal of World History*, vol. 26, no.3 (2015), pp443–489.

10 Kelly M. Askew, 'Female Circles and Males Lines: Gender Dynamics along the Swahili Coast', *Africa Today*, vol. 46 (1999), pp67–102, p84.

11 Barbara Freyer Stowasser, *Women in the Qur'an, Traditions and Interpretations* (Oxford: Oxford University Press, 1997).

12 Rosemary Muir Wright, *Sacred Distance: Representing the Virgin* (Manchester: Manchester University Press, 2006), p82.

13 For more on Aelfthryth, see Elizabeth Norton, *Elfrida, The First Crowned Queen of England* (Stroud: Amberley, 2013).

14 Sarah Duncan, *Mary I: Gender, Power, and Ceremony in the Reign of England's First Queen* (London: Palgrave Macmillan, 2012), p129.

15 Peter McClure and Robin Headlam Wells, 'Elizabeth I as a second Virgin Mary', *Renaissance Studies*, vol. 4, no.1 (1990), pp38–70.

16 Act 1, Scene 1.

CHAPTER 1

1   Jean-Pierre Patznick, 'Merit-Neith: in the footsteps of the first woman pharaoh in history' in *Egypt 2015: Perspectives of Research: Proceedings of the Seventh European Conference of Egyptologists*, eds. Mladen Tomorad and Joanna Popielska-Grzybowska (Oxford: Archaeopress, 2017), pp289–306.

2   Joyce Tyldesley, 'Foremost of Women: The Female Pharaoh of Ancient Egypt' in *Tausret: Forgotten Queen and Pharaoh of Egypt*, ed. Richard H. Wilkinson (Oxford: Oxford University Press, 2012), pp5–24.

3   Romer, *A History of Ancient Egypt*, p210.

4   *Gesta Stephani*, ed. and trans. K.R. Potter and R.H.C. Davis (Oxford: Clarendon Press, 1976), p119.

5   Vivian Etting, *Queen Margrete I (1353–1412) and the Founding of the Nordic Union* (Leiden: Brill, 2004), p49.

6   Etting, *Queen Margrete I*, p3. Etting has also written a later biography of Margrete in Danish: Vivian Etting, *Margrete 1. En Regent & Hendes Samtid* (Gyldendal, 2021).

ENDNOTES

7   Etting, *Queen Margrete I*, p4; Mary Hill, *Margaret of Denmark* (London: T. Fisher Unwin, 1893), p48; 'Ex Chronica Novella Hermanni Korneri' in *Scriptores Rerum Suecicarum Medii Aevi*, vol. 3., ed. Claudius Annerstedt (Uppsala, 1871–1876), p207.

8   'Ex Annalibus Danicis 1316–1389' in Annerstedt, *Scriptores Rerum Suecicarum Medii Aevi*, p126.

9   Etting, *Queen Margrete I*, p5; Hill, *Margaret of Denmark*, p33.

10 *Diplomatarium Norvegicum*, vol. I, ed. Christian C.A. Lange and Carl R. Unger (Christiana: P.T. Mallings, 1847), no.409, p342.

11 Hill, *Margaret of Denmark*, p54.

12 Etting, *Queen Margrete I*, p13.

13 Etting, *Queen Margrete I*, p15.

14 Steinar Imsen, 'Late Medieval Scandinavian Queenship' in *Queens and Queenship in Medieval Europe*, ed. Anne Duggan (Woodbridge: Boydell and Brewer, 1997), pp53–73, characterises her rule as 'an elected regent' p59.

15 Etting, *Queen Margrete I*, p55.

16 Barbara E. Mundy, *The Death of Aztec Tenochtitlan, The Life of Mexico City* (Austin: University of Texas Press, 2015), p1 suggests 150,000 people.

17 Mundy, *Death of Tenochtitlan*, p1; Leon, *Broken Spears*, pxxxviii.

18 Schroeder, *Tlacaelel Remembered*, p99.

19 Miriam Lopez Hernandez, *Aztec Women and Goddesses*, trans. Rose Vekony (San Pedro de Los Pinos: Fundación Cultural Armella, 2012), p13.

20 Lopez Hernandez, *Aztec Women and Goddesses*, p10.

21 Lopez Hernandez, *Aztec Women and Goddesses*; Hernan Cortes, *Letters from Mexico*, eds. Anthony Pagden and J.H. Elliott (Yale Universtiy Press, New Haven, 1986), p83; Susan D. Gillespie, *The Aztec Kings* (Tucson: University of Arizona Press, 1989), p19; Miguel Leon, ed., *The Broken Spears: The Aztec Account of the Conquest of Mexico* (Boston: Beacon Press, 1992); 'En este tiempo tenían los mexicanos por señor a Ilancueitl, una señora principal que les mandaba, y esta fue mujer de Acamapichi' (in *Historia de los Mexicanos por sus Pinturas*, ed. Joaquín García Icazbalceta (Mexico, 1891), p249.

22 Gillespie, *Aztec Kings*, pxvii–xix.

23 Lopez Hernandez, *Aztec Women and Goddesses*, p19.

24 Lori Boornazian Diel, ed., *The Codex Mexicanus: A Guide to Life in Late Sixteenth-Century New Spain* (Austin: University of Texas Press, 2018), p88; 'Sucedióle una hija legítima' in Toribio de Benavente Motolinía, *Relaciones de la Nueva España* (Mexico: Universidad Nacional Autónoma de México, 1964), p8; 'Muerto Montezuma el viejo, sin hijos varones, heredó el reino una su hija que estaba casada con un muy cercano pariente suyo' in Jerónimo de Mendieta, *Historia Eclesiástica Indiana* (Barcelona, 2011), p154; 'Axayacatl fué rey después de su madre' (Gomara, *Historia de las Conquistas*, p137).

25 Hanns J. Prem, Sabine Dedenbach-Salazar Sáenz, Frauke Sachse and Frank Seeliger, eds., *Relación de la Genealogia y Origen de los Mexicanos: Dos Documentos del Libro de Oro* (Mexico, 2015), no.636, p358: 'y decia mas aquel papel que fueron señores esta hija y su marido antes que Axayacaçi su hijo avnque por ser muger no le ponen en los anales syno a su hijo'; no.637: 'ovo esta hija de Moteççuma otros dos hijos Tiçiçicaçi Ahuicoçi junto con Axayaçi que fueron señores despues de Axacaçi'.

26 Leon, *Broken Spears*, p14.

27 Leon, *Broken Spears*, p31; Cortes, *Letters from Mexico*, p86.

28 Matthew Restall, *When Montezuma Met Cortés: The True Story of the Meeting that Changed History* (New York: Ecco, 2018), p345; David Carrasco, *Quetzalcoatl and the Irony of Empire: Myths and Prophecies in the Aztec Tradition* (University Press of Colorado, 2001); Donald E. Chipman, *Montezuma's Children: Aztec Royalty Under Spanish Rule, 1520–1700* (Austin: University of Texas Press, 2005).

29 Bernal Diaz del Castillo, *The True History of the Conquest of Mexico*, Maurice Keating ed. and trans. (London: J. Wright, 1880), p133.

30 Castillo, *True History*, p133.

31 Castillo, *True History*, p146.

32 Castillo, *True History*, p146; Cortes, *Letters from Mexico*, p103.

33 Castillo, *True History*, p138.

34 Karen E. Bell, 'Ancient queens of the valley of Mexico' in *Ancient Queens: Archaeological Explorations Walnut Creek*, ed. Sarah Milledge Nelson (2003), pp137–150, p137.

ENDNOTES

35   Donald Chipman, 'Isabel Moctezuma: Pioneer of Mestizaje' in *Struggle and Survival in Colonial America,* eds. David G. Sweet and Gary B. Nash (Berkeley: University of California Press, 1981), pp214–227; another source suggests 50 children, but only two legitimate – a son, Axayacatzin, and Tecuichpotzin, Prem, *et al, Relación de la Genealogia,* p58.

36   Leon, *Broken Spears,* p148.

37   Prem, *et al, Relación de la Genealogia,* p62.

38   Chipman, *Moctezuma's Children,* p67.

39   Chipman, 'Isabel Moctezuma', p225.

40   John Romer, *A History of Ancient Egypt, From the First Farmers to the Great Pyramid* (London: Penguin, 2013), p4.

41   Manetho, *Manetho,* ed. and trans. W.G. Waddell (1989), p29.

42   Joann Fletcher, *The Story of Egypt* (London: Hodder and Stoughton, 2015), p49.

43   Barry J. Kemp, 'Abydos and the Royal Tombs of the First Dynasty', *The Journal of Egyptian Archaeology,* vol. 52 (1966), pp13–22; Patznick, 'Merit-Neith', p289.

44   Tyldesley, 'Foremost of Women', p9 considers that 'Meritneith occasionally uses the serekh and this, combined with the fact that she was probably included on a broken section of the Palermo Stone (a record of the kings of Dynasties 1-5), suggests that she too ruled on behalf of her son. We may therefore regard her splendid tomb, set among the tombs of her fellow rulers, as a reward for her reign'; W.B. Emery, *Archaic Egypt* (Edinburgh: Penguin, 1961), p66 was tentative in his support for Merneith's rule, stating that 'she was more than a consort, but may herself have been a reigning monarch'. The contradiction in the way that Merneith has been interpreted has not gone unnoticed. Simphiwe Sesanti, 'Decolonized and Afrocentric Education' in *Journal of Black Studies,* vol. 50 (2019), pp431–449 points out the dominant role that Merneith's sex has played in interpretations of her political role.

45   Carola Hicks, *The Bayeux Tapestry: The Life Story of a Masterpiece* (London: Random House, 2006), pp83, 86; Charles Beem, *The Lioness Roared: The Problem of Female Rule in English History* (Basingstoke: Palgrave Macmillan, 2008), p26.

46   *Gesta Stephani,* p123.

47 Beem, *The Lioness Roared*, p26.

48 J. Evans, 'On some coins of the Empress Matilda, Queen of England', The *Numismatic Chronicle and Journal of the Numismatic Society*, vol. 14 (1851), pp66–71; Hanley, *Matilda*.

49 Marjorie Chibnall, *The Empress Matilda: Queen Consort, Queen Mother and Lady of the English* (Oxford: Wiley-Blackwell, 1991).

50 Etting, *Queen Margrete I*, p50.

51 *Die Lübekischen Chroniken in Niederdeutscher Sprache*, vol.1, F.H. Grautoff, ed. (Hamburg: Perthes under Besser, 1829) vol. 1, p344.

52 'Commentarii Historici super Nonnullis Revelationibus S. Birgittae de Rege Magno Erici et Successoribus Ejus' in *Scriptores Rerum Suecicarum Medii Aevi*, p20.

53 'Ex Annalibus Danicis 1316–1389' in *Scriptores Rerum Suecicarum Medii Aevi*, p127.

54 Etting, *Queen Margrete I*, p99; She has been called the Union's 'architect' (John P. Maarbjerg, '"Regimen Politicum" and "Regimen Regale": Political Change and Continuity in Denmark and Sweden (c.1450–c.1550)', *Scandinavian Studies*, vol. 72 (2000), pp141–162.

55 Tracey R. Sands, 'Saints and Politics During the Kalmar Union Period: The Case of Saint Margaret of Tentsa', *Scandinavian Studies*, vol. 80 (2008), pp141–66.

56 Etting, *Queen Margrete I*, p39.

57 *Corpus Juris Sueo-Gotorum Antiqui*, vol. IX, ed. Carl Johan Schlyter, (Lund, 1859) pp462–484.

58 https://www.kongehuset.dk/nyheder/80-fakta-om-hm-dronningen (date accessed 9 February 2024).

CHAPTER 2

1 Pius II, *Memoirs of a Renaissance Pope: the commentaries of Pius II, an abridgement*, ed. and trans. Florence A. Gragg and Leona C. Gabel (London: Putnam, 1960), p218.

2 See, for example, https://time.com/4268325/history-calling-women-shrill/ (date accessed 10 April 2025).

ENDNOTES

3   Homer, *The Iliad*, Book 1.

4   Tyldesley, 'Foremost of Women', p21; Sheila L. Ager, 'Familiarity breeds: incest and the Ptolemaic dynasty', *The Journal of Hellenic Studies*, vol. 125 (2005), pp1–34; Matthew L. Skuse, 'Coregency in the reign of Ptolemy II', *The Journal of Egyptian Archaeology*, vol. 103 (2017), pp89–101; Chris Bennett, 'Cleopatra V Tryphaena and the genealogy of the later Ptolemies', *Ancient Society*, vol. 28 (1997), pp39–66.

5   Chris Bennett, 'The chronology of Berenice II', *Zeitschrift fur Papyrologie und Epigraphik*, vol. 139 (2002), pp143–148.

6   Linda M. Ricketts, 'A dual queenship in the reign of Berenice IV', *The Bulletin of the American Society of Papyrologists*, vol. 27 (1990), pp49–60; Peter Green, 'The last of the Ptolemies', *Grand Street*, vol. 4 (1985), pp133–168.

7   Ricketts, 'A dual queenship', p55.

8   Cleopatra, unsurprisingly, has been the subject of many biographies, including Tyldesley, *Cleopatra* and Duane W. Roller, *Cleopatra: A Biography* (Oxford: Oxford University Press, 2011).

9   Joyce Tyldesley, *Cleopatra: Last Queen of Egypt* (London: Profile Books, 2008), p 42.

10 Tyldesley, *Cleopatra*, p44; Günther Hölbl, *A History of the Ptolemaic Empire* (London: Routledge, 2001), p231.

11 Pius II, *Memoirs*, p218.

12 Pius II, *Memoris*, p218.

13 Peter W. Edbury, *The Kingdom of Cyprus and the Crusades 1191–1374* (Cambridge: Cambridge University Press, 1991), p15.

14 George Hill, *A History of Cyprus*, vol. 3 (Cambridge: Cambridge University Press, 1948), p527.

15 Florio Bustron, *Chronique de L'Ile de Chypre* (Paris, 1886), p372.

16 *Excerpta Cypria: Materials for a History of Cyprus*, ed. Claude Delaval Cobham (Cambridge, 1908), p41.

17 Hill, *A History of Cyprus*, p527.

18 Laura Balletto, 'Ethnic groups, cross-social and cross-cultural contacts on fifteenth-century Cyprus' in *Intercultural Contacts in the Medieval Mediterranean: Studies in Honour of David Jacoby*, ed. Benjamin Arbel (London: Routledge, 1996), pp35–48.

19 Doctor Lorenzo Galindez de Carvajal, 'La Cronica del rey Don Juan el Segundo' in *Biblioteca de Autores Espanoles, Desde La Formacion del Lenguaje Hasta Nuestros Dias: Cronicas de Los Reyese de Castilla Desde Don Alfonso el Sabio, Hasta Los Catolicos Don Fernando y Dona Isabel*, vol. 2, ed. Don Cayetano Rosell (Madrid: M. Rivadeneyra, 1877), p565.

20 Galindez de Carvajal, 'La Cronica del rey', p567.

21 Galindez de Carvajal, 'La Cronica del rey', p567.

22 J. Vicens Vives, *Juan II de Aragon (1398–1479): Monarquia Y Revolucion en la Espana del Siglo XV* (Barcelona, 1953); Elena Woodacre, *The Queens Regnant of Navarre: Succession, Politics, and Partnership, 1274–1512* (New York: Routledge, 2013), p112.

23 Quoted from Vives, *Juan II de Aragon*, p143 (translation my own).

24 Elena Woodacre, 'Blanca, Queen of Sicily and Queen of Navarre: Connecting the Pyrenees and the Mediterranean via an Aragonese alliance' in *Queenship in the Mediterranean: Negotiating the Role of the Queen in the Medieval and Early Modern Eras*, ed. Elena Woodacre (London: Palgrave Macmillan, 2013), pp207–228.

25 Vives, *Juan II de Aragon*, p143.

26 *Memorias de don Enrique IV de Castilla*, vol. 2 (Madrid: Establecimiento Tipografico de Fortanet,1835–1913), p64.

27 Townsend Miller, *Henry IV of Castile, 1425–1474* (London: Littlehampton Book Services, 1972), p68.

28 '*Memorias de don Enrique IV de Castilla*, p62.

29 *Memorias de don Enrique de Castilla*, p64 ('tenia su verga viril firme').

30 Hill, *A History of Cyprus*, p534.

31 Pius II, *Memoirs*, p218.

32 *Excerpta Cypria*, p35.

ENDNOTES

33   Peter W. Edbury, 'Cypriot Society under Lusignan Rule' in *Caterina Cornaro, Queen of Cyprus*, eds. David Hunt and Iro Hunt (London: Trigraph, 1989), pp17–34.

34   The Chronicles of Enguerrand de Monstrelet in *Sources for the History of Cyprus, volume IV: Pero Tafur and Cyprus*, ed. and trans. Colbert I. Nepaulsingh (New York: Greece and Cyprus Research Centre, 1997), p51; Nicholas Coureas, 'Envoys between Lusignan Cyprus and Mamluk Egypt, 838-78 / 1435-73: the Accounts of Pero Tafur, George Boustronios and Ibn Taghri Birdi', in *Mamluk Cairo, A Crossroads for Embassies: Studies on Diplomat and Diplomatics*, ed. Frederic Bauden and Malika Dekkiche (Leiden: Brill, 2019), pp725–740 for the Egyptian invasion.

35   William Monter, 'Gendered Sovereignty: Numismatics and female monarchs in Europe, 1300–1800', *The Journal of Interdisciplinary History*, vol. 41, no.4 (2011), pp533–564.

36   Pius II, *Memoirs*, p218.

37   Coureas, 'Envoys between Lusignan Cyprus and Mamluk Egypt', p730.

38   Vives, *Juan II de Aragon*, p155.

39   Woodacre, *Queens Regnant of Navarre*, p112.

40   Jose Moret and Francois Aleson, *Anales del Reino de Navarra*, vol. 6 (Tolosa, 1890–92), p435.

41   Plutarch, *Plutarch's Lives*, ed. and trans. Bernadotte Perrin (Cambridge: Harvard University Press, 1919), p49.

42   Andre Raymond, 'Cairo's area and population in the early fifteenth century' *Muqarnas*, vol. 2 (1984) pp21–31.

43   Coureas, 'Envoys between Lusignan Cyprus and Mamluk Egypt', p731.

44   'The sultan has been told that he is the king's son and many are of the opinion that he shall take it' (George Boustronios, *A Narrative Chronicle of Cyprus, 1456–1489*, ed. and trans. Nicholas Coureas (Nicosia, 2005), pp 91–92). Holly S. Hurlburt, *Daughter of Venice: Caterina Corner, Queen of Cyprus and Woman of the Renaissance* (New Haven: Yale University Press, 2015), p22, considers that 'the gender of the candidates for rule almost certainly weighed more heavily with the sultan than did western notions of legitimacy'.

45   Coureas, 'Envoys between Lusignan Cyprus and Mamluk Egypt', p733.

46   Pius II, *Memoirs*, p221.

47   Archivo General de Simancas, Patronato Real, ES.47161.AGS/3.2.48/PTR, LEG, 12, DOC.12 (Protesta de la Princesa Doña Blanca, hermana del Príncipe de Viana, contra el pacto acordado por Don Juan II y Luis XI de Francia, sobre la sucesión al trono de Navarra).

48   Moret and Aleson, *Anales del Reino de Navarra*, vol. 6, p440.

49   Elena Woodacre, 'Leonor of Navarre: The Price of Ambition', in *Queenship, Gender, and Reputation in the Medieval and Early Modern West, 1060–1600*, eds. Zita Eva Rohr and Lisa Benz (London, Palgrave Macmillan, 2016), pp161–182, p166.

50   Moret and Aleson, *Anales del Reino de Navarra*, vol. 7, p44.

51   Tyldesley, 'Foremost of Women', p24.

CHAPTER 3

1   Joyce Tyldesley, *Chronicles of the Queens of Egypt* (London: Thames and Hudson, 2006), p97.

2   Monika Greenleaf, 'Performing Autobiography: the multiple memoirs of Catherine the Great (1756–96)', *The Russian Review*, vol. 63, no.3 (2004), pp407–426.

3   Cyril Mango, 'Introduction' in *The Oxford History of Byzantium*, ed. Cyril Mango (Oxford: Oxford University Press, 2002), pp1–18; Peter Sarris, 'The Eastern Roman Empire from Constantine to Heraclius (306-641) in *The Oxford History of Byzantium*, ed. Cyril Mango (Oxford, Oxford University Press, 2002), pp19–70.

4   Sarris, 'Eastern Roman Empire', p45.

5   Lynda Garland, *Byzantine Empresses: Women and Power in Byzantium AD 527–1204* (London: Routledge, 1999), p1.

6   Dominique Barbe, *Iréne de Byzance: La Femme Empereur* (Perrin, 1990), pp64–5.

7   Catherine the Great, *The Memoirs of Catherine the Great*, eds. Mark Cruse and Hilde Hoogenboom (New York: Random House, 2006), p7.

8   Catherine the Great, *Selected Letters*, eds. Andrew Kahn and Kelsey Rubin-Detleve (Oxford: Oxford University Press, 2018), p13.

ENDNOTES

9   Catherine the Great, *Selected Letters*, p7.

10 Catherine the Great, *Memoirs*, p9.

11 Carol S. Leonard, *Reform and Regicide: The Reign of Peter III of Russia* (Bloomington, 1993), p5.

12 Catherine the Great, *Memoirs*, p11.

13 Catherine the Great, *Memoirs*, p118.

14 Catherine the Great, *Memoirs*, p136.

15 Catherine the Great, *Memoirs*, p50.

16 Catherine the Great, *Memoirs*, p138.

17 Quoted from Tyldesley, *Chronicles of the Queens of Egypt*, p95.

18 Tyldesley, 'Foremost of Women', p6.

19 Vanessa Davies, 'Hatshepsut's Use of Tuthmosis III in her program of legitimation', *Journal of the American Research Centre in Egypt*, vol. 41 (2004), pp55–66.

20 Robert K. Massie, *Catherine the Great: Portrait of a Woman* (London: Apollo, 2019), p388; M. de Rulhiere, *A History or Anecdotes of the Revolution in Russia, in the Year 1762* (London, 1797), p9 for the quote.

21 For more on Peter, see Lindsey Hughes, *Peter the Great: A Biography* (New Haven: Yale University Press, 2002). Seven foot tall Peter was a man of extremes: he brought the theatre to Russia, but the fields remained tilled by serfs. Simon Sebag Montefiore, *The Romanovs: 1613–1918* (London: Orion, 2016) details the dynasty.

22 Marc Raeff (ed.), *Peter the Great Changes Russia* (Lexington: Heath, 1972) p30.

23 Lindsey Hughes, 'Catherine I of Russia, Consort to Peter the Great' in *Queenship in Europe 1660–1815: The Role of the Consort,* ed. Clarissa Campbell Orr (Cambridge: Cambridge University Press, 2004), p135.

24 Philip Longworth, *The Three Empresses: Catherine I, Anne and Elizabeth of Russia* (London: Constable, 1972), Brenda Meehan-Waters, 'Catherine the Great and the Problem of Female Rule', *The Russian Review*, vol. 34 (1975), pp293–307 notes that their coronations set Ekaterina I and her successors as empress apart from other women, raising their status.

25 The Heroic Tsar by Feofan Prokopovich in Raeff, *Peter the Great*, pp39–46.

26 Vera Proskurina, *Creating the Empress* (Academic Studies Press), p14; E.V. Anisimov, 'The question of women in power in the eighteenth century' in *Essays in Honor of Gary Marker*, eds. Maria di Salvo, Daniel H. Kaiser and Valerie A. Kivelson (Academic Studies Press), p192.

27 For English biographies of Elizaveta, see Robert Coughlan, *Elizabeth and Catherine: Empresses of all the Russians* (London: Purnell, 1974) and Tamara Talbot Rice, *Elizabeth Empress of Russia* (London: Weidenfeld and Nicholson, 1970). Both are considerably out of date.

28 Robert Nisbet Bain, *The Daughter of Peter the Great* (Westminster, 1899).

29 Anisimov, 'Question of Women', p196

30 Meehan-Waters, 'Catherine the Great and the Problem of Female Rule'; Cynthia H. Whittaker, 'The reforming Tsar: the redefinition of autocratic duty in Eighteenth-century Russia', *Slavic Review*, vol. 51, no.1 (1992), pp77–98.

31 Anisimov, 'Question of women', p199.

32 Longworth, *Three Empresses*.

33 Garland, *Byzantine Empresses*, p4.

34 Herrup, *Unrivalled Influence*, p203.

35 Herrup, *Unrivalled Influence*, p195.

36 For more on the state-ordered iconoclasm, see Patricia Karlin-Hayter, 'Iconoclasm' in *The Oxford History of Byzantium*, Cyril Mango, ed. (Oxford, Oxford University Press, 2002), pp153–168.

37 Herrup, *Unrivalled Influence*, p198.

38 Herrin, *Women in Purple*, p1.

39 Warren G. Treadgold, 'The unpublished saint's life of the Empress Irene (BHG 2205)' in *Byzantinische Forschungen*, vol. 8 (1982), pp237–251.

40 Theophanes, *Chronicle of Theophanes*, p140.

41 Garland, *Byzantine Empresses*, p23.

42 Catherine the Great, *Memoirs*, p182.

ENDNOTES

43 John T. Alexander, *Catherine the Great: Life and Legend* (Oxford: Oxford University Press, 1989), p4.

44 Marie-Henriette Fourmy and Maurice Leroy, eds., 'Laa Vie de S. Philaréte' Byzantion, vol. 9 (1934), pp113–167), p134 note that Irene chose the new bride, searching 'for a distinguished young girl who she would unite with her son' (*'une jeune fille distinguée qu'elle unirait á son fils'*); Theophanes speaks of Irene breaking off the betrothal to Rotrud and of Constantine's distress and unwillingness (Theophanes, *Chronicle*, p147).

45 Theophanes, *Chronicle*, p148.

46 Herrup, *Women in Purple,* p91.

47 Theophanes, *Chronicle*, pp154–155.

48 Warren Treadgold, *A History of the Byzantine State and Society* (Stanford: Stanford University Press, 1997), p430.

49 Garland, *Byzantine Empresses*, p75.

50 Theophanes, *Chronicle,* p151.

51 Edward L. Margetts, 'The masculine character of Hatshepsut, Queen of Egypt', *Bulletin of the History of Medicine*, vol. 25 (1951), pp559–562.

52 Joyce Tyldesley, *Hatchepsut, The Female Pharaoh* (London: Viking, 1996); Kara Cooney, *The Woman Who Would be King: Hatshepsut's Rise to Power in Ancient Egypt* (London: Oneworld, 2014).

53 Uros Matic, 'Gender in Ancient Egypt: Norms, Ambiguities, and Sensualities', *Near Eastern Archaeology*, vol. 79 (2016), pp174–183.

54 Amelia Blandford Edwards and Patricia O'Neill, 'The social and political position of women in Ancient Egypt' *PMLA*, vol. 120 (2005), pp843–857.

55 Manetho, *Manetho,* p3.

56 Elizabeth I, *Elizabeth I Collected Works,* eds Leah S. Marcus, Janel Mueller and Mary Beth Rose (Chicago: University of Chicago Press, 2002), p326.

57 Herrup, *Unrivalled Influence,* p200.

58 Theophanes, *The Chronicle of Theophanes,* ed. and trans. Harry Turtledove ((Philidelphia, 1982), p160.

59 Judith Herrup, *Unrivalled Influence: Women and Empire in Byzantium* (Princeton: Princeton University Press, 2013), p204.

60 Garland, *Byzantine Empresses*, p92.

61 Theophanes, *Chronicle*, p159.

62 Theophanes, *Chronicle*, p160.

63 Pearce Paul Creasman, 'Hatshepsut and the politics of Punt', *The African Archaeological Review*, vol. 31 (2014), pp395–405.

64 Davies, 'Hatshepsut's Use of Tuthmosis III', pp55–66.

65 Catherine the Great, *Selected Letters*, p17.

66 Catherine to Stanislas Poniatowski, 2 August 1762 (Catherine the Great, *Selected Letters*, p17).

67 Rulhiere, *History or Anecdotes*, p120.

68 Meehan-Waters, 'Catherine the Great and the Problem of Female Rule', pp293–307.

69 *Diaries and Correspondence of James Harris, First Earl of Malmesbury*, vol. I, ed. J.H. Harris (London, 1845), p146.

70 Meehan-Waters, 'Catherine the Great and the problem of female rule', p300.

71 Proskurina, *Creating the Empress*, p22.

72 Herrup, *Unrivalled Influence*, p2.

73 Catherine the Great, *Memoirs*, p211.

74 Greenleaf, 'Performing Autobiography, pp407–426.

CHAPTER 4

1 Robert Lindsay of Pitscottie, *The Historie and Cronicles of Scotland from the Slauchter of King James the First to the Ane Thousand Fyve Hundreith Thrie Scoir Fyftein Zeir*, vol. 1, A.J.G. MacKay, ed. (Edinburgh: William Blackwood and Sons, 1899), p407.

2 Archibald Alexander McBeth Duncan, *The Kingship of the Scots, 842–1292* (Edinburgh: Edinburgh University Press, 2002).

ENDNOTES

3 For a history of the region see Malcolm Barber, *The Crusader States* (New Haven: Yale University Press, 2012).

4 Bernard Hamilton, *The Leper King and his Heirs: Baldwin IV and the Crusader Kingdom of Jerusalem* (Cambridge: Cambridge University Press, 2015), p49.

5 Hamilton, *Leper King*, p54.

6 Bernard Hamilton, 'Women in the Crusader States: The Queens of Jerusalem 1100–90' in *Medieval Women*, ed. Derek Baker (Oxford: Wiley Blackwell, 1978), pp143–174, p148.

7 Hamilton, 'Women in the Crusader States', p150; Fulk was, by his first marriage, the father of Geoffrey of Anjou, husband of Empress Matilda (whom we met in Chapter 1).

8 Sarah Lambert, 'Queen of Consort: Rulership and Politics in the Latin East, 1118–1228' in *Queens and Queenship in Medieval Europe*, ed. Anne Duggan (Woodbridge: Boydell and Brewer, 1997), pp153–169, p153.

9 Cees Fasseur, *Wilhelmina De Jonge Koningin* (Balans, 1998), p41.

10 Arnout van Cruyningen, *The Dutch Royal Family* (2013), p20; Moniek Bloks, *Queen Wilhemina: A Collection of Articles* (2020), p129.

11 Queen Victoria's Journal for 21 June 1884 http://www.queenvictoriasjournals.org/search/displayItemFromId.do?FormatType=fulltextimgsrc&QueryType=articles&ItemID=18840621 (date accessed 1 August 2024).

12 Wilhelmina Princess of the Netherlands, *Lonely But Not Alone*, trans. John Peereboom (London, 1960), p17.

13 Princess Wilhelmina, *Lonely But Not Alone*, p21.

14 Princess Wilhelmina, *Lonely But Not Alone*, p23.

15 Hamilton, *Leper King*, p63.

16 *The Chronique d'Ernoul and The Colbert-Fontainebleau Continuation of William of Tyre, vol 2: The Continuation of William of Tyre*, ed. Peter Edbury and Massimiliano Gaggero (2023), p331; Edbury, *Conquest of Jerusalem*, pp154–5.

17 The Continuation of William of Tyre in *Chronique d'Ernoul*, p174.

18 The Old French Continuation of William of Tyre, in Edbury, *Conquest of Jerusalem*, p97.

19 Continuation of William of Tyre in Edbury, *Conquest of Jerusalem*, p115; Sarah Lambert, 'Queen or Consort', p163.

20 The Continuation of William of Tyre in *Chronique d'Ernoul*, p259.

21 Lambert, 'Queen or Consort', p162.

22 W.T. Pritchard, *Polynesian Reminiscences; or, Life in the South Pacific Islands* (London: Chapman and Hall, 1866), p29; Jorgen Jensen, 'A Danish visit to the Society Islands in 1846: Extracts from the diary of Cornelius Schmidt', *The Journal of Pacific History*, vol. 31, no.1 (1996), pp104–7, p106.

23 Queen Victoria's Journal, 24 February 1844 http://www.queenvictoriasjournals.org/search/displayItemFromId.do?FormatType=fulltextimgsrc&QueryType=articles&ItemID=18440224.

24 Pritchard, *Polynesian Reminiscences*, pp38, 40.

25 Karen Stevenson, 'Aimata, Queen Pomare IV: thwarting adversity in early 19th century Tahiti', *The Journal of Polynesian Society*, vol. 123, no.2 (2014), pp129–144, p135.

26 Neil Gunson, *Messengers of Grace: Evangelical Missionaries in the South Seas 1797–1860* (Oxford: Oxford University Press, 1978), p178.

27 Newbury, *Tahiti Nui*, p173–4; Stevenson, 'Queen Pomare IV', p140.

28 Jensen, 'Danish Visit', p107.

29 Colin Newbury, *Tahiti Nui: Change and Survival in French Polynesia 1767–1945* (Honolulu: University of Hawaii Press, 1980), p2 for the quote; Stevenson, 'Queen Pomare IV', p136 for attempts by Europeans to claim the islands.

30 Newbury, *Tahiti Nui*, p4.

31 Jensen, 'A Danish visit', p107.

32 Paul D'Arcy, *The People of the Sea: Environment, Identity, and History in Oceania* (Honolulu: University of Hawaii Press, 2006), p114–5; Douglas L. Oliver, *Ancient Tahitian Society, vol. 3: Rise of the Pomares* (Honolulu: University of Hawaii Press, 1974), p1211.

ENDNOTES

33 D'Arcy, People of the Sea, p115; Tati Salmon, *The History of the Island of Borabora and Genealogy of our Family from Marae Vaiotaha* (1904), p21; Anne Salmond, *Aphrodite's Island: The European Discovery of Tahiti* (Berkeley: University of California Press, 2009), p36.

34 *The Hamilton Papers: Letters and Papers Illustrating the Political Relations of England and Wales in the XVIth Century Formerly in the Possession of the Dukes of Hamilton Now in the British Museum*, vol. I, ed. Joseph Bain (Edinburgh, 1890), p337.

35 Arthur Clifford, ed., *Sadler State Papers*, vol. 1 (Edinburgh, 1809), p87.

36 *Hamilton Papers*, p328; Antonia Fraser, *Mary Queen of Scots* (London: Weidenfeld and Nicolson, 2018), p16.

37 Van Cruyningen, *Dutch Royal Family*, p39.

38 Wilhelmina, *Lonely But Not Alone*, p31.

39 Bloks, *Queen Wilhelmina*, p165.

40 Bloks, *Queen Wilhelmina*, p91; Wilhelmina, *Lonely But Not Alone*, p42–43.

41 Wilhelmina, *Lonely But Not Alone*, p43.

42 Guy Perry, *John of Brienne: King of Jerusalem, Emperor of Constantinople c.1175-1237* (Cambridge: Cambridge University Press, 2013), p40.

43 Perry, *John of Brienne*, p52

44 Continuation of William of Tyre in *Chronique d'Ernoul*, p270.

45 Perry, *John of Brienne*, p70–1; Barber and Bate, *Letters from the East*, no.58, p109.

46 Jacqueline Alio, *Queens of Sicily 1061–1266* (New York: Trinacria, 2018), p427; *Recueil des Historiens des Croisades, Historiens Occidentaux*, vol. 2 (Paris: Imperiale, 1859), pp343–4.

47 Uwe A. Oster, *Die Frauen Kaiser Friedrichs II* (Munich: Piper Verlag, 2008), p122 'und einen mächtigen Mann für seine Tochter finden'.

48 Colin Newbury and Adam J. Darling, 'Te Hau Pahu Rahi: Pomare II and the Concept of Inter-Island Government in Eastern Polynesia', *The Journal of the Polynesian Society*, vol. 76, no.4 (1967), pp477–514; Stevenson, 'Queen Pomare IV', p133.

49 Henry Byam Martin, *The Polynesian Journal of Captain Henry Byam Martin, RN, in Command of HMS Grampus – 50 Guns at Hawaii and on Station in Tahiti and the Society Islands August 1846 to August 1847* (Canberra: Australian National University Press, 1981), pp58, 73.

50 Martin, *Polynesian Journal*, p58.

51 Martin, *Polynesian Journal*, p73.

52 Martin, *Polynesian Journal*, p152.

53 Stevenson, 'Queen Pomare IV', p141.

54 Jensen, 'Danish Visit', p107.

55 Jensen, 'Danish Visit', p107.

56 Niel Gunson, 'Sacred Women chiefs and female 'headmen' in Polynesian history' in *The Journal of Pacific History*, vol. 22, no.3 (1987), pp139–172, p156.

57 'South Sea Isle Loses its Queen' (*Perth Mirror*, 4 February 1933).

58 Jensen, 'Danish Visit', p107.

59 Paul Gauguin, *Noa Noa: The Tahitian Journal* (New York: Dover Publications, 1985), p5.

60 Stevenson, 'Aimata, Queen Pomare IV', p141.

61 'French Annexation in the Pacific: A Fatal Misunderstanding', *Lyttelton Times*, vol. LXIX, Issue 8483, 16 May 1888.

62 'Queen Teriimaevarua II: Death in Tahiti', *The Pacific Islands Monthly*, 25 January 1934.

63 'Queen Teriimaevarua II: Death in Tahiti', *The Pacific Islands Monthly*, 25 January 1934.

64 Paul Gauguin, who had an assignation with Teri'imaevarua's sister in 1891 referred to her as a 'fallen princess', while also noting that she 'was a real princess, if such still exist in this country, where the Europeans have reduced everything to their own level' – Gauguin, *Noa Noa*, pp4–5.

65 Arthur Clifford, ed., *Sadler State Papers*, vol. 2 (Edinburgh, 1809), pp559–60.

66 *Hamilton Papers*, p633.

67 *Hamilton Papers*, p633.

ENDNOTES

68 Clifford, *Saddler State Papers*, vol. I, p289.

69 Fraser, *Mary Queen of Scots*, p27.

70 Perry, *John of Brienne*, p123; Oster, *Die Frauen Kaiser Friedrichs II*, p122.

71 Oster, *Die Frauen Kaiser Friedrichs II*, p124.

72 Perry, *John of Brienne*, p127.

73 Oster, *Die Frauen Kaiser Friedrichs II*, p126.

74 Oster, *Die Frauen Kaiser Friedrichs II*, p131; Jonathan Riley-Smith, *The Feudal Nobility and the Kingdom of Jerusalem, 1174–1277* (1973), p160.

75 William Patten, *The Expedicion into Scotlande (1548)* in *Fragments of Scottish History*, ed. J.G. Dalyell (Edinburgh, 1798).

76 Continuation of William of Tyre in *Chronique d'Ernoul*, p303.

77 Alio, *Queens of Sicily*, p425.

78 Continuation of William of Tyre in *Chronique d'Ernoul*, p354.

79 Natasha R. Hodgson, *Women, Crusading and the Holy Land in Historical Narrative* (Woodbridge: Boydell, 2007), p83.

80 The Marques of Northampton and the other ambassadors, to the lords of the Council, 20 June 1551, in *England Under the Reigns of Edward VI and Mary, with the Contemporary History of Europe, Illustrated with a Series of Original Letters Never Before Published*, vol. I, ed. Patrick Fraser Tytler (London, Richard Bentley, 1839), p388.

81 Quoted from Lambert, 'Queen or Consort', p153.

CHAPTER 5

1 *The Georgian Chronicle: The Period of Giorgi Lasha*, ed. Simon Qaukhchishvili and trans. Katharine Vivian (Amsterdam: Adolf M. Hakkert, 1991), pp91–2.

2 Antony Eastmond, 'Gender and Orientalism in Georgia in the age of Queen Tamar' in *Women, Men and Eunuchs: Gender in Byzantium*, ed. Liz James (London: Routledge, 1997), pp100–118, p101; Antonia Fraser, *The Warrior Queens: Boadicea's Chariot* (London, 1988) featured 'Queen Tamara', but the historical woman largely disappeared beneath the gloss.

3   *Georgian Chronicle*, p111.

4   Quoted from John Milton Potter, 'The development and significance of the Salic Law of the French', *The English Historical Review*, vol. 52, no.206 (1937), pp235–253, p237.

5   Jim Bradbury, *The Capetians: Kings of France 987–328* (London: Bloomsbury, 2007), p35.

6   Simon MacLean, *Ottonian Queenship* (Oxford: Oxford University Press, 2017), p47.

7   Woodacre, *Queens Regnant of Navarre*, p52.

8   Potter, 'The development and significance of the Salic Law', p325.

9   Charles Ingrao, *The Habsburg Monarchy* (Cambridge: Cambridge University Press, 1994), p129.

10 Charles W. Ingrao and Andrew L. Thomas, 'Piety and patronage: the empresses-consort of the High Baroque', *German History*, vol. 20, issue 1 (2002), pp20–43, p37.

11 Ingrao, *Habsburg Monarchy*, p129.

12 Barbara Stollberg-Rilinger, *Maria Theresa: The Habsburg Empress in her Time* (Princeton: Princeton University Press, 2021), p33.

13 R.J.W. Evans, 'Communicating Empire: The Habsburgs and their Critics, 1700–1919: The Prothero Lecture', *Transactions of the Royal Historical Society*, sixth series, vol. 19 (2009), pp117–138.

14 Ingrao, *Habsburg Monarchy*, p150; the quote is from Stollberg-Rilinger, *Maria Theresa*, p41.

15 Filippo Donvito, 'The lioness of the Caucasus', *Medieval Warfare*, vol. 4, no.2 (2014), pp19–24.

16 Ronald Grigor Suny, *The Making of the Georgian Nation* (Bloomington: Indiana University Press, 1994), p1.

17 Antony Eastmond, *Royal Imagery in Medieval Georgia* (Pennsylvania: Pennsylvania State University Press, 1998), p5; Mariam Lordkipanidze, *Essays on Georgian History* (Tbilisi: Mesniereba, 1994), p74.

18 Suny, *Making of the Georgian Nation*, pp34–35.

ENDNOTES

19 Lordkipanidze, *Essays on Georgian History*, p61; Mariam Lordkipanidze, *Georgia in the XI-XII Centuries* (Tbilisi: Ganatleba Publishers, 1987), p23.

20 Kalistrat Salia, *History of the Georgian Nation*, trans. Katharine Vivian (Paris, 1983), pp157–173.

21 Lordkipanidze, *Essays on Georgian History*, p149.

22 Eastmond, *Royal Imagery*, p106, 109–110.

23 Eastmond, 'Gender and orientalism', p102.

24 Stollberg-Rilinger, *Maria Theresa*, p61.

25 *Letters of an Empress: A Collection of Intimate Letters from Maria Theresia to her Children and Friends*, ed. G. Pusch and trans. Eilee R. Taylor (London: Massie, 1939), p177.

26 Maria Theresia, *Letters of an Empress*, p91.

27 Maria Theresia, *Letters of an Empress*, p106.

28 Robert Pick, *Empress Maria Theresa: The Earlier Years, 1717–1757* (New York: Harper and Row, 1966), p9.

29 Dénis-François Secousse, ed., *Recueil de Pieces Servant des Preuves aux Mémoires sur les Troubles Excités en France par Charles II, dit le Mauvais, Roi de Navarre et Comte d'Evreux* (Paris, 1755), pp6–10.

30 Woodacre, *Queens Regnant*, p55.

31 Woodacre, *Queens Regnant*, p58; Marguerite Keane, 'Louis IX, Louis X, Louis of Navarre: Family Ties and Political Ideology in the Hours of Juana of Navarre', *Visual Resources* vol. 20, nos.2-3 (2004), p238.

32 Jean Froissart, *Chronicles*, trans and ed Geoffrey Brereton (London: Penguin, 1978), p150.

33 Lordkipanidze, *Georgia in the XI-XII Centuries*, p137.

34 Donvito, 'The lioness of the Caucasus', p21.

35 *Georgian Chronicle*, pp59–60.

36 *Georgian Chronicle*, p60.

37 *Georgian Chronicle*, p60.

38 *Georgian Chronicle*, p62.

39 *Georgian Chronicle*, p62.

40 *Georgian Chronicle*, p114.

41 Monter, 'Gendered sovereignty', p538.

42 Monter, 'Gendered Sovereignty', p557.

43 Stollberg-Rilinger, *Maria Theresa*, p89.

44 For the War of the Austrian Succession, see M.S. Anderson, *The War of the Austrian Succession 1740–1748* (London: Routledge, 1995) and Reed Browning, *The War of the Austrian Succession* (New York: St Martins, 1993). For more on Maria Theresia in general, see Pick, *Empress Maria Theresa* and Edward Crankshaw, *Maria Theresa* (London: Constable and Robinson, 1969). Both are decades old, but provide reasonable narrative overviews of her life.

45 Ingrao, *Habsburg Monarchy*, p150.

46 *Georgian Chronicle*, p78.

47 *The Holy and Righteous King David the Restorer of Georgia and The Holy and Righteous Queen Tamar of Georgia: Lives Akathists Canons Works*, ed. John Townsend and trans. Irakli Beridze (Tbilisi, 2021), p95; *Georgian Chronicle*, p57.

48 Lordkipanidze, *Essays on Georgian History*, p55.

49 A.C.S. Peacock, 'Georgia and the Anatolian Turks in the 12th and 13th Centuries', *Anatolian Studies*, vol. 56 (2006), pp127–146.

50 *Georgian Chronicle*, p83.

51 Salia, *History of the Georgian Nation*, p181.

52 Stollberg-Rilinger, *Maria Theresa*, p122.

53 Ingrao, *Habsburg Monarchy*, p158.

54 Evans, 'Communicating Empire', p121.

55 Katherine Fischer Drew, trans and ed., *The Laws of the Salian Franks* (Philadelphia: University of Pennsylvania Press, 1991).

56 *Laws of the Salian Franks*, p122.

57 *Laws of the Salian Franks*, pp30, 44, 45.

58 Bradbury, *The Capetians*, p280 notes that 'its antiquity is dubious'; Potter, 'The development and significance of the Salic Law', p248.

ENDNOTES

59   Woodacre, *Queens Regnant*, p71.

60   Ingrao, *Habsburg Monarchy*, p160.

61   Maria Theresia, *Letters of an Empress*, p133.

62   Maria Theresia, *Letters of an Empress*, p22.

63   Ingrao, *Habsburg Monarchy*, p183.

64   Monter, 'Gendered sovereignty', p538.

65   Sargis Kakabadze, *Queen Tamar: Her Significance* (Tbilisi, 1912).

66   Eastmond, *Royal Imagery*, pp160–175.

67   Shota Rustaveli, *The Knight in Panther Skin*, trans. Katharine Vivian (London, 1977).

CHAPTER 6

1   Translation is taken from C.P. Fitzgerald, *The Empress Wu* (London: Barrie and Jenkins, 1956), p4.

2   Fitzgerald, *Empress Wu*, pv considers early Tang China to be 'one of the greatest ages of Chinese civilisation'.

3   R.W.L. Guisso, *Wu Tse-T'ien and the Politics of Legitimation in T'ang China* (Washington: Western Washington University, 1978), p127.

4   X.L. Woo, *Empress Wu the Great* (New York: Algora, 2008), p108.

5   Fay Beauchamp, 'Asian origins of Cinderella: The Zhuang Storyteller of Guangxi', *Oral Tradition*, vol. 25, no.2 (2010), pp447–496.

6   Dora Shu-Fang Dien, *Empress Wu in Fiction and History: Female Defiance in Confucian China* (2003), p30.

7   Guisso, *Wu Tse T'en*, pp11, 14–16; Nigel Cawthorne, *Daughter of Heaven: The True Story of the Only Woman to Become Emperor of China* (Sharpe Books, 2017), p10.

8   Bret Hinsch, *Women in Early Imperial China* (Maryland: Rowman and Littlefield, 2011), pp35–6; Cawthorne, *Daughter of Heaven*, p18; Hinsch, *Women in Early Imperial China*, p40.

9   Jonathan Clements, *Wu: The Chinese Empress who Schemed, Seduced and Murdered her Way to Become a Living God* (Albert Bridge Books, 2014), p22.

10   T.H. Barrett, *The Woman who Discovered Printing* (New Haven: Yale University Press, 2008), p4; Dien, *Empress Wu,* p31.

11   Carrie E. Reed, ed., *A Tang Miscellany: An Introduction to Youyang Zazu* (New York: Peter Lang, 2003), Entry 2, p79.

12   Howard J. Wechsler, *Mirror to the Son of Heaven: Wei Cheng at the Court of T'ang T'ai-tsung* (New Haven: Yale University Press, 1974), pp79–80.

13   *The Old Book of Tang*, volume 6, annals 6 (published online at https://chinesenotes.com/jiutangshu.html).

14   Anne Somerset, *Elizabeth I* (London: Weidenfeld & Nicolson, 1991) remains the most detailed biography to cover Elizabeth's entire life. For her early life see Elizabeth Norton, *The Temptation of Elizabeth Tudor* (London: Head of Zeus, 2015).

15   Clements, *Wu,* p85; Cawthorne, *Daughter of Heaven,* p134.

16   Leanda de Lisle, *The Sisters who would be Queen* (London: Ballantine, 2009).

17   McMahon, *Women Shall Not Rule,* pp1, 9, 11; Cawthorne, *Daughter of Heaven,* p58.

18   Mahon, *Women shall not rule,* p39.

19   Cawthorne, *Daughter of Heaven,* p65.

20   *Old Book of Tang,* Volume 6, Annal 6.

21   Science Museum: Sir Henry Wellcome's Museum Collection, object number A656209.

22   Clements, *Wu,* p68.

23   Dien, *Empress Wu,* p35 notes that 'the validity of this story cannot be ascertained'. The usual method of execution was either strangulation or beheading, although there are other examples of Wu apparently inflicting a crueller death on her opponents – Charles Benn, *China's Golden Age: Everyday Life in the Tang Dynasty* (Oxford: Oxford University Press, 2002), pp204, 207.

24   Clements, *Wu,* p76.

25   Denis Twitchett, '"Chen gui" and Other works attributed to Empress Wu Zetian', *Asia Major,* third series, vol. 16, no.1 (2003), pp33–109.

ENDNOTES

26 Denis Twitchett, *The Writing of Official History under the T'ang* (Cambridge: Cambridge University Press, 1992), p25.

27 Twitchett, 'Chen gui', p41.

28 Twitchett, 'Chen gui', p52.

29 Twitchett, *Writing of Official History*, p52.

30 Jessica Rawson, 'Ornament as System: Chinese bird-and-flower design', *The Burlington Magazine*, vol. 148 (2006), pp380–389, p383.

31 Dien, *Empress Wu*, p29.

32 Guisso, *Wu Tse-T'ien*, p202.

33 Christopher Haigh, ed., *The Reign of Elizabeth I* (London: Palgrave, 1984), pp1–26.

34 Guisso, *Wu Tse-T'ien*, p.127.

35 Fitzgerald, *Empress Wu*, p83.

36 Clements, *Wu*, p176.

37 Guisso, *Wu Tse T'ien*, p36.

38 N. Harry Rothschild, *Emperor Wu Zhao and her Pantheon of Devis, Divinities, and Dynastic Mothers* (New York: Columbia University Press, 2015).

39 Wendi L. Adamek, 'Robes purple and gold: transmission of the robe in the "Lidai fabao ji" (Record of the Dharm-Jewel through the Ages)', *History of Religions*, vol. 40 (2000), pp58–81.

40 T.H. Barrett, 'The woman who invented notepaper: towards a comparative historiography of paper and print', *Journal of the Royal Asiatic Society*, third series, vol. 21 (2011), pp199–210.

41 Barrett, *The Woman who Invented Printing*, p138.

42 Guisso, *Wu Tse-T'ien*, p57.

43 Guisso, *Wu Tse-T'ien*, p203.

44 Woo, *Empress Wu the Great*, p116.

45 Barrett, *The Woman who Invented Printing*, p75.

WOMEN WHO RULED THE WORLD

CHAPTER 7

1   Simonds d'Ewes, 'Journal of the House of Commons: November 1586' in *The Journals of All the Parliaments During the Reign of Queen Elizabeth* (Shannon, Ire, 1682), pp392–407. British History Online https://www.british-history.ac.uk/no-series/jrnl-parliament-eliz1/pp392–407 (date accessed 8 June 2024).

2   Herbert Lockyer, *All the Kings and Queens of the Bible* (Grand Rapids: Zondervan Publishing House, 1961), p207.

3   *The New Oxford Annotated Bible,* fifth edition, ed. Michael D. Coogan (Oxford: Oxford University Press, 2010), p494–495.

4   John Rogerson, *Chronicles of the Old Testament Kings* (London: Thames and Hudson, 1997), pp101–2.

5   For monotheism in the region and its effective backdating, see J. Alberto Soggin, *An Introduction to the History of Israel and Judah* (London: SCM Press, 1999).

6   Susan Ackerman, 'The Queen Mother and the cult in Ancient Israel', *Journal of Biblical Literature*, vol. 112, no.3 (1993), pp385–401.

7   Helena Zlotnick, 'From Jezebel to Esther: Fashioning images of queenship in the Hebrew Bible' *Biblica*, vol. 82, no.4 (2001), pp477–495, p479.

8   Lockyer, *Kings and Queens of the Bible*, p234.

9   Lockyer, *Kings and Queens of the Bible*, p241.

10 Edwin R. Thiele, *The Mysterious Numbers of the Hebrew Kings* (Grand Rapids: Zondervan, 1983); Rogerson, *Chronicles*, p129.

11 Flavius Josephus, *The Genuine Works of Flavius Josephus, the Jewish Historian*, ed. and trans William Whiston (1737), pp9, 96.

12 Lockyer, *All the Kings and Queens*, p240.

13 2 Kings 9:24, 27.

14 John Knox, *The Political Writings of John Knox: The First Blast of the Trumpet Against the Monstrous Regiment of Women and Other Selected Works*, ed. Marvin A. Breslow (Washington: Folger, 1985), p66.

15 Christopher Goodman, *How Superior Powers Ought to be Obeyed* (Geneva, 1558).

ENDNOTES

16 John Aylmer, *An Harborowe for Faithful and Trewe Subjectes* (1559).

17 Knox, *First Blast of the Trumpet*, p77.

18 Knox, *First Blast of the Trumpet*, p42.

19 Retha M. Warnicke, *Mary Queen of Scots* (London: Routledge, 2006), p59.

20 Jenny Wormald, *Mary Queen of Scots* (Edinburgh: Hamlyn, 1988), p21.

21 Antonia Fraser, *Mary Queen of Scots* (London: Wiedenfeld and Nicolson, 2018), p172.

22 Warnicke, *Mary Queen of Scots*, p71.

23 Sir James Melville, *The Memoirs of Sir James Melville of Halhill*, ed. Gordon Donaldson (London: Folio Society, 1969), p38.

24 William Shakespeare, *Antony and Cleopatra*, Act II scene V.

25 Shakespeare, *Antony and Cleopatra*, Act II scene III.

26 Helen Morris, 'Queen Elizabeth I "Shadowed" in Cleopatra', *Huntington Library Quarterly*, vol. 32, no.3 (1969), pp271–278, p272; Keith Rinehart, 'Shakespeare's Cleopatra and England's Elizabeth', *Shakespeare Quarterly*, vol. 23, no.1 (1972), pp81–86, p82.

27 Joyce Tyldesley, *Chronicle of the Queens of Egypt* (London: Thames and Hudson, 2006), pp201–2.

28 Günther Hölbl, *A History of the Ptolemaic Empire* (London: Routledge, 2001), p236.

29 Dio Cassius, *Roman History Books 41-5*, ed. and trans, Earnest Cary (Cambridge: Harvard University Press, 1916), p171.

30 Dio, *Roman History*, p175.

31 Melville, *Memoirs*, p35.

32 Robert Pitcairn, ed., *Ancient Criminal Trials in Scotland*, vol. I, part I (Edinburgh, 1829), p502.

33 *Prince Alexandre Labanoff, ed., Lettres et Memoires de Marie, Reine d'Ecosse*, vol. 2 (London: Charles Dolman, 1844), p3.

34 *Calendar of State Papers Foreign: Elizabeth*, vol. 8, 1566–1568, ed. Allan James Crosby (London, 1871), p185.

35 Labanoff, *Lettres et Memoires*, p38.

36 Melville, *Memoirs*, p64.

37 Warnicke, *Mary Queen of Scots*, p166.

38 Dio, *Roman History*, p175–177.

39 Dio, *Roman History*, p181.

40 Dio, *Roman History*, p183.

41 d'Ewes, *Journals of All the Parliaments*, pp205–221.

42 John Whitehorne, *Cleopatras* (London: Routledge, 1994), p182.

43 Dio, *Roman History*, p245.

44 Hölbl, *Ptolemaic Empire*, p237.

45 Clifford Weber, 'Intimations of Dido and Cleopatra in Some Contemporary Portrayals of Elizabeth I', *Studies in Philology*, vol. 96, no.2 (1999), pp127–143; *Calendar of State Papers, Spain (Simancas)*, vol. 4, 1587–1603 (London, HMSO, 1899), no.481.

46 John Hungerford Pollen, ed., *Mary Queen of Scots and the Babington Plot. Edited from the Original Documents in the Public Record Office, the Yelverton MSS, and Elsewhere* (Edinburgh, 1922), p18.

47 Pollen, *Mary Queen of Scots*, p21.

48 Pollen, *Mary Queen of Scots*, p26.

49 The National Archives State Papers 53/22, f.1 (Mary, Queen of Scots' Cipher Key).

50 David Harris Willson, *King James VI and I* (London: Jonathan Cape, 1956), p73.

51 Lloyd Llewellyn-Jones, *The Cleopatras: The Forgotten Queens of Egypt* (London: Wildfire, 2024), p286.

52 The National Archives SP 53/20, f.23.

53 Lockyer, *Kings and Queens of the Bible*, p1.

54 2 Kings 11.14; 2 Chronicles 23.12–15 presents an almost identical story.

ENDNOTES

55 Richard Nelson, *Interpretation, A Bible Commentary for Teaching and Preaching: First and Second Kings* (Louisville, 1987), p207.

56 2 Kings 9.33.

CHAPTER 8

1 Tormod Eide, Tomas Hägg, Richard Holton Pierce and Laszlo Török, eds., *Fontes Historiae Nubiorum: Textual Sources for the History of the Middle Nile Region Between the Eighth Century BC and the Sixth Century AD, vol. III: From the First to the Sixth Century AD* (Bergen: University of Bergen, 1998), p762.

2 David E. Jones, *Women Warriors: A History* (Washington: Potomac, 1997), px.

3 Nathanael J. Andrade, *Zenobia: Shooting Star of Palmyra* (Oxford: Oxford University Press, 2018) is probably as close as we can come to the historical Zenobia.

4 *Historia Augusta*, vol. 3, ed. and trans. David Magie and David Rohrbacher (Cambridge: Harvard University Press, 2022), p107.

5 Richard Stoneman, *Palmyra and its Empire: Zenobia's Revolt Against Rome* (Michigan: University of Michigan Press, 1992), p111.

6 Eric R. Varner, Transcending Gender: Assimilation, Identity, and Roman Imperial Portraits' *Memoirs of the American Academy in Rome*, vol. 7 (2008), pp185–205.

7 Michael H. Dodgeon and Samuel N.C. Lieu, eds., *The Roman Eastern Frontier and the Persian Wars AD 226–363* (London: Routledge, 1991), pp84–85.

8 Bergstein, 'Palmyra and Palmyra', pp13–38.

9 Roger Bland, 'The Coinage of Vabalathus and Zenobia from Antioch and Alexandria' *The Numismatic Chronicle*, vol. 171 (2011), pp133–186, p136.

10 *Historia Augusta*), p109.

11 Michael H. Dodgeon and Samuel N.C. Lieu, eds., *The Roman Eastern Frontier and the Persian Wars AD 226–363* (London: Routledge, 1991), pp84–85.

12 Quoted from Barbara F. Weissberger, *Isabel Rules: Constructing Queenship, Wielding Power* (University of Minnesota Press, 2003) pp82–83.

13 Weissberger, *Isabel Rules*, p82.

14   Elizabeth A. Lehfeldt, 'Ruling Sexuality: The political legitimacy of Isabel of Castile', *Renaissance Quarterly*, vol. 53 (2000), pp31–56.

15   Strabo, *Geography*, trans. Horace Leonard Jones (Loeb, 1932), p139. The Kandake in question is Amanirenas.

16   https://www.bbc.co.uk/news/entertainment-arts-67484645 (date accessed 8 December 2023).

17   Sarah B. Pomeroy, *Goddesses, Whores, Wives & Slaves* (London: Bodley Head, 1975), p149; https://www.nytimes.com/1992/07/15/garden/now-is-the-time-to-come-to-the-aid-of-your-favorite-cookies.html (date accessed 19 December 2023).

18   Pomeroy, *Goddesses, Whores*, p151.

19   https://www.bbc.co.uk/news/blogs-news-from-elsewhere-32736596 (date accessed 10 December 2023).

20   Andrade, *Zenobia*, p124.

21   *Historia Augusta*, pp43–45.

22   Mary Bergstein, 'Palmyra and Palmyra: Look on these Stones, Ye Mighty, and Despair' *Arion: A Journal of Humanities and the Classics*, vol. 24 (2016), pp13–38.

23   *Historia Augusta*, p130.

24   Samia Dafa'alla, 'Succession in the Kingdom of Napata, 900–300 BC', *The International Journal of African Historical Studies*, vol. 26 (1993), pp167–174; B.G. Haycock, 'The kingship of Cush in the Sudan', *Comparative Studies in Society and History*, vol. 7 (1965), pp461–480; P.L. Shinnie, 'The Nilotic Sudan and Ethiopia, c.660 BC to c. AD 600' in *The Cambridge History of Africa*, vol. 2, eds. J.D. Fage and Roland Oliver (Cambridge: Cambridge University Press, 1978), pp210–671.

25   Nwando Achebe, *Female Monarchs and Merchant Queens in Africa* (Ohio University Press, 2020) p75; Carolyn Fluehr-Lobban, 'Nubian Queens in the Nile Valley and Afro-Asiatic Cultural History', *Ninth International Conference for Nubian Studies, Museum of Fine Arts Boston* (1998).

26   Toyin Falola and Nana Akua Amponsah, *Women's Roles in Sub-Saharan Africa* (Santa Barbara, 2012), pp2–3.

27   Strabo, *Geography*, p145.

ENDNOTES

28 Angelika Lohwasser and Jacke Phillips, 'Women in Ancient Kush' in eds. Geoff Emberling and Bruce Beyer Williams, *The Oxford Handbook of Ancient Nubia* (Oxford: Oxford University Press, 2021), pp1015–1032, p1028.

29 Angelika Lohwasser, 'Queenship in Kush: Status, Role and Ideology of Royal Women' *Journal of the American Research Center in Egypt*, vol. 38 (2001), pp61–75.

30 Pliny the Elder, *Pliny Natural History with an English translation in ten volumes*, vol. II, ed. H. Rackham (London, 1942), p477.

31 Frank M. Snowden, Jr., *Blacks in Antiquity* (Cambridge: Cambridge University Press, 1970).

32 Strabo, *Geography*, p141.

33 Pliny, *Naturalis Historia* (quoted from *Fontes Historiae Nubiorum*, p856).

34 Fluehr-Lobban, 'Nubian Queens', p1.

35 John Coleman Darnell, *The Inscription of Queen Katimala at Semna: Textual Evidence for the Origins of the Napatan State* (New Haven: Yale University Press, 2006).

36 Barbara F. Weissberger, 'Questioning the Queen, Now and Then' in ed. Barbara F. Weissberger, *Queen Isabel I of Castile: Power, Patronage, Persona* (Woodbridge: Tamesis, 2008), ppxi–xxiv.

37 M. Lunenfeld, 'Isabella I of Castile and the company of women in power' *Historical Reflections*, vol. 4 (1977), pp57–99.

38 Alfonso de Palencia, *Cronica de Enrique IV*, 5 vols, ed. D.A. Paz y Melia (Madrid, 1908).

39 Giles Tremlett, *Isabella of Castile: Europe's First Great Queen* (London: Bloomsbury, 2017), p17.

40 Weissburger, *Isabel Rules*, p79.

41 Oscar Villarroel Gonzalez, *Juana La Beltraneja: La Construccion de Una Ilegitimidad* (Madrid, 2014), pp24–6 analyses the propaganda surrounding claims of Juana's illegitimacy, noting a 'political intentionality' behind works commissioned by Isabel.

42 Reynold A. Nicholson, *A Literary History of the Arabs* (London, 1907), p34.

43 Al-Tabari, *The History of al-Tabari, vol. IV: The Ancient Kingdoms*, ed. Moshe Perlmann (New York, 1987), pp139–40.

44 Dodgeon and Lieu, *Roman Eastern Frontier*, p85.

45 Zosimus, *The History of Count Zosimus, Sometime Advocate and Chancellor of the Roman Empire* (London, 1814), p23.

46 Bland, 'Coinage of Vabalathus and Zenobia', p137.

47 Zosimus, *History*, p27.

48 *Historia Augusta*, p125.

49 *Historia Augusta*, p130.

50 Gonzalez, *Juana la Beltraneja*, p19.

51 Susannah Humble Ferreira, 'Juana La Beltraneja, Dynastic Fears, and Threats of Marriage (1475–1506)', *Renaissance and Reformation*, vol. 43 (2020) pp79–100.

52 Ruy de Pina, *Chronica d'el-Rei D. Affonso V*, vol. I (Lisbon, 1901), pp130–131.

53 Pina, *Chronica d'el-Rei*, p136.

54 Hilaire Kallendorf, 'Inventing Isabel' in ed. Hilaire Kallendorf, *A Companion to the Queenship of Isabel la Catolica* (Leiden: Brill, 2023), pp1–33.

55 David A. Boruchoff, 'Isabel, her Chroniclers, and the Inquisition: Self-fashioning and historical memory' in Kallendorf, *A Companion to Queen Isabel*, pp34–71.

56 Michelle M. Hamilton, 'Hostile histories: Isabel and Fernando in Jewish and Muslim narratives' in Kallendorf, *Companion to Queen Isabel*, pp213–231.

57 Deborah Root, 'Speaking Christian: Orthodoxy and Difference in Sixteenth-Century Spain', *Representations*, vol. 23 (1988), pp 118–134; Enrique Rodriguez-Picavea, 'The military orders and the war of Granada' *Mediterranean Studies*, vol. 19 (2010), pp 14–42.

58 John Edwards, 'Windows into souls: Isabel, religion, and the Spanish Inquisition' in Kallendorf, *Companion to Queen Isabel*, pp232–253.

59 Nuria Silleras-Fernandez, 'Isabel's years of sorrow: consoling the Catholic Queen' in Kallendorf, *Companion to Queen Isabel*, pp254–278.

60 P.L. Shinnie, *Meroe: A Civilisation of the Sudan* (London, 1967), p158.

61 Yellin, 'Royal and elite cemeteries', pp562–588; David Sweetman, *Women Leaders in African History* (London: Heinemann, 1984), p12.

ENDNOTES

62   Strabo, *Geography*, p141.

63   Kandake Amanitare (*Fontes Historiae Nubiorum vol. III*, p903).

64   Janice W. Yellin, 'The royal and elite cemeteries at Meroe' in eds. Geoff Emberling and Bruce Beyer Williams, *The Oxford Handbook of Ancient Nubia* (Oxford: Oxford University Press, 2021), pp562–588, p562.

65   Bob Brier, 'The Other Pyramids', *Archaeology*, vol. 55 (2002), pp54–8.

66   Alberton A. Vela-Rodrigo, 'The sacred treasure of Queen Amanishakheto', *Ancient Egypt Magazine*, vol. 21 (2021), pp20–26.

67   Harkless, *Nubian Pharaohs*, p150.

68   James Bruce, *Travels to Discover the Source of the Nile*, vol. IV (London, 1790), pp531–536.

69   Alan Moorehead, *The Blue Nile* (New York, 1962), p39.

CHAPTER 9

1   Imatani Akira, 'The strange survival and its modern significance' in ed. Ben-Ami Shillony, *The Emperors of Modern Japan* (Leiden: Brill, 2008), p15.

2   Ben-Ami Shillony, *Enigma of the Emperors: Sacred Subservience in Japanese History* (Leiden: Brill, 2005), p278.

3   The Advisory Council on the Imperial House Law Report, 24 November 2005 (English translation) https://japan.kantei.go.jp/policy/koshitsu/051124_e.pdf

4   Ian Buruma, *A Japanese Mirror: Heroes and Villains of Japanese Culture* (London: Jonathan Cape, 1984), p53.

5   Shilomy, *Enigma*, p45.

6   Conrad Totman, *A History of Japan* (Oxford: Oxford University Press, 2005), pp208, 305.

7   E. Patricia Tsurumi, 'The male present versus the female past: historians and Japan's ancient female emperors', *Bulletin of Concerned Asian Scholars*, vol. 14, no.4 (1982), pp71–78, p72.

8   Joan R. Piggott, *The Emergence of Japanese Kingship* (Stanford: Stanford University Press, 1997), p15; Gina L. Barnes, *State Formation in Japan: Emergence of a 4th-Century Ruling Elite* (London: Routledge, 2007), p83.

9   Piggott, *Emergence of Japanese Kingship*, p34.

10 Richard Ponsonby-Fane, *The Imperial House of Japan* (Kyoto, 1959), p45.

11 Tsurumi, 'The male present versus the female past', pp71–78.

12 *Nihongi: Chronicles of Japan from the Earliest Times to A.D. 697*, vol. II, ed. W.G. Aston (London: The Japan Society, 1896), p121.

13 *Gukansho*, p37.

14 Totman, *History of Japan*, p55.

15 *Gukansho*, p26.

16 *Nihongi*, p122.

17 *Nihongi*, p122.

18 William Theodore de Bary, *Sources of Japanese Tradition* (London, 1958), p3.

19 G.B. Sanson, *Japan: A Short Cultural History* (Stanford: Stanford University Press, 1976).

20 'Michitsuna's Mother, *The Kagero Diary: A Woman's Autobiographical Text from Tenth Century Japan*, ed. and trans. Sonja Arntzen (Michigan: University of Michigan Press, 1997).

21 Lady Sarashina, *As I Crossed a Bridge of Dreams: Recollections of a Woman in Eleventh-Century Japan*, ed. and trans. Ivan Morris, (London: Penguin, 1975), p42.

22 Sarashina, *As I Crossed a Bridge*, p39.

23 Sarashina, *As I Crossed a Bridge*, pp46–47.

24 Murasaki Shikibu, *The Tale of Genji*, trans. Royall Tyler (London: Penguin, 2003).

25 Murasaki Shikibu, *The Diary of Lady Murasaki*, ed. and trans. Richard Bowring (London: Penguin, 1996).

26 Murasaki, *Diary*, p22.

27 Izumi Shikibu, *Heian Court Heroines: The Izumi Shikibu Nikki*, trans. Annie Shepley Omori and Kochi Doi and ed. William de Lange (TOYO Press: 2019).

ENDNOTES

28 Murasaki, *Diary*, p54.

29 Sei Shōnagon, *The Pillow Book*, ed. and trans. Meredith McKinney (London: Penguin, 2006), pp7–8.

30 William Wayne Farris, *Japan to 1600: A Social and Economic History* (Honolulu, University of Hawaii Press, 2009), p26.

31 Tsurumi, 'The male present', p73.

32 *Nihongi*, p174.

33 *Nihongi*, p192.

34 *Gukansho*, p30.

35 Michiko Y. Aoki, 'Jitō Tennō the Female Sovereign' in Chieko Irie Mulhern, ed., *Heroic With Grace: Legendary Women of Japan* (Armonk, 1991), pp40–76, p45.

36 *Nihongi*.

37 Aoki, 'Jitō Tennō', pp40–76.

38 *Gukansho*, p32.

39 Aoki, 'Jitō Tennō', p59.

40 Sarah Milledge Nelson, 'The Queens of Silla: Power and Connections to the Spirit World' in Sarah Milledge Nelson, ed., *Ancient Queens: Archaeological Explorations* (Walnut Creek: AltaMira, 2003), pp77–92.

41 Kim Pusik (ed.), *The Silla Annals of the Samguk Sagi*, trans. Edward J. Shultz and Hugh H.W. Kang with Daniel C. Kane (Korea, 2012), p149; Ilyon, *Samguk Yusa: Legends and History of the Three Kingdoms of Ancient Korea*, trans. Tae-Hung Ha and Grafton K. Mintz (Seoul, 1972), p74.

42 *Samguk Sagi*, p147.

43 Yung-Chung Kim, trans and ed, Women of Korea: A History from Ancient Times to 1945 (Seoul, Ewha Womans University Press), p5.

44 For example, *Samguk Sagi*, p159, 163, 165.

45 Kitabatake Chikafusa, *A Chronicle of Gods and Sovereigns: Jinno Shotoki of Kitabatake Chikafusa*, trans. H. Paul Varley (New York, 1980), p140.

46 Asserted in *Gukansho*, p32, written around 1220.

47 Chikafusa, *Chronicle of Gods and Sovereigns*, p140.

48 Sanson, *Japan*, p108; Farris, Japan to 1600, p31.

49 Sanson, *Japan*, p109.

50 Basil Hall Chamberlain, ed., *'A Translation of the "Ko-ji-ki" or Records of Ancient Matters'* (Yokohama, 1882), p4.

51 G. Cameron Hurst III, *Insei: Abdicated Sovereigns in the Politics of Late Heian Japan 1086–1185* (New York: Columbia University Press, 1976).

52 *Gukansho*.

53 Sanson, *Japan*, p183.

54 Sanson, *Japan*, p184.

55 Chikafusa, *Chronicle of Gods and Sovereigns*, p145.

56 Shilomy, *Enigma of the Emperors*, p54.

57 *Gukshanko*, p34.

58 Chikafusa, *Chronicle of Gods and Sovereigns*, p145.

59 For more on the shoguns, see Isaac Titsingh, *Secret Memoirs of the Shoguns: Isaac Titsingh and Japan, 1779–1822*, ed. Timon Screech (London: Routledge, 2006).

60 Roderigo de Vivero, *An Account of Japan, 1609*, ed. and trans. Caroline Stone (Edinburgh, Hardinge Simpole).

61 Vivero, *Account of Japan*, p91.

62 Vivero, *Account of Japan*, p83.

63 Vivero, *Account of Japan*, p85.

64 Shillony, *Enigma of the Emperors*, p278.

65 https://www.reuters.com/article/world/japans-crown-prince-ready-for-throne-but-no-fairytale-for-his-unhappy-princess-idUSKCN10L0UR/ (date accessed 10 October 2024).

66 Shilomy, *Enigma*, p280.

67 The Advisory Council on the Imperial House Law Report, 24 November 2005 (English translation) https://japan.kantei.go.jp/policy/koshitsu/051124_e.pdf p2.

68 Shilomy, *Enigma of the Emperors*, p277.

ENDNOTES

CHAPTER 10

1   Victoria's journals have been published online and can be found at http://www.queenvictoriasjournals.org/

2   Queen Victoria to Queen Liliuokalani, 8 March 1893, Hawaiian State Archives, Manuscript Collection, Lili'uokalani Manuscript Collection, Seized Documents, Box 18, M-93 Contents of Metal Box, Letter, 1893-03-08, Victoria of the United Kingdom of Great Britain and Ireland to Her Majesty Queen Lili'uokalani. Citation 18-143-S5.

3   Mark Twain, *Mark Twain in Hawaii: Rouging it in the Sandwich Islands, Hawaii in the 1860s* (Honolulu, Mutual Publishing, 1990), p62.

4   Twain, *Mark Twain in Hawaii*, p11.

5   Lili'uokalani of Hawaii, *Hawaii's Story by Hawaii's Queen* (1898), p18.

6   *Hawaiian Islands: Report of the Committee on Foreign Relations, United States Senate, with Accompanying Testimony, and Executive Documents Transmitted to Congress from January 1, 1893, to March 10, 1894*, vol. II (Washington: Government Printing Office 1894) gives the background to the relationship between Hawaii and the United States, with the first US consul appointed in September 1820.

7   E. Jensen Krige and J.D. Krige, *The Realm of a Rain Queen: A Study of the Pattern of Lovedu Society* (London: Routledge, 2020), p1.

8   S.S. Dornan, 'Rainmaking in South Africa', *Bantu Studies*, vol. 3 (1927), pp185–195. For a detailed discussion of the Rain Queens' role as spiritual leader, see Nwando Achebe, *Female Monarchs and Merchant Queens in Africa* (Ohio University Press, 2020).

9   Krige and Krige, *Realm of a Rain Queen*, p2.

10 Dornan, 'Rainmaking', p189; Menno Klapwijk, 'Pot- and Pit- Burials from the North-Eastern Transvaal, South Africa', *The South African Archaeological Bulletin*, vol. 44 (1989), pp65–69, p68.

11 Russell H. Kaschula, 'Alice in Wonderland: Translating to Read across Africa', *Journal of African Cultural Studies*, vol. 29, no 3 (2017), pp276–291, p283; Ann Jones, *Looking for Lovedu: A Woman's Journey Through Africa* (New York, 2001), p240.

12 Twain, *Mark Twain in Hawaii*, pp32–3.

13   Hawaii State Archives/ Manuscript Collection/ Lili'uokalani Manuscript Collection/ Seized Documents/ Lili'uokalani Collection, S#135-155: Letters and Documents Taken on Jan. 16, 1895, Folder 156/ Diary, 1887, Lili'uokalani (citation 19-156-S155).

14   Elfriede Höckner, *Die Lobedu Südafrikas: Mythos und Realität der Regenkönigin Modjadji* (Stuttgart: Franz Steiner, 1998), p32.

15   Hockner, *Die Lobedu Sudafrikas*, p35.

16   J.C. Smuts' Foreword to Krige and Krige, *Realm of a Rain Queen*, pvii.

17   Krige and Krige, *Realm of a Rain Queen*, p2.

18   Michael Nelson, *Queen Victoria and the Discovery of the Riviera* (London: I.B. Taurus, 2001).

19   Mary H. Krout, *The Memoirs of Hon. Bernice Pauahi Bishop* (New York, 1908), p193.

20   Krige and Krige, *Realm of a Rain Queen*, p17; Eileen Jensen Krige, 'The place of the North-Eastern Transvaal Sotho in the South Bantu Complex', *Africa: Journal of the International African Institute,* vol. 11, no.3 (1938), pp265–293, p267.

21   Julia Baird, *Victoria the Queen* (London, Blackfriars, 2016), p337.

22   Helena G. Allen, *The Betrayal of Liliuokalani: Last Queen of Hawaii 1838–1917* (Honolulu, 1982), p107.

23   Lili'uokalani, *Hawaii's Story*, p60.

24   Lili'uokalani, *Hawaii's Story*, p62.

25   Lili'uokalani of Hawaii, *The Diaries of Queen Liliuokalani of Hawaii*, ed. David W. Forbes (Honolulu: University of Hawai'i Press, 2019), pp147–8.

26   Lili'uokalani, *Hawaii's Story*, p66.

27   Lili'uokalani, *Hawaii's Story*, p66.

28   Lili'uokalani, *The Diaries*, p149.

29   Lili'uokalani, *Hawaii's Story*, p66.

30   Lili'uokalani, *Hawaii's Story*, p71.

31   Queen Victoria's Journal for 21 June 1887.

ENDNOTES

32 Gavan Daws, *Shoal of Time: A History of the Hawaiian Islands* (Honolulu: University of Hawaii Press, 1974), p209.

33 Kalākaua's reputation has suffered from the political difficulties of his reign, although attempts have been made to rehabilitate him in recent years. See, for example, Tiffany Lani Ing, *Reclaiming Kalākaua: Nineteenth-Century Perspectives on a Hawaiian Sovereign* (Honolulu: University of Hawai'i Press, 2019).

34 Lili'uokalani, *Hawaii's Story*, p94.

35 Johannes Meintjes, *The Commandant General: The Life and Times of Petrus Jacobus Joubert of the South African Republic 1831–1900* (Cape Town, 1971), p133.

36 H.J.C Pieterse, ed., *Volksaltare of 'N Veteraan van die Eerste Vryheidsoorlog Persoonlike Herinneringe van P.C. Joubert* (Kaapstad, Tweede Druk, 1948), pp87–92.

37 Pieterse, *Volksaltare*, p94.

38 Schlosser, *Rain-Queens*, p4.

39 Schlosser, *Rain-Queens*, plate 31.

40 Queen Victoria's Journal for 28 June 1838.

41 Hawaii State Archives/ Manuscript Collection / Lili'uokalani Manuscript Collection / Seized Documents/ Lili'uokalani Collection, S#61-85: Letters and Documents Taken on Jan. 16, 1895, Folder 151/ Note, 1893-01---, in Lili'uokalani's Handwriting (citation 19-151-S76).

42 Daws, *Shoal of Time*, p214.

43 Hawaii State Archives/ Manuscript Collection / Lili'oukalani Manuscript Collection/ Seized Documents/ Box 20/ Constitution (incomplete) (1893?) (Lili'uokalani)/ Constitution, 1893, Lili'uokalani (Citation 20-161-S196).

44 Daws, *Shoal of Time*, p251.

45 Traditionally historians have blamed Lili'uokalani for Hawaii's loss. Recent historians have been more favourable to her, while Hawaii's rich culture is more frequently depicted. For example, Gary Y. Okihiro, *Island World: A History of Hawai'i and the United States* (Berkeley: University of California Press, 2008) centres Hawaii in its relations with the US. Roger Bell, *Last Among Equals: Hawaiian Statehood and American Politics* (Honolulu: University of Hawaii Press) provides a nuanced assessment of Lili'uokalani's reign. J. Kehaulani Kauanui, 'Hawai'i in and out of America', *Mississippi Review*, vol. 32. No.3 (2004), pp145–

150, p146 notes the thriving independence movement in Hawaii today due to the illegal overthrow of the kingdom in a rebellion mounted by, effectively, thirteen white settlers. Tom Coffman, *Nation Within: The History of the American Occupation of Hawai'i* (London, 2016), p13 views Lili'uokalani as a patriotic figure.

46 Lili'uokalani, *The Diaries,* p317.

47 Hawaii State Archives/ Manuscript Collection/ Lili'uokalani Manuscript Collection/ Seized Documents / Box 18/ Lili'uokalani Collection, Lists of Seized Documents, Folder 142/ Schedule, 1895-01-16, Papers and documents found in the safe and writing desk of Lili'uokalani (citation 18-143-S0)

48 Lili'uokalani, *Hawaii's Story,* p119.

49 Michael Dougherty, *To Steal a Kingdom: Probing Hawaiian History* (Waimanalo, 1992).

50 Lili'uokalani of Hawaii, *The Kumulipo* (2020).

51 Lili'uokalani, *Hawaii's Story,* p136.

CHAPTER 11

1 Shaharyar M. Khan, *The Begums of Bhopal: A Dynasty of Women Rulers in Raj India* (London: I.B. Taurus, 2000), pp68–69.

2 Fatima Mernissi, *The Forgotten Queens of Islam,* translated by Mary Jo Lakeland (Cambridge: Polity, 1993).

3 Indira Iyengar, *The Bourbons and Begums of Bhopal: The Forgotten History* (New Delhi: Nihyogi Books, 2018), p48.

4 Ruby Lal, *Empress: The Astonishing Reign of Nur Jahan* (London: W.W. Norton, 2018).

5 Philip Harwood, ed., 'The Queen's Indian Title', *Saturday Review: Politics, Literature, Science and Art,* vol. 41 (1876), p396– 397; for more on Muslim women's status in early India, see Sudha Sharma's *The Status of Muslim Women in Medieval India* (New Delhi: Sage, 2016); Chimnabai II, Maharani of Baroda and S.M. Mitra, The Position of Women in Indian Life (London, 1911).

6 William Hough, *A Brief History of the Bhopal,* p1.

ENDNOTES

7   For a strident and highly important account of the evils of empire, see Shashi Tharoor, *Inglorious Empire: What the British Did to India* (London: Penguin, 2016).

8   Khan, *Begums of Bhopal*, p74.

9   P.K. De, *Bhopal* (New Delhi, 2015), p31.

10   Khan, *Begums of Bhopal*, p74.

11   Siobhan Lambert-Hurley, *Muslim Women, Reform and Princely Patronage: Nawab Sultan Jahan Begam of Bhopal* (London: Routledge, 2007).

12   Hough, *Brief History of Bhopal*, p132.

13   Miles Taylor, *Empress: Queen Victoria in India* (New Haven: Yale University Press, 2018), p2.

14   Taylor, *Empress*, pp75, 78.

15   Taylor, *Empress*, p90.

16   William Dalrymple and Anita Anand, *Koh-I-Noor: The History of the World's Most Infamous Diamond* (London: Bloomsbury, 2016), pp51–53.

17   Mervyn Brown, *A History of Madagascar* (Princeton: Princeton University Press, 2016), p39.

18   Keith Laidler, *Female Caligula: Ranavalona, the Mad Queen of Madagascar* (Chichester, 2005), p24.

19   Brown, *History of Madagascar*, p147.

20   Laidler, *Female Caligula*; Arianne Chernock, 'Queen Victoria and the "Bloody Mary of Madagascar"', *Victorian Studies*, vol. 55, no.3 (2013), pp425–449. Chernock does not agree with this comparison.

21   Bonar A. Gow, 'Independency among the Merina, 1833–1929', *The International Journal of African Historical Studies*, vol. 14, no. 2 (1981), pp229–253; Jocelyn Rabeson, 'Jesuits and Protestants in Nineteenth Century Madagascar' in eds. Robert Aleksander Maryks and Festo Mkenda, *Encounters Between Jesuits and Protestants in Africa* (Leiden: Brill, 2018), p172.

22   Stephen Ellis, 'Witch-hunting in central Madagascar 1828–1861', *Past and Present*, vol. 175 (2002), pp90–123, p102.

23   Chernock, 'Queen Victoria', p427.

24   Chernock, 'Queen Victoria', p426.

25 Laidler, *Female Caligula*, p103.

26 Chernock, 'Queen Victoria', p435.

27 Sambhu Chandra Mukhopa'dhya'ya, *The Career of An Indian Princess: The Late Begum Secunder of Bhopal, K.S.I.* (Calcutta, 1869), p6.

28 Khan, B*egums of Bhopal*, p88.

29 Mukhopa'dhya'ya, *Career of an Indian Princess*, p8.

30 Lambert-Hurley, *Muslim Women*.

31 Taylor, *Empress*, p199.

32 Clare Anderson, *The Indian Uprising of 1857–8: Prisons, Prisoners and Rebellion* (London: Anthem, 2007).

33 Lambert-Hurley, *Muslim Women*, p20.

34 Melinda Hinkson, *Aboriginal Sydney: A Guide to Important Places of the Past and Present* (Canberra: Aboriginal Studies Press, 2010), pxxi; Val Attenbrow, *Sydney's Aboriginal Past* (Sydney: University of New South Wales Press, 2010), p21.

35 Geoffrey C. Ingleton, ed., *True Patriots All: Or News from Early Australia as Told in a Collection of Broadsides* (Sydney, 1952), pp17, 45.

36 Hinkson, *Aboriginal Sydney*, p46; Greg Blyton, 'Harry Brown (c. 1819–1854): Contribution of an Aboriginal guide in Australian Exploration', *Aboriginal History*, vol. 39 (2015), pp63–82.

37 How people chose to be depicted and to dress was highly complex and active. Grace Karskens, 'Red coat, blue jacket, black skin: Aboriginal men and clothing in early New South Wales' *Aboriginal History*, vol. 35 (2011), pp1–36.

38 Ingleton, *True Patriots All*, p122.

39 https://rocksdiscoverymuseum.com/stories/cora-gooseberry (date accessed 21 March 2024).

40 Barratt, *Russians at Port Jackson*, p. 29; Jakelin Troy, *King Plates: A History of Aboriginal Gorgets*. The book was co-published by the National Museum and the Australian Institute of Aboriginal and Torres Strait Islander Studies (AIATSIS) in 1993. The book, long since out of print, has been published online at https://www.nma.gov.au/explore/features/aboriginal-breastplates/about; A. Hamilton, 'Equal to whom? Visions of destiny and the Aboriginal aristocracy', *Mankind*,

ENDNOTES

vol. 17, no.2 (1987), pp129–138, p138 notes the ways in which community hierarchical models were imposed on Aboriginal Australians for bureaucratic convenience; Peter Thorley, 'Self-Representation and Aboriginal Communities in the Northern Territory: Implications for Archaeological Research', *Australian Archaeology*, no.43 (1996), pp7–12 concludes that Aboriginal Australian communities have rarely been given the opportunity to 'self-represent' their culture and history.

41 Attenbrow, *Sydney's Aboriginal Past*, p60.

42 Troy, *King Plates*.

43 Barratt, *Russians at Port Jackson*, p34.

44 Barratt, *Russians at Port Jackson*, p32.

45 Barratt, *Russians at Port Jackson*, p35.

46 Barratt, *Russians at Port Jackson*, p36.

47 R.H.W Reece, 'Feasts and Blankets: The History of Some Early Attempts to Establish Relations with the Aborigines of New South Wales, 1814–1846', *Archaeology & Physical Anthropology in Oceania*, vol. 2, no.3 (1967), pp190–206, p197.

48 Hinkson, *Aboriginal Sydney*, p63.

49 Attenbrow, *Sydney's Aboriginal Past*, p83.

50 Mukhopa'dhya'ya, *Career of An Indian Princess*, p1.

51 Mukhopa'dhya'ya, *Career of an Indian Princess*, p2.

52 Taylor, *Empress*, p199.

53 Khan, *Begums of Bhopal*, p119.

54 Sunity Devee, Maharani of Cooch Behar, *The Autobiography of an Indian Princess* (London, 1921), p104.

55 Devee, *Autobiography of an Indian Princess*, p106.

56 Devee, *Autobiography of an Indian Princess*, p110.

57 William Dalrymple, *The Anarchy: The Relentless Rise of the East India Company* (London: Bloomsbury, 2019).

58 Lambert-Hurley, *Muslim Women*, p13.

59 Lambert-Hurley, *Muslim Women*, p13.

60 Shah Jehan, *Taj-ul Ikbal Tarikh Bhopal*.

61 Victoria called it a 'foolish marriage' (Taylor, *Empress*, p200); Sultan Jahan, Begum of Bhopal, *An Account of my Life*, vol. 1, trans. C.H. Payne (London, 1910), p39 also disapproved.

62 Sultan Jahan, *Account of my Life*, p92–93.

63 Khan, *Begums of Bhopal*, p126–127.

64 Devee, *Autobiography of an Indian Princess*, p219.

65 The Royal Collection Trust holds the volumes.

66 Shrabani Basu, *Victoria and Abdul: The Extraordinary True Story of the Queen's Closest Confidant* (Stroud: The History Press, 2010), pp80–81.

67 Basu, *Victoria and Abdul*, pp94, 109.

68 Basu, *Victoria and Abdul*, pp265–267.

69 Basu, *Victoria and Abdul*, p114.

70 Barratt, *Russians at Port Jackson*, p30.

71 Barratt, *Russians at Port Jackson*, p35.

72 Aiesha Saunders, Cora Gooseberry: https://rocksdiscoverymuseum.com/stories/cora-gooseberry (date accessed 21 March 2024).

73 The capitalisation of Queen apparently occurred on the original gravestone. The inscription is quoted from Vincent Smith, *King Bungaree*, p146.

74 Ellis, 'Witch-hunting', pp90–123.

75 Susan Bazargan, 'Leopold Bloom and William Ellis's Three Visits to Madagascar', *Joyce Studies Annual* (2017), pp65–93, p71.

76 Khan, *Begums of Bhopal*, p153.

77 Basu, *Victoria and Abdul*, p131.

78 Lambert-Hurley, *Muslim Women*, p4.

79 Khan, *Begums of Bhopal*, p175.

80 Quoted from Laidler, *Female Caligula*, p202.

ENDNOTES

CHAPTER 12

1   Harry Luke, *Queen Salote and her Kingdom* (London: Putnam, 1954), p16; for more on early Tongan society, see H.G. Cummins, 'Tongan society at the time of European contact' in ed. Noel Rutherford, *Friendly Islands: A History of Tonga* (Oxford: Oxford University Press, 1977), pp63–89.

2   Niel Gunson, 'The coming of foreigners' in Rutherford, *Friendly Islands*, pp90–113.

3   'Eseta Fusitu'a and Noel Rutherford, 'George Tupou II and the British Protectorate' in Rutherford, *Friendly Islands*, pp173–189, p176.

4   Basil Thomson, *The Scene Changes* (London, 1939), p196.

5   Elizabeth Ellem, *Queen Salote of Tonga: The Story of an Era 1900–1965* (1999), p3.

6   Wilhelmina Princess of the Netherlands, *Lonely But Not Alone*, trans. John Peereboom (London, 1960), p87.

7   Cees Fasseur, *Wilhelmina Sterker Door Strijd* (Balans, 2002), p65, p74, *'een echte Germaan'*.

8   William Hoffman, *Queen Juliana: The Story of the Richest Woman in the World* (London, 1980), p40.

9   Emerentia van Heuvan-van Nes, ed., *Darling Queen, Dear Old Bones: Queen Wilhemlina's Correspondence with her English Governess Miss Saxton Winter 1886–1935* (Amsterdam: Amsterdam University Press, 2017), p280.

10   Van Heuvan-van Nes, *Darling Queen*, p281.

11   Hoffman, *Queen Juliana*, p5.

12   A.H. Wood and Elizabeth Wood Ellem, 'Queen Salote Tupou III' in Rutherford, *Friendly Islands*, pp190–209, p193.

13   Hoffman, *Queen Juliana*, p40.

14   https://www.bbc.co.uk/news/magazine-33594809 (date accessed 11 September 2024).

15   Thomas Lyngby, 'Dronning af Danmark – et essay' in *Dronning af Danmark* (Der Nationalhistoriske Museum Frederiksborg Slot, 2010), p11.

16   'Den lille prinsesse var for mange danskere et lys I en mork tid' (Lyngby, 'Dronning af Danmark', p11).

17 https://www.theguardian.com/news/2000/nov/08/guardianobituaries2 (date accessed 2 September 2024).

18 Fasseur, *Wilhelmina Sterker Door Strijd*, p110: 'dat beest van een Hitler'.

19 Wilhelmina, *Lonely But Not Alone*, p151.

20 Hoffman, *Queen Juliana*, p107.

21 Hoffman, *Queen Juliana*, p86.

22 Hoffman, *Queen Juliana*, p35.

23 Fasseur, *Wilehmina Sterker Door Strijd*, p134.

24 Fasseur, *Wilhemina Sterker Door Strijd*, p139 'de onmenselijke behandeling, ja het stelselmatig uitroeien van deze landgenoten, die eeuwen met ons samenwoonden in ons gezegend vaderland'.

25 Henry L. Mason, 'Testing Human Bonds within Nations: Jews in the Occupied Netherlands', *Political Scient Quarterly*, vol. 99, no.2 (1984), pp315–343.

26 Andrew Buckser, 'Group identities and the construction of the 1943 rescue of the Danish Jews', *Ethnology*, vol. 37 (1998), pp209–226; Hans Kirchhoff, 'Denmark: A light in the darkness of the Holocaust? A reply to Gunnar S. Paulsson', *Journal of Contemporary History*, vol. 30, no.3 (1995), pp465–497; Leni Yahil's *The Rescue of Danish Jewry* (Philidelphia: Jewish Publication Society of America, 1969).

27 Andrew Morton, *The Queen* (London: Michael O'Mara, 2022), p73.

28 *The Way We Were*, BBC Radio 4, 24 December 1985.

29 Luke, *Queen Salote*, p82.

30 Wood and Ellem, 'Queen Salote', p205.

31 Moniek Bloks, *Queen Wilhemina: A Collection of Articles* (2020), p153.

32 Hoffman, *Queen Juliana*, p48, p50.

33 Wilhelmina, *Lonely But Not Alone*, p234–237.

34 John Hartley, *Accession: The Making of a Queen* (London: Quartet Books, 1992), p128.

35 Luke, *Queen Salote*, p76.

36 Kenneth Bain, *The Friendly Islanders* (London: Hodder, 1967), p23.

ENDNOTES

37 Elizabeth Wood-Ellem, 'Researching (w)riting, releasing, and responses to a biography of Queen Salote of Tonga' in eds. Brij V. Lal and Vicki Luker, *Telling Pacific Lives: Prisms of Process* (Canberra, 2008), pp139–148, p145.

38 Luke, *Queen Salote*, p119.

39 Lyngby, 'Dronning af Danmark', p12.

40 Lene Steinbeck, *Kings and Queens in Roskilde Cathedral* (2023), p152.

41 'Overalt er Hendes Majestaet Dronning Margrethe II med os' (Lyngby, 'Dronning af Danmark', pp9–14).

42 Torid Skard, *Women of Power: Half a Century of Female Presidents and Prime Ministers Worldwide* (Bristol: Policy Press, 2015), p7; Guida M. Jackson, *Women Leaders of Africa, Asia, Middle East, and Pacific: A Biographical Reference* (2009), pp173–5; Maureen Seneviratne, *Sirimavo Bandaranaike: The World's First Woman Prime Minister* (Colombo, 1975).

43 Seneviratne, *Sirimavo Bandaranaike*, p204.

44 Skard, *Women of Power*, p17.

45 Jana Everett, 'Indira Gandhi and the Exercise of Power' in ed. Michael A. Genovese, *Women as National Leaders* (Newbury Park: SAGE, 1993), pp103–134, p110.

46 Krishan Bhatia, *Indira: A Biography of Prime Minister Gandhi* (New York: Praeger, 1974); Indira Gandhi, *My Truth* (New York, 1980); Jackson, *Women Leaders*, pp207–209.

47 Sara J. Weir, 'Perónisma: Isabel Perón and the Politics of Argentina' in Genovese, *Women as National Leaders*, pp161–176.

48 Jackson, *Women Leaders*, pp158–159.

49 Charles Moore, *Margaret Thatcher: The Authorised Biography*, vol. 3 (London: Penguin, 2020), p290.

50 https://www.seoghoer.dk/kongelige/eksklusivt-interview-med-prins-henrik-hun-goer-mig-til-nar (date accessed 1 September 2024).

51 Steinbeck, *Kings and Queens*, p164.

52 https://www.abc.net.au/news/2024-01-07/queen-margrethe-ii-denmarks-longest-reigning-monarch/103282260 (dated accessed 1 September 2024).

53   Hoffman, *Queen Juliana*, p9.

54   https://www.pcgamer.com/queen-wilhelmina-leads-the-netherlands-into-civilization-6-rise-and-fall/ (date accessed 12 September 2024).

AFTERWORD

1   https://www.news24.com/News24/its-education-first-for-queen-modjadji-because-the-world-is-modern-20170611 (date accessed 14 August 2024).

2   https://www.news24.com/News24/its-education-first-for-queen-modjadji-because-the-world-is-modern-20170611 (date accessed 14 August 2024).

3   https://www.cogta.gov.za/index.php/2016/07/27/the-balobedu-queenship-recognised-and-dignity-restored/ (date accessed 14 August 2024).

4   https://www.timeslive.co.za/news/south-africa/2021-05-17-modjadji-royal-council-on-ascension-to-the-throne-that-caused-a-rift/ (date accessed 2 December 2024).

5   https://www.sabcnews.com/sabcnews/prince-lekukela-modjadji-installed-as-king-of-the-balobedu/ (date accessed 2 December 2024).

6   Margery Kempe, *The Book of Margery Kempe*, trans. Anthony Bale (Oxford: Oxford University Press, 2015), pp41–42.

7   Julian of Norwich, *Revelations of Divine Love*, trans. Barry Windeatt (Oxford: Oxford University Press, 2015).

8   Christine de Pizan, *The Book of the City of Ladies and Other Writings*, ed. Sophie Bourgault and Rebecca Kingston and trans. Ineke Hardy (Indianapolis: Hackett, 2018), p21.

9   Pizan, *Book of the City of Ladies*, p62.

10   Mary Beard, *Women and Power: A Manifesto* (London: Profile Books, 2018), p39.

11   They were the children of his illegitimate daughter, Juliane de Breteuil. Henry agreed to their blinding after Juliane's husband blinded the son of another nobleman. He also ordered that the tips of their noses be removed. Juliane later attempted to shoot her father with a crossbow, leading to her imprisonment.

12   Hossein Kamaly, *A History of Islam in 21 Women* (London: Oneworld, 2019), pp85–91.

ENDNOTES

13 Sarah Milledge Nelson, 'Ancient Queens: an introduction' in ed. Sarah Milledge Nelson, *Ancient Queens: Archaeological Explorations* (Walnut Creek: Altamira, 2003), pp1–18, p1.

14 Royal Collection Trust RCIN 980015.bl

15 https://edition.cnn.com/2024/09/05/world/new-maori-queen-anointed-intl-scli/index.html (date accessed 3 December 2024).

16 Origins of the Māori King Movement, URL: https://nzhistory.govt.nz/politics/the-maori-king-movement, (Manatū Taonga — Ministry for Culture and Heritage), updated 11-Sep-2024 (date accessed 3 December 2024).

17 https://www.news.com.au/world/pacific/new-zealand-crowns-new-27yearold-queen-in-surprise-choice/news-story/879d4a728b25603e313fd6e099d10274; https://www.telegraph.co.uk/world-news/2024/09/05/haka-teacher-masters-anointed-new-queen-maoris/?msockid=0d0cb096ae7d6eff08d6a022aa7d6053 (date accessed 2 December 2024).

18 https://www.bbc.com/future/article/20240307-the-160-year-mystery-of-the-stone-age-venus-figurines#:~:text=This%20is%20the%20Venus%20of%20Hohle%20Fels%2C%20and,back%20as%20the%2019th%20Century%3A%20the%20Venus%20figurines. (date accessed 3 December 2024).

19 Nicholas J. Conard, 'A female figurine from the basal Aurignacian of Hohle Fels Cave in southwestern Germany', *Nature*, vol. 459 (2009), pp248–252; Lawrence Guy Straus, 'The human occupation of southwestern Europe during the last glacial maximum: Solutrean cultural adaptations in France and Iberia', *Journal of Anthropological Research*, vol. 71, no.4 (2015), pp465-492.

20 Pizan, *Book of the City of Ladies*, p219.

ACKNOWLEDGEMENTS

Writing *Women Who Ruled the World* has been a labour of love, something which I hope is reflected in the text. It has been a long process and one which I could not have completed without the assistance of so many wonderful people.

First and foremost, I want to thank my agent, Donald Winchester at Watson Little for his enthusiasm and advice. Donald has been involved in this project at every stage and it could not exist without the hard work that he has put into it all the way through.

I would also like to thank everyone at Footnote Press. I am so grateful to them for giving me the opportunity to write the first comprehensive history of female kingship and for their advice and support throughout. Ellie Carr has been a wonderful and enthusiastic editor there and I am so glad to have had the opportunity to work with her. I would also like to thank Liz Marvin and Susan Pegg for their essential work on editing the text. Their questions and comments were often challenging, but always important (although Susan, you will never convince me that Henry VIII's six wives were not all doomed!).

I have, of course, spent a great deal of time in archives and libraries for my research. Firstly, I want to thank the staff at the British Library. Sadly, the research period for this book coincided with a devastating cyber-attack on the library, limiting access to many of their collections. Despite this, everyone there was unfailingly helpful. In particular, I would like to thank Aliki-Anastasia Arkomani, one of the British Library's Asian & African Studies Reference Specialists, who very kindly arranged for me to access some of the materials that the library holds on medieval Georgia.

I would also particularly like to thank the staff at Cambridge University Library, which became my go-to place to work and research. It is always a wonderful experience to explore the library's labyrinth of open shelves. I am always especially grateful that they let me borrow books!

I am very grateful to Rachel Peat Underhill, Curator of Decorative Arts at the Royal Collection Trust for providing me with the details of what is known about the fate of Hawaii's gift to Queen Victoria for her Golden Jubilee. I would also like to thank Sophie Jones of the Royal Collection Trust for introducing me to Rachel.

Research for the book has taken me around the world and along the way I have been assisted by too many guides, academics and researchers to include here. Mr Ashok, who expertly negotiated the Delhi traffic in rush hour is particularly memorable, but I would like to extend a general thank you to everyone involved.

Finally, I would like to thank my husband, David, and children Dominic, Barnaby and Ianthe, whom I have quite literally dragged around the globe on the trail of reigning queens. From hunting out royal breastplates in Sydney, avoiding the monkeys at the Baby Taj in Agra and visiting the Temple of Hatshepsut in Luxor in 45 degrees Celsius heat, they've remained good humoured throughout. David also provided very useful feedback on every chapter as it was written and endured many, many rants on the fates of female kings.

INDEX

Aelfgyva, 31
Aelfthryth, 14
Albert, Prince, 233, 278
Alexander the Great, 39
Aliquippa, ruler of the Seneca tribe, 8–9
Amazons, 3, 4, 6
Anchimaa, Khertek, 291
Ang Mei, 11
Argentina, 291
Arsinoë IV
   imprisonment, 173–4, 177
   marriage, 13
   rivalry with Cleopatra VII, 166–7, 172–4, 177–8
Athaliah of Judah
   and the dangers of female power, 157–8, 159, 161–2, 173, 178–9
   execution, 178–9
   knowledge of, 159, 161
   marriage to Jehoram, 161
   Mary Queen of Scots likened to, 157–8, 159, 173

   in the Old Testament, 160–1, 178
Atotoztli, 25
Australia
   Aboriginal Australian monarchs, 8, 260, 261, 262
   Bungaree, 260, 262, 269
   ceremonial 'king plates' (breastplates), 260, 261–2, 269
   colonisation, 259–61
   penal colonies, 257, 259
   see also Cora Gooseberry of Sydney
Austria
   female succession, 111–12, 117
   Habsburg dynasty, 110–11
   Karl VI, Holy Roman Emperor, 110–12, 115, 122
   War of the Spanish Succession, 122–3
   see also Maria Theresia of Austria-Hungary

Badenoch, Kemi, 302–3
Baldwin II, 85–6

Bandaranaike, Sirimavo, 290
Bayeux Tapestry, 30–1
Beard, Professor Mary, 301
Beatrix of the Netherlands, 11, 285, 298
Belgium, 305
Berenice III, 40
Berenice IV, 40
Bhopal
    independence from the Mughal Empire, 249
    nwab begums, 248, 265, 266, 272
    Sultan Jahan Begum, 257, 271–2
    see also Qudsia Begum; Shah Jahan Begum of Bhopal; Sikandar Begum
Bible
    Biblical knowledge in England, 158, 161
    historical accuracy of the Old Testament, 158–9
    Queen of Sheba, 187
    queens of the Old Testament, 159–60
    study of in England, 158
    see also Athaliah of Judah; Jezebel
Birgitta of Vadstena, 22
Blanca I, 44, 45
Blanca II of Navarre
    kingdom, 43–4
    male co-rulers, 49–50
    marriage to Enrique IV of Castile, 44–5, 46–7, 55, 190
    reign, 50, 54–5, 56
Blandford Edwards, Amelia, 73–4
Bogolyubsky, Yuri, 120–1
Bora Bora
    French colonisation, 98
    history, 91–2
    Tapoa's marriage to Pomare IV of Tahiti, 95–6
    see also Teri'imaevarua II of Bora Bora
Bothwell, James Hepburn, Earl of, 170–1
Boudicca, Queen of the Iceni, 5, 182, 188, 191
Bruce, James, 198–9
Buddhism
    in China, 150, 153–4
    in Japan, 204–5, 209, 216, 217
Bungaree (Aboriginal ruler), 260, 262, 269
Byzantium, 68–9; see also Irene of Byzantium

Calafia, 3–4
Cano de Saavedra, Juan, 28
Castile
    disenfranchisement of Juana (la Betraneja), 149, 190, 193–4, 199
    Enrique IV of Castile, 44–5, 46–7, 55, 189, 190, 192–3
    Juana 'La Loca', 9–10
    queens, 189
    see also Isabel I of Castile
Catharina-Amalia, Princess of Orange, 305, 306
Catherine de Medici, 102, 104, 163
Catherine II of Russia (Catherine the Great)
    autobiography, 58, 80–1
    children, 69–71
    male kingship images, 80
    marriage to Peter III, 59, 61–2, 69–71, 77
    on the Orthodox Church, 61, 62
    path to the throne, 6, 58–9, 69–70
    reign, 77–9, 81
    relationship with Empress Elizaveta, 62–3, 65, 80–1

INDEX

as 'unnatural', 78–9
Charlotte of Cyprus
    Egypt's support for, 52–3
    male co-rulers, 49, 52
    marriage to Joao of Coimbra, 47
    marriage to Louis of Savoy, 49, 54
    petition to the Pope for her throne, 37–8, 41–2, 52, 54
    political dexterity, 54
    reign, 48, 49, 54, 56
Chaucer, Geoffrey, 183–4
China
    Buddhism, 150, 153–4
    China-Japan-Korea relations, 213
    Emperor Gaozong, 138, 140, 141, 142–4, 146, 149, 213
    Emperor Taizong, 133–4, 137–8, 213
    and Japan, 203, 204, 206, 214
    Scholars of the Northern Gate, 145–6
    sexual behaviour at the imperial court, 141–2
    socio-cultural history, 134–5
    Tang Dynasty, 135, 136, 148, 154–5
    Zhou Dynasty, 154
    see also Wu Zetian of China
Christine de Pizan, 300–1, 307
Cleopatra VII of Egypt
    Elizabethan knowledge of, 166
    and Julius Caesar, 50–1, 167, 172
    male co-rulers, 5, 39, 41, 50–1, 56, 173
    and Mark Antony, 51–2, 177–8
    recognisability, 12, 39, 40–1, 52, 294
    rivalry with Arsinoë IV, 166–7, 172–4, 177–8
    in Shakespeare's Antony and Cleopatra, 52, 166, 179
    and Zenobia, Queen of Palmyra, 186
colonialism

in Australia, 259–61
British empire, 9, 230, 249–50, 252–4, 265, 286
concepts of monarchy, 8–9
East India Company, 248–9
in Hawaii, 224, 225–6, 230–1, 237–8, 245–6
in Madagascar, 254, 270
in New Zealand, 306
the nwab begums relations with, 9, 249, 250, 255, 258, 263–5, 266, 304
queens under, 249–50, 272–3
Constantine VI, 68, 71–2, 76
Constantinople, 59–60
Cook, James, 9, 198–9, 224
Cora Gooseberry of Sydney
    accommodation, 268–9
    colonialism's impact on, 263
    European monarchy applied to, 8, 260, 261, 262, 269
    as ruler, 260–1, 263
Cortes, Hernan, 9, 26, 27
Cyprus
    and Egypt, 48–9, 52
    female succession rights, 41–2, 43
    Helena Palaiologina, 42–3, 47
    history, 48–9
    Jacques the Bastard, 43, 49, 53–4
    see also Charlotte of Cyprus

Darnley, Lord Henry, 7, 168–70
Davit the Builder, 113, 114
Den, King, 18–19
Denmark
    herring industry, 34
    monarchy, 21–2, 270
    women's succession rights, 270–1, 289
    during World War II, 283

see also Margrete I of Denmark, Norway and Sweden; Margrethe II of Denmark
Dido, 4
Dominis, John Owen, 224–5, 233–4, 239–40
Dudley, Robert, 142, 168

East India Company, 248–9, 253, 265–6
Edward III, 118, 119, 128
Edward VI, 99, 104, 139
Egypt
    Alexandria, 173
    archaeology, 17–18
    Berenice III, 40
    Berenice IV, 40
    Cairo, 52
    and Cyprus, 48–9, 52
    Djeser-Djeseru temple, 57
    gendered roles, 73–4
    goddesses, 74
    and the Kingdom of Kush, 187
    Nile floods, 29
    Palermo Stone, 18–19
    pharaohs, 64–5
    pharaonic marriage practices, 29, 39, 40, 41, 57, 64
    Ptolemies, 39–40
    queens, 11–12, 40, 74
    and the Roman Empire, 41, 50–1, 167, 172, 173–4
    Saqqara, 17, 30, 197
    see also Arsinoë IV; Cleopatra VII of Egypt; Hatshepsut of Egypt; Merneith of Egypt
Ekaterina I of Russia, 10, 61, 66
Elagabalus, Emperor, 185
Eleanor of Aquitaine, 7

Elisabeth, Duchess of Brabant, 305, 306
Elizabeth I of England and Ireland
    absence of male rivals, 139–40
    accession, 105
    baths, 27
    birth, 138–9
    claim to the throne, 135–6, 150–1, 162, 164
    female rivals, 140–1
    grave, 156
    images of, 74, 134, 145, 147, 148–9
    and Mary Queen of Scots, 140, 144, 157–8, 164, 165–6, 174
    phoenix motif, 151
    reign, 134–5, 145, 155, 156
    religious beliefs, 14, 151–3
    Robert Dudley's status with, 142, 168
    self-propagandist, 147–9, 152, 195–6
    as Shakespeare's Cleopatra, 166, 179
    speculation over her sex life, 142
    titles, 156
Elizabeth II of the United Kingdom
    accession to the throne, 13, 285, 286
    childhood, 270
    coronation, 5–6, 286, 288
    death, 1
    decolonisation, 286
    marriage to Prince Philip, 279–80
    as a queen, 1–2, 291
    reign, 291–3
    succession rights, 270
    visit to Tonga, 288
    during World War II, 283–4
Elizaveta of Russia
    Catherine the Great's relationship with, 62–3, 65, 80–1
    character, 62–3, 67
    claim to the throne, 65–7, 80

INDEX

guardianship of Catherine's children, 69–71
male kingship images, 67, 80
support for Maria Theresia of Austria-Hungary, 126
Emma, Dowager Queen of the Netherlands, 93–4, 277, 279
Emma Rooke, Queen, 225, 231, 232
England
  Biblical knowledge, 158, 161
  Elizabethan, 134–5
  Elizabethan knowledge of Cleopatra, 166
  gender roles, 31
  succession rights, 20
  see also Elizabeth I of England and Ireland; Elizabeth II of the United Kingdom; Matilda of England; United Kingdom
Enrique IV of Castile, 44–5, 46–7, 55, 189, 190, 192–3
Ethiopia, 187, 188; *see also* Kandakes of Kush

female power
  Biblical tales of the dangers of, 157–8, 159, 161–2, 173, 178–9
  in the Kingdom of Kush, 188
  male subjugation of, 3, 4
  misogynistic responses to, 301–3
  in myth and legend, 3–4
  queenship's models for, 304, 306–7
  in the Roman Empire, 185–6
  as 'unfeminine' and 'unnatural', 15, 38, 72–3, 78–9, 139, 161–3, 185
Ferlini, Giuseppe, 197–8
Finnbogadóttir, Vigdís, 2, 291
France

female succession rights, 108–9, 127–8
  Isabella of France, 11
  Philippe of Poitiers, 108–9, 110
  Philippe of Valois, 118–19, 128
  Salic Law, 127–8
  see also Jeanne of France (Juana II of Navarre)
Frederick II, 101, 103–4, 126

Gandhi, Indira, 290
Gaozong, Emperor, 138, 140, 141, 142–4, 146, 149, 213
Genmei, Empress, 213–14
Genshō, Empress, 214–15
George V, 272
Georgia
  Davit the Builder, 113, 114
  Rusudan of Georgia, 130
  territories, 113–14, 123
  Trebizond Empire, 124
  see also Tamar of Georgia
Giorgi III of Georgia, 108, 112, 114, 115
Greek Orthodox Church, 42, 61, 62
Grey, Catherine, 140–1
Grey, Mary, 140–1
Guy de Lusignan, 48

Haggard, H. Rider, 229
Hatshepsut of Egypt
  depicted as a pharaoh, 73, 74–5
  early life, 63–4
  historical erasure of, 58, 65, 77, 81
  and the Kingdom of Kush, 188
  marriage to Thutmose II (half-brother), 57–8, 64
  mortuary temple, 57–8, 73
  path to the throne, 6, 57–8, 59, 64–5
  reign, 12, 76–7

Thutmose III, 64, 65
  as 'unnatural', 72–3
Hawaii
  Bayonet Constitution, 238, 239, 243
  colonisation, 224, 225–6, 227, 230–1, 237–8, 245–6
  constitutional monarchy, 238
  Kalākaua dynasty, 238
  Kamehameha dynasty, 224
  King Kalākaua, 225, 231–2, 234, 236, 238
  the 'Kumulipo', 244–5
  monarchy's relations with the UK, 230–2
  Queen Kapiolani, 234–5
  sugar plantations, 237–8
  US rebellion in, 223–4, 243–4
  see also Lili'uokalani of Hawaii
Helena Palaiologina, 42–3, 47
Henry I, 20
Henry VIII
  marriages, 134, 138
  and Mary Queen of Scots, 93, 99–100, 102, 105
  religious beliefs, 151
Himiko, shaman queen, 204, 222
Hippolyte, 3, 4, 6, 15

Iceland, 2, 291, 300
India
  British empire, 252–4, 265
  Koh-i-Noor diamond, 253–4
  Sunity Devee, Maharani of Cooch Behar, 264–5, 267
  women heads of state, 290, 300
  see also Bhopal
Ingrid Alexandra of Norway, Princess, 304–5, 306

Irene of Byzantium
  in Constantinople, 59–60
  involvement in religious matters, 69
  marriage to Leo IV, 51, 68, 69
  path to the throne, 59, 71–2, 75
  as queen regent, 6, 68–9, 72
  reign, 75–6
  son (Constantine VI), 68, 71–2, 76
  titles, 75
  as 'unnatural', 72
Isabel I of Castile
  claim to the throne, 189, 192–4
  Inquisition, 195
  male kingship imagery, 184–5
  marriage to Fernando of Aragon, 189, 193
  and the New World, 184, 195
  self-propagandist, 189–90, 194–6
  as a warrior queen, 189, 193–4, 195
Isabel II of Spain, 303
Isabella I of Jerusalem, 85, 88–9
Isabella II of Jerusalem
  as a child queen, 84, 86
  childhood, 95
  death, 103
  marriage to Frederick II, 13, 100–1
Isabella of France, 11
Israel, 159, 290–1

Jacques the Bastard, 43
Jadwiga, king of Poland, 7
James V of Scotland, 83
James VI of Scotland, 155, 156, 176
Japan
  abdications of sovereigns, 215, 220
  autobiographical literature, 207–9, 300

INDEX

bar on female inheritance, 202–3, 221–2
Buddhism, 204–5, 209, 216, 217
and China, 203, 204, 206, 214
China-Japan-Korea relations, 213
Emperor Meiji, 202–3
Genmei, Empress, 213–14
Genshō, Empress, 214–15
Himiko, 204, 222
Jitō, Empress, 211–12, 213, 214, 215
Kōgyoku, Empress, 210–11
Kōken, Empress, 215–18
Meisho, Empress, 220
Princess Aiko, 201–2, 220–1
the royal court, 208–9
royal family, 201–2
ruling empresses, 9, 15, 203
Shintoism, 204, 216
the Shoguns, 218–20
Shōtoku, Empress, 154, 217–18
Suiko, Empress, 205–7, 209–10, 212
Suiko's promotion of women's literature, 206–7, 209
Tenno (title), 206
Jean of Brienne, 94–5, 101
Jean of Ibelin, 89
Jeanne of France (Juana II of Navarre)
childhood, 109–10
female succession rights, 117–19, 128
reign, 119, 128–9, 131
Jerusalem
Baldwin II, 85–6
cosmopolitanism, 85
female succession, 85–6
Melisende, 85, 86
queen consorts, 85–6
Sybilla of Jerusalem, 48
see also Isabella II of Jerusalem;
Maria of Jerusalem
Jezebel
and the dangers of female power, 157–8, 159, 161–2, 173, 179, 195
evidence of the existence of, 159
Mary Queen of Scots likened to, 157–8, 159, 173
in the Old Testament, 159–60, 161
jezebel, term, 160
Jitō, Empress, 211–12, 213, 214, 215
Juan II of Aragon, 44, 45–6, 50, 55
Juana 'La Loca', 9–10
Juana of Castile (la Betraneja), 149, 190, 193–4, 199
Judah, 159; see also Athaliah of Judah
Juliana of the Netherlands, 279, 285, 294
Julius Caesar, 41, 50–1, 167, 172
Justinian I, 60, 69

Kalākaua, king, 225, 231–2, 234, 236, 238
Kandake Amanipilade, 198
Kandake Amanirenas, 195–6
Kandake Amanishakheto, 197–8
Kandakes of Kush
appearance, 187
male kingship imagery, 185
Meroë's pyramids, 197–8
Queen Katimala, 188
Queen of Sheba, 187
reigning Kandakes, 12, 188–9
as warrior queens, 181–2, 187, 196–7
Kapiolani, Queen, 234–5
Karim, Abdul, 267–8, 270–1, 273
Karl VI, Holy Roman Emperor, 110–12, 115, 122
Kempe, Margery, 300
Khan, Nazar Mohammad, 247
Kingdom of Kush, 12, 187–8; see also Kandakes of Kush

WOMEN WHO RULED THE WORLD

Knox, John, 161–2, 165, 167–8, 179
Kōgyoku, Empress, 210–11
Kōken, Empress, 215–18
Korea
    China-Japan-Korea relations, 213
    Kim Ju-ae in North Korea, 213
    Silla kingdom, 212–13

Laborde de Monpezat, Henri Marie Jean André de, 293–4
Leo III, Pope, 75
Leonor, Princess of the Asturias, 304, 306
Leonor of Navarre, 44, 50, 55–6
Leopoldovna, Anna, 66–7
Lili'uokalani of Hawaii
    childhood, 224
    journals, 228
    marriage to John Owen Dominis, 224–5, 233–4, 239–40
    new constitution, 243
    as queen regent, 232
    at Queen Victoria's Golden Jubilee celebrations, 234–5, 236–7, 238
    reign, 239–40, 243–5
    relations with Queen Victoria, 223–4, 235–6, 244, 245, 304
    translation of the 'Kumulipo', 244–5
    and the US settler rebellions, 223–4, 239, 243–4
Longinus, Cassius, 191
Louis of Savoy, 49, 54
Louis X, 108, 109

Madagascar
    colonisation, 254, 270
    religion, 255–6
    see also Ranavalona I of Madagascar

Makobo Modjadji VI, 297
Margrete I of Denmark, Norway and Sweden
    alliance with the Hanseatic League, 21, 22–3
    marriage, 13, 22
    queenship denied, 9, 18, 34, 280
    reign, 32–4
    titles, 7, 21, 23, 32, 34
    tomb, 293
Margrethe II of Denmark
    abdication, 297–8
    accession, 2, 289
    childhood, 281, 288
    marriage to Prince Henrik, 293–4
    reign, 34, 290, 293
    as the successor to Margrete I, 34, 289–90
    tomb, 293
Maria, king of Hungary, 7
Maria of Jerusalem
    as a child queen, 85, 86, 88
    death, 84, 85, 95, 104
    Jean of Ibelin's regency, 89
    marriage to Jean of Brienne, 94–5
Maria Theresia of Austria-Hungary
    accession to the Habsburg empire, 112, 117, 122, 125–7.7
    birth, 110
    Elizaveta of Russia's support for, 126
    images of, 121–2
    lack of political education, 112, 116
    male co-rulers, 79, 129–30, 131
    marriage to Francois-Etienne, 112, 116–17, 121–2, 126–7
    reign, 115–16, 125, 129–30
Marie of Guise
    dangers of female power, 161–2

INDEX

death, 162
governorship of Mary, 92–3, 99–100, 102, 103
Mark Antony, 51–2, 167, 177–8
Mary I of England and Ireland
   as Bloody Mary, 14, 255
   Catholicism, 151
   dangers of female power, 161–2
   death, 162
   grave, 156
   Marianism, 14
   marriage, 149
Mary Queen of Scots
   Babington Plot, 175–6
   birth, 83–4
   Bothwell's rape of, 170–1
   as a child queen, 84, 98–9, 105–6
   claim to the English throne, 164, 165–6
   and Elizabeth I, 140, 144, 164, 165
   escape plots, 174, 175–6
   execution discussions, 157–8, 173
   at the French court, 103, 163
   guardianship, 92–3
   imprisonment, 144, 171–2, 173, 174–6
   likened to Jezebel and Athaliah, 157–8, 159, 173
   marriage negotiations with Edward VI, 99, 102, 104
   marriage to Darnley, 7, 168–70
   marriage to Dauphin Francois, 104–5, 149, 163
   as a political pawn, 93, 99–100, 101–3, 105
   reign, 167–8
   religious beliefs, 165, 174
   return to Scotland, 163–5
   second marriage discussions, 167–8
   threat to Elizabeth I, 157–8, 174
   trial and execution, 176–7
   see also Marie of Guise
Masako, Crown Princess, 201–2, 220
Masalanabo Modjadji II, 228–9, 230, 232
   European literary depictions of as white-skinned, 229–30
   reign, 228–9, 240
   relations with the Boer, 240–1
   ritual suicide, 241–2
   rivalry with Chief Khasane, 229
   territories, 232
Masalanabo Modjadji, Princess, 297, 299, 304, 306
Maselekwane Modjadji I, 226–7, 228
Matilda of Boulogne, 6
Matilda of England
   character, 31, 303
   claim to the throne, 20–1, 31
   marriage to Heinrich V, 13, 19–20
   queenship denied, 6, 30, 31–2
   titles, 21, 32
Mecklenburg-Schwerin, Heinrich of, 277–8, 279, 281
Meiji, Emperor, 202–3
Meir, Golda, 290–1
Melisende, 85, 86
Merneith of Egypt
   queenship denied, 17–18, 30
   records of, 29, 30
   as a ruler, 18, 29–30, 32
   tomb, 17–18, 30
Mexica people
   Atotoztli's reign, 25
   empire, 23–4
   gender roles, 24
   Motecuhzoma II, 25, 26, 27
   rulers (Tlatoani), 24–5

Spanish Conquest, 25–7
Tenochtitlan, 23–4, 26–7, 29
see also Tecuichpotzin (Isabel
  Moctezuma)
Mughal Empire
  East India Company, 248–9, 253,
    265–6
  Empress Nur Jahan, 248
Mwana wa Mwana, 12

Naruhito, Crown Prince, 201–2, 220
Navarre
  female succession rights, 43–4, 128–9
  Juan II of Aragon, 44, 45–6, 50, 55
  Leonor of Navarre, 44, 50, 55–6
  see also Blanca II of Navarre; Jeanne
    of France (Juana II of Navarre)
Neithhotep, 18
Netherlands
  Beatrix of the Netherlands, 11, 285,
    298
  Catharina-Amalia, Princess of
    Orange, 305, 306
  Juliana of the Netherlands, 279, 285,
    294
  monarchy, 86–7, 278
  Nazi occupation, 281–2, 283
  see also Wilhelmina of the
    Netherlands
New Zealand, 305–6
Ngā Wai hono i te po Paki, 305–6
Norway, 304–5
Ntfombi, Queen of Eswatini, 11
Nur Jahan, Empress, 248

Palmyra *see* Zenobia, Queen of Palmyra
Papua New Guinea, 4
Perón, Isabel, 291

Peter III, 59, 61–2, 69–70, 77–8
Peter the Great, 59, 61, 65–6
Petrie, Flinders, 17, 18, 32
Philip of Greece and Denmark, Prince,
  279–80
Philippe of Poitiers, 108–9, 110
Philippe of Valois, 118–19, 128
Pius II, Pope, 37–8, 42, 52, 54
Podocataro, Peter, 52–3
Pomare IV of Tahiti
  as a child queen, 95–6
  French invasion of Tahiti, 89–90
  marriage to Tapoa, 95–6
  political acumen, 90, 91
  reign, 96, 97–8
  see also Teri'imaevarua II of Bora
    Bora
Ptolomy I, 39
Ptolomy II, 40

Qudsia Begum
  character, 250–2
  enforced abdication, 251, 257
  modernisation by, 250
  as a Muslim queen, 247–8, 251
  negotiations with the British, 249,
    250, 255
  political acumen, 248
  reign, 247–8, 249
queen, term, 6
queen regnants, term, 6, 7
queens
  attacks on women as rulers, 161–3
  child queens, 94, 98, 103, 105
  colonial-era concepts of, 8–9
  in Egypt, 11–12, 40, 74
  as female kings, 7, 74
  of the future, 304–6

INDEX

as heads of state, 8–10
historical denial of, 17–18
in the Islamic world, 13, 248
in the islands of the Indian Ocean, 12–13
limitations on, 11–12
male consorts, twentieth century, 278–80, 293–4
in myth and legend, 3–4
during the nineteenth century, 249–50
in the Old Testament, 159–60
only in the absence of male candidates, 38, 107–8
power of, 2–3
queen consorts, 6, 10, 14
queen regents, 10–11
queenship denied, 25, 34–5
rarity of, 4–5
spiritual roles, 14–15
terminology, 6–7, 18
threats from male family members, 38–9
travel and mobility, 13
as 'unnatural', 15, 38, 72–3, 78–9, 139, 161–3, 185
warrior queens, 181–2, 185, 199, 294
see also female power

Radiyya, Sultana of Delhi, 13
Rain Queens of the Balobedu
European literary depictions of, 229–30
Makobo Modjadji VI, 297
Masalanabo Modjadji II, 228–9, 230, 232
Masalanabo Modjadji, Princess, 297, 299, 304, 306
Maselekwane Modjadji I, 226–7, 228
Modjadji III, 242
Modjadji IV, 242–3, 298
queendom, 8, 298–9
ritual suicides, 228, 241–2
status as deities, 14–15
territories, 232
written records, 227–8
see also Masalanabo Modjadji II
Rameses II of Egypt, 11–12
Ranavalona I of Madagascar
accession, 254–5
character, 12, 269–70
expulsion of Protestant missionaries, 255–6, 270
queenship, 256, 269
relations with colonial powers, 12, 255, 256–7, 273
relations with Queen Victoria, 257
witchcraft tests, 269
religion
Charlotte of Cyprus's involvement in, 41–2, 52, 54, 6937–8
in Elizabethan England, 14, 151–3, 165, 174
in Madagascar, 255–6
Wu Zetian's religious backing for, 135, 136, 150–1, 153–4
see also Bible; Buddhism
Richard the Lionheart, 48
Roman Empire
Boudicca's revolt against, 5, 182, 188
and Egypt, 41, 50–1, 167, 172, 173–4
Emperor Elagabalus, 185
female power, 185–6
and the Kingdom of Kush, 188
in Palmyra, 183, 184, 191–2
Western, 60
Rukn-ad-Din, Sultan of Rum, 123–4

401

Russia
　Ekaterina I of Russia, 10, 61, 66
　Orthodox Church, 61, 62
　Peter the Great, 59, 61, 65–6
　queens, 67–8
　ritualised cross-dressing at court, 66–7
　see also Catherine II of Russia (Catherine the Great); Elizaveta of Russia
Rusudan of Georgia, 130

Salic Law, 127–8
Sālote Tupou III of Tonga
　birth, 275, 276
　at Elizabeth II's coronation, 5–6, 286, 288
　marriage to Prince Tungi, 278, 279, 284
　recognisability, 5–6, 287–9, 295
　reign, 286–8
　succession to the throne, 276, 278
　during World War II, 284
Scotland
　child sovereigns, 83–4
　Stewart dynasty, 83–4, 92, 105–6
　see also Mary Queen of Scots
Shah Jahan Begum of Bhopal
　and the colonial powers, 9
　education, 259
　reforms, 266
　relations with Queen Victoria, 264–5, 266, 304
　retreat into purdah, 266–7
Shah Jehan Mosque, Woking, 273
Shajar al-Durr, 13
Shakespeare, William, 135
　Antony and Cleopatra, 52, 166, 179
　Hippolyte in A Midsummer Night's Dream, 15
Sheba, Queen of, 187
Shōtoku, Empress, 154, 217–18
Sikandar Begum
　political acumen, 258–9
　reforms, 257–8, 270
　relations with colonial powers, 250, 258, 263–4, 271
Silla kingdom
　Chindŏk, Queen, 212, 213
　Jinseong, Queen, 213
　Sŏndŏk, Queen, 212–13
Soslani, Davit, 121
South Africa
　apartheid-era, 229–30, 242, 298
　Piet Joubert and Modjadji II, 240–1
　see also Rain Queens of the Balobedu
Spain
　Princess Leonor of the Asturias, 304, 306
　see also Castile; Navarre
Sri Lanka, 290
Stephen of Blois, 20, 21, 31
Stewart, James, Early of Moray, 165, 168, 170
Sudan
　and the Kingdom of Kush, 187, 188
　Meroë's pyramids, 196–7
　see also Kandakes of Kush
Suiko, Empress, 206–7, 209–10, 212
Sultan Jahan Begum, 257, 271–2
Sunity Devee, Maharani of Cooch Behar, 264–5, 267
Sybilla of Jerusalem, 48
Syria, 183, 184, 191–2; *see also* Zenobia, Queen of Palmyra

Tahiti

INDEX

colonisation, 89–91, 96, 98
   see also Pomare IV of Tahiti
Taizong, Emperor, 133–4, 137–8, 213
Tamar of Georgia
   death, 107, 130
   defeat of Rukn-ad-Din, Sultan of Rum, 123–4
   as a female king, 7, 115
   images of, 115, 130–1
   The Knight in the Panther Skin epic poem, 131
   marriage to Davit Soslani, 121
   marriage to Yuri Bogolyubsky, 120–1
   reign, 114–15, 119–20, 121, 123–4, 130–1
   succession to the throne, 108, 112–13
   Trebizond Empire, 124
Tecuichpotzin (Isabel Moctezuma)
   arrival of the Spanish Conquest, 25–6
   as heir to the Mexica throne, 28
   marriages, 27–8, 32
Teri'imaevarua II of Bora Bora
   as a child queen, 90–1, 92, 95, 96–7
   reign, 97–8
   see also Pomare IV of Tahiti
Thatcher, Margaret, 291
Theodora, 60, 69
Theophanes the Confessor, 69, 71–2
Thutmose II, 57–8, 64
Thutmose III, 64, 65
Tonga
   monarchy, 275–6
   postal service, 287
   Spanish Flu, 278–9
   see also Sālote Tupou III of Tonga
Trebizond Empire, 124
Tungi, Prince Uiliami Tupoulahi, 278, 279, 284

Tuvan People's Republic, 291
Twain, Mark, 227

United Kingdom
   female succession rights, 292
   women prime ministers, 291, 295
   women's rights, 279–80
   see also Elizabeth I of England and Ireland; Elizabeth II of the United Kingdom
United States of America
   California, 3
   US settler rebellions in Hawaii, 223–4, 239, 243–4

Victoria, Crown Princess of Sweden, 304, 306
Victoria of the United Kingdom
   accession to the throne, 5, 227
   childhood drawings of queens, 304
   colonial empire, 9, 230, 249–50, 252–4
   coronation, 242–3
   as Empress of India, 249–50, 252–3, 265, 266
   Golden Jubilee celebrations, 233, 234, 236–7, 238, 264–5
   images of, 5
   journals, 227, 267–8
   Koh-i- Noor diamond, 253–4
   marriage to Prince Albert, 233, 278
   memorial, 1–2
   queenship, 256
   reign, 232–3
   relations with Lili'uokalani of Hawaii, 223–4, 235–6, 244, 245, 304
   relations with Ranavalona I of Madagascar, 257
   relations with the Hawaiian royal

family, 230–2, 234–6
relationship with Abdul Karim, 267–8, 270–1, 273
Shah Jahan Begum of Bhopal's relations with, 264–5, 266, 272, 304
Urdu language skills, 267–8
Virgin Mary, cult of, 14
Vivero, Roderigo de, 218, 219

Walsingham, Sir Francis, 152, 174–6
Washington, George, 8–9
Wilhelmina of the Netherlands
abdication, 285
accession, 86, 87–8, 93–4
as a child queen, 88, 94, 105, 276–7
Emma as queen regent for, 93–4, 277, 279
marriage to Duke Heinrich of Mecklenburg-Schwerin, 277–8, 279, 281
as monarch, 278, 279
recognisability, 294
as a war leader during World War II, 281–3, 284–5, 294
women
autobiographical voices, 58, 80–1, 207–9, 300–1, 307
as heads of state, 2, 290–1, 299–300, 302–3
marriages, 13
'Venus' figures, 306–7
see also female power
women's rights
in Bhopal, 271–2
in the early twentieth century, 278
Sikandar Begum's reforms, 258
United Kingdom, 279–80
Wu Zetian of China, 147

Wu Zetian of China
Buddhism, 150, 153–4
character, 133–4
Chen gui (conduct guide for ministers), 145–6
childhood, 136–7, 139
claim to the throne, 136, 149–50
as a concubine at the imperial court, 10, 13, 137–8
and Emperor Gaozong, 138, 140, 142–4, 146, 149, 213
female rivals, 141, 142–4
images of, 134, 145, 190
legacy, 134, 146–7, 294
male rivals, 139–40, 155
peony imagery, 146–7
political writings, 145–6
promotion of women's rights, 147
reign, 145, 155, 156, 212
religious backing for her rule, 135, 136, 150–1, 153–4
speculation over her sex life, 142
titles, 156
tomb, 156
Zhou Dynasty, 154

Zenobia, Queen of Palmyra
legend of, 183–4
male kingship imagery, 183
marriage to Odanaith, 13, 183, 184
as queen regent, 184, 186
reign, 186
and the Roman Empire, 184, 191–2
Victoria's childhood drawings of queens, 304
as a warrior queen, 182–3, 191, 192